THE MAKING OF BRITISH COLONIAL
DEVELOPMENT POLICY 1914–1940

THE MAKING OF BRITISH COLONIAL DEVELOPMENT POLICY 1914–1940

STEPHEN CONSTANTINE
University of Lancaster

FRANK CASS

First Published 1984 in Great Britain by
FRANK CASS AND COMPANY LIMITED
Gainsborough House, 11 Gainsborough Road,
London, E11 1RS, England

and in the United States of America by
FRANK CASS AND COMPANY LIMITED
c/o Biblio Distribution Centre
81 Adams Drive, P.O. Box 327, Totowa, N.J. 07511

Copyright © 1984   Stephen Constantine

British Library Cataloguing in Publication Data

Constantine, Stephen
  The making of British colonial development
  policy 1914–1940.
  1. Economic assistance, British   2. Great
  Britain—Colonies—Economic policy
  I. Title
  338.91'41'01724   HC259

  ISBN 0-7146-3204-X

Typeset by Williams Graphics, Abergele, Clwyd.
Printed and bound in Great Britain by
A. Wheaton & Co., Ltd., Exeter

FOR WENDY

CONTENTS

LIST OF TABLES

ACKNOWLEDGEMENTS

In this book I return to a subject which I first began to examine several years ago in my Oxford doctoral thesis. That work has been substantially rewritten and shortened to form part of this larger study. I welcome this opportunity to record publicly my sincere thanks to Professor David Fieldhouse, the supervisor of that first project, for his guidance, encouragement and constructive criticism, and for his continuing interest in my work. I am also grateful for help received from Dr. A. F. Madden, Sir Norman Chester, Professor Michael Lee, Dr. Robert Pearce and colleagues at the University of Lancaster, especially Dr. John MacKenzie and Mr. Jeffrey Richards. I acknowledge with gratitude my debt to other scholars whose doctoral theses I have consulted, namely, Dr. Ann Burton, Dr. David Meredith, Dr. Curtis Nordman, Dr. Louis Nthenda and Dr. Dave Rampersad. My studies were enlivened by conversations with Sir Stephen Luke, formerly of the Colonial Office and the Crown Agents Office, and with the late Sir Gerard Clauson, whose distinguished career in the Colonial Office encompassed much of the period covered in this book. I also record with thanks the help given by the Library and Records Department of the Foreign and Commonwealth Office, by the Departmental Record Officer at the Treasury, and by the staff of the Public Record Office, Nuffield College Library, Bodleian Library, Rhodes House Library, University of Birmingham Library, Cambridge University Library, Churchill College Library and University of Lancaster Library. I am grateful to the Warden and Fellows of New College and to the Keeper of Western Manuscripts at the Bodleian Library for permission to consult and to quote from the Milner Papers, and to the Rt. Hon. Julian Amery M.P. for permission to examine and to quote from the Leo Amery Papers and from *The Leo Amery Diaries*. References to the Neville Chamberlain Papers are made with the kind permission of the Head of Special Collections at the University of Birmingham Library. Extracts from Crown-copyright material including the Niemeyer Papers kept at the Public Record Office appear by permission of the Controller of H.M. Stationery Office. My research was first supported as a postgraduate student by a D.E.S. studentship, and more recently I have received welcome assistance, which I happily acknowledge, from the British Academy Small Grants Research Fund in the Humanities, from the Department of History at the University of Lancaster and from the University of Lancaster Senate Research Fund. My greatest and abiding debt to the one who has provided most encouragement, comfort and assistance is simply but sincerely recorded in the dedication.

S.C.

ABBREVIATIONS

CAB	Cabinet
Cd., Cmd., Cmnd.	Command Paper
CDAC	Colonial Development Advisory Committee
CDF	Colonial Development Fund
CO	Colonial Office
CR	Colonial Report
E.A.P.	East Africa Protectorate
E.M.B.	Empire Marketing Board
E.R.D.C.	Empire Resources Development Committee
HC	House of Commons
HCP	House of Commons Papers
HL	House of Lords
Treas.	Treasury

I

INTRODUCTION

On 31 March 1970 the Overseas Development and Service Act of 1965 was allowed to expire. This brought to an end the Colonial Development and Welfare legislation which since 1940 had been central to the Imperial government's provision of financial aid for colonial territories. The conclusion of the Colonial Development and Welfare system did not, of course, end British aid to dependent colonies. Their needs were simply included within the government's more general schemes for aiding developing countries inside and outside the Commonwealth.[1] Nevertheless the decision in 1970 to allow specifically colonial development legislation to lapse marks a significant moment. It was symptomatic of the virtual completion of the process of political decolonisation which had by then left behind so few dependent territories. Since they alone were eligible for Colonial Development and Welfare aid, special legislation for them was no longer thought to be necessary. The Colonial Office itself had been merged with the Commonwealth Relations Office in 1966 to form the Commonwealth Office, and even that expanded department was fused into the Foreign and Commonwealth Office in 1968. Moreover, since 1964 the Colonial Development and Welfare Acts had been administered not by the Colonial Office but by the Ministry of Overseas Development until that body too was absorbed by the Foreign and Commonwealth Office in 1970. It seemed an appropriate time to review the record of Britain's colonial development policy. This was done, firstly and briefly, in a white paper issued by the Foreign and Commonwealth Office in 1971, and then by the publication in 1980 of a five volume official history.[2] While both these reports trace the origins of colonial development policy back to the 1920s, their main emphasis is placed on the operations of the Colonial Development and Welfare Acts and the evolution of policy since 1940. It is the purpose of this new study to contribute to a reappraisal of Britain's colonial record by a closer examination of an earlier phase of British colonial development policy running from before the First World War up to the passage of the first Colonial Development and Welfare Act in 1940. As will be shown, that legislation was preceded by almost half a century of vigorous debate on the merits and methods of colonial development and by a number of Imperial government decisions to finance such activities.

British colonial development policy and its derivative, overseas aid policy, have been and remain controversial topics. Since the Second World War attempts to generate economic growth in poorer societies inside and outside the colonial empires have led to demands for increasing the amount of assistance which should be given to them by richer countries, especially in the form of financial aid. Some contemporary commentators condemned as inadequate the amount of assistance made available by each of the post-war Colonial Development and Welfare Acts and by other overseas aid provisions. The Pearson Report produced by the Commission on International Development in 1969 criticised the developed world's record as aid donors and urged them to increase official development assistance to the level of 0.7% of their gross national product ideally by 1975 and no later than 1980.[3] Failure to achieve such targets was one complaint of the Brandt Report made by the Independent Commission on International Development Issues more than a decade later in 1980. They, too, proposed that the industrialised nations should set 0.7% of GNP as their target for official aid to be reached by 1985, but they wanted the rate to climb to 1% by the end of the century.[4] The level of colonial development assistance and overseas aid has, then, been a topic of some concern, and the virtue of such assistance has only been rarely questioned.[5] One feature of this study will be an attempt to calculate the amount of Imperial government assistance for colonial development in the period between the wars.

Further debates have centred on the motives of Imperial governments and other aid donors in providing assistance. The Pearson Report argued that the provision of aid by the rich to the poor was a moral responsibility which must be honoured. But they also defended aid as enlightened and constructive self-interest bringing mutual benefits to donor and recipient, for example through increased trade. Similar arguments were employed by the Brandt Commissioners. If human solidarity and international social justice were the principal motives for their proposals, mutual interests in economic growth, environmental protection and global peace were also cited as justifications.[6] Other observers, however, have detected little mutuality of interest and less morality behind the provision of aid. For example, the common practice of tying aid to the purchase of material from suppliers in the donor's country has been interpreted as a means of securing protected markets for the exports of industrial nations. The selection by the donor of the development projects deemed appropriate for financial support has been seen as a method of perpetuating the role of developing countries as primary producers dependent on the industrialised developed world. Moreover, in a world which since the Second World War has been divided into rival political spheres with conflicting ideologies and interests, the political advantages of drawing recipients of aid into the donor's camp have not gone unnoticed and uncriticized.[7]

An examination of colonial development policy between 1914 and 1940 raises similar issues. The records should enable us to explain not only the amount of money spent on that cause but also the imperial purpose behind it. Was the Imperial government motivated primarily by a moral obligation to provide benefits to colonial peoples? Or was the principal intention to secure advantages for the metropolis? Were they inspired by a civilising mission in the colonies or by an urgent need to obtain financial or economic gains for Britain or to salvage political interests? It would not, of course, be wise to assume that the objectives of colonial development policy remained unchanged. Some continuity may be claimed, stretching from a new initiative during Joseph Chamberlain's tenure of the Colonial Office to the passage and operations of Colonial Development and Welfare legislation during and after the Second World War. But some commentators have identified the Colonial Development Act of 1929 as inaugurating a new departure, while the claims of the Colonial Development and Welfare Act of 1940 have also been pressed. Did the aims of policy alter between 1914 and 1940 and if so, why, to what extent and in what ways?

Answering these questions may also throw some light on another issue. The history of Britain and the British Empire in this period seems to show differing even contradictory characteristics and to be open to rival interpretations. The nation emerged victorious from the First World War with an empire which in territorial extent reached its apogee with the absorption of former German and Turkish territories as mandated possessions. But it might appear that this triumph was followed by a rapid decline in Britain's economic strength and international authority. From 1921 to the outbreak of the Second World War governments were preoccupied by an economic depression which while fluctuating in intensity condemned on average 14% of the insured workforce to unemployment. During this period Britain's long-term relative decline as an industrial nation continued with her share of world manufacturing production going down to 9.2% by 1936–38.[8] External political challenges also revived after the First World War, most obviously in the 1930s, but even in the 1920s there was anxiety about the activities of Japan and the United States in the Far East and Pacific and of Bolshevik Russia particularly in Asia.[9] Within the formal empire, British authority seemed to be weakened by the national self-assertion of the dominions who obtained through the Imperial Conferences and by the Statute of Westminster in 1931 an equality of status and a freedom of action incompatible with older notions of imperial rule.[10] Nationalism in Ireland, in India, in Egypt and elsewhere in the Middle East also appeared to put the Imperial government on to the defensive. The concessions wrung from them in the Anglo-Irish treaty of 1921, the Government of India Acts of 1919 and 1935, and the Egyptian treaties of 1922 and 1936 and the abandonment of the mandate over Iraq in 1932 might seem but preliminaries to a more general imperial retreat. The discerning eye might also note signs of nationalist organisation in the Colonial Empire, for example in British West Africa from 1920 and in Ceylon from 1918.[11] Furthermore, some observers of cultural change in Britain have identified a declining faith in the imperial idea, a weakening of self-confidence in the civilising mission, and a greater unwillingness to employ British power against subject peoples and foreign nations.[12] In brief, it might seem that before the outbreak of the Second World War Britain was on a slippery slope likely to lead in the foreseeable future to the erosion of Britain's status as a world power and either the break up of the British Empire or at best its rapid evolution into the Commonwealth over which the Imperial government would have diminished control.

On the other hand, it might be argued that vigorous propaganda for the British Empire and exultation in its apparent political virtues and economic worth scarcely diminished after the First World War. Established organisations like the Royal Colonial Institute and the

Overseas Club were as active as ever and new initiatives like the British Empire Exhibition and the Empire Marketing Board aroused much attention. Through such agencies and by means of such media as cheap publications, children's literature, films, picture postcards, radio and exhibitions, it is probable that the imperial message achieved a deeper cultural penetration between the wars than ever before or since.[13] It has also been argued that the concessions apparently made to the dominions, India and Egypt were no more than tactical adjustments which maintained British interests and preserved the essentials of British control while defeating more radical and dangerous nationalist pressures. According to John Darwin, 'the besetting sin of the policy makers was not a galloping defeatism but, if anything, an excess of confidence in their ability, by a timely redeployment of the imperial factor, to outflank those elements in colonial nationalism which demanded a complete separation from Britain'.[14] Furthermore, historians generally agree that most contemporaries, including critics of British rule, assumed that imperial authority in the Colonial Empire could not and would not be abandoned for many years to come. The prospect of conceding self-government was in some cases ruled out entirely and elsewhere was regarded as a very remote possibility. In contrast with the problems facing the Indian Civil Service between the wars, there was little difficulty finding in Britain young recruits for the Colonial Service who evidently believed that they were embarking on lifetime careers. The inter-war years have been seen as a period of comparative quiet in the history of the Colonial Empire after completing the process of conquest and pacification and before the urgent improvising which accompanied the accelerating movement to decolonisation after the Second World War.[15]

The evolution of colonial development policy between the wars may illuminate this issue. Does it reflect confident assumptions about the future of Britain and the British Empire? Does it demonstrate an assumed faith in an imperial purpose, perhaps the fulfilment of a civilising mission in the colonies? Or do discussions and decisions indicate a growing disquiet and worry about the future? Was colonial development policy redesigned to revitalize British markets and repair Britain's economic fortunes? Or was it a response to political challenges and an attempt to restore a crumbling imperial authority?

As the title indicates, this is essentially a study of Imperial government policy-making. In particular it concerns the central role of the Colonial Office. It is not an attempt to assess in any systematic way the effect of policy upon the British or colonial economies or upon colonial peoples. It is based principally upon government records. The dangers of relying exclusively on such sources for a grasp of policy-making have recently been pointed out.[16] The official mind was not entirely cocooned and self-contained and might be affected by factors not immediately apparent from official records. Government departments were ultimately accountable to Parliament and might be influenced by the mood of M.P.s. Ministers were in addition not insensitive to the interests of their political parties. The lobbying of pressure groups might also be influential, while general political and economic conditions and the currents of intellectual and cultural change could also leave their mark. Such influences are often more implicit than explicit in the decisions taken and in the records left behind. Reference is therefore made to a wider range of contemporary material and to certain secondary sources in order, hopefully, to illuminate the nuances left in the official records. The emphasis of the study is nevertheless on intra- and inter-departmental discussions and negotiations. Amongst other things it examines the relationship between the political heads of the Colonial Office and their permanent advisers in order to determine their respective roles in the formulation and direction of policy. It also considers the influence of departmental structure and administrative method on the process of decision-making and on the decisions made. And much emphasis is placed upon the relationship between the Colonial Office and the Treasury. Throughout this period, as master of the purse strings, the Treasury retained considerable authority over other government departments. How it exercised that authority, how complete it was and how it might be circumvented by the Colonial Office are topics which will be examined. Research has suggested that in other contexts the Treasury do not deserve their reputation as short-sighted, unimaginative devotees of orthodoxy and that their views and strategies were actually subtle, flexible, reasonable and practical.[17] It remains to be seen whether the Colonial Office found them so.

The work is divided into analytical and narrative chapters. Because policy inevitably owed much to precedent it begins with an analysis of the origins and nature of colonial development policy in the generation before the First World War. The impact of the First World War is then examined before turning to a series of case studies dealing with new proposals for Imperial government expenditure on colonial development in the 1920s. Particular attention is then given to the origins and character of the Colonial Development Act of 1929. The operations of the act in the 1930s are then analysed, and this serves as a preliminary to a study of the origins in the late 1930s of the measure which was eventually to be realised as the Colonial Development and Welfare Act of 1940. There follows an estimate of total expenditure on colonial development between the wars. Finally, after a review of changes in Colonial Office structure and of Colonial Office–Treasury relationships, some conclusions are offered about the process of policy-making and the nature and purpose of colonial development policy from 1914 to 1940.

NOTES

1. For a review of these in 1970 see *Report from the Select Committee on Overseas Aid*, H.C.P. 299, 1970–71 Session.
2. *Colonial Development and Welfare Acts 1929–70. A Brief Review*, Cmnd.4677, June 1971; D. J. Morgan, *The Official History of Colonial Development*, 5 vols., London, 1980. Mr. Morgan's appointment was announced in a written parliamentary answer, *Hansard* H.C., vol.793, cols.411-12, 18 Dec. 1969.
3. *Partners in Development: Report of the Commission on International Development*, London, 1969, pp.136-52.
4. *North-South: A Programme for Survival. Report of the Independent Commission on International Development Issues*, Pan paperback ed., London, 1980, pp.224-6, 242, 255.
5. Though see, for example, M. Friedman, 'Foreign Economic Aid: Means and Objectives', *Yale Review* 47 (1958), reprinted in J. Bhagwati and R. S. Eckaus, eds., *Foreign Aid*, Harmondsworth, 1970; and P. T. Bauer, *Dissent on Development*, London, 1971, espec. pp.95-135.
6. *Partners in Development*, espec. 7-11; *North–South*, espec. pp.17, 64, 237-41.
7. See, for example, T. Hayter, *Aid as Imperialism*, Harmondsworth, 1971; B. Ward, J. D. Runnalls, L. D'Anjou, eds., *The Widening Gap: Development in the 1970s*, New York and London, 1971, pp.276, 296, 333. For a debate on the merits of bilateral and multilateral aid see Bhagwati and Eckaus, *Foreign Aid*, part 4.
8. S. Constantine, *Unemployment in Britain between the Wars*, London, 1980, p.3; D. H. Aldcroft, *The Inter-War Economy: Britain, 1919–1939*, London, 1970, pp.20-2.
9. P. Kennedy, *The Realities Behind Diplomacy*, Glasgow, 1981, pp.258-312; M. Howard, *The Continental Commitment*, Harmondsworth, 1974, pp.74-122; F. S. Northedge, *The Troubled Giant*, London, 1966, pp.200-7.
10. R. F. Holland, *Britain and the Commonwealth Alliance 1918–39*, London, 1981; N. Mansergh, *The Commonwealth Experience*, London, 1969, pp.159-86, 212-46.
11. W. D. McIntyre, *Colonies into Commonwealth*, London, 1966, pp.209-10; B. Porter, *The Lion's Share*, London, 1975, pp.251-5, 295-300.
12. C. Barnett, *The Collapse of British Power*, London, 1972, p.59; M. Beloff, *Imperial Sunset*, vol.1 *Britain's Liberal Empire 1897–1921*, London, 1969, pp.347-8; J. Morris, *Farewell the Trumpets*, Harmondsworth, 1979, pp.199-211.
13. T. R. Reese, *The History of the Royal Commonwealth Society 1868–1968*,

8 *The Making of British Colonial Development Policy 1914—1940*

London, 1968, pp.126-192, 204-8. I am grateful to my colleague Dr. John MacKenzie for discussions on this point: see his study *Propaganda and Empire*, Manchester, forthcoming.
14. J. Darwin, 'Imperialism in Decline? Tendencies in British Imperial Policy between the Wars', *H.J.*, 23 (1980) 678; see also Porter, *The Lion's Share*, pp.252-4, 295-300.
15. C. Cross, *The Fall of the British Empire*, London, 1968, p.154; R. Heussler, *Yesterday's Rulers*, Syracuse New York, 1963; Porter, *The Lion's Share*, pp.257-8, 290-5.
16. A. Booth and S. Glynn, 'The Public Records and Recent British Economic Historiography', *Ec.H.R.*, 32 (1979) 303-15; M. Beloff, 'The Political Blind Spot of Economists', *Government and Opposition*, 10 (1975) 107-12.
17. S. Howson, *Domestic Monetary Management in Britain 1919—38*, Cambridge, 1975; G. C. Peden, *British Rearmament and the Treasury 1932—1939*, Edinburgh, 1979.

II

COLONIAL DEVELOPMENT POLICY BEFORE 1914

One aim of this study is to trace the changes in the nature and purpose of British colonial development policy in the years after 1914. But in order to determine the extent to which policy was altered it is essential to describe as a contrast the kind of policy blessed by the Imperial government and operated by the Colonial Office in the period before the First World War. Moreover, another aim of this study is to explain changes in policy after 1914 by an examination of the policy-making process. Politicians and civil servants often feel constrained by precedent. As later chapters will show, reference back to pre-war policy was common. While not claiming that you cannot teach old dogs new tricks, it is at least probable that earlier experiences and practices affected later assumptions and behaviour. It needs to be remembered that in the period from August 1914 up to the introduction of the Colonial Development and Welfare Bill into the House of Commons in May 1940, there were twelve different Secretaries of State for the Colonies, but only Ormsby-Gore, born 1885, and Mac-Donald, born 1901, had not reached the age of thirty before the First World War. The same was true of all but four of the fourteen parliamentary under-secretaries, and all but one of the nine permanent and deputy under-secretaries.[1] Accordingly this chapter seeks to describe and explain the character of British colonial development policy before 1914.

The scramble for colonies after 1880 had hugely increased the size of the British Empire. Already by the time of Queen Victoria's Diamond Jubilee the formal empire covered nearly one quarter of the world's land surface and contained almost one quarter of its population. With the exception of a few territories still controlled by the Foreign Office, responsibility for supervising the affairs of this empire was divided between the India Office and the Colonial Office.

In practice, with the increasing self-assertion of the self-governing white settler colonies, the principal administrative concern of the Colonial Office was with the dependent colonies and protectorates. Since before the First World War this Colonial Empire already amounted to over 9¼ million square miles and contained nearly 57 million people, it was potentially a considerable responsibility.[2]

Around the turn of the century there were those who urged the Colonial Office to take seriously the development of these territories. The period of low prices for industrial products at the end of the 19th century, the fall in profits, the chill of American and German economic competition, and the reduction of the free trade world by tariff barriers alarmed some British businessmen and politicians. Moreover, there were political and military challenges overseas which seemed to threaten a Great Britain made vulnerable by limited and over-stretched resources. Meanwhile, trade union unrest and the formation of an independent working men's political party appeared to pose a socialist challenge to the *status quo* at home. An air of concern and crisis was generated. It may be that the emphasis placed on the economic value of the newly acquired territories was an *ex post facto* justification of British participation in the scramble for colonies. On the other hand, an increasing number of spokesmen claimed to see in the empire the solution to Britain's economic, political and social problems. Colonial markets and sources of raw materials were regarded as valuable assets to help the expansion of the metropolitan economy. The consequent wealth was seen by some as the essential basis to sustain Britain's military and political role overseas. Others, embracing doctrines of social imperialism, saw colonial resources as contributing to a cure for the social problems at home which seemed responsible for social unrest.[3]

What concerned some observers was the apparently underdeveloped potential of colonial resources. Annexation of territory was not enough. Trade to and from the Colonial Empire, especially with the newly acquired tropical territories, remained inadequate. Accordingly they wished to see the Colonial Office adopt a positive policy of colonial development, one which would increase colonial production and ease the process of trade between the colonies and the outside world. Before private enterprise could effectively tap these resources, however, railways, roads, harbours and other features of an economic infrastructure needed to be constructed and research into problems of production undertaken. These were among the tasks which entrepreneurs, chambers of commerce and such powerful Lancashire lobbyists as the British Cotton Growing Association, founded 1902, urged colonial governments and the Colonial Office to undertake.

The introduction of this approach into the Colonial Office was largely the work of Joseph Chamberlain.[4] As Secretary of State from 1895 to 1903 he campaigned to increase the amount of Imperial government aid for colonial development: 'I consider many of our Colonies as being in the condition of undeveloped estates, and estates which never can be developed without Imperial assistance.' He justified his crusade principally on the grounds of enlightened self-interest: Great Britain would benefit by the development of her colonial markets and sources of food and industrial raw materials. 'We have an Empire which with decent organisation and consolidation might be absolutely self-sustaining .... There is no article of your food, there is no raw material of your trade, there is no necessity of your lives, no luxury of your existence which cannot be produced somewhere or other in the British Empire.' Moreover, 'it is only in such a policy of development that I see any solution of these social problems by which we are surrounded. Plenty of employment and a contented people go together; and there is no way of securing plenty of employment for the United Kingdom except by developing old markets and creating new ones'.[5]

It was asserted by Chamberlain's supporters that his occupancy of the Colonial Office was a major turning point in the history of British colonial development policy. One enthusiast declared in 1906:

History will award to Mr. Chamberlain the credit of being among the first to realize that ... the economic salvation of the United Kingdom must be looked for in our undeveloped estates in the tropical regions of the earth .... He appreciated ... that ... the employment of the white man in the United Kingdom depends on the employment of the coloured man in the tropics.

Similarly Lord Milner claimed in 1914: 'Alike in East Africa, in West Africa, and in the West Indies, the years 1896–1903 were years of progress, and mark the transition from the old system of *laissez-faire* and stagnation to the new policy of activity and development.'[6]

This is a major claim, but at least one historian has been prepared to endorse it. Hyam writes that 'Before 1914 there was no slackening of the effort to continue the "constructive imperialism" initiated by Chamberlain.'[7] A close examination of colonial development policy in the period after 1895 does, however, reveal how partial were Chamberlain's successes and how limited was the legacy he left behind. It is true that after his departure the Colonial Office was responsible for a number of innovations similar to Chamberlain's own *achievements*. It cannot be said, however, that Chamberlain's successors were any more capable of putting into practice his more ambitious *proposals*.

The evidence shows for one thing how limited was the amount of money spent by the Imperial government on colonial development. Before 1914 no British government agreed to accelerate the economic development of the Colonial Empire by providing substantial cash grants or loans or other expensive aid. One estimate based on the annual Colonial Office accounts concludes that in the forty year period from 1875 to 1915 Parliament authorised a total expenditure of only about £1,400,000 for that purpose.[8] One might add the £5,502,592 lent by the Imperial government from 1896 for the construction of the Uganda Railway, the £3,351,820 made available under the Colonial Loans Act of 1899 but left substantially unspent and the £3 million to be advanced under the East African Protectorates Loans Act of 1914. Expenditure by the Imperial government on colonial development may have grown after 1895 but it remained small.

The obstacles which prevented more generous expenditure in the generation before the war and which limited the impact of Chamberlain's energies were deep-rooted. The one of which the Colonial Office most bitterly complained was the Treasury. Suspicion and hostility between the two departments was well-established. One parliamentary under-secretary's complaint about Treasury obstruction echoes down the years: 'This is not "Economy" but blundering stupidity and an absurd departmental crotchet productive of no result whatever except the exciting of a feeling of profound contempt for such miserable pettifogging proceedings.'[9]

Recent studies have, however, argued that the Treasury's powers of financial control have been exaggerated.[10] The Treasury's behaviour, it has been pointed out, was rooted in the tenets of financial orthodoxy and their authority came from the general acceptance of such views by those in government service and in Parliament. The Treasury were not speaking just for themselves. It was believed that economic and political necessity required the Treasury to keep down the rate of United Kingdom taxes and the extent and cost of Imperial government borrowing. In attempting to restrict departmental expenditure the Treasury were doing what was expected of them. It is certainly true that the Colonial Office staff did not object in any fundamental way to the role of the Treasury and the doctrines of financial orthodoxy. They agreed in principle that wherever possible annual budgets both imperial and colonial should be balanced, and they accepted that their expenditure on the Colonial Empire had to be carefully justified and kept as low as possible. The annual estimates of each colony had to be approved by the Colonial Office, and they were prepared to reject development projects proposed by colonial governors if they believed them to be excessively expensive.[11] Because the Colonial Office shared these common assumptions with the Treasury, they were therefore susceptible to 'moral suasion'.[12] The Treasury often deterred expenditure not by veto but by winning the intellectual arguments. Nevertheless, in spite of much common ground on financial theory there was still room for conflict over particular issues and items of expenditure. The bitter minuting on the departmental files and the exasperated exchanges between the two departments do suggest that the Colonial Office experienced and resented Treasury obstruction. The administrative difficulties involved in squeezing money out of the Exchequer acted as a deterrent to the Colonial Office, and the inevitable Treasury objections hardly encouraged the department to devise more ambitious programmes for colonial development.[13] A determined minister like Chamberlain was needed to give the lead.

It has also been argued that the Treasury did not seek to control Colonial Office policy but only to restrict the financial liabilities which might follow.[14] In practice, of course, the distinction was a fine one, and the Colonial Office certainly felt that the financial objections raised by the Treasury limited policy initiatives. It is true that the Treasury had no absolute veto over policy. If the Colonial Office insisted, then the Treasury alone could not block policy proposals. Often they gave way to repeated Colonial Office demands, but if they refused the Colonial Office could still appeal through the Secretary of State to the cabinet where ministers might be swayed by arguments other than those of financial orthodoxy. Political or economic issues might weigh more heavily. Conflict between Colonial Office and Treasury and the resolution of those conflicts by reference to cabinet arbitration was an established pattern before 1914. However, the value of Colonial Office appeals to the cabinet was limited by the generally higher prestige and influence of the Treasury and the Chancellor of the Exchequer. Their assertion of financial orthodoxy could be mighty effective, and it required a Secretary of State of unusual determination and/or with a particularly good case to win major concessions for his 'Cinderella' department.

Recent studies have also shown how the Treasury's specific powers to control the expenditure of colonial administrations were rationalized and reduced in the later nineteenth and early twentieth centuries. The notion that the Treasury had the authority to supervise the income and expenditure of all crown colony administrations was abandoned and the exact circumstances were defined in which Treasury control would operate.[15] Nevertheless, the Treasury retained formidable powers and many opportunities to influence the direction of colonial affairs. The annual estimates of the Colonial Office, like all other government departments, were still subjected to Treasury scrutiny and required their approval. The Treasury could only oppose increases in expenditure and could not compel reductions, but their objections and 'moral suasion' did exercise some control over the running costs and staff size of the Colonial Office and in that fashion indirectly over its functions and aspirations. The Treasury similarly scrutinized and attempted to prevent increases in expenditure on the Colonial Services vote, that is, the money spent by the Colonial Office on administrative, development and other services in or on behalf of the dependent empire. So, for example, Treasury sanction was required before the Colonial Office could make a grant for research into tropical diseases or to the British Cotton Growing Association. Since 1870 the Treasury had limited their powers to control the expenditure of colonial governments to those administrations in receipt of grants-in-aid, that is, the money grants enabling them to meet their administrative costs and avoid budget deficits. But in these circumstances Treasury approval of annual estimates had to be obtained so long as the grant-in-aid was required and for three years thereafter. The Treasury wanted to ensure that colonial budgets balanced as rapidly as possible so as to reduce the burden of grants-in-aid on the Imperial Exchequer. Chamberlain and his successors had to battle hard to increase grants to such hard-pressed colonies as the West Indies.[16]

In certain circumstances the Treasury also exerted their influence when colonies attempted to raise loans on the London market, as was often the case in order to finance large development projects. If a colonial government wished to raise a loan more cheaply by obtaining for it an Imperial government guarantee, then the Treasury had the power to ascertain that the colony could meet the interest and sinking fund payments on the loan. They feared that colonies might fail to meet their obligations and so oblige the Imperial government to honour the guarantee and pay these charges. Moreover, the Treasury argued that such guarantees should be granted only sparingly because they constituted additional burdens on the credit of the Imperial government and might therefore raise the cost of their own unavoidable borrowing. While the Treasury could justify their actions in the name of financial probity, their main purpose was to safeguard the financial interests of the Imperial Exchequer.

As an alternative, Chamberlain steered through Parliament in 1900 a bill which consolidated and amended the Colonial Stock Acts. His intention was to stimulate the development of colonies by reducing the cost to empire countries of borrowing on the London market. Only colonies and dominions, not protectorates and, later, mandated territories, were eligible. By making their stock trustee securities which could be acquired by British trust funds, it was hoped that their interest rates could be reduced. However, because the Treasury wished to be sure that the credit of trustee stocks in general would never be damaged by a defaulting colonial government, they subjected each colonial application to close examination, insisted on the establishment in the colony of a regularly provisioned sinking fund, and gave their approval to an issue only if they reckoned that the colony's financial position was sound. Lurking behind this rectitude was a Treasury suspicion that colonial borrowing under advantageous terms was competing with British government borrowing and raising the price. Although the Treasury claimed that the acts did benefit the colonies, the aid was at best marginal. In any case, while it possibly reduced interest charges on loans raised, an increase in colonial indebtedness could only be safely sustained by territories with reasonably buoyant economies.[17]

Chamberlain and his successors clearly regarded the existing mechanism for colonial borrowing as inadequate. But when they attempted to provide more generous help the Treasury's objections were a major obstacle. In 1895 Chamberlain succeeded in persuading the Prime Minister and even temporarily the Chancellor to use the dividends of the Suez Canal shares as a colonial development fund from which loans could be made to finance public works in the empire. But this attempt to upset the norms of financial management was attacked by the permanent officials at the Treasury who persuaded the Chancellor to oppose the scheme in cabinet where it was ultimately defeated. The Treasury later offered a Colonial Loans Fund Bill establishing an alternative colonial development fund, but predictably the purpose was primarily to ease a purely domestic problem concerning the investment of Post Office deposits and Local Loans fund capital, and loans to be offered to colonies would be firmly at the Treasury's discretion. Understandably Chamberlain was only lukewarm in his support. In the event, in 1899 the House of Commons rejected the bill at least in part on the grounds that it deviated from financial orthodoxy. The only apparent success which Chamberlain had in obtaining large loans for colonial development was the Colonial Loans Act of 1899, a measure authorising seventeen different loans totalling £3,351,820 to twelve colonies and needed in many cases to finance works already authorised by Chamberlain and under construction. But it is revealing of the Treasury's obstructionist role that the Treasury's interpretation of the terms was regarded as so onerous that, for example, the Gold Coast and Sierra Leone declined to tap this source and Lagos did so only on a limited and temporary basis.[18] Later, when Elgin requested a loan of £500,000 for railway building in Uganda, the Treasury would sanction an expenditure of only £200,000. Similarly, instead of providing an Imperial government loan for a railway in Northern Nigeria, the Treasury insisted that the money be raised on the credit of Southern Nigeria.[19] Obtaining some financial help from the Treasury in this period was obviously not impossible, but as Dumett concludes, Chamberlain's 'major policy aim of recasting the machinery of imperial development aid to crown colonies was abortive.'[20] His successors also found that the Treasury's influence was formidable.

It must not, however, be thought that the Colonial Office before 1914 were bursting with schemes for large-scale capital investment by the Imperial government in the colonies in order to trigger off economic growth. They were held in check not just by Treasury control but by their own understandable ignorance of modern concepts of economic growth. It was assumed that colonial production could be increased by scientific research, technical innovations and especially by an improved economic infrastructure, particularly the building of railways, roads and harbours. But for the most part the colonies would remain primary producers feeding the needs of industrialised economies. When they talked of economic development they meant an arithmetical increase in the production of staple primary products, not a structural change in the local economy, nor industrialisation. In explaining the limited role of the Imperial government in promoting the economic development of the colonies before 1914 this restricted vision of the purpose and character of colonial development is important.

Of equal significance is the Colonial Office's concept of their relationship with the Colonial Empire. It was neatly summed up by one officer: 'The Governor administers and the Colonial Office supervises.' This was a highly decentralised empire. Even though the sovereignty of the colonies was vested in the metropolis, the actual administration of territories was left in the hands of the appointed governor and his staff. While originally a matter of practical convenience, the largely supervisory role which the Colonial Office retained for themselves limited the office's view of their duties. Certainly the office did not regard themselves as having a responsibility to initiate proposals for the economic development of dependent territories. They did not cast themselves in the role of economic managers and devised no empire-wide strategy of colonial development. Instead they assumed that the initiative for development proposals would come from outside the Colonial Office, for the most part from the quasi-independent colonial governor and his staff. The Colonial Office would then respond and would scrutinize the projects submitted. As another official put it: 'The responsibility is on [the governor] to put forward positive proposals for the development of the country. The responsibility is on the Secretary of State to judge such proposals calmly and dispassionately, and with a long look ahead.' Significantly, he went on: 'If any mistake is to be made in the Colonial Office it should be that of excess caution, rather than the opposite'. The Colonial Office were evidently not in general anxious to encourage rapid change.[21]

It was also natural to assume, at a time when by modern standards government functions were limited, that it was private enterprise which would be mainly responsible for the economic development of colonial territories. It was argued that if the Colonial Office initiated schemes it was likely to obstruct the proper function of private businessmen by pre-empting the more economically viable propositions. Of course, colonial governments might have to provide certain basic facilities to attract private investors, and sometimes the provision of that infrastructure might require Imperial government assistance. But a major assumption of the Colonial Office was that their responsibility for development was to act as something of a long-stop, to become involved in projects only if private enterprise was unwilling or unable to intervene.

This did not, however, mean that the Colonial Office would invariably respond positively to the demands of private lobbyists and would unreservedly encourage private investment in the Colonial Empire. In part the discernible office prejudice against private businessmen was rooted simply in a Colonial Office preference for a quiet life. The primary responsibility of colonial governments and of the Colonial Office was for the maintenance of local law and order. Stability was the first priority. There was a suspicion in the office that trade and finance could be a disturbing factor in a colony. While colonial governments had an interest in increasing their taxable revenues, rapid economic change, it was thought, would upset established social and political order. There was also the prejudice felt by many members of the administrative middle class in government service against businessmen and sordid profit-making. Platt has argued that the official mind's contempt for trade and individual traders caused it to welcome laissez-faire economic policies as a means of avoiding soiling its hands with such business. Although this attitude was in decline from the last quarter of the 19th century, its influence remained, and the Colonial Office staff were not immune.[22] They remained, for example, highly suspicious of British concession-hunters in the Colonial Empire.[23]

But these prejudices were also strengthened by current Colonial Office understanding of the doctrine of trusteeship. The Colonial Office claimed that their primary administrative concern was with the welfare and rights of subject colonial peoples. However, interpretation of this responsibility could be contradictory. In the early 19th century, policy generally favoured a process of westernization, modernization and Christianization of the empire by European-controlled commercial developments, political rule and education. Some elements of this purpose remained at the end of the century and were indeed strengthened before the war. Part of the justification for British administration were the improvements in health and welfare brought to colonial people by imperial-financed research into tropical medicine and sanitation and the provision of services by paternalistic colonial governments.[24] Even those whose principal motivation for advocating colonial development was to secure benefits for the metropolis nevertheless often claimed like Chamberlain that the development of the dependencies was at least in part 'for the benefit of their population'.[25] Moreover, the Colonial Office accepted that economic development of territories was essential and not only to pay for these services and to raise local living standards: colonial rulers also had duty to the outside world, to expand and release colonial resources to industrial consumers. This too was part of their 'trust'.[26] The problem was how to reconcile such economic objectives with the maintenance of native rights, for by the end of the 19th century the confident conversionist interpretation of trusteeship was far less enthusiastically upheld in the Colonial Office and outside. Disappointments and a hardening of racial attitudes seem to have had most effect in reducing faith in the practicality and wisdom of such a programme. The civilising mission veered towards a more preservationist purpose concerned to restrain the pace of change and perpetuate where practical indigenous political, social and economic patterns.[27]

This can be seen most clearly in West Africa. Here, from the 1890s, the principle of peasant production was asserted. Most strikingly, the schemes of Lever to begin plantation production in Nigeria were rejected by the Colonial Office. Land in Northern Nigeria was vested in the governor as trustee, in order to prevent its alienation to European companies, while in Southern Nigeria it was vested in the native tribes. Leases were normally granted only for the purposes of mining and timber-felling, and there was very little scope for direct European economic activity except in the import and export business.[28] It has been rightly pointed out that this assertion of trusteeship in West Africa was appropriate in a region where peasant production was in any case proving economically highly successful,[29] and it is certainly true that the principle was not uniformly defended throughout the colonial empire. But it needs to be remembered that the Colonial Office was not omnipotent and that pressures from white settlers and local colonial governments were sometimes hard to resist. The ideal of protecting native rights nevertheless did influence land and labour policy elsewhere, perhaps especially after the horrors revealed in the Congo at the turn of the century made colonial rulers sensitive to charges of exploitation. Humanitarian and radical lobbies in and out of Parliament maintained a constant and critical eye on official behaviour.[30] Certainly the preservationist interpretation of trusteeship formed part of the mental baggage carried by the permanent staff at the Colonial Office before the war, and it constituted a standard against which to judge proposals for economic change. It seems to have induced a desire to moderate the pace of change and served therefore as another discouragement to the definition and assertion of a vigorous colonial development policy. Economic development was not the only nor indeed the main purpose of colonial administration.[31]

A further obstacle to the inauguration of ambitious economic development programmes requires emphasis. In the generation before 1914 there were no significant alterations in the structure of the Colonial Office and in the way it handled its daily business. The perpetuation of traditional administrative practices encouraged the preservation of traditional attitudes in the office and discouraged new approaches to colonial economic affairs. It has been argued that 'the Colonial Office was not up to the tasks Chamberlain set it' and that his failure to alter the administrative structure was a principal reason for the frustration of his policies.[32] Before the First World War the work of the Colonial Office was still primarily divided on a geo-graphical basis and handled by six separate departments responsible respectively for the dominions, West Africa and the Mediterranean, Nigeria, East Africa, the West Indies, and the East.[33] In view of the huge variety of regional characteristics around the empire there was a justification for this division of responsibilities, but the system required and created administrators who were above all specialists in particular territories, such as West Africa, rather than in particular problems of relevance to the Colonial Empire as a whole, such as economic development. The staff in each geographical department dealt with the full range of political, legal, military, cultural, social, financial as well as economic affairs of their colonies. It seems probable that as a result officials obtained a broad view of colonial conditions and could see the ramifications of, say, a change in economic policy on the political situation. Avoiding over-simplifi-cation of problems inspires a certain caution in decision-making, perhaps a reluctance to risk changes. A conservative approach was probably further encouraged when the workload of the Colonial Office increased considerably with the expansion of the empire. It has been suggested that 'the staff did not have the leisure to speculate on the future of the empire; they rarely had the opportunity of consciously moulding developments'.[34]

There was in addition a General department which did have contacts with organisations and individuals interested in economic and social developments in the Colonial Empire as a whole, but the department's involvement in such matters was swamped by its responsibilities for legal, establishment, patronage and other general matters. It was not a central storehouse of information on the economic potential and social needs of the Colonial Empire and was certainly not a central planning body. Furthermore, colonial development was likely to assume a low priority since with some honourable exceptions few recruits to the Colonial Office had much of the appropriate economic or scientific knowledge. Academically staff were of very high standing, but, for example, in 1903 only 5 of 43 officials in the upper division had been educated in the sciences.[35]

Some attempt was made to obtain technical advice when needed from professionally qualified people outside the Colonial Office. For example, medical specialists were occasionally consulted especially at the London and Liverpool Schools of Tropical Medicine, the first of which Chamberlain had helped create. The Tropical Diseases Bureau and the Entomological Research Committee (later Imperial Bureau of Entomology) were also on hand from 1909, and there were also contacts with the Imperial Institute. Other government departments such as the Board of Trade and the Ministry of Agriculture could also be asked to supply information. But most use seems to have been made of the Crown Agents. They acted in London primarily as the business and financial agents of all colonial governments. Their activities covered such matters as the raising of loans for colonial governments on the London Stock Market, the investing of surplus colonial funds, the assessment and planning of development proposals, and the inspection and purchase of materials for development works. On any economic or financial matter a good deal of correspondence took place between the Colonial Office and the Crown Agents. Although the Treasury frequently criticized the Crown Agents, an inquiry into their efficiency inaugurated in 1901 by Chamberlain vindicated their conduct, as did a later investigation which reported in 1909.[36]

Within the Colonial Office there were other sources of advice: a permanent legal adviser and, from 1902, the Director of Kew Gardens acting as botanical adviser. Chamberlain also appointed a medical adviser but that appointment lapsed. There were also a few advisory committees which brought together some officials with specialists from outside, the Advisory Committee of the Tropical Diseases Research Fund from 1904, the Colonial Survey Committee from 1905, the Colonial Veterinary Committee from 1907, and the Advisory

Medical and Sanitary Committee for Tropical Africa from 1909.[37] But in spite of these metropolitan sources of technical advice, the Colonial Office continued to rely heavily on the estimates and opinions of Colonial Service officers in the territories. Sir Cosmo Parkinson's comment on pre-war practices was an accurate summary: 'As regards specialist and technical advice, it was felt that each colony had its own staff in the Departments of Agriculture, Education, Public Health, etc., and that it was not for Whitehall to usurp functions which could, or at any rate should, be adequately performed in the colonies themselves.'[38] This reliance on the technical advice from the Colonial Service reinforced the tendency to expect initiatives for development to come from the colonies and not from the Colonial Office. It cannot be said that the Colonial Office was indifferent to economic and social improvements in the colonies, but it seems reasonable to conclude that the structure of the Colonial Office and the training and expertise of its staff were partly responsible for the rather low priority given to colonial development before 1914.

Given the Colonial Office's modest interest in colonial development and the obstacles presented by the Treasury to paying for it, under what circumstances could the Imperial government be persuaded to provide financial help for colonial development? It is noticeable that some of the expensive measures had substantial political connotations. Imperial aid accompanied major political settlements as in Canada after the British North America Act of 1867 and in South Africa after the Boer War. There were strategic considerations behind the imperial financing of some of the railways built in tropical Africa, especially the Uganda Railway, initially authorised at a cost of £3,000,000 in 1896.[39] Political and humanitarian arguments lay behind another type of provision, emergency aid to colonies battered by natural disaster, the fate, for example, of Jamaica devastated by an earthquake in 1907.[40]

However, much more central to the traditional Colonial Office view of the nature and purpose of colonial development policy was the provision of imperial aid to those financially hard-pressed colonial governments dependent on recurrent grants-in-aid. The aim of colonial development was to make them financially self-sufficient. Imperial assistance should enable a colonial government to build the railways, roads or other facilities needed to attract investment and stimulate exports, and the taxing of that business should provide the funds to meet future administrative running costs. This was a limited concept of colonial development, preoccupied with the balancing of colonial budgets. Further economic development and the provision of welfare services would be the responsibility of a now financially independent colonial government able to draw on its own revenue or raise loans on its own credit to finance new requirements. It is easy to understand why the Treasury was sympathetic to this kind of policy and also its attraction to the Colonial Office and colonial governments since it would free them from grants-in-aid and Treasury control.

Naturally the territories which looked for this kind of help were those least able to attract private capital or those least economically developed. Some of these were economic derelicts like the British West Indies, suffering from the decay of their once dominant sugar industry. Chamberlain went to a lot of trouble to try and ease their problems by tariff assistance, economic diversification, the funding of the West Indies Agricultural Department and the grant of £250,000 he squeezed out of the Treasury in 1902.[41] The other regions receiving substantial aid were the newly-acquired territories particularly in tropical Africa. Over half of the loans authorised under the Colonial Loans Act of 1899 were destined for West African territories, and later administrations provided development loans for Nigeria, Uganda and the East Africa Protectorate.[42] As Hyam concludes: 'The chief reason for interest in economic growth was the desire to relieve expense to the British tax payer, to get rid of imperial grants-in-aid, to make colonies self-supporting.'[43] That grants-in-aid to the tropical African territories were reduced as a result before 1914 helps explain the continued appeal after the First World War of what may be described as the West African model of colonial development policy.

However, the Chamberlainite thesis that colonial development in the interests of the metropolitan economy did justify imperial financial assistance also had some influence on the course of pre-war decision-making. The increased awareness of the value of colonial resources to the British economy was apparent in the lobbying to which Chamberlain had responded by urging railway development in West Africa,[44] and Hyam has shown how vociferous was the British Cotton Growing Association in its support for later programmes in Northern Nigeria, Uganda and the Sudan. Concern over the sufficiency of cotton supplies from the United States explains, for example, the £10,000 a year Treasury grant to the Association which ran from 1910 until the war, and the much more ambitious imperial guarantee of a £3,000,000 Sudan government loan in 1913, the first injection of funds into the Gezira cotton-growing scheme.[45] During the parliamentary debates on the latter, Bonar Law, the Leader of the Opposition, bluntly announced that 'if this experiment succeeds it is of direct advantage to the United Kingdom itself'.[46] Similar arguments might also be adduced to explain the small grants wrung out of the Treasury by Chamberlain and his successors to finance research into tropical diseases, entomology and tropical agriculture and to support the Imperial Institute.[47]

That Chamberlain's vision was an important but by no means predominant element in departmental decision-making on colonial development policy can be demonstrated by sketching the origins of the East African Protectorates Loans Act of 1914, the last significant proposal before the outbreak of war. The act sanctioned an Imperial government loan of £3 million to Nyasaland, Uganda and the East Africa Protectorate. It was passed days after the war began and remained moribund for the duration of hostilities. In keeping with the normal pattern, the proposal to provide aid to the three territories was made in response to pressures from outside the Colonial Office. Harcourt, the Secretary of State, informed the cabinet in June 1913 that M.P.s, visitors to East Africa and the press were complaining about the congestion on local railways which was affecting the production and export of local produce, especially cotton. It is also clear that the Colonial Office were still heavily influenced by the traditional concern to achieve the financial self-sufficiency of the territories. Harcourt explained that the economic dislocation caused by inadequate local communications risked increasing their burden on the Imperial Exchequer.[48] The formal Colonial Office request to the Treasury argued that

those Protectorates have now reached a critical stage in their development, where it appears to Mr. Harcourt to be essential that something should be done if only in the interests of the British taxpayer .... His Majesty's Government have, therefore, a direct pecuniary interest in devising means whereby the Protectorates can obtain funds to provide the necessary facilities for transport.[49]

This argument was not just a means of appeasing the Treasury. Harcourt explained to the House of Commons, 'we are only authorising a loan to the Protectorates at their own expense', and the objective was to prevent them becoming a charge on the British taxpayer.[50] The Colonial Office also took pains to ensure that the schemes authorised would be financially remunerative so that the territories would not find interest and sinking fund expenses too onerous. Projects in Uganda were cut down by the office lest their cost unbalance the local budget and force a renewed dependence on grants-in-aid.[51] Such caution did not lessen the degree of Treasury control. The £3 million eventually authorised was not to be handed over to the Secretary of State as a block grant for distribution at his discretion. The Treasury retained the power to authorise the apportionment and issue of the loans: they feared reckless expenditure.[52]

Harcourt had, however, been responding in part to those interested outsiders who wished to see better transport facilities in East Africa in order to improve supplies of empire cotton. In his cabinet submission he referred to the expansion of trade which would result from new development, and this was an argument in his defence of the proposal before the House of Commons. He did claim that the measure would benefit native producers and not just United Kingdom industrialists,[53] but what is striking about the parliamentary debate is the stress placed by many speakers on the advantages to the United Kingdom of the proposed loan. It was emphasized that the territories would provide raw materials and hence employment for Lancashire cotton operatives. 'The reason this money is being given ... is for the benefit of Lancashire.' The territories would also become better markets for British manufactured goods since purchasing power would be increased, and 'it is the workmen of this country who are going to find the railway material and the many things that the settlers will want out there'.[54] These arguments are not so obvious in the departmental negotiations which produced the bill but they seem to have been powerful agents in its passage.

It is then possible to discern in the generation before the First World War two main justifications for a policy of imperial-aided colonial development. The more traditional policy, the West African model, was firmly-rooted in the Colonial Office. It had as its main objective the financial self-sufficiency of colonial governments primarily by improving export facilities and raising local taxable resources. The alternative approach, most conspicuously launched by Chamberlain and fuelled by the evidence of foreign economic and political competition and social unrest at home, emphasized the metropolitan advantages to be derived from the development of colonial resources. But neither economic necessity nor Chamberlainite rhetoric had effected a fundamental change in development policy. The most that can be said is that outside pressure groups, politicians and Colonial Office staff had been provided with an additional argument, an appeal to national economic self-interest. The decision-makers of the war and post-war period were therefore equipped with both old and new concepts drawn from this earlier experience. Whether the re-examination of the economic value of the empire caused by the First World War had any lasting effect on the respective priorities of these concepts and on policy decisions must be the next subject for assessment.

NOTES

1. *Colonial Office Lists* and *Who Was Who*.
2. *Statistical Abstract for the British Empire 1899–1913*, Cd.7827, 1915, p.2, census returns of 1911.
3. See especially B. Semmel, *Imperialism and Social Reform*, London, 1960.
4. The best studies of Chamberlain's work at the Colonial Office are R. M. Kesner, *Economic Control and Colonial Development. Crown Colony Financial Management in the Age of Joseph Chamberlain*, Oxford, 1981; R. E. Dumett, 'Joseph Chamberlain, imperial finance and railway policy in British West Africa in the late nineteenth century', *E.H.R.*, 90 (1975), 287-321, and R. V. Kubicek, *The Administration of Imperialism: Joseph Chamberlain at the Colonial Office*, Durham, N.C., 1969; but see also S. B. Saul, 'The Economic Significance of Constructive Imperialism', *J.Ec.Hist.*, 17 (1957), 173-92; S. M. Hardy, 'Joseph Chamberlain and Some Problems of the "Under-developed Estates"', *Univ. of Birmingham Historical Journal*, 11 (1968), 170-90; and H. A. Will, 'Colonial Policy and Economic Development in the British West Indies 1895–1903', *Ec.H.R.*, 23 (1970), 129-47.
5. Quotations from Lord Milner, 'Mr. Chamberlain and Imperial Policy', a chapter in the *Life of Joseph Chamberlain* published immediately after Chamberlain's death by Associated Newspapers, London, 1914, pp.219-21, and B. Porter, *The Lion's Share*, London, 1975, p.189.
6. Sir Charles Bruce, 'The Colonial Office and the Crown Colonies', *Empire Review*, 11 (May 1906), 296, 298; Milner in *Life of Joseph Chamberlain*, p.219. See also Lord Milner, *The Nation and the Empire*, London, 1913, p.462.
7. R. Hyam, *Elgin and Churchill at the Colonial Office*, London, 1968, p.430. See also L. C. A. Knowles, *The Economic Development of the British Overseas Empire*, vol.1, 2nd ed., London, 1928, pp.56, 120; R. Robinson and J. Gallagher, *Africa and the Victorians*, London, 1961, p.396, and Kesner, *Economic Control and Colonial Development*, pp.45, 69.
8. E. R. Wicker, 'Colonial Development and Welfare, 1929–1957: The Evolution of a Policy', *Social and Economic Studies*, 7 (1958), 173. Kesner's figure of £23,656,267 covers expenditure by the Colonial Office between 1879 and 1914 on all services including grants to meet administrative costs and other non-developmental items, *Economic Control and Colonial Development*, Table 5, pp.34-43.
9. Knatchbull-Hugessen in 1871, quoted in H. L. Hall, *The Colonial Office*, London, 1937, p.36. For a later complaint see W. A. Baillie Hamilton, 'Forty-Four Years at the Colonial Office', *The Nineteenth Century and After*, 65 (1909), 610-12.

10. A. M. Burton, 'Treasury Control and Colonial Policy in the Late Nineteenth Century', *Public Administration*, 44 (1966), 169-92, based on her D.Phil. thesis 'The Influence of the Treasury on the Making of British Colonial Policy 1868–1880', Oxford, 1960; H. Roseveare, *The Treasury*, London, 1969, pp.133-50, 183-233; M. Wright, 'Treasury Control 1854–1914' in G. Sutherland, ed., *Studies in the Growth of Nineteenth Century Government*, London, 1972, pp.195-226.

11. Dumett, 'Joseph Chamberlain, imperial finance and railway policy', p.292; Hyam, *Elgin and Churchill at the Colonial Office*, p.470 note 2; Kesner, *Economic Control and Colonial Development*, pp.99, 117-18.

12. The phrase is Sir Robert Lowe's to the Select Committee on Civil Service Expenditure 1873, quoted in Roseveare, *The Treasury*, p.203.

13. B. L. Blakeley, *The Colonial Office 1868–1892*, Durham, N.C., 1972, pp.138, 150-1.

14. Burton, 'Treasury Control', p.176.

15. Burton, 'Treasury Control'; L-J.L. Nthenda, 'H.M. Treasury and the Problems of Nyasaland Public Finances 1919 to 1940', D.Phil. thesis, Oxford, 1972, pp.1-37.

16. Kubicek, *The Administration of Imperialism*, pp.76-9; Hyam, *Elgin and Churchill at the Colonial Office*, p.469.

17. For contradictory opinions on the value of the act see A. S. J. Baster, 'A Note on the Colonial Stock Acts and Dominion Borrowing', *Economic History*, 2 (1933), 602-8; Saul, 'Constructive Imperialism', p.189; I. M. Drummond, *British Economic Policy and the Empire*, London, 1972, p.43; and Kesner, *Economic Control and Colonial Development*, pp.81-8. See also D. Jessop, 'The Colonial Stock Act of 1900: A Symptom of the New Imperialism?', *J.I.C.H.*, 4 (1976) (Cass), 154-63.

18. Dumett, 'Joseph Chamberlain, imperial finance and railway policy', pp.302-20. For another account of these negotiations which ascribes the failure of the Colonial Loans Fund Bill to Treasury and not Parliamentary objections see Kesner, *Economic Control and Colonial Development*, pp.72-81. See also table in Kubicek, *The Administration of Imperialism*, p.81: less than half the amount sanctioned had been issued by 1910.

19. Hyam, *Elgin and Churchill at the Colonial Office*, pp.443, 447-8.

20. Dumett, 'Joseph Chamberlain, imperial finance and railway policy', p.321.

21. Quotations from R. Hyam, 'The Colonial Office Mind 1900–1914', *J.I.C.H.*, 8 (1979) 32. See also Hyam, *Elgin and Churchill at the Colonial Office*, pp.470-1, and R. C. Snelling and T. J. Barron, 'The Colonial Office and its permanent officials 1801–1914' in Sutherland, ed., *Studies in the Growth of Nineteenth Century Government*, p.165.

22. D. C. M. Platt, *Finance, Trade and Politics. British Foreign Policy 1815–1914* Oxford, 1968, pp.xx-xxx; L. H. Gann and P. Duignan, *The Rulers of British Africa 1870–1914*, London, 1978, p.53.

23. K. Sinclair, 'Hobson and Lenin in Johore: Colonial Office policy towards Concessionaires and Investors 1898–1907', *Modern Asian Studies*, 1 (1967), espec. pp.345-8.

24. See the enthusiasm for such work in 1909 described by Sir Cosmo Parkinson, *The Colonial Office from Within 1909–1945*, London, 1947, pp.47-50. See also R. E. Dumett, 'The Campaign against Malaria and the Expansion of Scientific, Medical and Sanitary Services in British West Africa, 1898–1910', *African Historical Studies*, 1 (1968), 153-95.

25. *Hansard* H.C., vol.36, col.642, 22 August 1895; see also Milner, *The Nation and the Empire*, p.xxxiii.

26. See, for example, C.O. minute quoted by Hyam, *Elgin and Churchill at the Colonial Office*, p.197.

27. R. Hyam, *Britain's Imperial Century 1815–1914*, London, 1976, pp.37-9, 78-85, 105-7, 287-9; D. A. Low, *Lion Rampant*, Frank Cass, London, 1973, pp.41-70.
28. W. K. Hancock, *Survey of British Commonwealth Affairs. Vol.II, Problems of Economic Policy 1918–39*, part 1, London, 1940, pp.53-72, part 2, London, 1942, pp.173-200; C. Wilson, *A History of Unilever* Vol.1, London, 1954, 165-7; D. K. Fieldhouse, 'The Economic Exploitation of Africa: some British and French Comparisons', in P. Gifford and W. R. Louis, eds., *France and Britain in Africa*, New Haven and London, 1971, pp.617-18.
29. A. G. Hopkins, *An Economic History of West Africa*, London, 1973, pp.210-14.
30. Hyam, *Elgin and Churchill at the Colonial Office*, pp.367-427, 464-8; Hyam, 'The Colonial Office Mind 1900–1914', pp.45-9; Porter, *The Lion's Share*, p.223; B. Porter, *Critics of Empire*, London, 1968, espec. chaps.6-9.
31. For similar attitudes in the Colonial Service see C. Ehrlich, 'Building and Care-taking: Economic Policy in British Tropical Africa, 1890–1960', *Ec.H.R.*, 26 (1973), 649-52.
32. Kubicek, *The Administration of Imperialism*, p.42; Snelling and Barron, 'The Colonial Office', p.158.
33. *Colonial Office List* 1914. The dominions department, set up in 1907, handled in addition the affairs of the South African Protectorates, Southern Rhodesia, Fiji and the Western Pacific. For a brief history of office organisation see R. B. Pugh, *The Records of the Colonial and Dominions Offices*, London, HMSO, 1964, pp.9-16.
34. Snelling and Barron, 'The Colonial Office', p.165. See also figures of papers registered in Kesner, *Economic Control and Colonial Development*, pp.56-7. For a contemporary comment on the increased work of the office see Sir John Brampton, 'The Colonial Office from Within', *Empire Review*, 1 (1901), 279-87.
35. Kubicek, *The Administration of Imperialism*, p.20; Hyam, 'The Colonial Office Mind', p.33.
36. A. W. Abbott, *A Short History of the Crown Agents and their Office*, London, 1959, pp.27-32; Dumett, 'Joseph Chamberlain, imperial finance and railway policy', pp.308-9; V. Ponko, 'Economic Management in a Free Trade Empire: the work of the Crown Agents for the Colonies in the 19th and early 20th Cen-turies', *J.Ec.Hist.*, 26 (1966), 363-77; R. M. Kesner, 'Builders of Empire: the Role of the Crown Agents in Imperial Development, 1880–1914', *J.I.C.H.*, 5 (1977), 310-30.
37. Parkinson, *The Colonial Office from Within*, pp.25-6; Sir George Fiddes, *The Dominions and Colonial Offices*, London, 1926, pp.33-9; *Colonial Office List* 1914.
38. Parkinson, *The Colonial Office from Within*, p.25.
39. Burton, 'Influence of the Treasury', p.107; J. Amery, *The Life of Joseph Chamberlain* Vol.IV, London, 1951, pp.316-18; Robinson and Gallagher, *Africa and the Victorians*, pp.308-9, 328, 350-1. See also Hyam, *Elgin and Churchill at the Colonial Office*, pp.444, 447, for military arguments in favour of a railway to Northern Nigeria.
40. Hyam, *Elgin and Churchill at the Colonial Office*, pp.459-61.
41. Will, 'Colonial Policy and Economic Development in the British West Indies 1895–1903'; Saul, 'Constructive Imperialism', p.188. See also Hyam, *Elgin and Churchill at the Colonial Office*, pp.461-2 for the continuation of this policy.
42. Dumett, 'Joseph Chamberlain, imperial finance and railway policy', p.312; Hyam, *Elgin and Churchill at the Colonial Office*, pp.435, 440-9.
43. Hyam, *Elgin and Churchill at the Colonial Office*, pp.469-70.
44. Dumett, 'Joseph Chamberlain, imperial finance and railway policy', pp.296-7.
45. Hyam, *Elgin and Churchill at the Colonial Office*, pp.444, 451-6. The Sudan was a responsibility of the Foreign Office.

46. *Hansard* H.C., vol.50, col.26, 10 March 1913. T. Barnett, *The Gezira Scheme: An Illusion of Development*, Frank Cass, London, 1977, p.4, asserts, without citing evidence, that the purpose was to enable the Sudan to finance its own administration. See also A. Gaitskell, *Gezira: a story of development in the Sudan*, London, 1959, p.66.
47. Saul, 'Constructive Imperialism', p.188; Hyam, *Elgin and Churchill at the Colonial Office*, pp.430-4. Milner stressed the value to Europeans of research into tropical diseases in *Life of Joseph Chamberlain*, pp.225, 227.
48. Harcourt, memo. to the cabinet, 7 June 1913, P.R.O. Treasury Board Papers, document 14326 of 1913 kept in box 11792, file 14101 of 1915, henceforth cited as T1/11792/14101. See also questions in the Commons, CO 533/128/HC 19563 and HC 27291.
49. Fiddes to Treas., 9 July 1913, CO 533/129/MO 23554.
50. *Hansard* H.C., vol.60, cols.1856, 1826, 7 April 1914.
51. Minutes by Read, 15 Jan. 1914, and Fiddes, 20 and 22 Jan. 1914, CO 533/125/Gov 1164.
52. Treas. to C.O., 19 Aug. 1913, CO 533/128/Treas. 29031; memo. by Behrens, 10 June 1913, T1/11792/14101.
53. *Hansard* H.C., vol.61, cols.45-6, 14 April 1914.
54. *Hansard* H.C., vol.60, cols.1840, 1870, 7 April 1914; vol.61, cols.52, 68, 14 April 1914.

III

WAR AND RECONSTRUCTION
1914—21

1. *THE ECONOMICS OF SIEGE*

The economic worth of the British Empire and the case for a more vigorous colonial development policy had been enthusiastically presented by neo-mercantilists like Joseph Chamberlain before 1914. But for many people the value of the empire was only to be revealed by the outbreak of the First World War. Colonial and dominion troops were then used extensively in Europe and elsewhere, and the financial and natural resources of the empire helped fuel the British economy and the war effort.[1] Prolonged warfare seemed to demonstrate the potential of the empire. The chances of realising its assets more fully by a more vigorous development policy also seemed to be increased by the political changes which took place in Britain during the war. Initially Asquith's government attempted to mobilise the nation for war broadly in accordance with free market methods and ideals, but the requirements of a protracted conflict between modern industrial nations frustrated those efforts. The formation of the Coalition government in conjunction with Bonar Law in May 1915 and Asquith's replacement as Prime Minister by Lloyd George in December 1916 were political land marks on a road which led to increasing state controls over the economy and the British people. The authority of the state was vastly increased by the creation of new government departments, by state production and services, and by extensive controls over finance, prices, supplies and labour.[2] Moreover, the war brought to power a number of ministers and officials who might well be tempted to use that authority to achieve their ideals of imperial expansion, unity and development. Lloyd George's five-man streamlined war cabinet contained the tariff reformer Bonar Law as Chancellor of the Exchequer, Curzon previously Viceroy of India and Milner recently High Commissioner in South Africa and a passionate advocate of imperial political consolidation and state-directed imperial economic expansion. Former members of Milner's South African staff like Curtis, Kerr and Buchan and other close associates like Waldorf Astor and Leo Amery came into official posts. Amery, like Milner, had been an ardent supporter of Joseph Chamberlain before the war: he was to devote most of his political career to the cause of imperial unity and economic development. W. A. S. Hewins, another supporter, became under-secretary at the Colonial Office in 1917, and John Hodge who was appointed Minister of Labour in 1916 remained until July 1918 a leader of the British Workers' National League, an organisation set up by Milner and other tariff reform Conservatives in 1916 to rally working-class support for imperial development and social reform. The waging of war diluted the forces of liberalism and ensured that policy fell increasingly under the sway of imperial enthusiasts.[3]

However, during the war years, the development of colonial resources depended almost entirely on colonial initiatives, energies and assets. In the immediate emergency, colonies could receive little help from the Imperial government. A scarcity of shipping restricted cargo space to the transport of essential goods and thus limited the supply of materials from Britain for public works in the colonies. Moreover, in an effort to preserve financial resources for urgent military purposes, the Treasury restricted access to the London Stock Market,[4] urged colonies to raise locally whatever loans they needed,[5] and insisted that the Colonial Office like other government departments exercise the greatest economy in carrying out their duties. Sustained pressure from the Treasury effected a reduction in expenditure on Colonial Services from £781,195 in 1913—14 to £605,257 in 1918—19.[6] In general the Colonial Office permanent and political staff accepted without complaint that the emergency of war required co-operation with the Treasury in reducing the financial cost of the Colonial Empire.[7]

The main aim of the Imperial government during the war was therefore to obtain those colonial supplies already available with little help to increase their production. But just as the war and political change stimulated ideas for post-war domestic reconstruction and reform,[8] so too it inspired various official plans for the future development of the colonies.[9] These took up considerable energies and aroused much interest in the later stage of the war. Hostility towards Germany and a desire to frustrate German recovery after the war was the first step towards a reappraisal of traditional British economic policy. A German economic offensive was feared when peace came, made more alarming by the recognition that free trade had left Britain vulnerable to German economic pressure. As Asquith told the Commons in August 1916:

We never realised, any of us, until the War broke out how we have allowed ourselves to become dependent with regard to ... essential ingredients for the prosecution of some of our most important industries on sources of supply that were not only not within our own control, but that could be absolutely controlled by the enemy.[10]

Policy changes were apparently needed to undo the damage, and this led the Board of Trade to prepare proposals late in 1915. More public was British participation in the Paris Economic Conference of allied powers in June 1916. Bonar Law insisted on being a member of the British delegation, and perhaps due to his influence the British government proposed the resolution accepted by the conference that in the post-war world the allies should 'render themselves independent of the enemy countries in so far as regards the raw materials and manufactured articles essential to the normal development of their economic activities'. It was understood that achieving this end might involve state enterprise or state encouragement for industry, financial assistance for scientific and technical research and for the development of national industries and resources, and tariff reform.[11]

The inspiration given by the experience of wartime state economic controls and activity was evident in these plans. This can also be seen in other official proposals at the time. For example, the Faringdon Committee set up by the Board of Trade 'to consider the best means of meeting the needs of British firms after the War as regards financial facilities for trade', recommended in August 1916 the creation by the Imperial government of a British Trade Bank to help British overseas traders open up new markets.[12] Such a scheme was in line with the revived neo-mercantilist enthusiasm for state encouragement for industry.

A further major inspiration for new proposals was the evidence of wartime imperial co-operation not only economically and on the battlefield but politically. Lloyd George in particular, by the creation of an Imperial War Cabinet meeting for the first time in March 1917 and by the summoning of Imperial War Conferences in 1917 and

1918, appeared to endorse the move towards imperial consolidation and post-war unity. Fuelling such ideals was Lord Balfour of Burleigh's Committee on Commercial and Industrial Policy. This committee had been set up in July 1916 to consider ways of putting the Paris Economic Conference resolutions into effect, and in an interim report in February 1917, substantially influenced by Hewins, a member of the committee, it broke with traditional government policy by recommending imperial tariff preferences to help in the recovery of trade lost during the war, to secure new markets and to consolidate the empire.[13] More far-reaching was the final report in March 1917 of the Dominions Royal Commission which had been appointed after the Imperial Conference in 1911 but whose deliberations were much affected by wartime anxieties and discussions. Although the bulk of its recommendations concerned the dominions, many involved the future development of the Colonial Empire. It argued that the empire's resources were enough to make it a self-sufficient unit 'which would enable it to resist any pressure which a foreign Power or group of Powers could exercise in time of peace or during war in virtue of a control of raw materials and commodities essential for the safety and well-being of the Empire'. To achieve this autarkic security, the commission recommended the establishment of an Imperial Development Board. This would represent the dependencies as well as the dominions. It would be advisory in its initial stages but would have considerable duties: to survey the resources and changing needs of the empire, to encourage scientific research and development plans, to direct empire capital towards the exploitation of empire resources, to publish statistical material, to study migration problems, to review imperial communications and to examine other trading questions. While the report did not recommend the creation of a state-financed imperial development fund or state enterprise, it did endorse the idea of a British Trade Bank to help finance new works on the lines of Lord Faringdon's proposals.[14]

Imperial enthusiasts in the British government and ministers from the dominions ensured that some of these post-war proposals were considered by the Imperial War Conferences. Although commitments were made in rather general terms, the conference did commit itself in April 1917 to the principle of imperial preference and did recommend that steps should be taken to encourage the further development and control of imperial resources.[15] Some detailed imperial preference proposals put forward by Walter Long, the Secretary of State for the Colonies, and by Hewins, his under-secretary, were accepted by the cabinet in July 1918,[16] and a number of other specific recommendations concerning, for example, the control of empire raw materials, emigration within the empire and inter-imperial shipping were approved by the next Imperial War Conference in 1918.[17]

It is then apparent that particularly in the later stages of the war there was a good deal of sympathy in official quarters for the reconstruction of British economic policy on novel lines which might involve after the war imperial tariff preferences and greater state support in various forms for imperial economic development. It is also clear that these proposals struck a responsive chord in many quarters outside government. Many journals and newspapers of the war period carried articles which thundered against German commercial practices and urged retaliatory action after the war.[18] Businessmen claimed that Germany controlled Britain's supplies of important commodities like sugar beet, dyes, jute and certain metals. Even British herb-growing, it seemed, was imperilled by the machinations of Central European producers.[19] It was widely believed that the war had exposed the inadequacy of pre-war policy and the need for a new departure. As one commentator put it, 'the attitude to be adopted in peace should always be considered in the light of its effect on the security and well-being of the State in war'.[20] Moreover, the phenomenon of imperial unity during the war inspired unofficial as well as official proposals. It was noted that in the pooling of imperial resources for the war effort 'we may ... find an irresistible argument for increasing a commercial association which is immune from political entanglements and the rival interests of neutral, even if friendly States'.[21] The logical conclusion of such arguments endorsed by many observers was the autarkic empire. The chairman of the British Cotton Growing Association recommended that 'we should grow as we can do, within the British Empire, all the cotton required by our mills, and so make them perfectly independent of all foreign countries', and the consulting engineer of the Burma Oil Company argued that the empire should attempt to produce all the oil supplies it needed in a major development effort. Sugar supplies could be obtained either from the West Indies or by developing a sugar beet industry in Britain. Timber supplies, badly needed in the war, should in future be obtained either by increasing colonial supplies or by afforestation in Britain.[22] In brief, the empire 'can supply every vital need of civilised man'.[23]

To achieve these targets unofficial commentators often emphasized the valuable wartime experience of extended state enterprise and economic organisation. Such 'War Socialism', it was felt, need not be a transitory phenomenon. 'After our experience of this war, it is out of the question to suppose we can again pursue a policy of complete laissez-faire, of complete laissez-aller, of freedom from all Government interference, Government assistance, or Government help in any form.' The extension of state control should be welcomed.[24] Most obviously this meant the acceptance of tariff reform since 'the day of Free Trade ... is now a thing of the past',[25] but there were also proposals for more extensive use of state credit, for improved government information and research services and for an Imperial Development Board. Many of those concerned particularly with the Colonial Empire urged an increase in Imperial government aid for the building of economic infrastructures in the colonies without which private enterprise in colonial production and marketing faced high risks and excessive costs.[26]

Such ideas on the need for imperial economic development and on the methods for securing it were embraced not just by such committed imperialists as the readers of the *Empire Review* or the members of the Royal Colonial Institute. They were also endorsed to varying degrees by a large section of the Conservative party such as those organised in 1915 by Hewins in the Unionist Business Committee,[27] by a few Labour leaders particularly those recruited to the British Workers' National League,[28] and by such substantial business interests as those represented in the British Empire Producers' Organisation and in the British Commonwealth Union.[29] To illuminate the aims and techniques of one such unofficial lobby it is worth examining more closely the activities of the Empire Resources Development Committee.[30]

The E.R.D.C. had three principal founders: Henry Wilson-Fox, Unionist M.P. for North Warwickshire from 1917 to 1921 and a director of the British South Africa Company, Alfred Bigland, Unionist M.P. for East Birkenhead from 1910 to 1922, an early adherent of the Tariff Reform League and an oils and fats controller during the war, and Moreton Frewen, formerly a cattle rancher in the American Wild West, briefly an M.P., an early supporter of the United Empire Trade League and a vice-president of the Imperial

Federation League.[31] Two articles in *The Times* in September 1916 written by Wilson-Fox were the first public statement of their ideas.[32] An inaugural meeting of the committee was held on 31 October 1916,[33] and a manifesto was published in the press on 29 January 1917. This was signed by thirty-three people made up of several current and former M.P.s, a few peers, several businessmen including four with interests in the British South Africa Company, a few writers on empire including Kipling, and four government ministers, John Hodge, Minister of Labour, Worthington-Evans, a junior at the Ministry of Munitions, Islington, a former under-secretary at the Colonial Office and currently at the India Office, and Macpherson the under-secretary at the War Office.[34] Walter Long and Lord Milner were initially members of the committee, the latter as the first chairman, but they resigned on taking office at the end of 1916.[35] Wilson-Fox, Bigland and Moreton Frewen, aided by other supporters, kept up a pamphlet, journal and newspaper campaign from 1916 to 1920. Their plans were backed by *The British Citizen and Empire Worker* and the British Workers' National League,[36] and their arguments were aired in the House of Commons, latterly by the Empire Development Parliamentary Committee which Bigland set up in 1920 and which claimed the support of over 200 M.P.s.[37] There was some development of the programme advocated by the E.R.D.C. but it remained constant in its major objectives and proposals.

'Within the Allied Empire are tremendous resources, capable of development by means of relatively small capital expenditure into assets of immense value.' Like many others during the war, members of the E.R.D.C. were impressed by the economic potential of the empire, and they too argued that 'the end to be attained is that the Empire should be self-supporting in all essentials'.[38] But more unusually they were conscious of the handicap which the war was imposing on British industry. The National Debt was rising massively and Wilson-Fox foresaw an annual charge of £210 million to service that debt. To avoid grinding post-war taxation which would discourage productive industry this burden would have to be lessened by the development of fresh sources of revenue.[39] But while this would lighten the load on the investing classes, the benefits would also inevitably be felt by British workers. Social imperialist ideas, close to Milner's views, were expressed for example by Bigland who argued that only the development of the empire's wealth could provide the

finance for social reforms.[40] Moreover, claimed Wilson-Fox, the war
had shown that 'there is no real reason why an unemployable class
should find a place in our social system'. 'The prosperity of the worker
during the war has been due to large State orders. If the State adopts
the Committee's plan it will become after the War a large buyer of
goods, materials and machinery.'[41] In the extreme form visualised by
one Labour party supporter imperial development would allow the
workers full employment, a six-hour day and two months holiday a
year.[42]

To achieve these delights, the committee envisaged considerable
state controls and enterprise. The principles of List and Naumann
were applauded, and there was praise for Bismarck's state socialism.
The interests of the individual must henceforth take second place to
the needs of the community.[43] The Imperial government would
benefit indirectly from empire development with a general rise in the
level of trade and therefore of taxable resources, but also directly,
for the committee intended that the state should be a public investor
and extract a profit. For example, they proposed state marketing of
fish, palm products, corn and electricity.[44] The committee were
seeking a partnership with private enterprise and denied any socialist
intent. For example, they argued that the state should invest in the
economic infrastructure of colonies and that this would open up opportunities for private business.[45]

Most imaginative was a plan to set up an Imperial Development
Board. This would have twenty members, mostly prominent businessmen, though including up to five civil servants, presided over by the
Secretary of State for the Colonies. The board would have executive
as well as advisory powers. In the first proposals it was to be given
an annual credit of £20 million by the Treasury.[46] Later it was
suggested that the money could come from that portion of the sinking
fund which would otherwise be used for paying off the National Debt.
In addition the fund could absorb the savings of the poorer classes.
And the state would guarantee all capital raised.[47] Another proposal
spoke of a supply from the Consolidated Fund of £10 million a year
for ten years after which time it was estimated that the fund would
be receiving an income sufficient to pay the interest on further loans
it could raise publicly.[48] However financed, the Imperial Development Board would then entrust capital to subsidiary Authorities which
would be constituted *ad hoc* to co-operate with private companies
engaged in particular activities. State funds would thus be expended

in conjunction with private capital and the profits of such enterprises shared. Subsidiary Authorities would, of course, be run by qualified businessmen who 'would be practically in the position occupied by directors of ordinary commercial companies, and the government of the day would have very little power of interference with them in the conduct of their business'.[49] The purchase of the Suez Canal shares, Churchill's purchase while at the Admiralty of a considerable interest in the Anglo-Persian Oil Company (B.P.), and the Development Commission responsible for the administration of the 1909 Development and Road Improvement Fund were quoted, not altogether accurately, as precedents for this sort of state enterprise.[50]

One assumption of the E.R.D.C. was that the empire, particularly the Colonial Empire, was a collection of undeveloped estates which the metropolis had definite rights to treat as imperial possessions. Bitter attacks on the committee came from those who suspected that their proposals would lead to gross infringement of native land rights in Africa. The sponsors protested that their proposals would be of equal benefit to all members of the empire, but their statements of good intent could not belie the implications of some of their proposals. It did not require an unduly cynical mind to interpret these as activated against native production. 'The adoption of sane, just, and practical views in regard to native ownership of land and native labour is above all essential', wrote Wilson-Fox.[51] Bigland agreed:

The proposed development scheme would afford a splendid means of facilitating the civilisation of the natives, as their labour would be harnessed to the chariot of progress and productiveness, and their purchases would to a greater extent than at present be under government control, thus in time enabling the disastrous gin traffic to be done away with entirely.[52]

Wilson-Fox was bluntly in favour of a planter's policy and hoped development would lead to an increase in the white population in tropical territories. And the broad justification was that 'at great sacrifice of life and treasure we have given millions of natives in Africa security of life and property. We can fairly claim that the natives shall in return bear their share of the Imperial burden'.[53]

If this was the seamier side of the committee's plans, there was also an important imaginative contribution to the ideas on empire development. The concept of a type of public corporation endowed with large state funds, employing experienced businessmen and using national credit for swift development of resources could be a vision of considerable attraction.

Looking into the future we can visualize the State as an owner of vast herds of cattle Overseas raised on lands which are today unutilised; as a proprietor of forests and valuable plantations of tropical shrubs and trees grown on areas which are still virgin; as the harnesser of mighty waterfalls fed by the eternal snows of India and Africa; as an organiser of great commercial air services; and as the reaper on an immense scale of the manifold harvest of the seas.[54]

2. COLONIAL OFFICE RESPONSES

The Colonial Office, like the rest of the country, became involved in considering post-war development problems during the summer of 1916. How did the permanent and political staff react to these official and unofficial proposals for radical innovations in imperial economic policy? What is remarkable is how little interest was shown in them by the permanent officials and how uncontaminated they were by the 'economics of siege' enthusiasms. Most matters were discussed primarily in the context of dominion rather than colonial affairs and even then without a great deal of eagerness.

Colonial governments were asked to give their views on the Paris Economic Conference recommendations and these were dutifully passed on to the Balfour of Burleigh Committee,[55] but senior staff in the office showed little desire to assist the investigations of the Dominions Royal Commission during the war and showed scant interest in their proposal to set up an Imperial Development Board.[56] Similarly, on being informed of the setting up of the Faringdon Committee on Financial Facilities after the war, Grindle, an assistant under-secretary, observed that 'this is not a matter in which we have any very direct interest', and the subject was 'put by'.[57] Equally dismissive was office reaction to a proposal by the Imperial Institute for forming committees in the Institute and in each colony to make surveys of the commercial resources of the territories. The minutes agree that such committees would serve no useful purpose since the needs of the dependencies were well known. As Read, another assistant under-secretary, put it, 'the main thing is to find the money'.[58] A similar hard-headed realism was shown in response to a Royal Colonial Institute programme for colonial development. A deputation from the institute proposed the creation of a committee to collate development schemes in different colonies and to suggest the ways in which imperial grants or loans could be spent to foster British trade. It received little encouragement. The official mind of the Colonial Office was revealed in one comment: 'I imagine that the duty of the C.O. is primarily to watch over the interests of the individual colonies, and not directly to foster British trade at their expense'.[59]

In March 1916 the Reconstruction Committee was created, to be turned into the Ministry of Reconstruction in July 1917.[60] Although its duties were to determine in advance the problems and possibilities likely to be brought up after the war, its formation generated little activity in the Colonial Office. A circular sent round the geographical departments produced few suggestions and the memorandum eventually drawn up mentioned the specific development needs of only British Guiana, Antarctica and the West Indies and the prospects for a handful of colonial commodities.[61] When in August 1917 the ministry asked the Colonial Office what action it was taking the chief clerk minuted that very little was being done.[62] Eventually after another reminder from the ministry a new memorandum sketching out the territories and products most in need of consideration was despatched in October.[63] But the Colonial Office did little more. Long, the Secretary of State, wanted to help the ministry but he admitted that it was not possible to do much because the office was already understaffed and overburdened.[64] More seriously, it seems clear that the Colonial Office and the Ministry of Reconstruction had quite different aims in mind. The ministry assumed that a serious economic depression would hit British industry with the ending of the war. As a counter-measure it sought to increase overseas demand for British goods in the immediate post-war period; hence its interest in colonial development proposals which would create such demand.[65] The Colonial Office did not share this preoccupation with the metropolitan economy. It was primarily concerned to obtain easier terms for financial aid for the development of the few territories dependent on Imperial government help. It was interested only in such proposals and did not consider its duties to include the pressing of economic development schemes on the financially independent territories of the Colonial Empire. This traditional attitude towards imperial development explains the desultory reaction of the Colonial Office to such overtures.

The same attitude can be seen in the permanent staff's response to the programme of the E.R.D.C. Wilson-Fox's two articles in *The Times* in September 1916 and his piece in the *Journal of the Royal Society of Arts* in December 1916 were filed and minuted in the Colonial Office.[66] They inaugurated a surprising amount of discussion in the office which ultimately revealed the permanent staff's conservatism and loyalty to established ideals and practices and their suspicion of grandiose imperial visionary schemes. It is noticeable that the political staff were more attracted to the E.R.D.C.'s programme.

Among many of the permanent staff, the first reaction was delight that somebody had acknowledged the value of the Colonial Empire's vegetable and mineral wealth. Harris, the chief clerk, commented that 'it is a great satisfaction to have the possibility of vigorous development pressed on us at a time when the dominant thought is thrift and parsimony'. However, Green, principal clerk of the West Indies department, observed that 'there is little in Mr. Wilson-Fox's paper that has not been common thought since Mr. Chamberlain's reference to "undeveloped estates", but constant failure has been disheartening'. The cause of this failure was identified by several officials. Strachey, head of the Nigeria department, was pessimistic about the future:

The annual fight with the Treasury over the estimates of the "grant-in-aid" Colonies I suppose still goes on. We are happily now free from it in Nigeria: but it is not long since we had to justify at length not only any large schemes (which were usually vetoed at once) but increases of £10 or £20 to the pay of deserving employees. In the year 1907−8 the whole amount sanctioned for buildings, roads, telegraphs and sanitary works in Northern Nigeria (a country about as big as France and Italy put together) was £49,857[67] − less than one third of what was announced in that year as the cost of the Camberwell Infirmary. Whether a new spirit will be breathed into the Treasury under the new conditions, when all the old arguments for "economy" will be a thousand-fold stronger, time alone will show.

Green added that 'the Treasury will not help unless they can control the whole expenditure of the Colony, in which case their ignorance of Colonial and industrial affairs may block all progress'. In general the Colonial Office permanent staff were not optimistic about the chances of obtaining capital for the poorer territories on easy terms after the war. Lambert, head of the Dominions department, pointed out that after the war there would be heavy demands on the money market by the dominions and for other domestic requirements, and that the loans Wilson-Fox advocated would be very hard to come by. Butler, principal clerk of the East Africa department, believed that the Colonial Empire would not get favourable financial terms and that it might be advisable to use the Trade Bank proposed by the Faringdon Committee. In other words, the Imperial government would have to provide the necessary facilities for easier borrowing, but there was no confidence that the Treasury would agree to that.

The next problem was the extent to which the state should involve itself in development works. One official argued that it should confine itself to roads and railways and perhaps hydro-electric power. He opposed state planting or involvement in agriculture. This was common ground in the office but he added: 'If the Imperial Government borrows the money needed for these purposes it should be charged upon the territory immediately benefited'. This was standard if ungenerous Treasury policy and differed from the opinion of many other officials. Moreover, the writer betrayed a most untypical Colonial Office attitude when he criticized the policy of upholding native claims to land.

This unqualified claim, supported by sentimentalists ..., hinders European development of the country, and perpetuates the wasteful and dangerous methods of native agriculture. It also prevents the native raising himself in the scale of civilization by the discipline of steady and continuous labour. In general I think that any scheme of State action which will prevent the industrious and adventurous man having an advantage over the lazy, wasteful and inefficient will be disastrous. Too much of our State action in this country has been in that direction.

This was pure Wilson-Fox and the more orthodox policy line on native agriculture was re-asserted by Butler, who argued that Wilson-Fox assumed resources in the colonies were at the disposal of the Imperial government: 'This, of course, is contrary to the principle on which we administer the Colonies and Protectorates'. Fiddes, the permanent under-secretary, put the case bluntly:

Before we even begin to ask if Mr. W. Fox's scheme is good we should have first to decide if we intend to turn our backs on our principles of colonization and to adopt instead the policy followed (I believe) by Holland – and by Belgium in the Congo – of exploitation for the direct pecuniary benefit of the metropolis.

Grindle argued for a compromise: 'If the Treasury are to supply money for development, they must be taken in as partners in the result, and given a fixed share of the profits. If their share went to the cancellation of war debt, colonies like British Guiana would not object'. Read, however, came out against the scheme as impracticable and urged a less ambitious programme of African colonial development: to improve communications, to investigate and control human, animal and plant diseases, to develop the agricultural and veterinary departments of the colonies so as to enable new industries and methods to be introduced, and to investigate mineral resources systematically. He stressed the considerable progress already made and was optimistic of the results if the £3 million East African Protectorates Loans Act was implemented after the war.

The general disapproval of the Wilson-Fox plan particularly in the upper echelons of the permanent staff did not deter Walter Long, the Secretary of State, and Arthur Steel-Maitland, his parliamentary under-secretary. Long was more optimistic than his permanent staff. He prophesied a new departure in public policy: 'Narrow Treasury control resulting in the blocking of all new enterprise or real development must surely come to an end'. Steel-Maitland did not think government development need be retrogressive or involve jettisoning principles on native agriculture, although he did not specify what he meant by 'government development'. He did say 'the Government ... would only be getting for the future the profits which Sir W. Lever *et hoc genus* get at present'. Since the Colonial Office had prohibited Lever from obtaining land in British West Africa for fear of its effects on native rights, this statement is both confused and indicative of a more favourable attitude to the Wilson-Fox line than that of most permanent officials. Long, obviously still sympathetic to his former colleagues on the E.R.D.C., proposed an unofficial conference with the committee. He informed the Colonial Office staff that they would hear arguments from some very able men with much knowledge and experience of imperial problems. This somewhat backhanded criticism of the Colonial Office's collective experience is indicative of the rift which existed between political and permanent staff at the office on this topic. Grindle minuted on Long's proposals that the E.R.D.C. plans were of no value to the colonies and that, for example, not one of the group knew that the Colonial Office could not do just as it liked in British Guiana — implying a criticism of the committee's studies, experience and ability, and, by implication, of Long's judgement.[68]

Did this conference take place? The records are silent. It may be significant that in May 1917 the government was urged to disavow any official approval of the E.R.D.C. proposals; it had been observed that the committee included several government ministers.[69] The minutes in the Colonial Office files on these questions are strangely quiet. The official answers, drafted by the permanent staff, disclaim any approval of the E.R.D.C.'s plans, and there is no sign that Long or Steel-Maitland protested. There seems to have been a complete victory for the views of the permanent officials.[70] Their opinions were on the whole those expressed by Steel-Maitland in the House of Commons in August 1917. He upheld the doctrine that Britain was a trustee both for the natives of the Colonial Empire and for the needs of the rest of the world, and he emphasised that development depended solely on financial supply: 'it is really a question of pounds, shillings and pence'. There was to be no colonial development solely in the interests of the British economy and the optimistic hopes that financial aid would be made available evaporated.[71]

The apparent retreat by the Colonial Office's political leaders was continued thereafter in spite of continued pressure by the E.R.D.C. The issues were reconsidered after the Armistice in the spring and summer of 1919. By this time not only had the immediate emergency of the war ended but Milner and Amery had taken charge of the Colonial Office, the former as Secretary of State, the latter at Milner's insistence as his under-secretary. Both men had past experience of colonial problems, both favoured extending state enterprise, both felt colonial development necessary for the economic and political future of Great Britain. Milner was particularly anxious to encourage reproductive expenditure, that is, government investment in development at home and especially in the Colonial Empire. Such investment would increase the resources available for social welfare at home and meet the costs of the war debt. He saw the colonies as sources of raw materials and as markets, and accepted that the state should participate in their improvement through the agency of an Imperial Development Fund.[72] It was clearly Milner's driving ambition at this time. After a cabinet meeting he made a private note that 'the only thing which keeps me in the Government at all is my desire to get the work of the C.O. on a somewhat better footing, and to give an impetus to the policy of development in the "dependent Empire". I mean to press forward as hard as I can on these lines'.[73]

These opinions were mirrored by those of Amery,[74] as can be seen in the reception he gave on 13 February 1919 in the House of Commons to the E.R.D.C.'s revived scheme for state enterprise in colonial development. Amery sympathised with their proposals to deal with the National Debt problem and agreed that the state could create new wealth 'certainly more quickly than if [individuals] were left to the ordinary course of the market, the hesitations of capital, and the fears of labour, in embarking on industry'. He tried to disarm critics by asserting that colonial administration must still be based on the principle of trusteeship:

We should not put ourselves in a position where there would be any conflict of interests between the Government of this country, which has the Colonial administration under its thumb, and the interests of the natives, or where our Government would be tempted in the direction of making a profit for the taxpayer here as against the interests of the natives for whom we are trustees.

But on the other hand, he argued, 'I do not think that there is necessarily any conflict between the two conceptions of utilising the development of the vast resources of the Empire in order to help forward trade in this country, and at the same time to help these peoples'.[75] This idea of a 'natural harmony' he repeated in the Supply debate of July 1919. He spoke of the vast potential wealth of the colonies, of the need for capital investment and of the trustees' duty to help the natives, 'but I am as sure as I stand here that we cannot develop them and help them without an over-spill of wealth and prosperity that would be an immense help to this country in the difficult times that lie ahead'. In answer to arguments that proposals for colonial development were in the interests of Great Britain only, Amery replied:

I do not see how you can create wealth and prosperity in one part of the Empire without creating it in another, and I am not prepared to accept in the least the doctrine that there is a diametric opposition in governing in the interests of the natives, and attempting to develop the country from the Imperial point of view.[76]

The difference between Amery's philosophy of state-aided colonial development and the permanent staff's traditional policy can be seen in their respective reactions to Wilson-Fox's Question to the House of Commons put down for 1 April 1919. This was framed in general terms, advocating state participation with private enterprise in colonial development on a profit-sharing basis. Grindle minuted that in this shape the scheme was free from the objection of causing unrest in native minds.

On the other hand it might well cause unrest among taxpayers at home at the prospect of losing money by participation in doubtful enterprise oversea. The proper way for the state to participate is by way of taxation: but I doubt whether the promoters of the movement realise that each colony has a separate purse distinct from that of the U.K. – that fact came as a revelation to Mr. Bigland when I was instructed to discuss somewhat similar proposals with him.

In other words, Grindle restated the Colonial Office view that colonial development was to be the responsibility of the colonial governments and depended mainly on their financial credit. Fiddes was similarly inclined to resist adding burdens to the British taxpayer's desperate case. Amery on the other hand was clearly sympathetic: 'There is no reason why the British taxpayers' money should not be profitably invested in development schemes either in conjunction with the local government or with private capital without in any way prejudicing native interests'. On this occasion the interest in colonial affairs was such that forty members not being present in the chamber, the House of Commons was adjourned and no motion was put.[77] Yet in spite of this setback and of the distinctly unenthusiastic attitude of the Colonial Office permanent staff this was not the end of the matter.

The debate of 13 February 1919 in which Wilson-Fox had put forward the E.R.D.C.'s latest proposals had important repercussions. Although the Colonial Office permanent staff had been on the whole critical of them, Amery told the Commons that the government would consider the plan for state participation in imperial economic development.[78] The Leader of the House, Bonar Law, had encouraged Wilson-Fox to see Austen Chamberlain, the Chancellor of the Exchequer. The Chancellor consulted the Minister of Munitions, the President of the Board of Trade and the Secretary of State for the Colonies, and certain objections to the E.R.D.C.'s plans were then submitted to Wilson-Fox. In reply the E.R.D.C. limited their proposals to a suggestion for a select committee to report on the state acquisition of land within the empire, on their fisheries plan, and on the development of the empire's petroleum resources. These matters were discussed by the cabinet on 18 June 1919. Chamberlain was inclined to support the first proposal if it was deemed compatible with current colonial policy. He confessed, however, that there was a dearth of capital available for even domestic needs. Milner denied this scarcity of capital.

He thought it should not be impossible to obtain capital for development of the more promising parts of what he would call our dependent Empire .... He doubted very much whether we should be able to get along on our old methods of finance; and we should have to look round for some new sources of revenue.

Bonar Law sympathised: 'He would like to say that, although it was impossible to find money for this purpose during the war when he was at the Colonial Office it had been constantly in his mind. He thought it was folly not to develop where we could and obtain a share in the profits'. The cabinet concluded that Milner should formulate definite proposals for their consideration.[79]

What are we to make of these developments? Most significantly, this rapid promotion of what the permanent staff of the Colonial Office had evidently considered to be the crank proposals of a minority committee to a subject for cabinet study and theoretical approval was brought about solely by personal pledges of politicians in the House of Commons. That is, the parliamentary system which brought ministers and M.P.s together side-stepped the process of departmental decision-making. Bonar Law, Austen Chamberlain, Amery and Milner were responsible for bringing to the cabinet's attention proposals of which the permanent staff in the Colonial Office continued to entertain strong suspicions. For example, the minutes in the Colonial Office records on this cabinet conclusion betray the antipathy of the permanent staff to the E.R.D.C. scheme for state acquisition of land within the empire. While recognising that in these new departures they must follow the lead of their political masters, the permanent staff did not disguise their reluctance.[80] This decision also makes an interesting contrast with the previous failure of the political staff to impose their views on the Colonial Office. More than anything this reflects the drive and ambition of the office's new political leaders. Milner and Amery knew clearly what they wished to achieve, and from the start Milner was determined to assert his authority over his staff. He told Amery that Fiddes, the permanent under-secretary, 'can't "run" me as he doubtless "ran" Long'.[81]

The success of Milner and Amery in obtaining cabinet encouragement for the preparation of colonial development schemes was tempered by their inability to do much about it in practice. The subject did not loom large in the attention of the cabinet. The Chancellor had made it clear that financial support would be difficult to obtain, and no further submissions were made by Milner to the cabinet on the subject. He did receive a deputation from the E.R.D.C. in October 1919,[82] but otherwise his attention was devoted to another innovation, the creation of a Colonial Development Committee. Its formation was announced to the press on 12 December 1919 and it subsequently held nine meetings, the first on 17 December 1919, the last on 24 November 1920. At most there were a dozen members. Amery was present at eight of the meetings, Milner, sidetracked by a crisis in Egypt, at only four. Read and Grindle as the principal Colonial Office representatives attended on each occasion and

colonial governors home on leave also joined in. There were representatives of the Crown Agents and of the Department of Overseas
Trade. But it was not just an official body for Milner made sure that
businessmen were also members. Geoffrey Dawson, editor of *The
Times* from 1912 to 1919 was perhaps an obvious choice as a former
private secretary to Milner in South Africa. John Ford Darling
brought to the committee financial expertise, a successful business
career culminating at this time as Managing Director of the London
Joint City and Midland Bank. Sir Owen Philipps, later Lord Kylsant,
was a conservative M.P. and also chairman of major British shipping
companies, soon to be President of the Chamber of Shipping of the
United Kingdom and of the London Chamber of Commerce. Sir John
Eaglesome, after a successful career as Director of Railways and
Public Works in Nigeria, had just returned to Britain while maintaining interests in transport and business. It must be stressed that by
contrast with the E.R.D.C.'s suggested Imperial Development Board
this committee was purely advisory. Its terms of reference were 'to
enquire into the opportunities of economic development in the
Colonies and Protectorates, to make recommendations as to the
principles and methods to be followed in such development, and to
examine and report on any particular schemes and suggestions which
may be submitted to them'. Moreover, there is no indication that the
proposals considered were in any way affected by the cabinet's request
to discuss schemes. The cabinet was contacted only after extensive
Colonial Office-Treasury negotiations, and then not until after Milner
had left office. Nevertheless, the committee's papers are interesting
because they reveal the thinking of its members and the type of
problem with which the Colonial Office was confronted.[83]

The committee was first presented with a 'Report on Economic
Development of Crown Colonies', prepared at the request of Milner.
It consisted largely of a survey of developments in each colony and
of particular commodities between 1901 and 1913. The conclusion
reached was that economic development in a colony depended on five
factors: (1) internal peace (2) adequate transport (3) health schemes
(4) agricultural education and research, and (5) a steady flow of capital
for agricultural and mineral development and to provide a sufficiency
of credit and marketing facilities. The Colonial Empire was regarded
as a huge potential market for manufactured goods and it was suggested that it 'will ultimately be capable of supplying the U.K. with
the bulk of the imported raw material it requires for its industries as

well as a great variety of foodstuffs'. Developing an enlarged imperial market was considered to be of considerable importance in the post-war world owing to the deterioration of the United States exchanges. Borrowings from the United States and the sale of securities in the war had reduced Britain's capacity to finance imports from the United States. To better Britain's trade balance the crown colonies could provide substitute raw materials of the kind imported from the United States as well as other goods which could be exported to that country. Fundamentally, it can be seen that the objective of colonial develop-ment was to support the British economy in the difficult post-war years. Significantly the author of the memorandum, Herbert Williams, was not a member of the Colonial Office but a business-man.[84]

Amery began at the first meeting by emphasizing the point made in the memorandum that the successful development of the colonies would be of direct assistance to the United Kingdom in the present conditions by promoting trade with this country and by providing raw materials for British industries. It 'would also by means of the "triangle of trade" contribute to the improvement of the American exchange'. Metropolitan considerations were of central importance in this re-assessment of colonial development. Only select areas of the empire, he argued, needed to be considered by the committee, the East African protectorates and British Guiana to begin with, Sierra Leone and Jamaica later. These were the territories whose develop-ment was dependent on imperial sources of capital. The problems eventually discussed concerned the West Indies sugar industry, Kilindini harbour, the Uganda, Central Africa and Nyasaland rail-ways and the general development needs of East Africa, British Guiana, British Honduras and the Federated Malay States.

A central topic for consideration when discussing these issues was the problem of finance. Amery confessed at the first meeting: 'There was, unfortunately, very little prospect of obtaining money for colonial development from the Treasury, and it would be necessary to face the problem of finding other ways and means, without de-parting from the principles of sound administration'.[85] If no money was likely to be forthcoming from the Treasury or if the terms of such loans were as onerous as was expected, then one possibility was to ob-tain Imperial government guarantees of loans raised by colonies in the open market.[86] It was also suggested that since the Colonial Stock Acts, which were designed to lower the cost of colonial borrowing, did not cover the protectorates, they should be amended or a portion of the territory of protectorates annexed to enable them to raise loans more cheaply. Alternatively, a system of concessions to private enterprise to work in partnership with the colonial government was proposed. This idea was similar to the plans of the E.R.D.C. One form was for a chartered bank to be set up in East Africa, preferably financed by the local government. In co-operation with the colonial government, investigations would be made, plans drawn up and then the bank would float a company thus drawing on private subscribers while taking up shares itself.[87] For developing British Guiana, the Anglo-Persian Oil Company was suggested as a model for joint government-private company development 'for it is obvious that no capitalists will risk their money in a country like British Guiana without full knowledge of government support, and, on the other hand, neither the Imperial Government nor the Colonial Government are today in the position alone to put up adequate capital for that purpose'. This British Guiana corporation would contain representatives of the Imperial government, the colonial government and British capitalists. The Imperial government would put up £1 million out of the £3 million capital and would obtain a block of ordinary shares to divide between itself and the colonial government.[88] Wilson-Fox sent in a memorandum and made an appearance before the committee advocating a similar scheme for the completion of a Cape-Cairo railway. Milner, not surprisingly, had much sympathy with his proposals.[89]

At first sight some of these discussions seem to have borne fruit in due course. Although the Colonial Stock Acts were not amended until 1929, part of the East Africa Protectorate was annexed to enable the territory in 1921 to raise a loan under the acts as a colony. The suggestion of Imperial government guarantees for colonial loans was followed in 1926 by the East Africa Loans Act. The 1920s also witnessed work on some of the African railways discussed by the committee. But it does not follow that the Colonial Development Committee materially accelerated such innovations. The Colonial Office departmental papers dealing with the origins of Kenya's loan in 1921, analysed in Chapter IV, contain a fleeting reference to the committee's discussions. But the financing of other developments, considered later in this study, does not seem to have been affected by the committee's labours. The committee was frustrated from the beginning by the realisation that the Treasury were not prepared to dispose generously of financial aid. Amery later recalled that he had hoped to strengthen the committee's hands with a Colonial Development Fund of over £500,000 drawn from the £1 million a year that Malaya offered the Imperial government for the navy. Malaya rejected the suggestion and Amery adds that at that date it would hardly have appealed to the Treasury either.[90] Consequently the committee remained only a talking shop; attempts to wring money from the Treasury followed normal departmental patterns.

The interest of the experiment is twofold. Firstly, it indicates the fresh approach of politicians like Milner and Amery to the issue of colonial development, an approach which contrasted with that of the Colonial Office permanent staff. Milner and Amery, like Joseph Chamberlain, sought to break with the traditional *ad hoc* response to colonial needs and to formulate and finance broad plans of development as much in the interests of the British economy as of the colonies. Significantly, to achieve his aims, Milner sought in this committee a partnership with business representatives and a departure from normal departmental decision-making. Secondly, the failure of the experiment draws attention to the fundamental obstacle which had similarly obstructed Chamberlain, the problem of finance. To conclude this chapter it is necessary to review this and the other factors which were responsible for limiting the practical effectiveness of the proposals for colonial development spawned during the war.

3. *CONCLUSION*

Given the bulk of neo-mercantilist proposals put forward by official and unofficial spokesmen during the war, some explanation must be found for the very limited number of innovations realised after the war. The establishment of the Imperial Shipping Committee, the Imperial Bureau of Mycology, the Imperial Mineral Resources Bureau[91] and the Colonial Research Committee[92] owed something to the war, and the origins of the Empire Settlement Act of 1922 may partly be traced back to wartime peace plans to encourage migration to the dominions.[93] But these were peripheral to the perceived essential needs of the Colonial Empire. That the elephantine labours of the Paris Economic Conference, the Balfour of Burleigh Committee, the Imperial War Conference, the Dominions Royal Commission and the Empire Resources Development Committee gave birth to the

Colonial Development Committee mouse reflects the nature of the proposals and the obstacles they faced.

In the first place it should be stressed that the 'economics of siege' ideas were not unchallenged during the war. Tariff policies, for example, remained a divisive issue. The recommendations of the Paris Economic Conference were bitterly contested in the House of Commons, and Lloyd George remained sceptical of them.[94] Free trade, some argued, was a basic right of colonial native producers. Others queried the economic wisdom of adopting imperial self-sufficiency as a target. Even the Balfour of Burleigh Committee in its final report in December 1917 concluded that 'any attempt to make the Empire self-supporting in respect of [all necessary supplies] would probably be both impracticable and economically unsound'.[95] It was argued by several commentators that autarkic and protective policies would limit total world trade and damage Britain's export-orientated economy.[96] For this reason the Federation of British Industries could not accept the imperial preference objectives of the British Empire Producers' Organisation and the British Commonwealth Union.[97] The strength of the free trade movement after the war was sufficient to deter Lloyd George and later Bonar Law from adopting tariff reform as an election platform and their governments did no more than tinker with customs duties.[98]

Further opposition to schemes of state-directed colonial development came from defenders of the principle of trusteeship. Their ideals were revitalised at the end of the war with the establishment of the League of Nations Permanent Mandates Commission whose standards ostensibly set a measure against which to judge colonial administrations.[99] Foremost among the opponents of the E.R.D.C. was the Aborigines Protection Society. Against the implications of the doctrine of imperial estates, the society stressed that colonial rule was justified only if it acted in the interests of the native population, a philanthropic, humanitarian, civilizing and preservationist mission. Economic development had to be made compatible with the retention of traditional native forms of production, land tenure, and social and political cohesion. The war-time development proposals stressed the importance of the colonies to the metropolitan economy, but, said Sir Victor Buxton, 'we ought to remember that these dependencies are not our estates, but protectorates; that they have no representative institutions; and that we have the greater responsibility, therefore, not to exploit them for our own gain'.[100]

The society's ideals were supported by a number of individuals and organisations predominantly of a Liberal or Labour party allegiance. Attacks were made in the House of Commons on 'the new doctrine that has already started to creep in ... that the native should not produce for himself but for a master'.[101] The *Manchester Guardian* criticized the E.R.D.C.'s proposals for 'treating the Empire not as a trust but as an estate to be exploited for the benefit of the British taxpayer'. It opposed depriving the natives of their land rights and concluded that the schemes had 'the characteristic features of the system under which King Leopold devasted the Congo'.[102] Amongst other opponents of the scheme it is interesting to observe the Association of West African Merchants, Liverpool, whose critical letter was published with approval in *The Economist*.[103] Another major critic was Lord Lugard, the former Governor of Nigeria, who attacked the E.R.D.C. in an article in 1920 and in his book *The Dual Mandate in British Tropical Africa*, published in 1922. His preservationist, even patronizing,[104] attitude to the natives and their social, economic and political traditions led him to favour a system of indirect rule which would limit the impact of European control on African society. Given this major concern to preserve stability in the colonies, Lugard was suspicious of the proposals for rapid state-aided economic development. A process of steady and regulated investment by private enterprise and by independent colonial governments was preferable. Such economic benefits as resulted should be enjoyed equally by the local people and by the rest of the world: 'the power in control in dealing with subject races should in no remote way seek her own advantage at their expense'.[105] This was a denial of the concept of imperial estates.

These were views with which the Colonial Office permanent staff greatly sympathised, and their allegiance to them was in part responsible for the failure of the E.R.D.C. and other imperial visionaries to win much support in the Colonial Office. The right of financially self-sufficient colonial governments to maintain their economic independence was upheld by Colonial Office permanent staff and by the governors. But they were not the main reason for the failure to implement the new schemes after the war. Determined men, like Milner and Amery, who refused to believe that a conflict could exist between the interests of colony and metropolis, failed to realise their ambitions less because of the pressure from the critics and much more because of the rapid change in circumstances after the Armistice.

Much of the planning during the war had been based on the assumption that with peace would come economic depression and a crippled British economy. The 'economics of siege' planners were preparing to fight a new campaign in a dislocated post-war world. In practice, their pessimistic assumptions seemed to have been belied when following a short depression, the economy boomed in late 1919 and early 1920. The fragility of that boom was not foreseen. Apparently Britain's economy had survived remarkably well. The necessity therefore for major state involvement in economic affairs had evaporated. This relief reinforced the already existing reaction against wartime state controls to hasten the process of dismantling the structure of government intervention and to speed up the 'return to normalcy'. The years 1919 and 1920 therefore witnessed a rapid retreat of the state from its position of economic planner and controller. Most industrialists and financiers favoured a return to the pre-war system of private enterprise and limited government interference in economic affairs, and their influence after the general election of 1918 on a Conservative-dominated Coalition government ensured that their views were not ignored.[106]

Such a backlash against the plans born of the wartime emergency necessarily caused an ebbing of the support for Imperial government involvement in colonial development. With the wartime crisis safely passed, the necessity for such innovations was removed. But in addition the final obstacle to such schemes was the budgetary crisis, which the Imperial government believed it faced. In 1913 central government expenditure at current prices was £169 million. By 1920 it had risen to £1275 million.[107] To contemporary decision-makers these figures were central to the two basic economic problems with which the government had to deal. Firstly, the figures were symptomatic of inflation. The rise in prices during the war continued afterwards during the boom. The expected result was that British goods would be priced out of overseas markets and serious repercussions would be felt at home. It was believed that if the government cut its expenditure this would go some way towards reducing inflation. Secondly, the figures represented an absolute increase in total government expenditure as a proportion of the gross national product, an increase from 12.4% in 1913 to 26.2% in 1920. (It had been 51.7% in 1918.)[108] In order to release capital for productive investment by industry and in order to reduce taxation so as to encourage savings and investment, then it was again essential to cut government expenditure. The great fear was of an unbalanced central government budget. Not only would this force the government to borrow more money on the open market in competition with industry but it was felt that it would reflect adversely on British financial credit. For these reasons the period immediately after the war was dominated by a drive to cut government expenditure. Behind the government's decisions lay a growing public pressure for decontrols and reductions in taxation. In the face of this attack, Milner's hopes of reproductive government expenditure especially on colonial development were dissipated.

After four years of soaring government expenditure the Treasury were determined to restore their authority over spending departments.[109] Their requests for annual departmental estimates insisted on strict economy. 'It is urgently necessary that immediate steps should be taken by all Public Departments to reduce the expenditure from funds under their control .... It is not sufficient that the object of proposed expenditure may be in itself desirable; it is necessary in the present emergency to consider how far even desirable expenditure can be postponed.' 'The provision to be made for the year 1920—1 must then be restricted within the narrowest limits consistent with the carrying out of essential public services.' 'In the present financial situation the need for economy is more than ever pressing.'[110] Ministers were subjected to a similar barrage at cabinet level. Austen Chamberlain, the Chancellor, told the cabinet that 'If we cannot balance revenue and expenditure next year, our credit — national and international — will be seriously shaken and the results may be disastrous'.[111] A Treasury memorandum circulated to ministers by Lloyd George urged that 'All Departments should receive peremptory instructions from the Cabinet to subject every item of their Votes to a most rigorous scrutiny'.[112]

The effects this had on proposals for increasing imperial expenditure on colonial development can be simply demonstrated. In January 1919 the Colonial Office asked the Treasury to increase imperial aid to the East Africa Protectorate.[113] Treasury officials agreed amongst themselves that such a request was impossible. Niemeyer, assistant secretary at the Treasury, minuted that to increase such aid would strain the capital resources of the country. Bradbury, the deputy controller of finance, summed up: 'I am very much afraid that any attempt during the next few years to find any appreciable amounts of capital for ''Empire Development'' will lead to grave disaster'. He feared inflation on the one hand and a collapse of the foreign exchanges on the other. In reply to the Colonial Office's request the Treasury admitted that colonial development was 'in the long run broadly and indirectly remunerative, even if not so immediately and directly'. But increased demands for capital for reconstruction and development at home had to have priority. It was suggested that the Colonial Office should draw up a programme of development work in the Colonial Empire in order of priority which the Chancellor could discuss with Milner in an attempt to meet some of the Colonial Office's needs.[114] Although some attempt was made by the Colonial Office to provide such a programme it was never sent to the Treasury. Amery still pressed for a general development fund. He wanted money available for the Secretary of State to spend at his discretion.[115] But Milner seems to have recognized the impossibility of obtaining such financial aid and the contemplated general development fund, the Chamberlain concept, was passed over.[116]

Throughout 1919 and 1920 the obstacle of the financial crisis continued to restrict attempts to put wartime plans into operation. When the cabinet gave Milner approval to consider the E.R.D.C. schemes in June 1919 he was reminded that no capital was available. During the Supply debate in July 1919 Amery admitted that government money was not available for investment in colonies.[117] The Colonial Development Committee was always conscious of the limited chances of obtaining financial help from the Treasury; this more than anything probably explains its quiet demise. It certainly helps explain Milner's resignation from the government in February 1921. In a private note he recorded that in the economy drive

all hope of a forward policy of Colonial development ..., by timely expenditure, of the new forms of potential wealth revealed by the war, had become hopeless. I could do nothing much for the Crown Colonies, hence my only reason for remaining in a Government with which I was fundamentally out of sympathy was gone.[118]

It is true that after the war some imperial aid for colonial development was provided, but the new projects, to be examined in the next chapter, followed the *ad hoc* traditional lines of before the war. The broadly-conceived schemes of colonial development to create a self-sufficient empire and increase the assets of the British economy were ignored. Victory and the economic boom eradicated the phobias which had made the new development proposals popular. The financial detritus of the war made their application impossible.

NOTES

1. P. Kennedy, *The Realities Behind Diplomacy*, Glasgow, 1981, pp.165-6; C. E. Carrington, 'The Empire at War, 1914–1918' in E. A. Benians, Sir J. Butler and C. E. Carrington, eds., *The Cambridge History of the British Empire*, vol.3, Cambridge, 1959, pp.605-44.
2. S. J. Hurwitz, *State Intervention in Great Britain*, New York, 1949; reprinted Frank Cass, London, 1968.
3. P. Guinn, *British Strategy and Politics 1914 to 1918*, Oxford, 1965, pp.191-4; P. A. Lockwood, 'Milner's Entry into the War Cabinet', *H.J.*, 7 (1964) 120-34; J. O. Stubbs, 'Lord Milner and Patriotic Labour 1914–1918', *E.H.R.*, 87 (1972) 717-54. For some reservations concerning this interpretation see M. Beloff, *Imperial Sunset*, vol.1 *Britain's Liberal Empire 1897–1921*, London, 1969, pp.214-17. Also for Milner see his *The Nation and the Empire*, London, 1913, and *Questions of the Hour*, London, 1923, and A. M. Gollin, *Proconsul in Politics*, London, 1964; for Amery see *My Political Life*, 3 vols., London, 1953–5; for Hewins see *The Apologia of an Imperialist*, 2 vols., London, 1929; for Hodge see P. S. Gupta, *Imperialism and the British Labour Movement 1914–1964*, London, 1975, pp.20, 22, 26.
4. CO 323/686/CO 3257; CO 323/681/Treas 5875.
5. CO 323/682/Treas 16644.
6. CO 323/718/Treas 2935; CO 431/143/Treas 50026; CO 431/144/Treas 48734; CO 431/145/Treas 47275; *Annual Appropriation Accounts* in parliamentary papers.
7. See, for example, minute by Harding, 26 September 1914, CO 323/643/CO 37934.
8. P. B. Johnson, *Land Fit for Heroes*, Chicago and London, 1968; A. Marwick, *The Deluge: British Society and the First World War*, London, 1965.
9. This theme was first explored by W. K. Hancock, *Survey of British Commonwealth Affairs*, vol.II, *Problems of Economic Policy*, part 1, London, 1940, pp.94-110, who coined the phrase 'The Economics of Siege'.
10. *Hansard* H.C., vol.85, col.335, 2 Aug. 1916.
11. V. H. Rothwell, *British War Aims and Peace Diplomacy 1914–1918*, Oxford, 1971, pp.267-9; *Recommendations of the Economic Conference of the Allies*, Cd.8271, 1916, p.18; Asquith, *Hansard* H.C., vol.85, col.340, 2 Aug. 1916.
12. *Financial Facilities for Trade. Report to the Board of Trade by Committee Appointed to Investigate*, Cd.8346, 1916.
13. *Resolutions passed by the Committee on Commercial and Industrial Policy on the Subject of Imperial Preference*, Cd.8482, 1917. For Hewins' role see *Apologia of an Imperialist*, vol.II, pp.93-4, 104-5, 114-15, and for Amery's exultation see J. Barnes and D. Nicholson, eds., *The Leo Amery Diaries*, vol.1, London, 1980, 15 Feb. 1917, p.143.
14. *Royal Commission on the Natural Resources, Trade and Legislation of Certain Portions of His Majesty's Dominions, Final Report*, Cd.8462, 1917.
15. *Extracts from Proceedings and Papers laid before the Imperial War Conference*, Cd.8566, 1917, resolutions XVI and XXI.
16. I. M. Drummond, *British Economic Policy and the Empire 1919–1939*, London, 1972, pp.57-8, 150-4. See also W. Long, *Memories*, London, 1923, pp.242-3, and Hewins, *Apologia of an Imperialist*, vol.II, pp.168-71.
17. *Imperial War Conference, 1918. Extracts from Minutes of Proceedings and Papers laid before the Conference*, Cd.9177, 1918.
18. For example, Sir H. Wilson and H. T. Montague Bell, 'German Trade Methods', *United Empire*, 9 (Feb. 1918) 50; Sir G. Makgill, 'Industrial Organisation and Empire', *Nineteenth Century and After*, 82 (July 1917) 114.

19. E. Saunders, *A Self-Supporting Empire*, London, 1918, p.30; Rev. W. Greswell, 'Our Colonies and the War', *Fortnightly Review*, 104 (Oct. 1915) 709; C. C. McLeod, 'The Indian Jute Industry', *J.R.S.A.*, 64 (Dec. 1915) 117; J. C. Shenstone, 'Herb-Growing in the British Empire; its Past, Present and Future', *J.R.S.A.*, 65 (May 1917) 445-54.

20. D. A. E. Veal, 'Problems of Today and Tomorrow', *Empire Review*, 30 (March 1916), 57.

21. P. Hurd, 'Next Steps in Empire Partnership', *J.R.S.A.*, 64 (April 1916) 419. See also W. Lang, 'The Economics of Empire', *United Empire*, 9 (Sept. 1918) 390.

22. J. A. Hutton, 'The Effects of the War on Cotton-Growing in the British Empire', *J.R.S.A.*, 64 (Jan. 1916) 221; E. H. Cunningham-Craig, 'Oil Producing Deposits of the Empire', *United Empire*, 9 (May 1918) 208-14; E. R. Dawson, 'Trade after the War. The West India Point of View', *Empire Review*, 30 (July 1916) 261-5; J. Watson Grice, *The Resources of the Empire*, London, 1917, pp.3, 5, 30.

23. Makgill, 'Industrial Organisation', p.111. See also J. C. Simpson, 'The Natural Resources of the Empire', *The British Citizen and Empire Worker*, 1 (Oct. 1916) 114.

24. Sir C. Kinlock-Cooke, 'Financial Facilities and British Trade', *Empire Review*, 30 (Dec. 1916) 481-9.

25. McLeod, 'Jute Industry', p.117.

26. R. O. H. Spence, 'The Development of British Guiana', *United Empire*, 9 (Feb. 1918) 63; F. M. B. Fisher, 'Imperial Trade', *ibid.*, p.73; J. J. Terrett, 'A Self-Supporting Empire?', *B.C.E.W.*, 2 (April 1917) 202, 208.

27. Hewins, *Apologia of an Imperialist*, vol.II, espec. pp.7-8, 11-12.

28. For the reactions of organised labour see Stubbs, 'Lord Milner and Patriotic Labour'; Gupta, *Imperialism and the British Labour Movement*, pp.18-26; and the columns of *The British Citizen and Empire Worker* founded August 1916.

29. Both were founded in 1916; for the B.E.P.O. see D. Killingray, 'The Empire Resources Development Committee and West Africa 1916–20', *J.I.C.H.*, 10 (1982) note 6, and for the B.C.U. see J. A. Turner, 'The British Commonwealth Union and the General Election of 1918', *E.H.R.*, 93 (1978) 528-59.

30. The first examination of the E.R.D.C. was by Hancock, *Survey of British Commonwealth Affairs*, vol.II, part 1, pp.106-9: the latest study is Killingray, 'The Empire Resources Development Committee and West Africa 1916–20', pp.194-210.

31. *Who Was Who*; A. Bigland, *The Call of Empire*, London, 1926; M. Frewen, *Melton Mowbray and other Memories*, London, 1924; A. Leslie, *Mr. Frewen of England*, London, 1966.

32. *The Times*, 28 Sept. 1916, p.6, and 29 Sept. 1916, p.4. A leader on 28 Sept., p.9 was broadly sympathetic to Wilson-Fox's views.

33. Lord Milner presided at a meeting at the Rhodes Trust convened to discuss a scheme by Frewen for an 'Empire Farm'. This meeting resolved to establish the E.R.D.C.: Milner's Diary 31 Oct. 1916, Milner Papers 279; H. Wilson-Fox, 'The Development of the Empire's Resources', *The Nineteenth Century and After*, 82 (Oct. 1917) 835; Bigland, *Call of Empire*, pp.89-96.

34. *The Times*, 29 Jan. 1917, p.7; also quoted in Wilson-Fox, 'The Development of the Empire's Resources', p.836.

35. Milner Papers, Box 166, contain letters and reports from Wilson-Fox and the E.R.D.C. to Milner which make it clear that Milner and Long were members of the original committee. See also Bigland, *Call of Empire*, p.96. There is one E.R.D.C. document of 18 April 1917 concerning currency matters in the Worthington-Evans Papers, Mss.Eng.Hist. c.900.

36. See, for example, 'Our Empire Estate', *B.C.E.W.*, 2 (Feb. 1917) 69.

37. Bigland, *Call of Empire*, pp.96-9, 219-223; CO 525/91/Gov 57571.
38. A. Bigland, 'The Empire's Assets and How to Use Them', *J.R.S.A.*, 65 (March 1917) 356, 361.
39. H. Wilson-Fox, 'The Development of Imperial Resources', *J.R.S.A.*, 65 (Dec. 1916) 78-81; 'The Development of the Empire's Resources', pp.839-40; 'Payment of War Debt by Development of Empire Resources', *United Empire*, 9 (April 1918) 169-82. Bigland too argued that heavy taxes on the wealthy would destroy capital, *Call of Empire*, pp.92-3.
40. Bigland, 'The Empire's Assets', p.356.
41. Wilson-Fox, *The Times*, 28 Sept. 1916; 'The Development of the Empire's Resources', p.840.
42. Jesson, *Hansard* H.C., vol.112, cols.429-30, 13 Feb. 1919.
43. M. Frewen, 'The Structure of Empire Finance', *Nineteenth Century and After*, 88 (Nov. 1920) 882; Wilson-Fox, 'Development of Imperial Resources', p.82; Frewen in *J.R.S.A.*, 65 (Dec. 1916) 89; Wilson-Fox, 'Payment of War Debt', p.177.
44. Wilson-Fox, 'Payment of War Debt', pp.173-5. Reports on the oils and fats and the fish proposals can be found in the Milner Papers, Box 166.
45. Wilson-Fox, 'Development of Imperial Resources', pp.78-9, 84.
46. Wilson-Fox, *The Times*, 29 Sept. 1916.
47. Wilson-Fox, 'Development of Imperial Resources', p.88.
48. Wilson-Fox, 'The Development of the Empire's Resources', p.849.
49. Wilson-Fox, 'Payment of War Debt', p.178.
50. Wilson-Fox, *Hansard* H.C., vol.112, col.410, 13 Feb. 1919, and 'The Development of the Empire's Resources', p.843.
51. Wilson-Fox, 'Development of Imperial Resources', p.85.
52. Bigland, 'The Empire's Assets', p.359.
53. Wilson-Fox, 'Development of Imperial Resources', pp.85-6.
54. Wilson-Fox, 'Payment of War Debt', p.175.
55. CO 885/25/Misc.No.330.
56. S. Buckley, 'The Colonial Office and the Establishment of an Imperial Development Board: The Impact of World War 1', *J.I.C.H.*, 2 (1974) 308-17.
57. CO 323/724/CO 31389.
58. CO 323/717/II 46378.
59. CO 323/732/MO 48594; CO 323/726/CO 53536 and minute of 22 Nov. 1916.
60. For the work of committee and ministry see Johnson, *Land Fit for Heroes* and K. O. and J. Morgan, *Portrait of a Progressive. The Political Career of Christopher, Viscount Addison*, Oxford, 1980, pp.70-82.
61. CO 323/728/MO 14927A; CO 323/725/CO 40053.
62. Minute by Harris, 30 Aug. 1917, CO 323/763/MO 41713.
63. CO 323/763/MO 47780.
64. Minute by Long, 16 Sept. 1917, CO 323/763/MO 41713.
65. See, for example, CO 323/787/MO 22050.
66. CO 323/726/CO 61941.
67. He added in the margin: 'the '57' shows how close the estimating was'.
68. *Ibid.*, minutes of 30 Dec. 1916 to 7 Feb. 1917.
69. *Hansard* H.C., vol.93, col.323, 2 May 1917; col.472, 3 May 1917; cols.870-1, 8 May 1917; cols.1219-20, 10 May 1917.
70. CO 323/746/HC 22335, 22336, 23060, 24026. Long continued to show some, unproductive, interest in the affairs of the E.R.D.C., Killingray, 'The Empire Resources Development Committee', p.198.
71. *Hansard* H.C., vol.97, cols.1053-7, 14 Aug. 1917.
72. Milner's views can be traced in Milner Papers, Boxes 156, 174, 175, 177, 246-9,

and in his book *Questions of the Hour*, espec. 146-73. His determination to have Amery as his under-secretary is recorded in Milner's Diary 8 Jan. 1919, Milner Papers 282, and in *Leo Amery Diaries*, 7, 9 and 10 Jan. 1919, pp.250-2.

73. Note of 4 Nov. 1919, Milner Papers, Box 246.
74. See *My Political Life; National and Imperial Economics*, Westminster, 1923; 'The Economic Development of the Empire', *United Empire*, 16 (March 1925) 143-9.
75. *Hansard* H.C., vol.112, cols.408-30, 13 Feb. 1919 for E.R.D.C. proposals and cols.431-4 for Amery's reply.
76. *Hansard* H.C., vol.118, cols.2172-85, 2230-40, 30 July 1919.
77. CO 323/796/HC 17226, and minutes of 19 March 1919.
78. *Hansard* H.C., vol.112, col.431, 13 Feb. 1919.
79. CO 323/814/MO 36576; memo. by Chamberlain, CAB 24/5/G.248, 5 June 1919 and cabinet minutes CAB 23/10/580(3), 18 June 1919.
80. CO 323/814/MO 36576, minutes of 24, 25 and 30 June 1919.
81. Milner to Amery 12 Jan. 1919, Amery Papers, Box 54, Folder B. Fiddes had been Milner's Imperial Secretary in South Africa 1897–1900.
82. E.R.D.C. to Milner, 4 Oct. 1919, Milner Papers Add.Mss.Eng.Hist. c.704.
83. For the formation of the committee see minutes of 8 Oct. to 24 Dec. 1919, CO 323/814/MO 36576; for its membership, *Who Was Who*; and for its work see CO 885/26/Misc.No.348 and Amery, *My Political Life*, vol.2, pp.197-8. Milner was away from London 29 Nov. 1919 to 25 March 1920, see his diaries, Milner Papers 282 and 283.
84. CO 885/26/Misc.No.348, Paper 1, pp.28-9. Williams became secretary of the Empire Economic Union, Director of the Empire Industries Association and Conservative M.P. for Reading 1924–9, see *Who Was Who*. For the origins of the memorandum see the correspondence between Milner and Williams in Sept. 1919 in Milner Papers Add.Mss.Eng.Hist. c.705.
85. Minutes of 1st Meeting, 17 Dec. 1919, CO 885/26/Misc.348. He had reached the same conclusion in a letter to Milner 3 March 1919, Amery Papers, Box 54, Folder B.
86. *Ibid.*, minutes of 9th Meeting, 24 Nov. 1920.
87. *Ibid.*, paper 2, pp.63-5.
88. *Ibid.*, paper 19, p.94.
89. *Ibid.*, minutes of 4th and 5th Meetings, 17 March, 29 April 1920; Wilson-Fox to Milner, 11 Nov. 1919 and Milner to Amery 2 Dec. 1919, Amery Papers, Box 54, Folder B.
90. Amery, *My Political Life*, vol.2, p.198. He related Malaya's rejection of the plan in a letter to Milner on 14 Jan. 1920, Amery Papers, Box 54, Folder B.
91. *Imperial War Conference 1918*, Cd.9177, resolutions VII, XVI, XXIV; K. H. Burley, 'The Imperial Shipping Committee', *J.I.C.H.*, 2 (1974) 208-9; Johnson, *Land Fit for Heroes*, pp.123-4.
92. Sir C. Jeffries, *A Review of Colonial Research 1940–1960*, London, HMSO, 1964, pp.13-14; *First Annual Report of the Colonial Research Committee*, Cmd.1144, 1921. The committee began on a grant of £1000 in 1919–20.
93. I. M. Drummond, *Imperial Economic Policy 1917–1939*, London, 1974, pp.43-54.
94. *Hansard* H.C., vol.85, cols.349-58, 380-89, 415, 439, 2 Aug. 1916; Hewins, *Apologia of an Imperialist*, vol.2, pp.132-3.
95. *Final Report of the Committee on Commercial and Industrial Policy after the War*, Cd.9035, 1918, p.123.
96. D. Clerk, 'Inaugural Address', *J.R.S.A.*, 65 (Nov.1916) 5-19; H. D. Gregory, 'British Trade Policy After the War', *Empire Review*, 30 (May 1916) 163-70; E. Cannan, *An Economist's Protest*, London, 1927, pp.54-62, 120-33 (these essays were written in 1916 and 1917).

97. V. A. Malcolmson to Milner, 14 Nov. 1919, Milner Papers Add.Mss.Eng.Hist. c.705; Turner, 'The British Commonwealth Union'.

98. See, for example, election manifestos for 1918 and 1922 in F. W. S. Craig, ed., *British General Election Manifestos 1918–1966*, Chichester, 1970.

99. Hancock, *Survey of British Commonwealth Affairs*, vol.2, part 1, pp.111-12; K. Robinson, *The Dilemmas of Trusteeship*, London, 1965, pp.19-21.

100. Discussion of Wilson-Fox's proposals at the Royal Colonial Institute, *United Empire*, 9 (April 1918) 183. See also Killingray, 'The Empire Resources Development Committee', pp.202-6.

101. Wedgwood, *Hansard* H.C., vol.118, col.2219, 30 July 1919.

102. *Manchester Guardian*, 15 May 1917, quoted by Wilson-Fox, 'The Development of the Empire's Resources', p.856.

103. *The Economist*, 85 (22 Dec. 1917) 985-6.

104. 'The virtues and the defects of this race type are those of attractive children, whose confidence when once it has been won is given ungrudgingly as to an older and wiser superior, without question and without envy', Sir F. D. Lugard, *The Dual Mandate in British Tropical Africa*, London, 1922, p.70. For the attack on the E.R.D.C. see p.273.

105. Sir F. D. Lugard, 'The Crown Colonies and the British War Debt', *The Nineteenth Century and After*, 88 (Aug. 1920) 242. See also M. Perham, *Lugard, The Years of Authority 1898–1945*, London, 1960, pp.571-3.

106. W. Ashworth, *An Economic History of England 1870–1939*, London, 1960, pp.384-8; C. L. Mowat, *Britain between the Wars*, London, 1955, pp.28-9; R. H. Tawney, 'The Abolition of Economic Controls, 1918–21', *Ec.H.R.*, 13 (1943) 1-30; Johnson, *Land Fit for Heroes*.

107. A. T. Peacock and J. Wiseman, *The Growth of Public Expenditure in the United Kingdom*, 2nd ed., London, 1967, p.201.

108. *Ibid.*, p.190, central plus local government expenditure at current prices.

109. H. Roseveare, *The Treasury*, London, 1969, pp.243-9, 258-60; CAB 23/20/CAB 1(20)2, 6 Jan. 1920.

110. 26 Aug. 1919, CO 431/146/Treas. 50105; 1 Oct. 1919, CO 431/146/Treas. 56605; 1 Oct. 1920, CO 431/147/Treas. 48754.

111. Note by the Chancellor of the Exchequer, 26 July 1919, CAB 24/5/G 257.

112. Treas. memo. 20 Sept. 1919, Milner Papers, Box 157.

113. Grindle to Treas., 4 Jan. 1919, CO 533/196/Gov. 41421.

114. Minutes of 3 Feb. and 10 Feb. 1919 and Treas. to C.O. 13 Feb. 1919, Treas. 755 on T1/12495/9552 of 1920.

115. Minutes of 19 Feb. to 29 March 1919, CO 323/804/Treas. 9775.

116. Milner always expected the Treasury to be an obstacle, see *Leo Amery Diaries*, entry 8 Jan. 1919, p.251.

117. *Hansard* H.C., vol.118, col.2239, 30 July 1919.

118. Note of 23 June 1921, Milner Papers, Box 246.

IV

IMPERIAL POLICY AND THE DEVELOPMENT OF EAST AFRICA 1918–21

1. *APPLICATIONS FOR ISSUES UNDER THE EAST AFRICAN PROTECTORATES LOANS ACT OF 1914*

The previous chapter concluded with an account of the failure to implement after the war the 'economics of siege' proposals for colonial development. No commitments were made by the Imperial government to accelerate the development of the Colonial Empire in the interests of the British economy. The Colonial Office disregarded such grandiose schemes and instead focused their attention in traditional fashion on the needs of financially vulnerable territories. Hence the significance of the case studies examined in this chapter: colonial development policy reverted to its pre-war pattern.

The Colonial Office became preoccupied after the war with the needs of East Africa: all British possessions in the region seemed financially precarious. Tanganyika was a new responsibility, drawing on an imperial grant from the beginning, Somaliland an old one, in need of grants-in-aid after the war as previously to service its administration. Nyasaland's government had also needed grants-in-aid to balance its budget right up to the war but had been given no extra help with its development. Uganda also needed grants-in-aid before the war but had been given more substantial assistance with loans for railway building in 1910, 1911 and 1912. The East Africa Protectorate fared rather better, helped by the Imperial government's largesse in building the Uganda Railway and by the provision of extra loans to finance extensions in 1911 and 1912. It received its last grant-in-aid in 1912–13 and alone of the East African territories was by the end of the war free of Treasury financial control. And yet the Colonial Office remained anxious about its financial prospects. By contrast, the territories of West Africa were free of Treasury control by 1918.

Nigeria had been the last to receive attention following the conquest of the northern territory and its unification with the south: the government had once received substantial grants-in-aid but they were now a thing of the past. The Colonial Office saw this as the model to be emulated and hoped that with appropriate imperial aid most of the East African territories would follow suit. They wished to avoid the fate of other possessions, for example, in the West Indies and Pacific, condemned to dependence on grants-in-aid by economic dereliction or a perception of poor economic potential.[1]

Milner and Amery did not challenge these Colonial Office objectives: freedom from Treasury control and a future of financial independence were laudable colonial targets. But they brought to their contemplation of East African problems additional imperial interests. Both men wished to encourage white settlement in East Africa after the war, particularly in the E.A.P.. Amery especially saw the white community there as the focus for a large, united, white-dominated East African dominion. Improving communications in East Africa would be a stimulus to white settlement and success. They also recognised the economic potential of the region. Milner was 'convinced that if we can once get the country fairly started we might see a development there almost as great as that of the West Coast'. Amery was equally optimistic, and likened their task to the reconstruction in South Africa after the Boer War.[2] Prospects for the cultivation of cotton, sisal and flax seemed good. If not already aware of the prospects for white settlement and economic development, ministers would have been quickly informed by the organisations which in Britain and in East Africa, particularly in the E.A.P., were anxious to see these causes promoted. The London and Manchester Chambers of Commerce had sub-committees concerned with East Africa active by 1919, settlers' interests were well-aired in Parliament by sympathetic Conservative M.P.s like Sydney Henn and some interested parties also opened direct communications with the Secretary of State.[3]

The colonial administrations in East Africa were also concerned about the future. For them, the war had meant not a revolutionary reappraisal of the value of colonies to the imperial economy, but an enforced disruption in the pattern of their development. In particular, Uganda, Nyasaland and the E.A.P. felt cheated of their allowances under the 1914 act, wartime financial restrictions having cut off this source of aid almost as soon as it was opened. The inadequate roads, railways and harbours which had produced the pressures leading to the 1914 act had not, of course, been improved by a legislative sop and continued financial hardship. All three territories were still dependent on imperial assistance to obtain investment capital, and therefore they were anxious to draw at once upon their entitlement.

In the later stages of the war the government of the E.A.P. several times requested permission to begin major public works,[4] but it was not until December 1918 that these proposals were given sympathetic consideration in the Colonial Office. Bottomley, principal clerk of the East Africa department, then agreed that certain projects were indeed urgent. But he noted that rising prices plus the new items the governor wished to add to the programme meant that the cost would exceed the territory's allocation of funds under the 1914 act. He concluded that the Treasury should be asked to approve the additional projects and release funds for immediate works, and, more daringly, should consider increasing the total amount of money made available under the pre-war legislation. The Secretary of State agreed with the proposal without comment, and a letter was sent to the Treasury in January 1919 along with a vast batch of despatches and reports from the protectorate's government, the material upon which the Colonial Office had reached their conclusions. As a further argument, attention was drawn to proposed post-war white settlement in the territory. To accomplish these aims financial help was needed.[5]

This request drew two replies from the Treasury in February 1919. The first, analysed in the previous chapter, stressed the general financial problem facing the Imperial government and the difficulty of finding funds for colonial development, and urged the Colonial Office to provide a complete programme of the schemes throughout the empire which needed imperial aid.[6] The second was a specific refusal to ask Parliament to increase the total allowance of loans for the East African territories above the £3 million fixed by the act in 1914. Moreover, of that total only £500,000 could be issued in present circumstances to all three protectorates and the interest would be not less than 5½%. The Treasury 'must ask that no capital commitments involving any further assistance from this country may be entered into at the present time'. The Colonial Office were understandably dismayed by this response.[7]

Meanwhile, Governor Northey of the E.A.P. had again reassessed the needs of his territory. He argued in February 1919 that settlement and development were being seriously retarded by lack of capital expenditure on communications and that a total loan of £3 million was needed for his projects alone. This meant a further £1,100,000 was required in addition to the E.A.P.'s allocation under the 1914 act and the unissued balances of smaller loans authorized in 1911 and 1912. After consideration, the Colonial Office forwarded this new request to the Treasury accompanied by what they hoped would be weighty supporting arguments. Emphasis was placed on the importance for imperial purposes of the raw materials produced in the territories, sisal, flax and coffee. Further, there was a moral liability to help ex-officer settlement in the E.A.P. as part of the Imperial government's post-war reconstruction plan. Finally, it was pointed out 'that a large proportion of the money will be spent in this country on steel work and other necessaries for the construction of the railways, harbour works, etc., and that the expenditure will therefore be of direct assistance in reducing unemployment in the United Kingdom'.[8] The Treasury rejected the application out of hand. They could not consider the E.A.P.'s proposals until they had been sent, as requested earlier, a programme of all the development schemes in the Colonial Empire which needed imperial aid.[9]

A lull in negotiations with the Treasury then ensued. In view of the Treasury's reluctance to issue capital even under the 1914 act, the Colonial Office had already asked the governors of the other two East African territories to submit revised programmes for loan expenditure in order of priority.[10] The reply from Nyasaland was received in April 1919: it outlined a five-year programme of railway, road and harbour works costing £659,000 of which £81,000 was needed for 1919–20.[11] Uganda, like the E.A.P., had already pressed for an issue under the 1914 act, but in response to the Colonial Office telegram Governor Corydon submitted a further proposal: he wanted an additional loan from imperial funds of not less than £750,000. 'Mature consideration shows no other possible measure for even moderate developments of this country.' In a later despatch, received by the Colonial Office in June 1919, he explained that the sums which could be set aside from general revenue for capital works were insufficient and also that the 1914 act was inadequate for present needs. The war had revealed the need to increase production of raw materials in the empire, and cotton, rubber and other supplies could be obtained from Uganda if loan funds were obtainable. £750,000 plus the 1914 act allowance would at least suffice for the next few years.[12]

Thus, by the summer of 1919, Uganda and the E.A.P. had compounded the Colonial Office's problem by requesting loan funds additional to the supply to which they were nominally entitled under the 1914 act. Reviewing all proposals, Bottomley concluded that the Treasury should be asked to provide £1 million at once under the 1914 act, mainly for expenditure in the E.A.P. However, embarking on this programme assumed that more money would be available later to complete the works; but only Nyasaland at this stage could manage on the amount assigned to it under the act, the E.A.P. needed an additional £1,100,000 and Uganda had asked for £750,000. Since the government revenues of the protectorates were not strong, interest on the loans would have to be paid out of the capital for the first three years. Bottomley therefore suggested that the Colonial Office should seek additional loans for these territories of at least £2½ million. With this reasoning Read, an assistant under-secretary, and Fiddes, the permanent under-secretary, agreed but wanted additional loans of £3 million. Some consideration was given to the possibility of using private capital for railway building in the E.A.P. but this, as expected, turned out to be even more expensive than obtaining funds from the Treasury. Before anything further could be done the Colonial Office was informed that Uganda wished to increase its additional loan plan to £1 million, that the Nyasaland railway extension programme was calculated to cost £1,409,492, and that a development programme for Tanganyika would require initially about £200,000.[13] A noticeable feature of these negotiations is the rapidity with which colonial estimates and programmes escalated.

In October 1919 at Milner's request, Bottomley costed once again the development proposals of the three protectorates: £2,863,680 for the E.A.P., £1,394,000 for Uganda and £1,585,492 for Nyasaland. With an allowance of interest for three years at 5½% this made a total of £6,950,000. In other words some £4 million was now required in addition to the amount unissued under the 1914 act. £1,400,000 was needed in 1919–20. Amery suggested that the Colonial Office should concentrate on getting £1,400,000 out of the Treasury at once and the balance of the £3 million already sanctioned as early next year as possible.

As for the money required to complete those schemes ... we shall have to have recourse to entirely new financial devices, I fancy, and I should like to have a comprehensive development loan for the whole area (including German East Africa) from the public: but I would first have a High Commission to give us a policy.[14]

This was the distinctive Amery touch again, a marked contrast with the readiness of the permanent staff to put individual proposals to the Treasury as they were prepared by the colonial governments and the Colonial Office.

On this occasion Milner was rather less breezy. Early in November he went over the proposals individually with Bottomley and selected those urgent items costing only £740,000 for which the Treasury should be asked to advance capital at once under the 1914 act; some other matters could be dealt with by other loan funds, but most were delayed pending further discussions with the governors. It was nearly twelve months since the Colonial Office began serious study of the post-war needs of East Africa. Milner must have accepted the necessity for drawing up such a minimum programme in order to obtain some funds for the more pressing requirements of the protectorates. Above all he recognized the Imperial government's firm insistence on economy in expenditure. Only the most mature plans would obtain financial aid from the Treasury and consequently this was the programme submitted to the Treasury on 19 November.[15]

The Treasury were nevertheless alarmed that the amount asked for was, with interest, 70% more than the maximum of £500,000 they had previously offered in February 1919. What displeased the Treasury in addition was that at the same time the Colonial Office was obliged to ask for a loan of £150,000 from imperial funds to help the E.A.P. get over a temporary deficit on its annual account. The Treasury feared that grants-in-aid were likely to rise next year; they suspected that the East African territories would fall back on imperial funds when they could not meet the interest payments on the loans they seemed eager to take up.[16]

Milner was evidently anxious to reach a settlement before he departed for Egypt, so on 26 November he had a talk with Austen Chamberlain, the Chancellor, and won a sympathetic hearing. When the Treasury staff still dragged their feet, Chamberlain intervened and in December reached an agreement personally with Amery. £862,927 was to be advanced under the act providing capital of £565,680 to the E.A.P., £110,850 to Uganda and £28,000 to Nyasaland. The Chancellor did, however make it quite clear that he did not pledge himself to give further funds when the £3 million loan was exhausted.[17]

The negotiations reveal important aspects of the financial situation after the war and of government decision-making. After the Armistice the Treasury were determined to stabilize the economy by a rapid reduction of government expenditure. Inflation was their constant fear: one eye was constantly cocked on the exchanges, and programmes of long-term imperial development left them unmoved. They assumed that short-term inflation would ruin the country before long-term colonial development had any effect on increasing Britain's export trade or supplies of cheaper raw materials and food. To Milner and Amery, this was a narrow-minded appraisal of the situation. Government expenditure, if well-directed, would be an important impetus to post-war reconstruction. The colonies had an important role to fulfill in this. In addition they shared with their permanent staff a genuine concern for the damage done to the standard of life and trade in the colonies by the war. There was a duty to be performed in helping the colonies in the difficult period after the war. The difficulty was that they could not at a time of rapid price changes and unsettled colonial programmes draw up the classified imperial development programme on which the Treasury insisted.

The deadlock was broken only by the intervention of the political staff and by compromise. The Treasury, of course, gained most of what they required in the settlement since immediate issues under the 1914 act were limited and there was no pledge to provide additional funds. Chamberlain must have felt that the minimum programme was justified by the details presented by Milner. But the agreement was largely based on the co-operation of political leaders. Personal appeal to a cabinet colleague was evidently a more effective way of settling problems than the epistolary combats of the departments. The negotiations over a development loan for Uganda confirm this.

2. *THE UGANDA DEVELOPMENT LOAN 1920*

Amongst the items which Milner deferred pending further consultation with the Governor of Uganda was the additional Imperial government loan which Coryndon had originally proposed back in April 1919. He pressed for this while negotiations still continued over issues under the 1914 act. The amount requested grew from an initial £750,000 to £1 million; at one stage Coryndon even hoped to increase the total to £1,250,000. By January 1920 Coryndon was home on leave, but he continued to bombard the Colonial Office with letters from his Surrey home, stressing the urgency and value of loan aid for Uganda and clarifying the terms he proposed. He settled on a total expenditure of £1 million, spread probably over seven years and requiring a maximum provision of £200,000 in any one year. He warned that the protectorate could not support heavy sinking fund and interest charges and therefore requested that interest on the new loan should initially be paid out of capital. The money, he emphasised, would be used only for public works and not for balancing the ordinary budget.[18] Meanwhile, in Uganda a local Development Commission also reported on the necessity of obtaining capital for railway projects from the Imperial government on generous terms, namely, free of interest for 15 years and thereafter charges to be shared equally between the Imperial and Protectorate governments.[19]

The governor's proposals were given little consideration in the Colonial Office until negotiations had been completed with the Treasury over issues under the 1914 act, and further delay ensued until Milner returned from Egypt and could discuss the matter personally with Coryndon. The governor was, however, warned that 'it is really difficult at present to obtain loan funds from the Treasury'.[20] Eventually, in April 1920, Milner had several meetings with Coryndon discussing Ugandan needs and finances,[21] and on 7 May he wrote personally to Austen Chamberlain that 'there are some Colonial matters of the *greatest urgency* with which I can't get on – I am absolutely stuck – unless I can induce the Treasury to give me rather more latitude'. He asked that the Treasury should send someone to help him frame proposals in a shape acceptable to the Treasury.[22]

At a meeting on 11 May, Barstow, controller of supply services at the Treasury, and Niemeyer, principal assistant secretary, heard Milner explain that a £1 million development loan for Uganda would enable the territory in future to be financially self-sufficient and independent of grants-in-aid. The Treasury officials seem to have been attracted by this idea and agreed to the proposal in principle. They even suggested that a repayable grant-in-aid on the Colonial Services Vote would be the simplest method of finance. Chamberlain, however, on receiving their report insisted that before he could give his approval he needed to know the terms, purposes, amount and duration of the loan proposals. Furthermore, he argued that in view of the urgent need to reduce government expenditure, he could only agree to the plan if Milner answered the questions Chamberlain had asked a year ago: what were the total costs of the imperial development schemes Milner wished to undertake and how much money would be spent in each colony? He minuted to Barstow:

The list supplied to you for Uganda is merely another way of saying that the money asked for is needed as a grant in aid of Uganda finance in general and that it is an impertinence on the part of the C/E to enquire what is done with the British taxpayer's money. I do not accept this view of the Chancellor's position.[23]

This apparent check to a settlement was again resolved by the personal co-operation of the politicians. Milner had a long talk with Chamberlain on 9 June and persuaded him to supply £200,000 a year for five years for development works in Uganda.[24] In this first agreement interest at 5% would be issued in addition, making a total debt to the Imperial Exchequer of £1,105,126 to be paid off in 1925 by a loan that Uganda itself would raise. All Exchequer grants would then be repaid. If this was not possible, interest would be paid by the territory until repayment was made. Sums unexpended in one year would be available in the following. In a final settlement in August there were some modifictions. £250,000 a year would be issued for four years, interest being paid out of capital and included in the total of £1 million.[25]

This would seem to have been a concession made by Milner. The co-operation of the political chiefs made the settlement possible and such compromise was its essence. This explains Chamberlain's acceptance of the plan. His concern was to defend the Imperial Exchequer from drains on its resources at a time when economy was considered imperative. What Milner was requesting was the minimum amount of aid necessary to enable Uganda to become self-financing for its future development: no further calls on imperial aid were foreseen. Moreover, Chamberlain welcomed Milner's assurance that except possibly for the Imperial Institute no more Colonial Office applications for money would be made in the current financial year. Milner had conceded that 'under present conditions much very desirable and eventually remunerative work must be postponed'. Finally, Chamberlain explained to his staff:

I have been influenced by the fact that this is the first time that the policy of the Colonial Secretary — though for convenience it takes the Parliamentary form of a Grant in Aid — is based upon the grant being an interest-bearing loan instead of a free gift. This is an important principle, the acceptance (or, I should rather say, the offer) of which by the Colonial Office it is worth our while to meet.

And, he confessed, 'we should probably have been driven to make a free gift if the Secretary of State himself had not spontaneously adopted this new policy'.[26] In the Colonial Office Bottomley would have been upset to read those words; in April 1920 he had reluctantly concluded that 'there is no possibility of getting a free gift for this particular section of the Colonial Empire'.[27]

Why did the Colonial Office accept these terms, a settlement which was to be the precedent for later agreements? In the first place the urgency of providing aid to Uganda was recognized. It seems clear that Milner and the Colonial Office permanent staff accepted in the light of the financial policy of the Imperial government that such a compromise was necessary. But they were encouraged also by the hope that by obtaining such a loan and accelerating the territory's development they could guarantee Uganda's future freedom from grants-in-aid. In this, of course, they were in accordance with the Treasury's own ambitions, and hence an agreement could be reached.

3. *THE KENYA LOAN 1921*

The Imperial government's *ad hoc* response to Uganda's development needs and the objective of using imperial financial aid as a means of securing the financial self-sufficiency of the protectorate were the two traditional aspects of the new agreement. Similar traditional characteristics dominated the more complex negotiations relating to Kenya's requirements. Once again we can see the emphasis on ensuring colonial self-development, on restricting imperial liabilities and on *ad hoc* responses to local colonial needs.

In April 1919 Governor Northey of the E.A.P. reminded the Colonial Office of the request he had submitted in February for an increase up to £3 million in the total loan provision of his territory. Development seemed dependent upon it: he deleted additional public works from his budget for 1919–20 because the government's revenues were proving insufficient after the war to sustain the cost of development works.[28] The Colonial Office was not entirely happy with this expedient but it was recognised that the war had increased government burdens and disrupted development. Bottomley minuted:

Personally I think that in a new country, where it is certain that large expenditure on works will be necessary year after year, it is very much the best course to provide for them out of revenue, but there is so much leeway to be made up in East Africa, both as regards the offices and accommodation of staff, and the construction of hospitals etc., that I think recourse to a loan is inevitable. It will have to be a new loan because the £3,000,000 loan of

1914 is definitely ear-marked for improving communications and trade facilities.[29]

Evidently the feeling was that slow, steady development expenditure out of revenue was financially less risky than dependence on loans which added a fixed burden to local revenues with the consequent threat of a deficit and recourse to Treasury grants-in-aid and financial control.

The governor's suggestion for a new loan was accepted in principle by the Colonial Office. The negotiations over the next two years concerned the source of the money and the terms on which it was to be raised. Would the Treasury supply financial assistance, should part at least of the territory be annexed so that the colony could obtain a favourable loan under the Colonial Stock Acts, or could the terms of the acts be extended to allow protectorates to take advantage of them? These were the first questions to be decided. The issues were complicated by the protectorate's immediate financial problems and by the Imperial government's claims for war expenses from the East African protectorates. The governor was meanwhile informed that there would be considerable difficulty in obtaining a loan and terms would in any case be onerous.[30]

Negotiations got off to an unpromising start. Early in August 1919 the governor upset the Colonial Office by announcing that, because of a depression in trade, customs revenue and railway earnings had fallen by £250,000, that expenditure had risen, that the budget would not balance and that the Treasury should be asked for a loan of £600,000. There followed an exercise in Colonial Office financial control. All agreed that economies must be made. One officer minuted that the governor had failed to understand the financial position of this country and the Treasury's point of view. Fiddes concluded: 'This is a light-hearted telegram. Sir E. Northey seems to think that the Treasury have a bottomless purse into which he can dip when he likes'. The distant Northey received no favours even from Amery: 'I am inclined to agree with Sir G. Fiddes. Our chances of getting the loan money we want for development will be increased if we can show real efforts at economy are being made locally'. Predictably though, Amery had a further imaginative comment to make. He concluded that the governor should have a good financial adviser: 'What is really needed, I submit, is an absolutely first rate finance man for Eastern Africa as a whole i.e. I come back always to my old idea that the whole of E. Africa should now come under a regime like that of T[rans]v[aa]l and O[range] R[iver] C[olony] after 1902'. Milner agreed: 'Could not there be something like a 'Financial Adviser' for the whole E. African block? We want something more than the local Treasurer.' Such far-reaching ideas of regional planning received intermittent discussion throughout the 1920s. For the time being though, Northey was left 'to cut down expenditure drastically and to discover fresh sources of revenue'.[31]

Northey did balance his budget. At least he submitted proposals which would have given him financial harmony, but these involved increasing the railway rates on the Uganda Railway. Protests from the Uganda government and from merchants who depended on this pipeline to the sea obliged the Colonial Office to instruct the governor to suspend the increases.[32] In reply Northey responded by renewing his request for financial help. Thus cornered, the Colonial Office were forced to apply to the Treasury, stressing that assistance was required only because of the disturbances caused by the war, that it was only a temporary difficulty and that a loan of £150,000 and not a grant-in-aid (which involved financial control by the Treasury) was required.[33] The Treasury were inevitably displeased by the request,[34] but before battle could be properly joined it was realized in the Colonial Office that the protectorate actually needed more than £150,000. The question of the E.A.P.'s war debt had to be resolved.

The East African protectorates involved in the campaigns against Germany's African possessions had agreed in the early stages of the war to bear the cost of their respective forces of King's African Rifles on the basis of pre-war establishments. They also agreed to finance volunteer local forces needed for defence. Other troops in the area were to be an imperial responsibility. In practice it had become impossible to distinguish between the expenses incurred by local and by imperial troops. Common accounts were used and the liabilities of the protectorates, it was agreed, should be allocated after the war. Meantime the War Office had footed the entire bill. Consequently the War Office pressed after the Armistice for a financial settlement with the territories. The Colonial Office then argued that the war had been an imperial and not a colonial responsibility and that the greater share of the burden for the East African campaigns should therefore be borne by the Imperial government. Neither the War Office nor the Treasury accepted this argument and the dispute dragged on into the 1930s.[35]

The Colonial Office's immediate concern was to accelerate the development of the E.A.P.. The territory was currently paying an annual allocation out of revenue to the War Office to cover some of these military expenses and this was upsetting normal budgeting arrangements and therefore militating against more productive use of revenue. Pending a final settlement of the question, it was decided to ask the Treasury for a loan to cover the war debt. This would make the task of balancing annual budgets easier, although the territory would be saddled with interest and sinking fund payments on the debt incurred. Accordingly in December 1919, in place of the original request for £150,000, the Colonial Office asked the Treasury to supply a loan of £550,000 to cover war expenses and the budget deficit.[36] In response, the Treasury acknowledged that some assistance would have to be given but they were determined that the terms should be strict so as to drive the protectorate into financial independence as soon as possible, an expression rather indicative of the Treasury's approach to colonial finance. Their offer, conditional on increased taxes and railway rates, was an advance of only £150,000 at 6% simple interest repayable in five years and involving full Treasury control of the territory's finances.[37] It was, the Colonial Office decided, unacceptable. 'We should have all the hampering obstruction of Treasury control without any of the advantages.' Bottomley concluded that nothing more could be done until Milner returned from Egypt.[38] The Treasury's proposal was rejected and the deficit was met by Crown Agents advances.[39]

By early 1920, Colonial Office attempts to obtain further financial assistance from the Imperial Treasury for the development of the E.A.P. had failed. Because of the E.A.P.'s existing debts, unbalanced budget and economic problems, the Treasury did not feel that more aid would lead in the near future to the financial self-sufficiency of the protectorate. Hence they refused to commit more of their precious funds to the territory. Thus it became clear to the Colonial Office and to the governor of the E.A.P. that the protectorate would have to raise its own loan independently, both to solve immediate budgetary problems and to accelerate long-term development.

However, it was accepted without question in the Colonial Office that if the E.A.P. was to raise an independent loan successfully it would have to be covered by the Colonial Stock Acts. Since the existing Colonial Stock Acts were applicable only to colonies, Amery contemplated amendments which would extend their cover to include

protectorates and mandated territories. This proposal was resoundingly rejected by the Treasury who claimed, among other things, that
'to do as you wish would ... depreciate all existing British Government securities'.[40] By the time this refusal was received, alternative
arrangements were already well under way, namely, to annex some
of the E.A.P.. The annexation of the protectorates in East Africa had
been considered during the war.[41] The objective then had been
political, but in December 1919 Bottomley noted that 'the case for
annexation has been strengthened by the necessity of obtaining loans'.
Amery and the Colonial Development Committee gave their blessing in February 1920. Because the Sultan of Zanzibar's province on
the coast was subject to complicating treaties with France, the
intention was to annex only the interior of the protectorate. Preparing
the appropriate legislation took some time, and the Order-in-Council
declaring the new Colony of Kenya was not published until 23 July
1920.[42]

Meanwhile, the territory's problems had not eased. By February
1920 the overdraft with the Crown Agents stood at £1 million,
although £580,000 was due to be advanced by the Treasury under the
1914 act. The Agents were keeping the account in funds by advances
at bank rate, 6%, but they were anxious to see preparations made for
raising a public loan.[43] Unfortunately the administration's financial
position did not improve: in March 1920 it was reported that once
again the budget would not balance and that a deficit of £250,000
was expected in the financial year 1920–21. The Colonial Office
uniformly agreed that in the light of the Treasury's previous response
there was no virtue in asking for help in that quarter. Economies
would have to be made.[44] Here was another reason for accelerating
arrangements for raising an independent loan. Annexation had first
to be completed, but in May 1920 the Colonial Office instructed
Deputy Governor Bowring (Northey was home on leave) to pass the
necessary loans ordinance.[45]

Nevertheless, the first Kenya loan was not issued until 10 November
1921, eighteen months later. The delays were caused by vacillations
of the Kenya government on the projects to be financed, changes in
the financial position of the colony, and lengthy and occasionally
short-tempered negotiations between the Colonial Office and the
Treasury principally on the settlement of outstanding debts.

Estimates of Kenya's loan requirements continued to rise. Northey's original request back in February 1919 had been for an increase

in his loan provision up to £3 million, but in May 1920 while still on leave he submitted further proposals bringing his requirements up to £5 million.[46] In July Bowring proposed another addition to cover extra building works.[47] Northey reconsidered his plans on his return to East Africa and in September produced a new schedule for loans totalling £7 million to be raised over three years. This escalation worried the Colonial Office. Northey had set aside only £600,000 to cover interest payments for three years; the interest on most of the items listed, he reckoned, could be borne on the colony's revenues. But the unfavourable budgets of 1919–20 and 1920–21 had not been forgotten in the Colonial Office, and doubts were expressed about the adequacy of the administration's income to support such costs.[48] It should, moreover, be noted that the sums being requested did not include money to pay off the war debt in the fashion proposed by the Colonial Office in December 1919. There was another worry. The Colonial Office realised that the price of any loan raised on the open market would be affected by the extent of prior charges for interest on the territory's revenues. If the indebtedness of the colony was increased by accepting further loans from the Imperial government under the 1914 act, this would prejudice the market chances of an independent public loan. Accordingly it was decided that no further issues would be made to Kenya from that source or from the small allocation authorized in 1911 and not yet exhausted.[49] However, the Crown Agents pointed out a further difficulty: so long as the interest on the colony's existing debts to the Treasury incurred by such earlier measures ranked as prior charges on the colony's revenues, the rate of interest on a new public loan would have to be high in order to make it attractive. To avoid making the new loan expensive therefore, it would have to rank with the debts to the Treasury as an equal charge on the colony's revenues. If the Treasury would not agree to this arrangement, they suggested that the new loan should be increased in amount and the debts to the Treasury paid off from it. They concluded, acutely and accurately: 'It will no doubt be appreciated in that Department that they have an interest in helping the colonies to borrow money in the open market at reasonable rates'. The Colonial Office took up the suggestion of paying off the debts to the Treasury from the new loan, and informed them of this intention. Because the old debts had been incurred at low rates of interest and interest rates had since risen, they also requested that the debts be revalued and the totals accordingly reduced.[50]

While awaiting Treasury reactions, the Colonial Office and the Crown Agents completed the other preparations for the raising of a loan. It was decided to increase the total to £8 million, but with a first issue of only £4 million. The Bank of England arranged this for 6 December 1920, and the Treasury were so informed. The price would be steep, 6% at 95, though the operation of a sinking fund would be postponed for three years.[51] Everything now seemed to hinge on the Treasury.

Officials in the Treasury recognised that Kenya's attempt to raise an independent loan at least eased demands upon them. Indeed, this might be a useful precedent in dealing with crown colonies in the future. Moreover, if Kenya repaid its debts to the Exchequer this would actually help the Imperial government by topping up the credit of the Local Loans Fund at Kenya's expense. But all this assumed that the Treasury would not have to come to Kenya's support later on. Before they could approve the issue, particularly as a trustee security under the Colonial Stock Acts, they had to be sure that the colony's revenues could support large interest payments. Some Treasury officials emphasized that Kenya's finances were in fact in a 'rocky condition', and that, with the additional burden of the new loan, budget deficits could be expected, to be met by Treasury grants-in-aid. Furthermore, bringing up an old score, if Kenya was made to bear its proper war liabilities, this would be a further considerable debt charge. Given their fears it was inevitable that these officials would also protest at the Colonial Office's intention to allow Kenya's earnings from the Uganda Railway to be diverted from the administration's general revenue into additional development works. 'The Colonial Office do not seem to recognise that very desirable development may have to be postponed in the face of urgent necessity.' Senior staff were, however, a little more accommodating. Niemeyer confessed: 'I am in sympathy, even in present circumstances, with putting something into East African Development: it is probably wise even from the narrowly financial standpoint'. He accepted, that is, the Colonial Office argument that financial aid would improve general revenues and reduce the risk of requiring grants-in-aid. But he argued that some revenue should still be used to repay the war debt, and that railway revenue should swell general income. Barstow agreed with this assessment.[52]

At this critical juncture matters took a sudden turn. The Colonial Office, who had been badgering the Treasury to reach a rapid settlement of outstanding problems, received a telegram from Governor Northey on 26 November 1920 requesting a postponement of the loan until June 1921. Further surveys needed to be carried out, new items for inclusion in the loan had been produced. The colony would get by on Crown Agents advances in the interim. The Colonial Office were left with the duty of informing the Treasury of the postponement. Montagu Norman, Governor of the Bank of England, complained to Niemeyer about the upset caused by this postponement, and Sir Warren Fisher, permanent secretary at the Treasury, ticked off the Colonial Office. Fiddes rejected the accusation that the delay was the Colonial Office's fault and sent him a copy of the admonishment already sent by the Colonial Office to Northey. Niemeyer concluded this little bout of back-biting by reassuring Norman that the Colonial Office had been told off and would not offend again.[53]

The Colonial Office still urged the Treasury to complete negotiations, and so on 5 January 1921 the Treasury despatched their first formal response to the loan proposals. They accepted such a loan in principle and welcomed the repayment to the Imperial Exchequer of Kenya's outstanding debts. But while the money advanced in 1912 could be repaid at its present lower value they were obliged for legal reasons to ask for the repayment in full of the amounts borrowed under the acts of 1911 and 1914. Moreover, they also reminded the Colonial Office that the colony still faced the prospect of shouldering its share of the East African war expenditure. That was one reason why they insisted that income from the Uganda Railway should add to Kenya's general revenue and should not be used for development works. They claimed this was a concession since under the original agreement made for building the railway with Imperial government funds, income from it should in fact be transferred to the Imperial Exchequer. Finally they demanded assurances that in spite of the colony's present financial position and the existing burdens upon its revenue it could still support a loan of the magnitude proposed.[54]

The Colonial Office were understandably unhappy with this reaction. While they accepted as unavoidable the terms for the repayment of Kenya's existing debts, they denied the Treasury's right to restrict Kenya's use of its Uganda Railway revenue. They argued that accelerating development was the way to ensure that the territory would not need future Imperial government assistance. For similar reasons they rejected the Treasury's suggestion that Kenya's war liabilities should be a prior consideration: so far from the issue of the loan being dependent on the financial ability of the colony to meet war expenditure, the colony's ability to pay such debts depended on the development of the territory.[55] Milner's last contribution to these negotiations was to give his approval to the office's reply to the Treasury. Frustration on this business completed the disillusionment which in February 1921 induced him to resign. Amery served under his successor, Churchill, until in April he too departed, transferred to the Admiralty as Financial Secretary.

The Treasury, no longer feeling the matter urgent, responded slowly to the Colonial Office's complaints. Officials were evidently displeased by the Colonial Office reply and toyed with the idea of claiming for the Imperial Exchequer the income from the Uganda Railway 'in present financial circumstances', but in the event they decided merely to use their claim as a bargaining counter to bring the Colonial Office to heel over the war debt question. But it took over two months, until 1 April 1921, before they wrote back to the Colonial Office, stressing that Kenya's war debt liabilities had still to be determined, and pointing out that the Imperial government had not yet waived its claim to the Uganda Railway.[56]

Bottomley realized at once that this reference to imperial claims on the Uganda Railway was a debating weapon to force the Colonial Office to reach a settlement on the war debt. Nevertheless, he did not under-estimate the Treasury's ability to undermine the loan plan:

If the Treasury choose to consider that Kenya's resources are not sufficient to bear both the loan charges and the War bill they will not approve the loan for the purposes of the Colonial Stock Acts, and there will be no loan; and, further that if a definite (even if future) liability is laid on the Colony for war expenditure, it will have to be stated in the Prospectus, as a matter of good faith with the investing public, and the result will be − no money.[57]

The capacity of Kenya's finances to support both a new loan and war debt liabilities looked even less certain when in April 1921 a despatch from Governor Northey proposed yet another increase in the size of his intended loan to £9 million.[58] This made it more imperative to ease other burdens on the colony's revenues. Bottomley gloomily observed, 'unless ... we are to advertize the place as bankrupt we must get the military expenditure question settled before we issue the prospectus'. Sir James Stevenson, the recently appointed Business Adviser at the Colonial Office,[59] explained the difficulties to Churchill: given the barely balanced budget, 'I see great difficulty in floating a loan of £9 million either now or in the near future ... except at a high rate of interest'. The war debt issue would have to be settled first and the territory's development plans carefully re-examined. Churchill agreed: 'The flotation of this large loan and the objects will have to be further considered. It will probably cost 8% at present rates'.[60] The Crown Agents reported that underwriting might be difficult: Kenya had a bad press and this was new stock; 6% at 96 was possible. The permanent staff, Stevenson, Read, Bottomley and Mercer of the Crown Agents, then gathered to consider the problem and agreed that raising a £9 million loan was impossible at the present time. £4 million only should be applied for, of which £1,100,000 would go to the Treasury and £1 million would repay advances from the Crown Agents, but a further issue might be possible in the following year.[61]

It was time for the Secretary of State to intervene. On 25 May Churchill and Stevenson discussed the matter with two Treasury officials, Sir Warren Fisher and Upcott. Churchill accepted the view that the Uganda Railway was indeed the property of the British taxpayer and he agreed not to press the plan to repudiate the war debt. Although he refused immediate payment on either account, his views differed markedly from those expressed earlier by Bottomley and other members of the permanent staff. But tactically this move was successful in easing the log-jam in negotiations. Progress was made at further inter-departmental discussions on the following day, after which both sides withdrew to their respective departments to clarify their differences.[62] These still proved to be serious.

The Colonial Office wanted to obtain Treasury consent to a total loan of £9 million. Most importantly, the interest and sinking fund charges on this amount should have priority over whatever payments became due in any war debt settlement. Without such priority the cost of the loan was likely to be excessive since the investing public would fear the colony might default on the interest of their loan. The Treasury objected that this would excessively postpone payments on the war debt and, rejecting Colonial Office compromises, they insisted that the portion of the Kenya loan with priority over the war debt should be restricted to £4 million. At best they would consider later a moderate further issue. Bottomley minuted despondently that nothing had been achieved. One major project, the Uasin-Gishu Railway, could not be started since there was no certainty of obtaining the second loan needed to complete it.

A further obstacle was the Treasury's refusal to allow interest to be paid out of capital for the first three years. This was harsh. Normal commercial practice approved of this method and it had been part of the recent settlement on the Uganda Development Loan. By insisting that the interest and sinking fund be met from revenue from the outset, the Treasury were forcing an extra burden on the already overstrained income of the colony. Bottomley estimated that the territory would have to raise an extra £250,000 of fresh revenue in the next twelve months and that this was impossible. But the Financial Secretary at the Treasury argued that capital outlay which would not produce an almost immediate return could not be justified under present conditions when the market 'is starved for capital that is needed for immediately productive purposes'.

The third major conflict was over the question of the interest and sinking fund charges on the war debt. It was agreed that a government inter-departmental committee should be set up to determine the actual size of this debt. Meanwhile, the Treasury proposed that the colony should pay on account half of any future increase of its revenue above a datum-line. This line would be fixed at the level of the existing colonial revenue plus an allowance to cover the charges arising out of the new loan. In return the Treasury agreed to allow income from the Uganda Railway to be used to support the colony's revenue. What was given with one hand, was taken away with the other. Bottomley argued that the datum-line allowed no margin for the normal growth of ordinary colonial expenditure: for example, while the railway and marine service revenue would increase as the country developed, so would expenses, and under this proposal these expenses would be balanced by only half their reciprocal increase in revenue. He suggested that only a third of increased revenue should be earmarked for war debt servicing until a certain figure, an extra £300,000 a year, was reached. Thereafter the half and half principle might apply. But the Treasury stuck to their original offer. On 31 May 1921 Bottomley concluded that the terms offered were unacceptable: it simply meant that the Treasury would get back £1 million's worth of long-dated loans. It was suggested that Churchill should see the Chancellor.[63]

On the following day a telegram arrived from Governor Northey which shattered the negotiations. Northey regretted that instead of his predicted surplus revenue by the end of the year, there was to be an estimated deficit of £300,000. Later he reported an estimated deficit by 1 January 1922 of £570,000 and an estimated deficit for the 1922 Budget of £600,000. There was no possibility of raising additional revenue or of lowering expenditure and he requested a grant-in-aid. This financial crisis, 'resulting from abnormal trade depression', postponed the Kenya loan for the second time.[64] Shortly afterwards, and possibly as a result of this emergency, Bottomley broke down through overwork.[65]

It was understood in the Colonial Office that the loan could not be simply suspended indefinitely. It was too late to draw back. Development materials had already been ordered and there was an overdraft of over £1 million with the Crown Agents, costing £62,000 a year. A loan had to be raised as soon as possible, but with an unbalanced budget in the colony it could prove an expensive disaster. The governor was urged to make every effort to get his administration solvent.[66] In August, recuperated and back in harness, Bottomley was proposing to cover all needs with a total loan of £10 million, but with a first issue of £5 million. To attract investors the price must be high, 6% at 95. Interest must be paid out of capital. In fact this loan would then realise capital of only £3,779,200, under £2 million for new works and the rest to pay off old debts. But at least Bottomley was confident that the Treasury would sanction the loan: the only alternative would be a grant-in-aid and the postponement indefinitely of any chance of repaying previous imperial loans or bearing any part of the war debt.[67]

The Treasury must have been equally aware of this: it was the key to the success of the negotiations. They had no intention of actually preventing the loan being raised, but were determined to ensure that the terms agreed were as favourable as possible to their interests. Hence the ease with which the last stage of the settlement was reached. Prodded by Churchill, the Treasury met representatives of the Colonial Office and agreed on final terms. The Treasury raised from £4 million to £8 million the extent of the loan which would take priority over war debt liabilities. The appointment of an inter-departmental committee to establish the size of the East African war debt was confirmed, and a complicated compromise was reached on the datum-line which determined the amount to be paid by Kenya on account. It seems to have been quietly accepted that interest and sinking fund could be paid out of capital for the first three years and that income from the Uganda Railway could be used for development purposes.[68]

These were the principles of the agreement which enabled the loan to be issued as a trustee security. The necessary legislation and announcements were made early in October, but details needed for schedules not being supplied by the Kenya government in time, the date of issue was postponed once more from 17 October until 10 November when the loan was raised at 95 and 6%. It was not a popular issue: only £2,100,000 was subscribed by the public and £2,900,000 was taken up by the underwriters.[69]

There was no neat conclusion to these negotiations. The datum-line question was still in its details unresolved and provoked some further exchanges, and at one stage it seemed likely that the Treasury would query the terms for debt repayments. Meanwhile, the inter-departmental committee was meeting to allocate the amounts of the East African territories' war liabilities. Its report was not made until 1927 by which time the decision had already been taken to postpone war debt repayments until 1934.[70]

The initiative for the Kenya loan came from the governor of the territory, and this is the first important point to note about the negotiations. The Colonial Office were not however just passive agents, for it was they who insisted on local economy, a balanced budget and a careful assessment of the ability of the colony's revenue to bear the servicing charges of the loan. It was the Colonial Office who reprimanded the governor for his unprofessional postponement of the issue. But the Colonial Office agreed with the governor that local revenues were insufficient to finance development works and that a loan was necessary to obtain capital. The Treasury's insistence on strict economy in Imperial government expenditure and their refusal to offer aid to the territory except on the most formidable terms made it inevitable that this loan would be raised independently in the London market. The Treasury showed themselves to be sympathetic, in principle, to such a move since it relieved them of the necessity of providing aid. But they insisted on obtaining their pound of flesh in the repayment of old debts before they would give their blessing. In addition they shared the Colonial Office's fears that the colony might overburden its revenue with interest and sinking fund payments. They therefore tried to limit loan expenditure not because they opposed colonial development or open market issues, but because they feared such commitments would lead ultimately to dependence on Exchequer grants-in-aid. So long as the Imperial government's main economic policy was to reduce government expenditure, this type of obstructionism was difficult to circumvent.

4. CONCLUSION

The three studies contained in this chapter illustrate a number of significant aspects of immediate post-war policy and decision-making. The first important feature is that the pressure to obtain financial issues under the 1914 act, the suggestions for a general loan for Uganda, and the programme for increasing development expenditure in Kenya all came from the respective governments of the territories concerned. Although the Colonial Office was anxious to further such proposals it did not initiate them. It acted as the agent, a critical and supervisory agent, of the colonial governments. It was not acting as an initiatory development office.

Moreover, it is clear from the cases considered that the projects financed and the purposes behind them were of the same character as the pre-1914 *ad hoc* development schemes. They were designed to lay down basic railway networks, build roads and improve harbours and so improve the export potential of the territories. Their objective was to foster increased colonial revenues so as to secure the territories' freedom from galling Treasury grants-in-aid and financial control. Imperial aid had achieved this target in West Africa before 1914 and enabled those colonies to finance their own development after the war. This was the model of colonial development policy which Colonial Office staff wished to follow in East Africa in the difficult post-war years. The contrast with the schemes outlined in the previous chapter is clear. While occasional appeals were made to metropolitan interest in the products of these territories, the basic value of the schemes was not that they were part of a general economic development programme but that they removed a potential financial burden from the Imperial Exchequer.

In other words, in the decision-making process financial benefits to the Imperial Exchequer rather than economic benefits to the imperial economy were of prime concern. This was the reason why the Imperial Treasury could be persuaded to sanction the schemes. The emphasis upon the Imperial government's financial interests also explains the stubborn restrictiveness of the Treasury's proposals. They saw little advantage in encouraging long-term economic development if it was likely to involve more immediate short-term financial burdens on the Imperial government. Excessive loan expenditure would lead to unbalanced local budgets and dependence on grants-in-aid. A compromise was therefore sought by the Treasury as by the Colonial

Office: enough financial encouragement for economic development to promote local financial self-sufficiency without risking so great a local financial burden as to exceed the increases in local government revenue.

One other point needs to be made. The Colonial Office and the Treasury did in practice share very similar views as to the purpose of Imperial government aid for colonial development. Their conflicts stemmed from the different perspectives of the two departments. The Colonial Office were concerned with obtaining the best possible financial assistance for the territories which dominated their attention. The Treasury, on the other hand, necessarily regarded the requirements of the dependencies as but one of many pressing financial demands upon the limited resources of the Imperial Exchequer. Given the state of the imperial budget, the burden of the national debt and high taxation, and in view of the external popular and political pressures for economy, the Treasury's difficulties become apparent. If the necessity for reducing Imperial government expenditure is assumed, then very convincing reasons had to be presented to justify waiving debts to the Imperial Exchequer and increasing imperial expenditure. Only the argument of avoiding the burden of grants-in-aid convinced the Treasury at this time. In the next chapter we must consider how altered circumstances presented the Colonial Office with a new lever with which to open the imperial purse.

NOTES

1. See Table 6 below, p.273, for a list of post-war grants-in-aid.
2. Amery to Milner 12 Feb. and 4 June 1919, Milner to Amery 2 and 30 Dec. 1919, Amery Papers, Box 54, Folder B; J. Barnes and D. Nicholson, eds., *The Leo Amery Diaries*, vol.1, London, 1980, 8 and 26 Feb. 1919, pp.255, 257; L. S. Amery, *My Political Life*, vol.2, London, 1953, pp.360-2; R. M. A. van Zwanenberg and A. King, *An Economic History of Kenya and Uganda 1800–1970*, London, 1975, pp.233-6.
3. E. A. Brett, *Colonialism and Underdevelopment in East Africa*, London, 1973, p.63; Major E. S. Grogan to Milner 21 Nov. 1919, Milner Papers Add.Mss.Eng. Hist. c.704.
4. CO 533/193/Gov 9782; CO 533/194/Gov 13427 and Gov 13555; CO 533/195/Gov 38661 and Gov 38671; CO 533/196/Gov 41419 and Gov 41421.
5. Minute by Bottomley, 24 Dec. 1918, and C.O. to Treas., 4 Jan. 1919, CO 533/196/Gov 41421; Treas 755 on T1/12495/9552 of 1920.
6. Treas. to C.O. 13 Feb. 1919, CO 323/804/Treas 9775; see above pp.55-6.
7. Treas. to C.O. 13 Feb. 1919 and minutes, CO 533/219/Treas 9776.

8. Northey to C.O. 27 Feb. 1919 and Grindle to Treas. 20 March 1919, CO 533/207/Gov 13354.
9. Heath to C.O. 4 April 1919, Treas 12663 on T1/12495/9552 of 1920; CO 533/219/Treas 20714.
10. C.O. to Govs. of Nyasaland and Uganda 18 March 1919, CO 533/207/Gov 13354.
11. Duff to C.O. 14 April 1919, CO 525/82/Gov 23055.
12. Coryndon to C.O. 24 Jan. 1919, CO 536/93/Gov 5754; 12 March 1919, CO 536/93/Gov 23883; 29 April 1919, CO 536/93/Gov 27068; 5 May 1919, CO 536/94/Gov 37443.
13. Mema. by Bottomley, minutes 11 Aug.–15 Oct.1919 and Byatt to Parkinson 15 Aug. 1919, CO 533/226/G 45697.
14. Memo. by Bottomley 15 Oct. 1919 and minutes of 15 and 20 Oct. 1919, *ibid.*.
15. Note of Discussion with Secretary of State 8 Nov. 1919, minute by Bottomley 12 Nov. 1919 and C.O. to Treas. 19 Nov. 1919, CO 533/222/CO 65566.
16. Treas 49585 and Treas 48402 on T1/12495/9552 of 1920.
17. Minute by Chamberlain 26 Nov. 1919, minutes of 1 Dec. 1919, Fiddes to Barstow 22 Dec. 1919, Barstow to C.O. 6 Jan. 1920, Treas 49585 and Treas 4403, *ibid.*; CO 533/243/Treas 1303 and Treas 10342; Fiddes to Milner 17 Dec. 1919 and Milner to Fiddes 5 Jan. 1920, Milner Papers Add.Mss.Eng.Hist. c.700.
18. Coryndon to C.O. 29 April 1919, CO 536/93/Gov 27068; Coryndon to Milner 5 May 1919, CO 536/94/Gov 37443; Coryndon to Milner 6 Sept. 1919, CO 536/95/Gov 60497; Coryndon to C.O. 18 Feb., 3 April, 6 May 1920, CO 536/107/C 9131, C 17322 and C 22861.
19. Para 329 of report, CO 536/99/Gov 17962.
20. Parkinson to Bottomley 30 Jan. 1920, CO 536/95/Gov 60497.
21. Milner's Diary 14, 22, 30 April 1920, Milner Papers 283.
22. Milner to Chamberlain 7 May 1920, T 161, box 2, file S.119 henceforth cited as T 161/2/S.119.
23. Minutes by Barstow and Chamberlain 12–20 May 1920 and Barstow to Milner 14 May 1920, *ibid.*.
24. Chamberlain to Barstow 9 June 1920, *ibid.*; Milner Diaries 9 June 1920, Milner Papers 283.
25. Mema. on Uganda Development Grant, Chamberlain to Barstow 15 July 1920 and Barstow to C.O. 7 August 1920, T 161/2/S.119; CO 536/101/Gov 33533; CO 536/106/Treas 39577 and Treas 42126.
26. Chamberlain to Barstow 9 June and 15 July 1920, T 161/2/S.119. The Treasury did exploit this new agreement: from 1921–22 most grants-in-aid of local administrations in fact took the form of repayable loans.
27. Bottomley to Thornton 13 April 1920, CO 536/107/C 22861.
28. Northey to C.O. 16 April 1919, CO 533/209/Gov 28670.
29. Minutes by Parkinson 11 June and by Bottomley 14 June 1919, *ibid.*.
30. C.O. to Northey 17 July 1919, *ibid.*.
31. Northey to C.O. and minutes 9–15 Aug. 1919, C.O. to Northey 19 Aug. 1919, CO 533/212/Gov 45780. Amery had a fairly low opinion of Northey's ability: he was 'keen and well-meaning but without the experience or brains to handle the problem in a big way': Amery to Milner 25 Feb. 1920, Amery Papers, Box 54, Folder B.
32. Northey to C.O. 24 Sept. 1919 and C.O. to Northey 15 Oct. 1919, CO 533/213/Gov 56218.
33. Northey to C.O., and C.O. to Treas. 12 Nov. 1919, CO 533/215/Gov 64193.
34. Craig to Bottomley 2 Dec. 1919, Treas 48402 on T1/12495/9552 of 1920.
35. Minutes of 11 June – 6 July 1919, CO 533/209/Gov 28670; memo. by Machtig 13 April 1921, CO 533/245/CO 23629; Report of the Inter-departmental

Committee on the Apportionment of the East African War Expenditure, 1927, T 161/64/S.4648/2. The views of the Colonial Office, War Office and Treasury on this issue may be found in CAB 24/112/CP 1926, CAB 24/118/CP 2454 and CAB 24/114/CP 2002 respectively.

36. Bottomley to Read 13 Oct. 1919, CO 533/213/Gov 56218; C.O. to Treas. 17 Dec. 1919, CO 533/227/N 69315.

37. Minute by Millar 24 Jan. 1920 and Barstow to C.O. 31 Jan. 1920, Treas 54373 on T1/12495/9552 of 1920.

38. Minutes of 2 and 3 Feb. 1920, CO 533/243/Treas 5576.

39. C.O. to Northey 26 Feb. 1920, CO 533/239/CA 8491. The Crown Agents frequently made small loans from the cash reserves deposited with them by other colonial governments to tide an administration over temporary crises. Larger advances might be made if the colony intended to raise a public loan in the near future.

40. Minutes 10–19 Dec. 1919, Amery to Chamberlain 4 March 1920 and Chamberlain to Amery 25 March 1920, CO 323/839/CO 2832. The Treasury had rejected a similar proposal in 1912.

41. CO 533/190/CO 33858; CO 533/196/Gov 41444.

42. CO 533/214/Gov 70819; CO 533/240/FO 2323; CO 533/248/M1 15088; minutes of Third Meeting of Colonial Development Committee 20 Feb. 1920, CO 885/26/Misc 348.

43. C.A. to C.O. 16 Feb. 1920, CO 533/239/CA 8491.

44. Bowring to C.O. 6 March 1920, minutes 12–13 March 1920, CO 533/231/Gov 13183.

45. C.O. to Bowring 12 May 1920, CO 533/245/CO 23629. Milner had several meetings discussing East African problems with Northey while he was on leave: Milner Diaries 31 March, 13 and 22 April, 3 June 1920, Milner Papers 283.

46. Northey to C.O. 28 May 1920, CO 533/253/N.26417.

47. Bowring to C.O. 2 July 1920, CO 533/234/Gov 36903.

48. Northey to C.O. 7 Sept. 1920 and Parkinson to Bottomley 13 Sept. 1920, CO 533/236/Gov 44987.

49. Memo. by Bottomley 21 June 1920 and minutes by Bottomley 21 June and 29 Sept. 1920, CO 533/245/CO 30441.

50. C.A. to C.O. 19 Oct. 1920, minute by Bottomley 23 Oct. 1920, Read to Treas. 4 Nov. 1920, CO 533/240/CA 51578.

51. C.A. to C.O. 22 Nov. 1920 and minute by Bottomley 22 Nov. 1920, CO 533/240/ CA 57419; minute by Bottomley 19 Nov. 1920, Read to Treas. and C.O. to Gov. 20 Nov. 1920, CO 533/247/CO 57427.

52. Minutes of 27 Oct. — 4 Dec. 1920 and mema. by Skevington and by Upcott 25 Nov. 1920, T 161/64/S.4648/1.

53. Northey to C.O. 25 Nov. 1920, minutes and letters 26 Nov. — 10 Dec. 1920, CO 533/237/Gov 58080; minutes and letters 30 Nov. — 15 Dec. 1920, T 161/64/ S.4648/1.

54. Read to Treas. 30 Nov. 1920 and Meiklejohn to C.O. 5 Jan. 1921, T 161/64/ S.4648/1.

55. Minute by Bottomley 20 Jan. 1921, C.O. to Treas. 28 Jan. 1921, CO 533/268/Treas 631.

56. Minutes of 28 Feb. and 29 March and Treas. to C.O. 1 April 1921, T 161/64/ S.4648/1.

57. Minute by Bottomley 9 April 1921, CO 533/268/Treas 15879.

58. Northey to C.O. 14 March 1921, CO 533/257/Gov 19686.

59. Sir James Stevenson, 1873–1926, was a private businessman who served in the Ministry of Munitions 1915–17 and as Colonial Office Business Adviser 1921–3, *Who Was Who.*

60. Minutes 27 April — 5 May 1921, CO 533/257/Gov 20180.
61. C.A. to C.O. 12 May 1921, Stevenson to Churchill 24 May 1921, CO 533/266/CA 23565.
62. Minute by Upcott 28 May 1921, T 161/64/S.4648/1.
63. Minutes and papers 28 — 31 May 1921, *ibid.*; minutes and papers 27 — 31 May 1921, CO 533/266/CA 23565.
64. Northey to C.O. 28 May 1921, CO 533/266/CA 23565 and CO 533/259/Gov 27224; Northey to C.O. 13 June 1921, CO 533/260/Gov 30096.
65. Minute by Skevington c.23 June 1921, T 161/64/S.4648/1.
66. Minute by Fiddes 17 June, C.O. to Gov. 22 June 1921, CO 533/260/Gov 30096; C.A. to C.O. 13 July 1921, CO 533/266/CA 35060.
67. Minute and memo. by Bottomley 4 Aug. 1921, CO 533/270/CO 41691.
68. Minutes and letters 11 Aug. — 1 Sept. 1921, T 161/64/S.4648/1; note by Stevenson 18 Aug. 1921, CO 533/270/Co 41691; minutes and letters 19–26 Sept. 1921, CO 533/268/Treas 42161.
69. CO 533/271/CO 51030 and CO 51475; CO 533/266/CA 57426; M. F. Hill, *Permanent Way. The Story of the Kenya and Uganda Railway*, 2nd ed. Nairobi, 1961, p.395.
70. CO 533/274/R 49009; T 161/64/S.4648/2; for the war debt problem see below pp.134-5.

V

UNEMPLOYMENT AND COLONIAL DEVELOPMENT POLICY: THE TRADE FACILITIES ACTS 1921–24

1. *UNEMPLOYMENT AND GOVERNMENT EXPENDITURE*

After the war, novel and expensive colonial development proposals were rejected and policy reverted to its limited pre-war mould. The Imperial government became preoccupied with its immediate financial problems. Beyond this primary consideration, they left the development of colonial resources substantially to the joint endeavours of colonial governments and private enterprise and the maintenance of the nation's economic interests to the normal operation of market forces. But the Imperial government faced a new worry from the end of 1920 when those market forces created high levels of unemployment in Britain. Attempts to alleviate the depression were to have a profound effect on the Colonial Office's efforts to obtain financial support for colonial governments from the Imperial Treasury. The unemployment problem seriously modified colonial development policy.

The percentage of insured workers registered as unemployed rose rapidly in 1921 to leave an annual average of 16.9%. There were over two million out of work in December 1921. Although there was subsequently some improvement, the average was still over 10% in 1924. These figures were higher than anything recorded before the war.[1] A cyclical downturn in the international economy had badly affected a British economy which was heavily export-orientated and susceptible to fluctuations in overseas demand. The volume of British exports in 1921 was 50% below the level of 1913, and the depression in the staple export industries of cotton, iron and steel, coal and shipbuilding inevitably infected the rest of the economy. But the unemployment figures also contained within them the victims of a structural economic problem. When world economic recovery began in 1924, the permanent decline in overseas demand for the products of Britain's staple industries was revealed in the unprecedentedly large numbers in those trades who remained out of work.[2]

It became a political as well as an economic necessity for the government to suggest some solution to the unemployment problem. Rival party proposals featured in all the general election campaigns of the 1920s, and other, often more radical, alternatives were put forward by concerned individuals and organisations. Ministers and party leaders were subjected to pressures from backbench M.P.s and from bodies like the Bank of England and the F.B.I. and from new groups such as the Empire Development Union, formed in 1922, and the Empire Industries Association, formed in 1924. The Advisory Committee to the Board of Trade, which represented the banks and major British industries, also spoke directly to ministers. Moreover, causing much concern to those in authority was the voice of the unemployed themselves, expressed through the National Unemployed Workers Movement established in 1921 and in demonstrations, hunger marches and sporadic violence.[3]

The initial reactions of the Imperial government to the slump were not helpful to the Colonial Office. The conventional wisdom of the Bank of England, the City of London and most industrialists was fully supported by the Treasury: sound monetary conditions were a prerequisite for economic recovery. In particular this meant that the post-war inflation of British prices had to be reversed. Such a step would stimulate purchases of British goods at home and, more importantly, overseas. Moreover, it would facilitate exchange stabilization, preferably at pre-war parities, the reintroduction of the gold standard and the restitution of London as the control centre of international finance. The government could help by lowering taxation. The reduction of government borrowing would also assist by leaving more capital available for the private investment which was expected to lead the economy out of the depression. But to achieve these desirable targets government expenditure would have to be still further reduced. Hence the immediate effect of the slump was to subject the expenditure of government departments to closer scrutiny.[4]

In the preparation of annual departmental estimates, the Treasury circulars increased the pressure for economy. On 13 May 1921 the attention of the departments was drawn to the severity of the government's financial crisis. Estimated revenue for 1922–23 would be about £950 million. Of this, £465 million was required for debt servicing. Since on other items current government expenditure amounted to £603 million, drastic reductions would be essential to keep expenditure for 1922−23 down to £490 million. Otherwise, the Treasury pointed out, more money would have to be borrowed, interest charges would rise, there would be intensified inflation and the £ sterling would be depressed. Alternatively, taxes would have to rise and this would hamper the recovery of British industry and commerce and damage employment prospects. Parliament and the country would not tolerate this. To achieve the necessary economies it was recognized that not only must new expenditure be ruthlessly controlled but that 'a reduction of expenditure on the requisite scale may only be obtained by the sacrifice of services in themselves desirable'. Departments were urgently requested to submit provisional estimates for Treasury inspection.[5]

In response the Colonial Office made an honest effort to co-operate. The permanent staff proposed and Churchill approved the formation of an Economy Committee which began on 1 June 1921 a genuine search for savings. The report eventually submitted on 27 July pointed out, however, that as a result of 'the insistent demands for economy during and since the War', further reductions in expenditure were made difficult. Cuts in grants-in-aid, necessary to reduce expenditure by 20% as the Treasury had requested, could only be done at the cost of retarding development. Reducing expenditure on research into tropical diseases and entomology was equally short-sighted. Nonetheless, grants-in-aid were reduced and other estimates pared down to give a reduction of 15% overall on Colonial Services. The Treasury were sent these provisional estimates in August and the proposed savings were detailed. At the same time the particular needs of the East African dependencies were stressed: it would be false economy to cut off their supply of development aid since, adequately assisted, they were expected to become 'not only self-supporting, but flourishing portions of the Empire'. The first objective, it will be noted, was to make these territories independent of Treasury support.[6]

In spite of these efforts, the Treasury circular of 1 October 1921 requesting the final (not provisional) estimates for 1922−23 explained that the deteriorating situation meant that the reductions previously requested would now prove inadequate.

You are therefore asked to consider the expenditure of your Department with a view to eliminating all services without exception which are not absolutely and directly necessary .... At the present time it is necessary to justify afresh both to the Treasury and to Parliament the continuance of any Government activity which, however desirable in itself, is not essential to the national welfare.

One irritated Colonial Office clerk minuted: 'So far as I know, it is not *"absolutely and directly necessary"*, or *"essential* to the national welfare"*, that this country should have any Colonies or Protectorates at all, still less a Colonial Office'.[7]

Meanwhile, the Geddes Committee was scrutinizing the provisional estimates. Confronted by a backbench and newspaper agitation against waste in government expenditure, the cabinet had appointed in August 1921 a parliamentary Committee on National Expenditure chaired by Sir Eric Geddes to propose further reductions. The committee's third report, submitted to the cabinet in February 1922, dealt with Colonial Services. The settlement of Uganda's war debt and the use of the profits from the Uganda Railway were queried, but the only cut proposed, a compliment perhaps to the Colonial Office's tight budgeting, was a reduction by £200,000 in the aid to Tanganyika and its change from a grant to a loan. The committee commented:

It has been urged before us that capital expenditure in [Tanganyika], as in other British Protectorates in East Africa, will materially promote their development, and that the provision of funds by the British Taxpayer would be a sound investment. We would, however, observe that the British Exchequer has, in present circumstances, no surplus funds for investments of this nature. At the present time, the provision of Public Funds must necessarily be limited to urgent requirements, and the development of these countries ought, in our opinion, to be regulated mainly by the ability of local governments and private undertakings to raise funds independently. As in the case of this country, these Territories, ought, we think, to deny themselves expenditure, even on laudable objects, until by rigid economy and taxation they have balanced their Budgets.[8]

This was no transitory pressure. In June 1922 the Treasury again requested provisional estimates for the financial year 1923–24. Further reductions in expenditure were necessary because 'the unfavourable industrial and commercial situation of the past year will be reflected in next year's Revenue Receipts'. The provisional estimates provided by the Colonial Office were studied by a cabinet subcommittee, while once again in October 1922 the Treasury circular on estimates urged further reductions on these provisional figures.[9]

In October 1923, the Treasury maintained the demand for economy in the estimates for 1924–25. Remissions of taxation were going to cut revenue by £23,750,000 and income tax returns would be lower. To balance the books, 'very substantial reductions on this year's Estimates must therefore be made'. It was unlikely that this sustained anti-waste campaign throughout the 1920s allowed any laxity in estimating. As one member of the Colonial Office commented: 'this Office is run on the cheap, if ever an Office was'.[10] The pressures for economy inevitably affected its work.

2. THE TRADE FACILITIES ACT 1921

With the Treasury, the cabinet, the House of Commons and much of the public apparently adamant for restrictions on expenditure, the prospect of the Imperial government aiding colonial development seemed limited. The paradox of the economic depression, however, was that it generated more than the restrictive pressures of the economy campaign: it created also an additional set of arguments which encouraged increased government expenditure. Discussions on colonial development reflected the conflict between these two reactions.

The economy campaign would have been more ruthless had it not become politically essential for the governments of the 1920s to demonstrate their concern over unemployment by policies giving direct relief. While it is true that by post-Second World War criteria the experiment in government provision of employment was derisory, it did nonetheless consume a certain amount of public funds and a considerable proportion of government discussion. It was the basic dilemma of governments that while toeing the Treasury's orthodox financial line designed to solve unemployment by a long-term cure for the economy, yet they were pressed politically to effect short-term cures by measures often at variance with that orthodoxy.

Even at the height of the anti-waste campaign the government had felt compelled to extend the unemployment insurance scheme and meet the additional cost. At the same time modest funds were advanced for domestic relief works to provide some employment, particularly during the winter. Subsidising the emigration of surplus labour also attracted ministers and enabled Amery to win cabinet approval for an expensive Empire Settlement Act against the protests of the Chancellor. And, significantly, by the Overseas Trade (Credit and Insurance) Acts of 1920 and 1921 the government authorised the Board of Trade to guarantee bills drawn by British exporters up to a maximum of £26 million. It was in this context of government encouragement for the depressed export trades that colonial development policy was reassessed. Assisting development projects in the colonies might relieve unemployment in Britain by boosting immediate purchases of British materials and by expanding markets for British goods.[11]

The idea was floated in September 1921. At the beginning of the month the Colonial Office discussed the loan requirements of the self-financing colonies and the arrangements for their issue on the London market.[12] This was a purely routine discussion quite unconnected with the economic problems of Great Britain, but it seems to have stimulated Churchill's imagination. At the end of September in an address to the Gold Coast Civil Service Club he argued that the development of the crown colonies could help solve the temporary collapse and breakdown of overseas markets. Over the next ten years profitable investments of £200 million could be made by the state and private investors.[13] The following day Churchill put the same case in a memorandum to the cabinet. In the economic crisis, he argued, mere economy was insufficient. He favoured a policy of stimulating trade by aiding public utility companies and by export credits schemes. But in addition, 'the Treasury should assist the Colonial Office to increase the loans they propose to issue in the near future for the development of the various Crown Colonies'.[14]

To strengthen the proposal, the geographical departments of the Colonial Office were asked in October 1921 to give information on contemplated colonial development projects, whether colonial governments could finance further works, and what other developments could be begun if some assistance was provided by the Imperial Treasury. Churchill was evidently anxious to justify the policy as an emergency unemployment measure since it was requested that note should be taken of the amount of expenditure that could be made in Great Britain in the next six months. The departmental replies are instructive. They showed colonies would be reluctant to accelerate development projects simply to serve imperial interests. Even rich colonies like Ceylon which could raise capital without imperial help would be reluctant at present to engage in further schemes unless the Imperial government met interest charges. Other territories like Nigeria could contemplate additional works only if the Treasury provided a free grant to meet the costs. Many territories were already too committed to consider anything further: they would need considerable inducements.[15]

Drawing on these replies two proposals were eventually put forward by the Colonial Office. The first was drawn up by Sir James Stevenson, the Business Adviser, and was submitted to the cabinet's Unemployment Committee with Churchill's approval. It was argued that while colonial development schemes were already being busily pursued, much more could be done if the Imperial government helped poorer territories meet the cost of loan charges. An expenditure of £2 million over two years was proposed to meet part at least of these costs.[16] The second rather more radical scheme which went straight to the cabinet owed much to Grindle, assistant under-secretary. He drew an important distinction between the richer financially self-sufficient colonies which could raise loans on fairly favourable terms and the proper dependencies which could not afford interest charges even if they could raise loans. It was typical of the permanent staff's approach that Grindle was much less concerned with the financially independent colonies: he had no plans to make them part of an imperial economic system to ease Britain's depression. Like Stevenson, he was primarily concerned with the poorer territories, dependent on imperial aid to accelerate their development. He drew up a list of works costing nearly £8 million which the Imperial government might assist. The cabinet was asked either to advance money free of interest for a period, or to meet loan charges for two or three years, or to make a grant of part of the total cost of projects. An appeal was made to metropolitan self-interest:

It is submitted that the present circumstances justify the expenditure of Imperial funds on such works. A large amount of work would be provided in this country without delay, for it would, of course, be a condition of Imperial assistance that any plant or materials required should be ordered in this country. The works would benefit the Colony, develop markets for British goods, and enhance the purchasing power of individual inhabitants in the Colonies with future benefit to British trade.[17]

Although there was some support for these schemes inside and indeed outside the cabinet[18] and although the Prime Minister himself at this time favoured large-scale government borrowing and expenditure to combat the depression,[19] neither Colonial Office plan won approval. On 17 October 1921 the particular needs of the poorer colonies were swamped in cabinet by the overriding concern with the

British budget. Since the Colonial Office had acknowledged that the Colonial Empire as a whole was already doing a great deal to alleviate unemployment in Britain through existing development projects, it was argued that no additional imperial aid was necessary. Besides, 'any proposal to enable the Colonies to borrow cheaply at the expense of the British Treasury involved a further depreciation of Government Stocks and a consequent outcry from Banks and other large holders of these stocks'. The cabinet had just agreed as part of its unemployment programme to guarantee loans raised for capital undertakings up to a maximum of £25 million, and it was decided merely to allow colonies to apply for assistance under this scheme.[20]

The Colonial Office still hoped to modify this decision by influencing the committee set up to administer the £25 million guarantee bill then being drafted. The Colonial Office were even considering early in November 1921 a number of colonial development projects which could be started if the Imperial government provided free grants.[21] These optimistic hopes were quite at variance with the cabinet's intentions, and they came crashing down when Grindle saw Sir Basil Blackett, the controller of finance at the Treasury, and discovered the limited scope of the Trade Facilities Bill. It adhered to the cabinet's original decision and simply authorised the Treasury to guarantee the payment of interest and principal of loans up to a maximum of £25 million. Moreover, the Treasury had instructed the committee which would administer these terms not to accept any scheme unless it showed reasonable prospect of financial success.

He made it plain that the Treasury would look to the Colonial Office and the Committee to see that the guarantee if given would never become operative. The sort of guarantee he had in mind as one that could be given was a guarantee to a perfectly solvent Protectorate to enable it to borrow more cheaply. Further, if a loan were guaranteed under the Act, and the guarantee became operative, the Treasury would insist on treating the defaulting Colony as a grant-in-aid Colony – i.e. would insist on full control of all its finances.

Stevenson commented:

This of course entirely disposes of any idea of our being able to assist unemployment by putting up any schemes for undeveloped colonies which are not in a position to meet the standing charges on the loans .... It appears to me that most people will prefer to exhaust other means of raising money for financing sound schemes than going to the Treasury, where they will be subject to some considerable control by the Treasury.

He saw no merit in the bill and thought it futile to put colonial development schemes to the Trade Facilities Committee. Churchill, however, thought otherwise. He argued that if a good enough case were made out, the Treasury could make a grant-in-aid for the partial payment of the standing charges in addition to the guarantee. Stevenson disliked this plan. In particular he was adamantly against allowing the colonies to fall under Treasury control:

You will appreciate what this will involve: how it will hinder any other developments in the Colony and to what difficulties it will lead as between the Colony, the Colonial Office and the Treasury in the adjustment of Revenue and Expenditure. It would in fact involve a surrender of some of the most important functions of the Colonial Office.

This clear statement of the departmental view failed to move Churchill. At his insistence, a selection of development schemes was submitted to the Trade Facilities Committee and the assistance they needed in addition to a guarantee was explained. Predictably the committee turned them down, and sent a copy of the act by way of explanation. Stevenson told Churchill that his instructions had been carried out: 'Unless, therefore, you are disposed to raise the question at the Cabinet, we cannot pursue these schemes any further at the present time'. Churchill did not press the matter.[22]

A number of points deserve emphasis. In the first place it is clear that in Imperial government decision-making those who favoured deflation as a first priority continued to hold the whiphand over those who advocated government expenditure to assist colonial development in order to stimulate British exports. At this stage it must be recognized that the Imperial government could not be aware of the lasting character of the depression, nor had they any experience of the inefficacy of the moderate measure they proposed. On the other hand, the Colonial Office permanent staff were well aware that guarantees for loans were unnecessary for prosperous solvent colonies and would not tempt them into accelerating development work. Nor did guarantees remove the burden of interest and sinking fund payments from the poorer colonies who had most difficulty in raising the finance for development works. It is quite clear that whereas the Imperial government were anxious to encourage purchases of British products by the Colonial Empire as a whole, the Colonial Office permanent staff were concerned to obtain assistance primarily for that handful of territories dependent on Imperial government aid. They were suspicious of suggestions that the primary purpose of colonial development policy was to ease Britain's economic problems.[23] Their main concern was not to cure British unemployment but to achieve a basic level of colonial development while avoiding Treasury grants-in-aid and control. It is also significant that it was Churchill, the political chief, not the permanent staff who pursued the idea. His advisers were from the beginning highly sceptical of the suggestion. In this first example, the effect of economic depression had proved of little benefit to the Colonial Office in their endeavours to find the finance for developing the poorer dependent territories.

3. *THE TRADE FACILITIES ACT 1922*

The continued depression in British overseas trade, high levels of unemployment at home and Lloyd George's concern about social and political consequences led to the appointment in July 1922 of a Cabinet Trade Policy Committee. In view of Churchill's existing workload, Amery, although by then Financial Secretary at the Admiralty, was appointed to the committee as the Colonial Office representative.[24] The cabinet's decision therefore gave the Colonial Office and the principal political enthusiast for colonial development fresh opportunities to put their plans before the government.

As an initial shot the Colonial Office explained to the Trade Policy Committee the inadequacy of Trade Facilities guarantees as an inducement to colonial development.[25] This was followed by another internal office review of colonial needs. As in the previous October, the permanent staff emphasised the danger of overburdening colonies with excessive loan charges and the consequent need for free Treasury grants or loans without interest for a period of years if colonial development projects were to be accelerated.[26] Armed with these conclusions Amery then drew up proposals for the consideration of the Trade Policy Committee. Following the Colonial Office line he stressed that the Trade Facilities Act of 1921 only offered guarantees for schemes in colonies which had no difficulty raising money without them. More substantial aid was needed. Over £34 million had been raised by the colonies in the last 2½ years, most of which had been spent in Britain thus generating employment, but little more could be done unless the Imperial government met interest charges for several years or made a free gift of some at least of the cost of new schemes. With typical boldness he concluded:

A large Imperial loan spent on a comprehensive plan of development would, on a balance of successful and unsuccessful schemes, and including all the indirect advantages resulting from the development, probably prove in the long run a profitable investment, as well as provide a considerable volume of direct employment over the next 10 years.[27]

The case presented also drew some modest support from the Advisory Committee which administered the Trade Facilities Act. They too agreed that the offer of a guarantee was an insufficient inducement to colonial governments in present circumstances.[28]

Faced with these criticisms and new proposals, the Trade Policy Committee did the natural thing and set up a sub-committee to examine the question. Amery's presence on this sub-committee probably explains why it reported in favour of two expensive proposals: that the Imperial government should pay for three to five years the whole or part of the interest charges on loans to be raised for new works and that where raising a public loan would be a problem the Imperial government should lend the capital required. In turn the Trade Policy Committee accepted these recommendations and forwarded them to the cabinet.[29]

The momentum of these new proposals now began to slacken. At a cabinet meeting on 12 August 1922, Horne, the Chancellor, succeeded in postponing a decision on the critical issue. Then on 14 August, he openly opposed the most radical suggestion that the capital needed might be advanced by the Imperial government. The Prime Minister 'emphasized the importance of assisting the development of the Empire on a considerable scale', but the cabinet concluded only with an agreement to pay the whole or part of the interest charges for three years on loans raised, to raise to £50 million the maximum amount of loans to be guaranteed and to extend the operations of the Trade Facilities Act for a further twelve months.[30]

Although this still constituted something of a setback for the Treasury's rigid demand for economy, it was but a slight departure, and the Colonial Office were not enthusiastic. Grindle commented that they did not want the colonies to raise loans unless they were confident that they could meet the interest costs involved. 'A promise of the interest for a few years does not help us, as we have no guarantee that a Colony which cannot pay interest this year will be able to do so in a few years hence.' Much more generous terms were wanted: the Crown Agents should be authorised to place orders for development material, the Treasury should meet these costs and the colony should then repay the Treasury several years later the full amount advanced, but without interest. This would give the colonies the materials they required in advance and also the time to raise the finance needed.[31]

Amery too was naturally disappointed, and in reaction devised an even more radical 'Programme of Empire Development' for the Trade Policy Committee. It was a typical Amery blueprint, couched in the neo-mercantilist mould which had become so prominent during the war.

The restriction of our foreign markets by fluctuating exchanges and almost prohibitive tariffs, and the need for keeping down our foreign imports, especially those from the United States, in order to pay off our foreign debt, are compelling us to concentrate our attention on the development of our own Empire.

The objectives of such efforts should be steady trade and employment and immediate relief from the present acute unemployment crisis. There must be substantial inducement to encourage development, 'but it will be less costly, and far more remunerative ultimately, than money thrown into the sink of unemployment insurance and other forms of unproductive relief'. The heart of the plan was 'an Empire Development Bill giving Parliamentary authority for the expenditure of £10,000,000 a year for 15 years on the promotion of development schemes within the Empire'. From this fund not only could interest payments be met but alternatively or in addition substantial amounts of the capital cost of development works could also be financed. 'Such a continuous policy', he concluded, 'would also make it possible to deal on a systematic plan of development, without being tied down by local revenue considerations.' Since the scheme threatened to impose no burdens on colonial revenues it was, not surprisingly, heartily welcomed by Colonial Office staff.[32]

Unfortunately these grand visions suddenly became irrelevant. On 19 October 1922 Lloyd George's Coalition Government collapsed and Bonar Law became Prime Minister of a Conservative administration. The Trade Policy Committee was simultaneously wound up and its activities taken over by a new Unemployment Committee. The cabinet's decision of 14 August to amend the 1921 Trade Facilities Act had not as yet reached legislative form and the issue was reconsidered by the Unemployment Committee. The Treasury had another chance to deploy their arguments against increased government expenditure: in the words of the new Chancellor, Baldwin, 'money taken for Government purposes is money taken away from trade'. The Unemployment Committee and the new cabinet accepted this thesis. Accordingly the revised Trade Facilities Act of 1922 did not allow the government to meet interest charges for the first three years and merely empowered the Treasury to guarantee the principal and interest of loans up to a new maximum of £50 million and within a period up to November 1923.[33] On receipt of these terms, the Colonial Office felt it hardly worthwhile informing the Colonial Empire.[34]

There had been moments during the course of the 1922 discussions when the Colonial Office seemed likely to obtain more generous financial aid for underdeveloped dependencies. With the continuation of the depression the political support for colonial development schemes had widened. The Trade Policy Committee and Lloyd George's cabinet had accepted the need for greater government commitments to ease the depression. Amery had pressed hard for favourable terms and the Prime Minister and some other colleagues were obviously sympathetic.[35] Because of these political pressures the Treasury had been less able to resist proposals involving some government expenditure. The concessions made were not, however, very large and the subsequent change of government had provided the Treasury with the opportunity to restore their authority. Government economy still had priority over schemes to stimulate British exports. The reversal of the cabinet's decision of 14 August was not serious insofar as the Colonial Office did not consider the proposed revised terms for Trade Facilities a sufficient stimulus to colonial development. The permanent staff in the Colonial Office together with more adventurous politicians like Amery consistently argued that only generous financial aid justified accelerating colonial development plans. Colonial Office determination to avoid over-burdened colonial revenues explains their sceptical reception of proposals to encourage colonial development in order to ease British unemployment. These considerations were central to the office's subsequent examination of similar proposals.

4. *THE TRADE FACILITIES ACT 1924*

Bonar Law's government had not initially shown much willingness to increase imperial aid for colonial development. Given the general acceptance of the orthodox economic and financial theses presented by the Treasury, it was very difficult for the government to justify expenditure on the promotion of British exports to ease unemployment. But the continuation of the economic depression made a reconsideration of policy unavoidable. Ministerial appointments also made likely the submission of more positive, and more expensive, proposals than the system of guarantees offered under the Trade Facilities Acts of 1921 and 1922. The Duke of Devonshire as Secretary of State for the Colonies was to show himself sympathetic to the views of his advisers, and he was energetically supported by Ormsby-Gore, his under-secretary, who had clear views on the virtues of colonial development.[36] Since the extension of imperial aid would require cabinet approval it was valuable that Amery was now a member as First Lord of the Admiralty. And a major role was also played by the new President of the Board of Trade, Lloyd-Greame, who was also convinced that 'the solution of unemployment depends on finding and developing new markets for our industry. The great opportunity for this lies within the British Empire.'[37] It is, however, important to recognise that during the negotiations which led to the Trade Facilities Act of 1924 there were important distinctions between the objectives of the Colonial Office permanent staff and those of most of their political allies. The former still regarded colonial economic development as a means of creating colonial financial independence and avoiding future reliance on Treasury aid. The latter were attracted to the idea of colonial development much more because they hoped to maximize overseas demand for British manufactured goods and sought to integrate colonial economies with the ailing British economy.

High levels of unemployment during the winter of 1922–23 led the Prime Minister to request the President of the Board of Trade to suggest new solutions. A memorandum drawn up by Lloyd-Greame in consultation with Devonshire was sent to the cabinet on 8 February 1923. It is worth noting that the general tenor of their programme suggests that they regarded the primary purpose of increasing imperial aid for colonial development as a *long-term* solution to Britain's loss of overseas markets: immediate relief for domestic unemployment was not prominent in their arguments. They dwelt on the deep-seated difficulties of the British economy. In the past year the export trade had been 31% below the 1913 level, population was increasing and permanent unemployment would result unless trade and emigration levels improved. Before the war more than one-third of British trade was with Europe, and indirectly even more, because credits created by Indian and Chinese sales in Europe were used to finance Eastern purchases from Britain. But the revolution in Russia, the collapse of Germany, production uncertainties, tariff barriers and other restrictions prevented Europe's recovery. These conditions 'make it essential for us to develop new markets'. It was also desirable for exchange reasons to purchase more raw materials from the empire and less from the U.S.A.. Development of imperial markets and resources would be slow without imperial aid, but such investment would be profitable since expenditure on unemployment relief would be reduced and orders and emigration to new markets increased. It was proposed that the Secretary of State for the Colonies should be given up to £2 million a year for the next ten years to spend at his discretion, advancing for up to fifteen years the whole or part of the interest on loans raised by colonies for development works and/or lending the capital required at cheap rates.[38]

Amery responded at once with his own memorandum, basically endorsing the scheme but typically proposing to raise the annual allowance to £5 million and wishing its terms to cover also India and the dominions.[39] It was also predictable that the Treasury would be less happy, and an internal memorandum condensed their grumbles. They denied the severity of the unemployment problem, claiming that figures were 'not much' above pre-war averages. 'In 1919 (after demobilisation) we were actually short of domestic servants.' Besides, the birth rate had fallen and that would reduce the future labour force. The proposals put forward were also unnecessary because the Trade Facilities Act of 1922 still had much unused capacity, and the dominions and protectorates could borrow what they needed. More harm than good would result since increased empire loans on the London market would force up interest prices for the Imperial government and British industry, and increased public expenditure 'is the most certain way of hampering British industry and limiting its power of competing in world markets'. There would in any case be budgetary problems in 1923–24. 'It seems to be forgotten that we are a Government pledged to economy.' As Sir Warren Fisher, permanent secretary at the Treasury, bluntly put it to the Chancellor and the Prime Minister, 'I believe these proposals to have no merits'.[40]

Some whiff of the Treasury's objections possibly disturbed the cabinet's examination of the new plans in February 1923. Though ministers were evidently worried by the unemployment problem and expressed general support for the principle of colonial development as a cure, they avoided any commitment to expensive new policies and settled for a cheaper alternative, words. Ministers were authorised to announce in the House of Commons that the government's main policy lay in the direction of developing trade and industry 'and more particularly of Empire Development and Empire Settlement'.[41]

This was obviously unsatisfactory to Amery, and he tried unsuccessfully to raise the matter at a later cabinet meeting. Rather more effective was an episode in March 1923 when Amery, Lloyd-Greame and Devonshire cornered the unfortunate Chancellor on his own and persuaded him to agree at least in principle to finance colonial development schemes.[42] But Baldwin was a tough customer especially when backed by the officials in the Treasury, and the offer which was eventually grudgingly made was hardly generous. The Imperial government would provide a maximum of £250,000 a year to pay up to half the interest charges for five years on loans raised by the colonies in the next two years for the purchase of development materials in Britain. Applications for grants should be made to an advisory committee of businessmen representing the Treasury, Board of Trade and Colonial Office who would ensure that the schemes approved would be ultimately remunerative and could not be undertaken in the next two years without imperial assistance. These terms were discussed by Devonshire and his senior officials and resoundingly rejected. In the first place the necessity of submitting Colonial Office plans to an advisory committee was an indignity:

When a scheme has been settled, after due deliberation and consultation of experts, and commends itself to the responsible government on the spot, to my advisers, and to me as Secretary of State, I cannot see that an outside committee, necessarily ignorant of local conditions and needs, can add anything of value to it.

Moreover, the terms proposed were derisory: aid in the form of half interest payments would exclude the poorer colonies which most needed developing and were unnecessary for the richer which 'can finance themselves on their own terms at their own time'. And finally, Baldwin's evident preoccupation with immediate short-term gains to British industry aroused the Colonial Office's hostility.

To remove any possible misapprehension I want to make it clear that, so far as we are concerned, there is no urgency whatever about any of the new schemes which we have put forward. They were formulated at the request of the Prime Minister as a Colonial Office contribution to the problem of unemployment ... and from the strictly Colonial Office point of view I am not anxious to urge the Colonial Governments to accelerate their programmes.

And with this somewhat disingenuous observation the correspondence closed. The reply was a perfect reflection of the permanent staff's views which Devonshire, in contrast with Churchill, seems to have accepted completely.[43]

Meanwhile, preparations were underway for the forthcoming Imperial Economic Conference. This gathering was primarily designed by the British government to foster closer economic co-operation with the dominions and India, and the question of imperial aid for the development of dependent territories was not intended to be a primary topic of discussion. However, since the Board of Trade was heavily involved in the preparations, this gave Lloyd-Greame the opportunity to steer proposals in that direction. In March 1923 a Board of Trade plan was aired which envisaged an Imperial government expenditure of £2 million a year, advancing for up to ten years the whole or part of the interest on capital raised for development works not only in the dominions but in the colonies too. The proposal inevitably drew Treasury criticism,[44] but Lloyd-Greame was not deterred, and in May he elaborated on the scheme for the cabinet committee which was responsible for preparing the agenda for the Imperial Economic Conference. While keeping annual expenditure at £2 million, he now suggested the scheme should run for fifteen years and that while the payment of interest would be the normal form of assistance, guarantees of interest could also be given and, more radically, capital might be loaned to meet the needs of smaller colonies. The attractions of the scheme included 'the additional employment afforded to our population from the orders placed in the United Kingdom in connection with the scheme'.[45]

This was too much for Niemeyer, recently promoted controller of finance at the Treasury. His first objection was that Lloyd-Greame was lumping together proposals for financial aid to the dominions with the different question of aid for the dependencies. He reminded the Chancellor that the Treasury's only concession to date was contained in Baldwin's proposal to Devonshire in April concerning *colonial* development. He protested that the cabinet had not as yet decided in favour of financial assistance to the *dominions*. However, he evidently sensed that the political pressures were building up and therefore proposed to limit the damage by offering terms similar to the April offer but relating solely to the dominions: the provision of up to £1 million a year to meet up to half the interest for five years on loans raised by the dominions in the next two years for the purchase of development materials in Britain. These terms were, of course, far less generous than those detailed by Lloyd-Greame, and as a further saving Niemeyer suggested that the money required should come out of the £3 million a year already set aside under the Empire Settlement Act of 1922.[46]

In May 1923 Bonar Law was forced to retire with cancer of the throat. Baldwin took over as Prime Minister while remaining, until August, Chancellor of the Exchequer. He accepted Niemeyer's main argument and in his new role authorised Devonshire to inform the dominions that the Imperial government did favour a scheme to help development works: but only by guaranteeing loans or advancing part of the interest payments for a limited period. This telegram was despatched on 16 July.[47] However, on 10 July the Cabinet Committee on the Economic Conference began considering Lloyd-Greame's more expensive proposal. Amery rather distressed the Financial Secretary by proposing that the £2 million a year suggested should be increased to £10 million: 'I assured him that like Clive I was astounded at my own moderation'. The committee could not be drawn that far, but they did in the end forward to the cabinet their approval of Lloyd-Greame's scheme as a way of encouraging developments in the dominions. In an attempt to warn the cabinet of the implications, the Financial Secretary produced a memorandum the following day spelling out the budget problem for 1923–24 and urging, as Niemeyer had proposed, a maximum expenditure of £1 million drawn from the sum authorised by the Empire Settlement Act.[48] Niemeyer also tried to recover the ground by alerting the new Chancellor, Neville Chamberlain, to the dangers. He claimed that a fifteen year commitment to dominions' development would cause excessive competition for capital in London to the detriment of domestic British interests, and that the only justification for a scheme was as an immediate unemployment measure, accelerating orders for British goods in the next few years.[49] These arguments were persuasive and explain the restricted terms eventually proposed and approved at the Imperial Economic Conference in November 1923: the Imperial government would make a maximum grant of three-quarters of the interest for five years on loans raised for public utility schemes in the empire, but only on projects approved in the next three years and only on that portion of the capital which would be spent on orders in Britain.[50]

It should be remembered that these terms were devised, essentially by the Treasury, to meet the needs of the comparatively wealthy dominions. Niemeyer had succeeded in blocking Lloyd-Greame's attempts to launch at the Imperial Economic Conference an ambitious and expensive plan to cater for the colonies as well as the dominions. But meanwhile the question of assisting colonial development was being discussed in another context. Since June 1923 the Cabinet Committee on Unemployment had been anxiously seeking ways of alleviating the distress expected in the forthcoming winter, and the Colonial Office were repeatedly asked if the Colonial Empire could generate employment by expediting orders for development materials in Britain.[51] The Colonial Office, by now inured to these requests, responded cautiously. 'This question is now a hardy annual which bursts into flower every autumn.' Much depended on whether the Imperial government would offer financial help and on what terms. Departmental heads noted, for example, that Tanganyika, Nyasaland and Kenya could not commit themselves still further unless capital was given as a free grant or as a loan with interest payments postponed perhaps indefinitely.[52] Stevenson bluntly identified the problem:

Considerable progress can be made by a policy of confidence in the C.O. but no Government is in my judgement in a position to surmount the inherent jealousy of the Dept. of Treasury Control, because it must be appreciated that immediately the smallest "grant-in-aid" is made no further schemes can be considered by the C.O. without the consent of the Treasury whose duty it is *to avoid* expenditure.[53]

These observations were then patiently relayed to the Unemployment Committee. In July Ormsby-Gore described to them several urgent schemes which would provide immediate orders in Britain but which the colonies could not begin to finance. Ormsby-Gore later explained that before the Colonial Office could sanction new works they had to be sure that the cost of interest and capital repayments on any loan required would not overburden a colony's finances.[54]

He went over the ground again in October. The richer colonies like Nigeria, which could raise capital themselves without difficulty, were already fully occupied and could not be tempted into additional works simply by the offer of imperial loans. As for poorer territories like Nyasaland, they 'cannot afford to raise loans for any purpose merely on the basis of part or whole payment of interest for a limited period'.

If the Unemployment Committee were seriously anxious to create employment, very considerable inducements would be necessary. He recommended a scheme put forward by the Crown Agents. In the case of prosperous territories, the Imperial government should pay up to a fixed amount the whole cost including freight charges of any materials purchased in Britain for colonial development works in the next two years. But poorer territories could not even afford local labour costs and the Imperial government would have to meet those too. Perhaps understandably taken aback by these terms, the committee requested further information on the cost of schemes, the amount of expenditure expected in Britain, the extent of assistance required and, rather hopefully, the prospects of subsequently recovering from the colony any of the sums advanced.[55]

Irritated by this response and anxious to press matters to a conclusion, Ormsby-Gore consulted Devonshire, Colonial Office staff and the Crown Agents and then drafted a letter clarifying the Colonial Office's views. Although this was addressed to the chairman of the Unemployment Committee, its real target was the Treasury to whom a copy was sent. Ormsby-Gore placed a judicious emphasis on metropolitan interests in colonial development. Because the vast bulk of the trade with African colonies was with Britain, expenditure on their development inevitably eased the British unemployment problem.

To my mind, the whole thing boils down to this. Is the British government prepared, instead of giving a dole to workmen in this country in return for no work whatever, to give a dole in return for work in the Iron and Steel trade in this country, the result of which would mean the increase of the purchasing power for British goods of our oversea possessions?

However, colonial interests also had to be considered. Already the colonies had been persuaded to embark on public works which were for the moment straining their financial stability.

It is no exaggeration to say that there is a real danger of attempting to force too much on those Colonies which are already themselves developing their resources as rapidly as their finances permit, and the question as far as these Colonies are concerned must be approached purely from the point of view of unemployment in Great Britain and not from that of any advantage to the Colonies.

But if the colonies were to help Britain in this fashion, generous financial assistance must be given: the Imperial government should pay for half the cost of development works including local expenditure or provide a free gift of the materials ordered in the United Kingdom and meet the freight charges involved in transporting them. The terms proposed at the Imperial Economic Conference in connection with developments in the dominions were specifically condemned as inadequate.[56]

As noted earlier, the Treasury had previously defined the scheme to be proposed at the Imperial Economic Conference solely in relation to the dominions. Similarly the Colonial Office had always insisted that it was inapplicable to the Colonial Empire: Board of Trade documents upon it which inadvertently referred to the colonies as well as the dominions had been corrected at the Colonial Office's insistence.[57] But when Ormsby-Gore's letter came up for discussion at the Unemployment Committee on 9 November 1923, the Financial Secretary was ready with the Treasury's response: the colonies and protectorates should be invited to apply for aid under the plan offered to the dominions at the Imperial Economic Conference. This manoeuvre was evidently intended to head off 'more generous alternatives' and it aroused understandable hostility. Various more expensive schemes were batted about the meeting with the Financial Secretary resisting them all. The committee's decision to set up a sub-committee to investigate such plans was later roundly condemned by the Chancellor, who insisted that the colonies should be asked to consider only the 'extremely liberal' terms already approved. With this request the Colonial Office grudgingly complied.[58]

The Colonial Office's prediction that the offer of three-quarters of the interest for five years on loans raised by the colonies would not induce territories to accelerate their development projects was soon revealed. The only governors who replied enthusiastically seem to have misunderstood the terms and were rapidly disillusioned.[59] In December 1923 the Colonial Office once again explained to the Unemployment Committee why these terms were inadequate and what kind of assistance was needed to get certain major railway schemes underway. The committee listened sympathetically and did indeed recommend to the cabinet some proposals requiring imperial assistance.[60] But decisions were not taken hastily, ministers being busy with a general election in December and thereafter expecting the imminent resignation of the administration.

On 22 January 1924 Baldwin's government finally fell and Ramsay MacDonald's first Labour government took office. But on this issue little changed. Only the signatures altered; policies and attitudes were reproduced. So we find on 27 January the President of the Board of Trade, Sidney Webb, like his predecessor, urging the Colonial Office to expedite the placing of orders from the colonies for development materials in an effort to relieve unemployment in Britain. And we find J. H. Thomas, Secretary of State for the Colonies, and Lord Arnold, his under-secretary, anxious like previous ministers to push forward the schemes which their advisers, perhaps rather wearily, had dug out for them.[61] Colonial development had become a popular remedy for Britain's economic depression. And we also encounter a similar obstacle: Philip Snowden as Chancellor of the Exchequer was no more generous than Neville Chamberlain. Indeed, in Churchill's happy phrase, 'the Treasury mind and the Snowden mind embraced each other with the fervour of two long-separated kindred lizards'.[62]

The in-coming administration also inherited a Trade Facilities Bill. This had been drafted in November partly to amend the 1922 act and extend the duration of its operations and increase the total value of the loans which could be guaranteed. But it also embraced the Imperial Economic Conference resolution committing the Imperial government to pay three-quarters of the interest for five years on loans raised for public utility development schemes in the empire. A modest £1 million was to be set aside for this purpose. Following Chamberlain's instructions these terms were extended to cover colonies as well as dominions.[63] On 30 January 1924 Niemeyer offered the new Chancellor some advice on this business. There was, he claimed, much in the proposal to be condemned, but it would on balance be too much trouble to drop: 'Economically, and vis-a-vis unemployment, I should attach no importance to it; financially it is open to obvious objection; but politically there may be something to be said for it. I think it is on that point that your decision will have to be taken'. Niemeyer observed that the Labour government intended to reject the imperial preference resolution approved at the Imperial Economic Conference; they would not wish to cause extra offence to the dominions by ignoring another conference recommendation. Besides, the government was eager to demonstrate its energetic tackling of unemployment by early action, and, probably, in Snowden's view this was financially less objectionable than some other suggestions. Accordingly Snowden agreed that the scheme should go ahead.[64] The bill was approved by the cabinet without difficulty and went to the House of Commons in February to be given sporadic debate in March and April and to receive the Royal Assent on 15 May 1924.[65]

The debates emphasize that it was completely understood on all sides of the House that the 'main purpose of this proposal is to stimulate orders for goods which will be supplied from this country and to help to some extent the unemployment from which we are now suffering'.[66] Critics of the measure tended to be doctrinaire Liberals opposed to interference with normal financial credit operations, or Labour backbenchers who wished to see the expenditure made at home. Generally it was accepted on the grounds that immediate orders for materials could be expected and also, particularly with respect to a Sudan cotton-growing scheme, that increased cotton supplies would result. The latter was expected to have a favourable effect on the American exchange.

Some critics, including not surprisingly Lloyd-Greame, suggested that greater aid would be required for the colonies and protectorates than payment of three-quarters of the interest for five years on loans raised, but Graham, the Financial Secretary, defended the clause, adding that the matter was purely experimental: 'only time can tell how far public utility undertakings in the Colonies and Dominions and Protectorates will avail themselves of this arrangement'.[67] As far as the colonies and protectorates were concerned the Colonial Office could have suggested an answer, for on the day before the Money Resolution of the bill was introduced in the Commons, the Colonial Office summarized the replies of the dependencies to the terms offered. The dominant note was one of indifference. As Read minuted to Lord Arnold, the response 'amounts to very little'. British Guiana suggested a light railway or road programme, and there was a tentative proposal from Uganda. Otherwise the terms offered were still under consideration or had been ignored.[68]

In July 1924 Niemeyer confided to Grindle, his sparring partner at the Colonial Office: 'I doubt myself if much will come of this business'. The secretary of the advisory committee set up to administer the terms had been equally pessimistic even before the bill was passed: 'I do not think that the grant of part of the interest for five years will of itself enable any scheme to be carried out which on its financial merits cannot be put through today'.[69] The accuracy of these predictions was revealed over the three year operations of the measure. A report was produced in January 1926. In the words of a Treasury official, 'the results have been quite trifling'. The committee had considered only twelve applications in over eighteen months. There were only two from the Colonial Empire, one from Ceylon for an electrical lighting scheme which did not comply with the terms of the act and was rejected, and one from the Sudan for a railway project which succeeded in obtaining a grant of three-quarters of the interest for four years on the loans required. Two other schemes in Australia and Newfoundland were also accepted but altogether the three schemes approved involved an expenditure of only £480,653 at a cost of £86,090 to the Imperial Exchequer. Since the act had provision for an expenditure of £1 million a year, the advisory committee recommended a relaxation of its terms. The Treasury, 'having regard to the paramount need for economy' refused.[70] Amending acts in 1925 and 1926 merely extended the duration of the measure and increased marginally the amount of the loans which could be guaranteed, and in April 1926 the cabinet accepted the Chancellor's recommendation that the scheme should be allowed to expire in 1927.[71] The Trade Facilities Act died unwept.

5. *CONCLUSION*

It is a striking feature of the three Trade Facilities Acts that as attempts to encourage colonial development in order to stimulate British exports they were singularly useless. As revealed in departmental discussions there were many advisers both in the Colonial Office and in the Treasury who were perfectly aware of the inadequacy of the terms. In view of their almost total ineffectiveness it is legitimate to ask why the schemes ever became law.

The answer undoubtedly lies in the political necessity felt by the politicians of all persuasions to concoct some policy to deal with unemployment. Coalition, Conservative and Labour governments felt obliged to justify their existence by attempting to deal with this pressing problem. This had become especially the case by 1923–24 when there was less room for believing that the slump was a passing phase. Since the loss of overseas markets was easily indentifiable as a principal feature of Britain's economic problem, a programme of encouraging the development of new markets sprang readily to mind. It seemed a natural policy, best suited to the export-orientation of British industry. If markets had been lost in Europe and Latin America, then it was tempting to find recompense in those areas of the globe where Britain retained some political influence, namely in

the empire. Discussions at the Imperial Economic Conference emphasised that the greatest hopes were placed on the market capacities of
the dominions, but the Colonial Empire was regarded as a useful
additional asset. There is no doubt that the ideas stimulated during
the war of empire development and empire unity obtained an attractiveness in the depression which they had not had in the immediate
post-war days. Thus by October 1923, Baldwin's Conservative
government had decided to commit itself at the general election to
a programme of empire development and protective tariffs.[72] While
the tariff proposals were dropped in the light of the election results,
the Conservatives maintained, and the Labour government took over,
their pledges for empire development as a cure for unemployment.[73]

Analysis of the discussions leading to the three Trade Facilities Acts
shows that the idea of such development was attracting more and more
politicians. It was a policy which cabinet Trade Policy and Unemployment Committees were instinctively drawn towards in a search for
solutions. It is, however, a striking feature of the discussions and of
the legislation passed that emphasis was put at this time almost entirely
on the short-term value of colonial development. Regard was paid
by Lloyd-Greame, Amery, Devonshire and the Colonial Office
permanent staff to the long-term advantages which would accrue to
Britain by increasing imperial resources, especially of cotton, and by
increasing colonial purchasing power. Hence they favoured relatively
large annual expenditure by the Imperial government over many
years. Lloyd-Greame argued for an expenditure of £2 million a year
for 15 years. By contrast the Trade Facilities Act of 1924 offered a
maximum of £1 million a year for a mere five years. But other government ministers in the cabinet and on the Unemployment Committees
were anxious to obtain immediate relief for British unemployment
by immediate increases in colonial purchases of British goods. Expenditure on colonial development was for the most part not regarded
as an investment but as an equivalent to domestic public works programmes, as short-term relief for economic distress.

This emphasis on short-term British needs made the government
as a whole insensitive to colonial interests. The Colonial Office staff
were constantly forced to emphasise that accelerating colonial
development works might accentuate two colonial problems: an
increase in existing surpluses of primary products and an overburdening of colonial government revenues with long-term debts. The
Colonial Office remained adamant that all schemes for colonial

development should decrease rather than increase the dependence of the poorer territories on Treasury grants-in-aid. For these reasons the political and permanent staff of the office concluded that schemes for colonial development required much more Imperial government assistance before they could be encouraged.

For ministers to propose more generous aid was not made any easier by their basic acceptance of the economic and financial policy of the Treasury. The prestige of that department and the lack of alternative economic theses powerfully restricted the type of assistance which the cabinet felt it could offer to the British export trade. These limitations explain the unhappy and ineffective compromises embodied in the three Trade Facilities Acts.

These acts were not, however, without their importance. Although they failed entirely to meet the needs of the colonies as the Colonial Office said they would, they were, especially the act of 1924, interestingly distinct from the traditional *ad hoc* proposals for colonial development. Instead of being tailored to the known existing needs of specific territories such as the Uganda Development Loan of 1920, the Trade Facilities Acts were general development schemes available to all territories with suitable projects. As we shall see, the general nature of the schemes and the arrangements for their administration were important precedents for the Colonial Development Act of 1929.

It is also worth noting that the Trade Facilities Acts were hardly the result of colonial or Colonial Office initiatives. The schemes originated in 1921, 1922 and 1923 from outside the office, in cabinet committees, the Board of Trade and, for some details, the Treasury. The Board of Trade rather than the Colonial Office had dominated these discussions. It is indicative of the Colonial Office's preference for tested approaches and of their understanding of the problems of colonial development that, contemporaneously with the drafting of the Trade Facilities Acts, the Colonial Office were pursuing with more vigour more traditional and more effective proposals for development in East Africa. These will be examined in the next chapter.

NOTES

1. Department of Employment and Productivity, *British Labour Statistics Historical Abstract 1886–1968*, London, H.M.S.O., 1971, p.306; for problems associated with comparing unemployment rates, A. E. Booth and S. Glynn,

'Unemployment in the interwar period: a multiple problem', *J.C.H.*, 10 (1975), 611-36.

2. S. Constantine, *Unemployment in Britain between the Wars*, London, 1980, pp.2-16.

3. *Ibid.*, pp.46-57; F. W. S. Craig, *British General Election Manifestos 1918–1966*, Chichester, 1970, pp.11-61; L. S. Amery, *My Political Life*, vol.2, London, 1953, p.291; W. A. S. Hewins, *The Apologia of an Imperialist*, vol.2, London, 1929, pp.252, 265, 288; W. Hannington, *Unemployed Struggles 1919–1936*, London, 1936. For the Board of Trade Advisory Committee see, for example, CAB 24/161/CP 312 and CP 360, para.42 and Viscount Swinton, *I Remember*, London, 1948, p.27.

4. Constantine, *Unemployment in Britain*, pp.46-53; D. Winch, *Economics and Policy*, Fontana ed., Glasgow, 1972, pp.102-9.

5. Treasury Circular 13 May 1921, CO 431/147/Treas 24036.

6. Minutes of 19, 24 and 25 May 1921, *ibid.*; minutes and report of Colonial Office Economy Committee and C.O. to Treas. 29 Aug. 1921, CO 431/148/Treas 39529.

7. Treasury Circular 1 Oct. 1921, minute by Fiddian 6 Oct. 1921, CO 431/149/Treas 48996.

8. For the appointment of the Geddes Committee see C. L. Mowat, *Britain between the Wars 1918–1940*, London, 1955, pp.129-30. For the report see CAB 24/133/CP 3774, also published as *Third Report of the Committee on National Expenditure*, Cmd.1589, 1922.

9. Treasury Circular 16 June 1922, CO 431/150/Treas 29009; for the appointment of the Sub-Committee of the Cabinet Committee on Civil Estimates see memo. by Horne, Chancellor of the Exchequer, 26 May 1922, CAB 24/136/CP 3997 and Scott to C.O., 18 Aug. 1922, CO 536/120/Gov 39674; Treasury Circular 2 Oct. 1922, CO 431/150/Treas 49180.

10. Treasury Circular 1 Oct. 1923, minute by Fiddian 9 Oct. 1923, CO 431/151/Treas 48133.

11. Constantine, *Unemployment in Britain*, pp.52-5; K. J. Hancock, 'The Reduction of Unemployment as a Problem of Public Policy, 1920–1929', *Ec.H.R.*, 15 (1962), 328-43; I. M. Drummond, *Imperial Economic Policy 1917–1939*, London, 1974, pp.54-85.

12. Minutes of Group Council, 1 Sept. 1921, CO 323/875/CO 55839.

13. *The Times*, 28 Sept. 1921.

14. Memo. by Churchill, 28 Sept. 1921, CAB 24/128/CP 3345.

15. Minutes by Grindle 3 Oct. 1921 and by departments CO 323/875/CO 55839.

16. Memo. for Committee on Unemployment, 10 Oct. 1921, CAB 27/120/CU 268.

17. Memo. by Grindle, 10 Oct. 1921, CO 323/875/CO 53456 and memo. by Churchill 17 Oct. 1921, CAB 24/129/CP 3415.

18. See, for example, memo. by F.B.I., 12 Oct. 1921, CAB 24/129/CP 3421, and letter of Alfred Bigland, chairman Empire Development Parliamentary Committee to Sir James Masterton-Smith, permanent under-secretary at the C.O., 3 Oct. 1921, copy in Milner Papers 175.

19. For Lloyd George's Gairloch proposals see B. B. Gilbert, *British Social Policy 1914–1939*, London, 1970, pp.46-8.

20. Cabinet minutes, 17 Oct. 1921, CAB 23/27/CAB 80(21) 2 and 4.

21. Leake to Grindle, 26 Oct. 1921, CO 323/875/CO 53456; memo on Unemployment Scheme n.d. and minute by Grindle 8 Nov. 1921, CO 323/875/CO 57824.

22. Minutes by Grindle, Stevenson and Churchill 14–18 Nov. 1921, memo. for Advisory Committee of Trade Facilities Act, CO 323/875/CO 57824; Sainsbury to C.O. 29 Nov. 1921 and minute by Stevenson 19 Dec. 1921, CO 323/882/MO 59713. The act was passed on 10 Nov. 1921, 11 and 12 Geo.V ch.65.

23. See reactions to a proposal from the British Engineers Association in Oct. 1921, CO 323/881/MO 49494.
24. Cabinet minutes 24 July 1922, CAB 23/30/CAB 41(22) 2.
25. C.O. memo. 31 July 1922, CAB 27/179/TP 5.
26. C.O. mema., CO 323/894/CO 39959.
27. Empire Development Schemes, memo. by Amery, 3 Aug. 1922, *ibid.* and CAB 27/179/TP 13.
28. Provisional Report of Trade Facilities Act Advisory Committee, 3 Aug. 1922, CAB 27/179/TP 14.
29. Minutes of 2nd meeting Trade Policy Committee 4 Aug. 1922 and 3rd meeting 11 Aug. 1922, Report of Sub-Committee TP 21, Interim Report of Trade Policy Committee 12 Aug. 1922, CAB 27/179 and CAB 24/138/CP 4159.
30. Cabinet minutes 12 and 14 Aug. 1922, CAB 23/30/CAB 45(22)3 and CAB 47(22); CAB 24/138/CP 4162.
31. Memo. by Grindle, 26 Sept. 1922, CO 323/894/CO 39959.
32. A Programme of Empire Development, memo. by Amery 6 Oct. 1922, CAB 27/179/TP 43; Stevenson to Amery 6 Oct. 1922, CO 323/894/CO 39959; Amery, *My Political Life*, vol.2, pp.222-4.
33. Necessity for National Economy, memo. by Baldwin, Chancellor of the Exchequer, 20 Nov. 1922, CAB 24/140/CP 4314; recommendations of Sub-Committee of Unemployment Committee 20 Nov. 1922, CAB 27/129/CU 485; accepted by Unemployment Committee 21 Nov. 1922, CAB 27/191/CU 54th concl.; reported to cabinet 27 Nov. 1922, CAB 24/140/CP 4319; approved by cabinet 29 Nov. 1922, CAB 23/32/CAB 68(22)3. The act was passed on 15 Dec. 1922, 13 Geo.V ch.4.
34. Minutes of 17–19 Jan. 1923, CO 323/913/MO 2761.
35. Amery records that Lloyd George had talked of a £100 million loan for Empire Development, J. Barnes and D. Nicholson, eds., *The Leo Amery Diaries*, vol.1, London, 1980, 18 Sept. 1922, pp.291-2. Sir Alfred Mond, Minister of Health, had earlier proposed something similar, and he criticised the Trade Facilities Act as inadequate in a memo. of 5 Oct. 1922, CAB 24/139/CP 4267.
36. According to the late Sir Gerard Clauson, during Devonshire's tenure of office most of the work was done by Ormsby-Gore and the departmental heads, interview with the author, July 1971. See also W. Ormsby-Gore, *The Development of Our Empire in the Tropics*, Nottingham, 1927.
37. Sir Philip Lloyd-Greame, *The Imperial Economic Conference*, National Unionist Association, Westminster, 1924, p.6; see also Lord Swinton, *I Remember*, London, 1948, p.31 and A. Earl, 'The Political Life of Viscount Swinton 1918–1938', Manchester M.A. thesis, 1960. The Swinton papers contain little of value on this topic.
38. Memo. by Lloyd-Greame registered in C.O. 24 Jan. 1923, minute by Grindle 7 Feb. 1923, CO 323/906/CO 4233; memo. prepared by Secretary of State and President of the Board of Trade, 8 Feb. 1923, CAB 24/158/CP 90.
39. Memo. by Amery 12 Feb. 1923, CAB 24/158/CP 93.
40. Minutes by Niemeyer and Barstow 14–27 Feb. 1923, Fisher to Financial Secretary, Chancellor and Prime Minister, 14 Feb. 1923, Niemeyer Papers T 176/11; memo. n.d., filed with papers of May–June 1923, T 161/196/S.18578/1, originally intended as a memo. for the cabinet.
41. Cabinet minutes 14 Feb. 1923, CAB 23/45/CAB 9(23) 4; *Leo Amery Diaries*, 14 Feb. 1923, p.320.
42. *Leo Amery Diaries*, 24 Feb. and 20 March 1923, pp.321-2, 324.
43. Baldwin to Devonshire 10 April 1923, Devonshire to Baldwin 16 April 1923, CO 323/908/CO 19432. There is a copy of Baldwin's letter in Baldwin Papers vol.92,

in Niemeyer papers T 176/11 and on T 161/196/S.18578/1, but no other material on this episode has been found.

44. Amery claimed credit for persuading Lloyd-Greame to put forward this plan, N. Chamberlain Papers NC 2/21 Political Diaries, 24 March 1923; Outline Scheme for Imperial Co-operation for Financial Assistance to Imperial Development, 2 March 1923, minute by Niemeyer 15 March 1923 and Baldwin to Lloyd-Greame 20 March 1923, T 161/196/S.18578/1.

45. Co-operation in Financial Assistance to Imperial Development, 12 May 1923, *ibid.*, printed as appendix III to CAB 24/161/CP 360.

46. Empire Development Pledges, memo. by Niemeyer 28 May 1923, re-dated 20 June 1923, T 161/196/S.18578/1.

47. Devonshire to dominions, 16 July 1923, *ibid.*.

48. *Leo Amery Diaries*, 10 July 1923, p.333; Report of Imperial Economic Conference (Documents) Committee, 30 July 1923, CAB 24/161/CP 360; The Budget Situation 1923–4, memo. by Joynson-Hicks, 31 July 1923, CAB 24/161/CP 370.

49. Niemeyer to Chancellor, 27 Sept. 1923, T 161/196/S.18578/1.

50. *Imperial Economic Conference, Record of Proceedings*, Cmd.2009, 1924, resolution 2, p.13.

51. Lloyd-Greame to Devonshire 22 June 1923, CO 323/903/BT 31316; Francis to Marsh 13 July 1923, CO 323/909/CO 39731; Lloyd-Greame to Devonshire 26 July 1923, CO 323/913/MO 34696; minutes of 64th meeting Cabinet Committee on Unemployment 27 July 1923, CO 323/875/CO 53456; Worthington-Evans to Ormsby-Gore, 4 Sept. 1923, CO 323/910/CO 46434.

52. Minutes 23–29 Aug., 5 Oct. 1923, CO 323/910/CO 46434.

53. Stevenson to Ormsby-Gore, 18 Oct. 1923, CO 323/916/E 50514.

54. Minutes of 64th meeting Cabinet Committee on Unemployment, 27 July 1923, CO 323/875/CO 53456; Ormsby-Gore to Worthington-Evans 20 Sept. 1923, CO 323/910/CO 46434.

55. Statement made by Ormsby-Gore and Crown Agents memo. read by Ormsby-Gore to Unemployment Committee 23 Oct. 1923, CO 323/911/CO 51934; Minutes of 68th meeting Cabinet Committee on Unemployment, 23 Oct. 1923, CO 323/875/CO 53456.

56. Ormsby-Gore to Worthington-Evans and Devonshire to Chamberlain 25 Oct. 1923, CO 323/911/CO 51934, circulated to Committee on Unemployment CU 595, copy in T 160/184/F 6984/1.

57. Minutes by Grindle and Ormsby-Gore, 12–13 July 1923, CO 323/913/MO 34696; letters and minutes 15–24 Sept. 1923, CO 323/910/CO 47220.

58. Minutes of 69th Meeting Cabinet Committee on Unemployment, 9 Nov. 1923; minutes of 70th Meeting, 15 Nov. 1923 and appendix, letter from Chamberlain to Worthington-Evans 12 Nov. 1923, Worthington-Evans papers Mss.Eng.Hist. c.924, file no.1 and T 160/184/F 6984/1; minute by Ormsby-Gore 9 Nov. 1923 and Chamberlain to Devonshire 12 Nov. 1923, circular telegram C.O. to colonies and protectorates 21 Nov. 1923, CO 323/912/CO 56382.

59. See letters and minutes in, for example, CO 323/901/Gov 58934, CO 323/875/CO 53456, CO 323/901/Gov 61686.

60. Minutes of 71st Meeting Cabinet Committee on Unemployment, 18 Dec. 1923, memo. for committee on railway projects, 31 Dec. 1923, CO 323/912/Co 63020; minutes of 72nd Meeting Cabinet Committee on Unemployment, 8 Jan. 1924, CO 323/929/MO 1900.

61. Webb to Arnold 27 Jan. 1924, mema., and Arnold to Webb 30 Jan. 1924, CO 323/920/BT 4556.

62. W. S. Churchill, *Great Contemporaries*, London, 1939, p.293.

63. Minutes of Home Affairs Committee, 1 and 8 Nov. 1923, CAB 26/5/HAC 16(23)

8 and 17(23) 2; cabinet papers 30 Oct., 7 Nov. 1923, CAB 24/162/CP 434 and CP 445.

64. Niemeyer to Chancellor, Grigg to Niemeyer, 30 Jan. 1924, T 160/184/F 6984/2; Trade Facilities Bill, memo. by Chancellor, 31 Jan. 1924, CAB 24/164/CP 40.

65. Cabinet minutes 8 Feb. 1924 , CAB 23/47/CAB 11(24) 4; *Hansard* HC, vol.169, cols.1594-1660, 1928-1946; vol.170, cols.560-90, 642, 1268-95, 1343, 1437-1504, 2387-2457, 2503; vol.172, cols.1058-81, 1193-1251, 1299-1324, 1439-45; *Hansard* HL, vol.57, cols.278, 319-25, 358, 392, 481; 14 Geo.V ch.8.

66. W. G. Graham, Financial Secretary, 27 Feb. 1924, *Hansard* HC, vol.170, cols.560-1.

67. W. G. Graham, 19 Feb. 1924, *Hansard* HC, vol.169, col.1658.

68. Memo. by Machtig 18 Feb. 1924 and minute by Read 20 Feb. 1924, CO 323/929/MO 6694.

69. Niemeyer to Grindle 1 July 1924, T 160/184/F 6984/2; Sainsbury to Cuthbertson 20 Dec. 1923, T 160/184/F 6984/1.

70. Sainsbury to Treas. 28 Jan. 1926, minute by Phillips 2 Feb. 1926, Niemeyer to Sainsbury 6 Feb. 1926, T 160/184/F 6984/2.

71. CAB 23/49/CAB 7(25) 3; CAB 23/52/CAB 3(26) 15 and CAB 17(26) 1.

72. Cabinet minutes 23 Oct. 1923, CAB 23/46/CAB 50(23)4 and 16 Nov. 1923, CAB 56(23)1 and CAB 57(23)1.

73. King's Speech 15 Jan. 1924, *Hansard* HC, vol.169, col.79; cabinet minutes 18 Dec. 1923, CAB 23/46/CAB 59(23) 1 and 8 Feb. 1924, CAB 23/47/CAB 11(24) 4.

VI

THE DEVELOPMENT OF EAST AFRICA 1921–26

1. THE UGANDA DEVELOPMENT LOAN AND THE EAST AFRICAN WAR DEBT 1921–24

The debates described in the last chapter reflected the Imperial government's dilemma in the face of economic depression and high levels of unemployment. It was acknowledged that colonial development would be of advantage to the faltering British export trade, but the problem was to foster the growth of colonial markets without upsetting the regimen of strict national economy at home. The resulting compromise rendered the Trade Facilities Acts ineffective. The Colonial Office permanent staff were not particularly distressed by this outcome because they remained suspicious of attempts to accelerate development schemes in the colonies to meet imperial needs and because they preferred to meet real colonial requirements by traditional *ad hoc* arrangements. This priority can be further illustrated by examining the Colonial Office's continued preoccupation in the 1920s with the needs of East Africa.

Their concern with the East African dependencies reflected primarily the Colonial Office's anxiety about the finances of the local governments. These territories were vulnerable to fluctuations in the prices of their principal exports and this left government revenues at best in precarious balance. Moreover, Uganda remained under the galling financial control of the Treasury as the price for her £1 million development loan.[1] Nyasaland too was entangled with the Treasury, her finances having been gravely disturbed by the commitment to the Trans-Zambesia Railway recently foisted upon her.[2] Tanganyika's needs following the transfer of the territory from Germany also much preoccupied officials in these early post-war years. Kenya likewise remained a worry; controversy over race relations in the colony was apparently partly responsible for the failure of the administration's first attempt to raise capital independently on the London market.

But there were also other parties interested in East Africa and anxious to bring its needs and potential to the notice of the Secretary of State. The region's value as a market and as a source of raw materials, especially of cotton, was emphasized by lobbies in the colonies and in the metropolis. Chambers of Commerce in Lancashire, for example, representing the cotton industry, were a powerful economic and political force, and the Joint East Africa Board established in 1923 was an additional voice, one which expressed many of the concerns and aspirations of white settlers in the region. These pressure groups had their spokesmen in Parliament and within the political parties. Labour as well as Conservative ministers were to show themselves sensitive to their demands.[3]

However, the prospects of obtaining adequate Imperial government assistance for the East African dependencies were not initially improved by the onset of Britain's economic depression. As described in the previous chapter, the Treasury's anxiety about government finances in the summer of 1921 had persuaded the Colonial Office to set up an Economy Committee to propose reductions in expenditure on the Colonial Empire. This was evidently an uncongenial task, and the committee included in their report to Churchill in July 1921 a firm expression of faith in the virtues of their traditional colonial development policy and their concern with the needs of East Africa:

We take leave to observe here as regards East Africa, excluding Somaliland, that these territories possessing as they do magnificent natural resources, are just in that stage of development where assistance is essential to their material progress, and that it may be confidently expected that with the growth of their development, greatly retarded by the War, and with the progress of world trade to more normal conditions, they will ultimately become not only self-supporting but flourishing portions of the Empire. In saying this we have in mind the parallel case of the West African possessions, all at one time in receipt of Parliamentary grants and now all standing alone above the necessity for outside help. East Africa has the addded advantage that it benefited at the outset by enormous improvements brought about largely through the efforts of your predecessors in the cause of tropical hygiene and sanitation, whereas West Africa had to achieve her advancement in this respect through many years of painful practical experience. It is then we fear unavoidable that during the process of development these East African dependencies will have to look to Parliament for assistance in a greater or lesser degree as circumstances may require.[4]

The example of West Africa's success, the value of research into tropical hygiene, the objective of a self-supporting territory and the interim dependence on Imperial government aid, these remained the principal ingredients of the Colonial Office's preferred policy in the 1920s.

Nevertheless, it was conceded that cuts would have to be made in the short-term. It will be recalled that under the terms of Milner's agreement with Austen Chamberlain, Uganda was entitled to a loan of £250,000 a year for four years. In response to an earlier Treasury request for economies the first issue of that loan had already been postponed until August 1921.[5] Now the governor was asked if that allowance for 1921–22 would suffice also for the following financial year; failing that, he was instructed to submit at once a minimum requirement. When the governor delayed, the Colonial Office threatened to impose an arbitrary cut. This tough line brought an immediate request for an instalment of £150,000 in 1922–23.[6] The Colonial Office sent this figure on to the Treasury. In reply they were asked if Uganda could make do in 1922–23 on temporary borrowings from their surplus balances: 'the financial position was such that every £100,000 or even £50,000 was worth saving'. Even with this proposal the governor and the Colonial Office were initially prepared to comply, provided that inquiry proved that the colony's finances could sustain it and provided the full £1 million was made available within the original four year period if Uganda so desired. The Colonial Office evidently felt unable simply to reject the demands for economy.[7]

However, Churchill's sudden decision late in September 1921 to adopt colonial development as a remedy for unemployment gave a toehold to Colonial Office resistance and reinvigorated the staff. The Treasury were now told that

the position has been considerably altered since the correspondence began by recent developments in connection with the unemployment question, and it now looks as though we shall want for Uganda Development Schemes every penny we can lay our hands on, in addition to next year's reduced instalment of £150,000 .... In fact the question has been raised whether we should not ask you to increase that instalment.[8]

Silence followed, the Treasury pulled in their horns, and the £150,000 was retained in the 1922–23 estimates. Already the policy of linking the argument for colonial development with the problem of unemployment was showing signs of effectiveness.

But the major conflict between Treasury and Colonial Office was about to begin. The issue was Uganda's war liability.[9] In December 1920, the head of the East Africa department received the Uganda estimates for 1921, and was at once aware of the exposed flank left by the governor in crowing over his healthy finances. Bottomley was not so confident of Uganda's prosperity, and 'if I were, I should not be inclined to let the Treasury know my confidence until they have given up the idea that the Protectorate can possibly contribute to the cost of the war'.[10] In November 1921 the Colonial Office sent on to the Treasury the final estimates of Uganda for 1922, happily in balance and a sixth year free from the need for a Treasury grant-in-aid. Rising revenue was foreseen which would finance some new development works. Because of this the Colonial Office suggested that the protectorate might need a development loan issue of only £110,000.[11] This observation was a mistake. Instead of receiving a pat on the back, the Colonial Office and the Uganda government were treated to a vigorous demonstration of Treasury control.

Treasury officials regarded these Uganda estimates as evidence of local prosperity and this as a justification for imperial economy. They claimed that the development loan had been promised when the protectorate's financial position had been 'rocky'; if this healthy situation had been foreseen, no imperial aid would have been granted and the protectorate would have been left to develop out of its own resources. 'The financial position has changed − Uganda's for the better and our own for the worse.' The promise to provide a development loan could not be broken, but it was recalled that Uganda's war debt was still unsettled. Here was a way of easing the burden on the Imperial Exchequer: a proportion of Uganda's financial surplus should be used to pay off the debt on the lines of the repayment agreement recently reached with Kenya.[12]

These instructions were not only sent to the Colonial Office; the Treasury also alerted the Geddes Committee. The Committee on National Expenditure ignored a Colonial Office proposal to postpone the question or to settle Uganda's war debt with a modest final payment of £100,000, and instead concluded that 'in view of the strength of the Protectorate's financial position, if the Exchequer is called upon to provide capital for development purposes, arrangements should be made at the same time for the liquidation of the war expenditure liability'.[13]

The Colonial Office reacted in unison. Bottomley objected to the Treasury's policy of 'robbing the child's money-box'. Read, assistant under-secretary, insisted that payment of war liability must be postponed until the capital requirements of Uganda had as far as possible been satisfied. Sir John Masterton-Smith, permanent under-secretary, and Sir James Stevenson, the Business Adviser, urged the Colonial Office to dig their heels in. The political staff appeared equally firm. The Duke of Sutherland, the acting parliamentary under-secretary, minuted: 'The greatest care is necessary not to retard or permanently injure the growth and develpment of a young country like Uganda by false economy or appropriation of funds saved by strict economies in the past'. Churchill concurred: 'Certainly I refuse categorically without a Cabinet decision'. And this message was despatched to the Treasury.[14] The Colonial Office's concern for Uganda's future was increased in March 1922 when the acting governor sadly reported an estimated drop of 30% in annual customs revenue, decreased cotton and poll taxes and the need for consequent cuts in expenditure. The trade depression had not after all ended; indeed, primary producers were experiencing a severe downturn. Colonial Office pessimism about the territory's prospects proved justified, and this increased their zeal to withstand Treasury claims on Uganda's surplus balances.[15]

The Treasury, however, were not deflected. Their response to the Colonial Office was uncompromising. Although they had previously used Uganda's apparent prosperity as the basis for their actions, they still insisted on a repayment of the war debt in spite of the fall in Uganda's fortunes. There was a more pressing priority: 'whilst appreciating the aspirations of the Uganda Government in the matter of development', a settlement was urgent, they claimed, 'in the interest of the British taxpayer'. They would not postpone war debt repayments without cabinet direction, insisted that the issue of development loan money depended on a satisfactory settlement, and claimed that Uganda's finances if properly husbanded were still adequate to satisfy obligations to the Imperial Exchequer.[16]

Conflict had now apparently come to a head, and the Colonial Office set about preparing and polishing a memorandum for the cabinet. This was a lengthy process requiring consultation with the governor through the summer and the feeding in of extra evidence to support Colonial Office arguments. By August 1922 the case was ready: it protested against the Treasury holding up the 1922 issue of the development loan, denied their right to insist on a prior settlement of the war liability and stressed the danger of raiding Uganda's surplus balances when they were needed for public works and possibly for essential services if the depression lasted. In brief, the Colonial Office insisted that Uganda's requirements must take priority over the settlement of the war liability.[17]

This final version was printed but still not circulated to the cabinet: instead, Churchill personally sent a copy to the Chancellor and suggested settling the matter inter-departmentally.[18] Treasury officials were still not very accommodating. Their comments included the observation that taxation in Uganda was trifling compared with the burden in Great Britain. Their response was to propose that the full amount of the Uganda loan could be issued but in smaller annual amounts, and over a longer period up to 1927. Moreover, they still required Uganda to pay something out of her surplus on account of the war liability, preferably on the lines of the datum line scheme recently accepted in the case of Kenya. 'If Uganda is making a surplus, we think that, in our desperate financial position, we have a right to some of it.' Bottomley, roused from his summer holiday to comment, was inclined to scrap the development loan altogether rather than accede to this sort of exaction.[19] However, the Treasury's case was backed by the weight of the cabinet sub-committee which the Chancellor had appointed to scrutinise provisional estimates for 1923–24. The Colonial Office had pencilled in a request for £350,000 as Uganda's legitimate allocation of the development loan; the original annual allowance of £250,000 plus the £100,000 arrears from 1922–23. In August the committee informed the Colonial Office that 'the Protectorate cannot reasonably expect to carry out the original programme of development to time, at the expense of the British taxpayer, when many desirable and even necessary services in this country are being cut down or postponed through lack of funds to finance them'.[20]

In view of all that had gone before, the Colonial Office's next step was rather remarkable. Bottomley went before the cabinet sub-committee on 28 September 1922 and offered considerable concessions: the development loan should be paid out at £150,000 a year over an extended period, Uganda would at the same time pay the Imperial Exchequer a moderate amount each year to cover the controversial war debt, and the balance of the debt and the development loan would be repaid to the Treasury when Uganda eventually raised her first public loan. Some of these terms are readily comprehensible: the governor had concluded that lower annual instalments of the development loan would better suit Uganda's needs. But the other proposals were put forward reluctantly: there were inescapable precedents in the Kenya case for payments to meet the war debt and also for the idea of repaying imperial aid out of a future public loan, although 'the appreciation with which [this idea] was met by the Treasury representative at the Committee is my chief reason for thinking there may be something wrong with it'. Admittedly, Bottomley hoped that in return Uganda would be released from Treasury financial control. Moreover, the pressures from the Treasury, Geddes Committee and cabinet sub-committee were difficult to defy. But it is also clear that it was Churchill himself, as Secretary of State, who was primarily responsible for this initiative. Although he had shown himself to be anxious to tackle the unemployment problem, like most other politicians he was unable to provide an economic rationale to justify increased expenditure. Accepting the logic of orthodoxy, he acquiesced in the Treasury's arguments. Hence his reluctance to appeal to the cabinet in spite of his earlier protestations. Instead, as Masterton-Smith explained to Stevenson, the Secretary of State wanted an amicable settlement with the Treasury. A later minute by Bottomley puts the responsibility firmly on Churchill who gave instructions that the Colonial Office must come to terms with the Treasury. The proposals to the cabinet sub-committee were the result.[21] This was Churchill's last contribution to the negotiations. The following month Lloyd George's government fell and Churchill and Wood were replaced by the more determined leadership of Devonshire and Ormsby-Gore. The initiative of the political staff effected many changes in colonial development policy. This example, retrogressive in the eyes of the Colonial Office, may explain the lasting resentment of the office towards Churchill, expressed especially, as we shall see, when Churchill later became Chancellor of the Exchequer.

The Treasury agreed that the terms Bottomley had offered to the cabinet sub-committee could form the basis of a settlement, but important particulars still had to be decided: the amount of Uganda's annual war liability payment and of the initial contribution for 1922–23. In December 1922, the Colonial Office offered in the light of Uganda's draft estimates for 1923, a maximum annual payment of only £25,000, in return for which they wanted the territory to be released from the Treasury's financial control. The Treasury in reply insisted on the operation of the datum line principle worked out in the Kenya case, that is, a payment to the Treasury of half the revenue earned by the Uganda government in excess of the expenditure met from local revenue in 1922, in this case about £32,000. But the sting was a demand for a lump sum payment of £250,000 as the contribution for 1922—23. Without this the Treasury would not relax their financial control.[22]

The Colonial Office were not pleased. They rejected the datum line idea and the demand for £250,000 as impracticable and damaging to Uganda's development: instead they passed on the governor's suggestions for a maximum annual payment of £30,000 and an initial contribution of £100,000, but with a warning that the governor's financial preditions might be optimistic. In turn the Treasury found these terms unacceptable. They had their eyes fixed on Uganda's surplus funds, and in their reply claimed £200,000 of which £150,000 should be handed over at once, and they insisted on the operation of the datum line principle.[23] Bottomley was indignant and resented the way the compromise with the Treasury, insisted upon by Churchill, was turning out: 'We have had to get what satisfaction we can out of the knowledge that the British taxpayer gains what the Uganda taxpayer loses'. Ormsby-Gore was equally concerned and approved a response to the Treasury which complained at this subordination of Uganda's interests to those of Great Britain. The only Treasury reaction was to insist on their demands and to hint that the payment demanded might actually be increased to £250,000.[24]

Negotiating positions altered slightly in May. The Treasury accepted another Colonial Office suggestion that the interest on Uganda's development loan should be paid from the protectorate's annual revenue instead of from the capital as in the original terms. This would leave more money available for investment. But it would also increase the burden on the territory's annual revenue, and the Colonial Office began to fear that the fixed annual payment for war liability they had been requesting might actually be dangerously inflexible. If a datum line was calculated to take account of the interest payments on the development loan, Uganda might pay less on the half and half system, especially in years of poor trade and low income, than under a fixed sum arrangement. The governor agreed, and the Treasury snapped up the Colonial Office's offer to settle on these lines.[25]

But the annual amount to be paid on this basis and the size of the initial payment were still unagreed. The governor rather spoilt the

Colonial Office's case by offering an initial payment of £200,000 for 1922–23 and £50,000 as the sum for 1923–24 pending the fixing of the datum line. Bottomley was unhappy with the opportunities this gave the Treasury: 'When the Treasury have finished with Sir G. Archer's proposals for a half and half pinciple, he may recognize them as little as I do the results of my proposals ... a year ago'. Bottomley was prepared to accept the £50,000 offer but insisted that £150,000 must be the limit for the first payment. Since it was the practice to transmit to the Treasury copies of the Colonial Office correspondence with the governor, the Treasury were fully aware of the restraint being exercised by Colonial Office staff. As one Treasury official observed, it looked as though the Colonial Office were more anxious than the Uganda government to limit the initial lump sum payment, and this confirmed their belief that £200,000 was a just contribution and that even £250,000 could probably be paid. Hence they once more stuck to their claim for £200,000 and to the operation of the datum line system up to a maximum of £50,000 a year.[26] Not surprisingly relations between the two departments were by this time rather strained. 'Why is it,' wrote one Colonial Office man to his opposite number, 'that you at the Treasury seem to want to bleed Uganda as if it were an ex-enemy Government instead of part of the Empire that did more than its share in a war which happened to spread to the East of Africa and in which Uganda as such had no interest?'[27]

Further disruption came in October when the governor conceded that his earlier financial predictions were over-optimistic and that Uganda could only afford £150,000 as an initial payment from surplus balances. This setback seems to have provoked a general review of East African problems in the department. Finally, with Ormsby-Gore's support, Bottomley informed the Treasury that in the light of Uganda's difficulties, the Colonial Office could not approve any initial payment above £100,000, 'until we see our way clearer'. Not unexpectedly the Treasury resented this stubbornness, and they threatened in response to cut off supplies of the development loan and maintain their control of Uganda's finances until a larger contribution of at least £175,000 was forthcoming. They saw the issue with stark clarity: 'if Uganda keeps her balances, she does not need our Development money'.[28]

At this point, late November 1923, the forthcoming general election delayed matters. The Colonial Office required ministerial authority to offer more than £100,000, and it was the end of December before the political staff reconsidered the papers. By then the permanent staff felt that in order to secure future instalments of the development loan, they must agree to the Treasury's terms, an initial war contribution of £175,000 and an annual contribution on the half and half principle amounting to £50,000 for 1923–24. Read, assistant under-secretary, reluctantly capitulated to the Treasury's demands, 'but I think that it is short-sighted policy to extract from Uganda these heavy contributions on account of war liability at a time when its prospects of development are so promising. Uganda will, however, be free from Treasury control and that is something to be thankful for'. Churchill, judging by his previous role in these negotiations, would probably have accepted this advice, but much depended on the character of ministers, and Ormsby-Gore now intervened:

I protest most strongly and I personally cannot possibly concur in the penny wise and pound foolish policy of the Treasury. All that Mr. Ramsay Macdonald and Sir Alfred Mond and the Daily Express said in the election about the starvation of Crown Colony development under the Conservative Government will be true if ministers accept and agree to this malicious attempt of the Treasury to wring money for war contributions out of struggling Colonies and Protectorates that need every penny for development. The whole policy seems to me to be utterly wrong and foolish: I have spoken to several Cabinet Ministers about it and they entirely agree, and nothing short of a cabinet decision would make me concur in what is now proposed. When I first came to the Office Lord Milner said that his experience at the Colonial Office had left one outstanding impression on his mind, namely that the Treasury continuously and by tradition do everything they can to make Colonial development difficult. To my mind this Uganda case is an outstanding example.

With these sentiments Devonshire agreed, and requested that a personal letter expressing the Colonial Office case be prepared for despatch to the Chancellor, Neville Chamberlain. This letter, sent on 4 January 1924, was carefully framed as an appeal to enlightened metropolitan self-interest. Depriving Uganda of financial resources was 'quite incompatible with our settled policy that we should develop these African Dependencies to the utmost not merely in their own interests but also in those of the mother country'. Uganda had great possibilities especially as a cotton growing country, but 'it really needs more liberal expenditure than that arranged between Milner and your brother in 1920 by means of a Development Loan'. It followed that it was indefensible for the Treasury to threaten to cut that loan in retaliation for the Colonial Office's refusal to accept their terms for the repayment of the war debt.[29]

The trouble with these personal letters was that they were first received and dissected by the permanent officials in the Treasury. The touch of ministerial camaraderie was rapidly obscured by critical minuting. Treasury staff pointed out that the governor of Uganda had offered as much as £200,000 out of his surplus balances as a war liability payment, and they claimed that large balances were unnecessary when 'no emergency expenditure is in sight'. (It might be argued that if emergency expenditure was in sight there would be no emergency.) In the event the Treasury did prepare a reply to Devonshire offering some sort of compromise: a payment of £150,000 as a war debt contribution would secure Uganda's release from the Treasury's financial control, but in return the next instalment of the development loan would be cut to £100,000. What they conceded with the one hand they intended to recoup with the other.[30]

The letter was not sent. The negotiations concerning Uganda's war liability pursued through several files over almost exactly two years were rapidly concluded on an entirely new basis within the space of a week. To explain this twist in events it is necessary to piece together proposals for further development in East Africa. To this point the story of Uganda's development loan and her war liability illustrates the conflict between the protectorate's financial needs and the financial orthodoxy of the Imperial Treasury. The next stage shows how arguments emphasising the economic needs of Britain in a period of high unemployment helped resolve this conflict between colonial and metropolitan interests.

2. THE £3,500,000 LOAN TO KENYA AND UGANDA 1924

Discussions between the Colonial Office and the governors of Kenya and Uganda concerning railway developments in their territories and methods of financing them shadowed the negotiations just examined. The pressures for such developments, which culminated in an Imperial government loan of £3,500,000, came from three sources. In the first place both governors on their own initiative or stimulated by interested groups in their territories formulated proposals for railway building and other public works which they forwarded to the Colonial Office for consideration and sanction. Secondly, the Colonial Office received proposals from interested parties in the metropolis. Thirdly, the political structure itself spawned initiatives; that is, in the context of the economic depression, politicians strove to meet political pledges to alleviate Britain's distress. Colonial development as a remedy for unemployment proved to be a crucial proposition in overcoming Treasury resistance to expenditure.

It will be recalled that Kenya issued her first independent loan of £5 million on the London market in November 1921. It was expected that a second loan of £3 million would be raised shortly afterwards to cover other planned works, notably the completion of the Uasin-Gishu Railway. This was discussed early in 1922, further additions were made to the programme, and the necessary loan ordinance was passed. But it was agreed that the loan would not be raised until the market appeared suitable.[31] Delay ensued when depression hit Kenya and unfavourable revenue figures made the chances of a cheap loan remote. In addition, the agitation over the Indian question in Kenya was judged likely to damage an issue of stock.[32] Meanwhile, other proposals, distinct from those originally contemplated for this £3 million loan, were also being examined, including one large project to relay the Uganda Railway (which ran through Kenya).[33]

Similarly, Uganda had its contemplated developments. The protectorate's needs were stressed in a despatch received in the Colonial Office early in 1923 and amplified in later correspondence. It was stressed that Uganda's development depended very much on cotton, and the cultivation of this and other export products was dependent on effective communications by road and especially by rail to help the flow of goods to the Uganda Railway and out through Kenya to the sea. Governor Archer argued that it was necessary to create a co-ordinated service. This was an important point in that it suggested the linking of the development proposals of the two territories.[34]

Such projects were also encouraged by pressure groups in the metropolis. For example, in September 1923 the Oldham Chamber of Commerce played host to a cotton ginner from Uganda who gave a lecture on the necessity for empire development. He stressed the value of Uganda as a source of raw cotton supplies for Lancashire and as a market for British goods. After the lecture a resolution was passed and forwarded to the Colonial Office: 'That the Oldham Chamber of Commerce, in view of the extreme urgency of increasing the production of cotton, are of the opinion that more development work should be done in Uganda and in the basin of the Victoria Nyanza, as offering one of the finest fields for increased production'. Colonial Office staff were sympathetic, but Bottomley commented that increasing production required expenditure on transport improvements.[35]

By the autumn of 1923, therefore, both East Africa administrations already had planned works in hand and other projects under consideration, and there was much colonial and metropolitan support for such proposals. For the Colonial Office, the problem lay not in the economic validity of the schemes put forward but in their financing. As Bottomley pointed out in October 1923 in a memorandum on 'Obstacles to Transport Developments in Kenya and Uganda', these territories lacked the means to meet loan charges on big projects. The initial expenses would be high, and he was concerned that their cost might overstretch local revenues. Both governments were already substantially burdened by earlier commitments. Generous imperial aid was therefore needed. Parkinson, principal clerk in the East Africa department, observed: 'If H.M.G. were to make a free gift of funds to Kenya — or at any rate advance money with postponement of all loan charges for a very long period of years, there are presumably other works which could be put in hand'. The difficulty was, of course, to persuade the Treasury of the need.[36]

Colonial Office attempts to obtain adequate imperial assistance for Kenya and Uganda need to be seen in the context of the negotiations analysed in the previous chapter. In June and again in September 1923 an anxious Cabinet Committee on Unemployment had asked the Colonial Office if the Colonial Empire could accelerate orders for development materials to ease the expected distress in Britain in the coming winter. The Colonial Office took this as an opportunity to make a bid for generous terms. The needs of Kenya and Uganda featured in the proposals they put forward in reply, but, as described, the Chancellor's determined resistance obliged the Colonial Office in November 1923 to offer to Kenya and Uganda, along with other territories, the terms of assistance proposed at the Imperial Economic Conference: an imperial grant of three-quarters of the interest for five years on loans raised in the next three years for expenditure in Britain.[37]

The governors of Kenya and Uganda, catching wind of the Colonial Office's efforts to obtain aid, had meanwhile put their heads together and come up with a joint programme of railway and harbour works in the two territories and requested approval of their plans plus imperial aid to service the £6 million loan required. The scheme absorbed the projects originally put forward to help the Uganda cotton industry and the works to be covered by Kenya's second and much postponed independent loan. Further information was sent later that month and, in justification of the proposal, a judicious emphasis was placed on the employment consequences for Britain as well as on the needs of the territories. The financial requirements were also explained: 'It is essential that financial assistance should be available for these enterprises from Imperial Funds and that the Railway Administration should not be called upon to meet full interest and sinking fund charges during the initial stages'. What the General Manager of the Uganda Railway had in mind was an imperial loan free of interest for perhaps ten years.[38]

The Colonial Office were sympathetic to the need for such generous aid but were despondent about the chances of obtaining it. They were therefore somewhat taken aback when Governor Coryndon reacted enthusiastically to the Imperial Economic Conference terms for aid of three-quarters of the interest for five years. 'Offer of assistance greatly appreciated by this Colony and will further stimulate economic and agricultural progress', he telegrammed. 'I hope he understands its limited scope', a Colonial Office official minuted.[39] The governor's response rather blunted the Colonial Office's insistence on more generous terms, but another chance arose to press their case when Ormsby-Gore was once again invited to appear before the Unemployment Committee to discuss colonial development plans. On 18 December 1923 he explained that no definite proposals had yet resulted from the offer to pay three-quarters of the interest for five years. The committee therefore invited the Colonial Office to prepare a memorandum describing railway projects in tropical Africa which might relieve unemployment and detailing their financial needs. This opportunity was eagerly taken and by the end of the year the Colonial Office had prepared their case, describing projects in Nyasaland, Tanganyika, Gold Coast and Nigeria as well as in Kenya and Uganda, and condemning as inadequate the aid already offered. Although the governor of Kenya had welcomed these terms, the Colonial Office doubted if the colony could sustain the charges, and they supported instead the General Manager's proposal for an Imperial government loan free of interest for ten years. Moreover, they insisted that the charges on the new loans must have priority over Treasury claims for war debt repayments.[40]

Before the memorandum reached the Unemployment Committee, the Treasury were given an opportunity to study it. They acknowledged readily the pressures to which the depression subjected them: 'Generally on these schemes ... we are handicapped by approaching them from the unemployment aspect, which enables the Colonial Office to say that if you want these works you must pay for them, the Colonies cannot'. But they obviously did not accept the validity of such arguments, for 'it may help employment as much to leave these millions in the pockets of the British taxpayer as to abstract them and apply them to unprofitable ventures born before their time'. Niemeyer, the controller of finance, also denied the need: 'steel trade is looking up as it is .... There is therefore no real need to be black-mailed by the C.O. into wholly uneconomic expenditure on schemes which haven't been properly thought out'. They naturally seized on Governor Coryndon's willingness to use the terms offered. They also accepted that the proposal to extend the Uganda Railway was a viable scheme, but argued that since the Uganda Railway already generated enough revenue to meet interest payments, Kenya should therefore raise the capital needed as part of the postponed £3 million loan. The Imperial government would help on the basis of the terms agreed at the Imperial Economic Conference. Other schemes were criticized as not paying propositions: 'We are prepared to help the lame dog with some chance of recovery, but not the dog with no legs at all'.[41]

The Cabinet Unemployment Committee, however, were sympathetic to the Colonial Office memorandum, perhaps more sensitive to political needs and less optimistic about unemployment prospects. The committee reported to the cabinet on 9 January 1924 that they approved in principle the proposals to build the Uasin-Gishu Railway and relay part of the Uganda Railway at a cost of £6,150,000. The scheme would 'not only assist in the relief of unemployment, but will when completed contribute materially towards the solution of the British cotton shortage problem'. But the Treasury representative had urged that imperial aid should be on the basis of the three-quarters interest scheme and the committee had ducked out of a decision on finance by recommending that the Treasury and Colonial Office should meet to examine the financial aspects and agree on terms as favourable as circumstances would permit.[42]

A meeting between Colonial Office representatives led by Ormsby-Gore and Treasury representatives led by Walter Guinness, the Financial Secretary, did take place on 10 January but seemingly without progress being made. The cabinet was due to debate the Unemployment Committee's report the following day, so Ormsby-Gore took pains to brief Devonshire on the line he was to take. He should explain that the total needs of Kenya and Uganda amounted to £8 million, over half of this concerned with developments intended to improve cotton output. But the two territories were already shouldering considerable loan burdens, and therefore for these essential works to take place imperial aid was needed. Ormsby-Gore recommended asking for a grant of £210,000 a year to pay all the interest on half the programme for five years, or half the interest on all the programme for five years. 'This is the minimum cash assistance required.' Although this looks less generous than the Imperial Economic Conference terms of three-quarters of the interest, it should be remembered that the latter would cover only the capital spent in the United Kingdom; Ormsby-Gore imposed no such limitation. Moreover, he also urged Devonshire to insist that the question just reopened by the Treasury of Kenya repaying the capital advanced for the building of the original Uganda Railway should be postponed for five years. More radically, the Treasury should also waive and never raise again their demands for contributions from Kenya and Uganda to meet war liabilities.[43]

The matters outlined in the first section of this chapter at this point merged with the proposal to find new development funds for East Africa. Negotiations over Uganda's war liability had stumbled over the Colonial Office's desire to avoid overburdening the territory when attempts were being made to accelerate development proposals, and over the Treasury's refusal to abandon their financial claims. The long drawn out talks had shown no sign of conclusion during the first week of January 1924.

But Devonshire must have been fairly persuasive at the cabinet which met on 11 January 1924. Ministers approved the recommendations of the Unemployment Committee including the request that the Colonial Office and the Treasury should agree to assist Kenya and Uganda on the most generous financial terms possible, and the Chancellor of the Exchequer agreed to discuss with the Secretary of State his proposal to remit the territories' war liabilities.[44]

Faced with this request Treasury officials seem to have accepted that some provision was unavoidable. And having realised that, they sought the most effective method. They drew up their own rather novel proposal. It was realised that East Africa would have problems raising capital on the open market at reasonable rates, even with an imperial guarantee. Moreover, Kenya could not raise a loan with a guarantee without depreciating her credit and damaging her chances of raising a second independent loan. Therefore it was proposed that the Imperial government should provide a loan of £3,500,000, free of interest for five years, as a supplementary parliamentary vote. This was, of course, less capital than the Colonial Office had proposed but the Treasury reckoned that Kenya could itself raise the other £4,500,000 later when needed.[45] This plan was accepted in the Treasury with no apparent dissent and was passed on by Walter Guinness at a meeting with Ormsby-Gore on 14 January 1924.

The basis for a settlement now seemed apparent to the Colonial Office. On the same day they wrote to the Treasury accepting the offer of £3,500,000 even though it was less than they had originally sought and still left Kenya to raise an additional loan later. They even offered to ask Uganda if she could do without her development loan instalments after 1924–25 and possibly accept a reduced issue for 1923–24. But in return the Treasury must make further concessions. They were asked to drop their claim for half the balance of net revenue earned by the Uganda Railway as a contribution to the repayment of the capital cost: the drain on the railway's resources was prejudicial to its improvement, and development should take priority. Furthermore, the Colonial Office argued that it was the cabinet's wish to see the war debt claims on East Africa abandoned and the Treasury were asked to make this concession.[46]

The Treasury were being asked to forego claims on two sources of revenue from East Africa, war debts and railway profits, and this struck Treasury officials as an imperfect balance. They argued that if the developments generated the prosperity claimed for them there was no need to abandon their demands. Instead it was suggested that the question of repayment should merely be postponed for ten years. However, the Colonial Office's offer to abandon the Uganda Development Loan should still be insisted upon since, freed from immediate war debt payments, Uganda would have sufficient income to meet intended schemes.[47] These were the terms upon which the Chancellor insisted when he met Ormsby-Gore on 17 January. They were accepted by the Colonial Office. Colonial Office staff were not happy that the war debt claims had only been postponed and not abandoned and they regretted the loss of the Uganda Development Loan. But at least Uganda was now freed from Treasury financial control. On the other hand one Treasury official, while glad that the war liabilities were not waived, concluded that 'C.O. appear to have beaten the Treasury'.[48] Honours were probably even.

A press announcement on the new loan was published on 22

January, and Baldwin's government resigned the same day. This did not affect the settlement. The new political chiefs at the Colonial Office, Thomas and Arnold, accepted the scheme at once and the Labour government absorbed it into their unemployment proposals. The new Cabinet Unemployment Committee blessed it on 7 February, the cabinet gave their formal sanction the following day and the supplementary estimate authorising the £3,500,000 loan to Kenya and Uganda passed through Parliament on 3 March 1924.[49]

In some respects this was a remarkable conclusion to the negotiations so far described in this chapter. There is a sharp contrast between the months of futile haggling between Colonial Office and Treasury about the size of Uganda's initial war liability payment, a disagreement of £50,000 and the rapid decision-making which produced a £3,500,000 Imperial government loan and postponed the whole question of war debts for ten years together with the secondary disputed issue of the Uganda Railway revenues. The responsibility for this transformation lies with the persistence of high levels of unemployment in Britain and the political and economic exigencies it created. These pressures explain the Colonial Office's ability to circumvent Treasury demands for economy and also the Treasury's attempts to relieve the problems of the British Exchequer by recovering outstanding debts from the East African territories. There are obvious similarities here with the parallel negotiations which led to the Trade Facilities Act of 1924.

But it is also necessary to recognise an interesting contrast. In the case of the Trade Facilities Acts the value of the proposals had primarily been regarded as lying in the immediate provision of work for the British unemployed by accelerating the purchase of materials needed for colonial development. In spite of the Unemployment Committee's continued faith in this strategy neither Colonial Office nor Treasury staff seem to have been convinced by it. Parkinson in the Colonial Office was anxious to see Kenya given generous aid, 'but I should say that there would be no prospect of affecting unemployment here this winter by means thereof'. Read pointed out that surveys must precede railway building, 'so that no relief for unemployment can be hoped for in this direction during the coming winter'. Unwittingly they agreed with Niemeyer in the Treasury, who commented on the Colonial Office's memorandum on railway projects in Africa, 'Nothing that is done now can make any difference to present unemployment'.[50] In fact, in the case of the Kenya-Uganda loan the attraction of obtaining immediate orders for the iron and steel industry was only a secondary consideration. Railway building would increase the supplies of quality cotton for another crippled British industry. Kenya and Uganda were regarded more as sources of supply than as immediate purchasers of British goods. During the House of Commons debate on the loan the Secretary of State for the Colonies did stress its value for accelerating immediate orders for British goods and he did insist that the purchase of materials with the loan had to be made in Britain.[51] But in the Colonial Office and in the House of Commons most emphasis was put upon the value of stimulating increased cotton production. Ormsby-Gore told Devonshire that 'You can assure the Cabinet that the Uganda production alone can be brought up to half a million bales a year'. A Colonial Office memorandum summarising the negotiations to date for the information of the new Labour government similarly emphasised the importance of cotton growing and the needs of Lancashire.

It is well known that the supply of cotton from the United States of America cannot be relied on to supply Lancashire, owing to the increasing consumption of American cotton in America, the ravages of the boll weevil and the shortage of labour on account of the restriction of immigration and the consequent movement of the negro population from the Southern States to the towns in the Northern States where extremely high wages are obtainable.

The explanatory note to accompany the Supplementary Estimate, designed obviously to win the approval of the House of Commons, described the purpose of the loan as being 'for the relief of unemployment at home and also for furthering the development of the cotton growing industry and of communications generally'. And during the debate speakers defended the proposal in similar terms: 'As Lancashire is dependent upon cotton and as we can grow the cotton within the Empire, it is to our obvious advantage to do what we can in that way', 'We are bound once again to recur to the policy of a century and a half ago and create our own supply within our own territory'.[52]

The advantages of this colonial development scheme were not therefore limited to short-term benefits for the British unemployed. The economic depression had led to a revival of the idea that British economic security lay in the integration of colonial and metropolitan economies. This was an important advance along the path to regarding colonial development and Imperial government aid for colonial development as a long-term solution to Britain's economic needs and not just as a measure for immediate unemployment relief. The idea was encouraged by the clear compatability between the aid requirements of Kenya and Uganda and the cotton supply needs of Lancashire. The negotiations leading to the East Africa Loans Act in 1926 repeated this assessment.

3. THE EAST AFRICA LOANS ACT 1926

The imperial government's decision to commit £3,500,000 to the development of railways in Kenya and Uganda, while generally welcomed by the cotton and colonial lobbies in East Africa and in Britain, did not completely satisfy their requirements. Indeed, within a month of its announcement, the Secretary of State for the Colonies was faced on 4 April 1924 by a formidable delegation. A body of Lancashire M.P.s and members of the British Cotton Growing Association expressed their concern for the ailing textile industry and their interest in East African solutions. They were accompanied by representatives from such humanitarian groups as the Aborigines Protection Society, anxious to protect native rights should developments be accelerated. Economic arguments were most forcefully expressed: 'If this country is going to maintain its position in the world as an industrial nation, it is to Africa that we shall have to look for our raw materials, and again it is to Africa that we shall have to look for our customers for manufactured goods'. The delegation proposed an investigation both of the opportunities for economic development in East Africa and of the associated issues of land tenure, trusteeship and native rights. In response Thomas did inaugurate such a wide-ranging inquiry by appointing the Southborough and Islington Committees, but the only body to fulfil their allotted task was the East Africa Commission, originally only a roving sub-committee sent to examine East African conditions on the spot and with a more restricted brief. In particular they considered measures to accelerate economic development and to secure closer co-ordination of policy between East African administrations on transport, cotton growing and disease control. The impact of the East Africa Commission's investigation owed much to the appointment of Ormsby-Gore as the chairman.[53]

Their report, signed in April 1925, contained among other matters a strong emphasis on the need for further transport developments in the region. It was observed, however, that private enterprise was unwilling to undertake such investments. Moreover, the responsibility which as a result fell on the local administrations was too onerous for them to carry. Kenya alone, as a colony, was qualified to raise her own loans in London under the Colonial Stock Acts. Even if the acts were amended to cover the other territories visited, Uganda, Nyasaland, Tanganyika and Northern Rhodesia, there was a danger of overburdening local revenues by interest charges during the period of construction. Evidently, imperial aid was needed, but the commission was critical of the system of grants or loans-in-aid made available in the past. Not only did this involve intolerable Treasury control of local finances, but it 'is dependent entirely on the amount of money which the British Chancellor of the Exchequer is willing or able to divert from the Sinking Fund from time to time for colonial development'. The commission reached a clear conclusion: 'unless the Imperial Government is prepared to assist liberally in this matter, little or nothing can be done'. Generous terms must be granted; therefore they recommended that an East African Transport Loan Guarantee Bill should be introduced. This would authorise the issue of a £10 million loan, guaranteed as to principal and interest by the Imperial government and ranking as a trustee security: as a result the interest charges would be low. In addition, for the first five years, that is during the construction period, interest on this loan should be paid by the Imperial Exchequer. Finally, after ten years, the amount advanced as interest in the first five years could be repaid, by the now revenue-earning new transport systems.

While reference was made to Britain's moral obligation to develop her tropical possessions in the interests of their inhabitants and the wider world, the major weight was placed on metropolitan economic benefits to justify the proposal. There were some immediate advantages: half the capital raised would be spent on materials in Britain 'which at this time would provide work for the engineering industries ... and so lessen unemployment charges'. But in addition 'the indirect benefits of increased trade and production within the Empire will more than counterbalance any initial sacrifice'. The plan could therefore be defended 'as a business proposition which will redound not merely to the credit but also to the economic advantage of Great Britain'.[54]

These proposals struck a responsive audience. During the spring and summer of 1925 congestion on the Uganda Railway and at the ports of Kilindini and Kisumu in Kenya alarmed such colonial producers and exporters as the Uganda Company, the Magadi Soda Company and the British East Africa Corporation, and they complained to the press and directly to the Colonial Office. Their laments were echoed by textile manufacturers in Britain who were anxious to increase supplies of good quality raw materials at low prices, increases which they too realised were dependent on transport developments in East Africa. Voices were raised in Parliament, and in July 1925 a delegation to the Colonial Office by the East Africa sections of the London, Liverpool and Manchester Chambers of Commerce endorsed the proposals of the East Africa Commission.[55]

The discontented had also expressed their worries to the Committee on Industry and Trade, appointed by the Labour government to enquire into the means of improving Britain's export trade and so relieving the depression. The committee gathered evidence from various concerned organisations such as the Cotton Spinners' and Manufacturers' Association, the Empire Cotton Growing Corporation, the British Cotton Growing Association, the Provisional Emergency Cotton Committee, the Agricultural Engineers' Association, and the Iron and Steel Trades Confederation. Many testified to the need for more and cheaper raw materials for the cotton industry from an alternative source to the United States. The need for fresh orders to be placed on the home market was also stressed by the Locomotive Manufacturers' Association. The Shipping Merchants' Committee of the Manchester Chamber of Commerce argued that something 'big in comparison with what has already been done but small from a national budget point of view, would be justified as a measure against unemployment and a stimulus to national recovery', and Ormsby-Gore, invited to give evidence to the committee, suggested what that might be, a £10 million guaranteed loan for transport developments in East Africa. In the event this proposal received the weighty backing of the Committee on Industry and Trade in July 1925 in its interim report on *Transport Development and Cotton Growing in East Africa*. Long-term as well as short-term advantages were stressed:

there appears to be no reasonable doubt that British trade and employment would substantially benefit not only from the immediate demand for the products of the iron and steel and engineering industries and the prospective increase of raw cotton supplies but also, eventually, in many other ways, through the added purchasing power of the population of African territories affected.[56]

The chances of this proposal receiving sympathetic consideration by the government were enhanced by the return of a Conservative administration under Baldwin in November 1924. The party had committed itself in the general election, albeit in general terms, to a policy of empire development,[57] and Baldwin had taken at least one step towards honouring that pledge by appointing Amery as Secretary of State for the Colonies. At last the principal imperial enthusiast of the period had control of the office he had long coveted. He wrote to Milner, his former chief and mentor, 'I succeed to the tradition which Chamberlain and you have created'. In return he received Milner's blessing, 'You are, of all men in the world, the best fitted'. As before, Amery energetically promoted the policies of colonial development, empire settlement and imperial preference. He was convinced that with unemployment in the mid 1920s still around the 10% mark and with socialism apparently gaining credibility, constructive imperialism was the only viable economic and political alternative. In the case of East Africa, however, he retained his earlier interest in the promotion of development works as the preliminary to the creation of a self-governing federation of territories dominated by the white settlers.[58] Enthusiastic support for imperial financial assistance to East Africa could, of course, be expected from his under-secretary, the former chairman of the East Africa Commission, Ormsby-Gore. Certain cabinet colleagues might also prove obliging, particularly Cunliffe-Lister at the Board of Trade, who since the last Conservative government had changed his name from Lloyd-Greame but had not altered his views on the virtues of empire development. But Amery was to find Churchill as Chancellor of the Exchequer less sympathetic. Churchill was for the most part to accept the orthodox economic and financial views of his advisers, and the Treasury staff in the light of their previous experience of Amery and Ormsby-Gore were expecting demands on their funds and were prepared to resist.[59]

In July 1925 Amery made his first approach to the Treasury. He asked Churchill to approve in general terms a government commitment to a policy of railway construction in East Africa. He mentioned the immediate benefits to British exports if such works were expedited, but laid more emphasis on the longer-term gains from improving the supply of raw cotton 'for our main industry' and from increasing the wealth and purchasing power of East Africa. He enclosed a copy of the report just issued by the Committee on Industry and Trade to add weight to his case, and indicated the political interest in this matter by referring to deputations of Lancashire and Cheshire M.P.s he would be meeting later in the month. He concluded, 'this at any rate is not a question of asking you to find cash for employment but only a guarantee of very moderate sums spread over several years'. Since the Ormsby-Gore Commission had recommended that the Imperial government should advance the interest on these guaranteed loans for the first five years, this interpretation of the proposal was either careless or dishonest. Furthermore, Amery's apparent failure to grasp the intricacies of the financial system never ceased to annoy the Treasury. Although 'only a guarantee' was requested, Churchill insisted that full information about the proposed new schemes should be given before the Imperial government could pledge its credit to their financing. Debt conversions, capital for telephone construction, trade facilities schemes, electricity development and agricultural developments – all these, he pointed out, were competing with East Africa for the Exchequer's limited credit.[60]

What was probably intended as a Treasury brush off was interpreted by Amery as a request for actual schemes; and these after a fashion he supplied. By contrast with the situation leading to the £3,500,000 loan to Kenya and Uganda, no detailed plans were as yet available, and Bottomley was conscious that the Secretary of State was advocating premature schemes. Against one suggestion he minuted: 'It may be urgent, but the work leading up to it will take us at least two years from now'. Amery was not deterred. Drawing on the report of the East Africa Commission, a list of proposed railways, harbour improvements and road schemes was despatched to the Treasury on 7 August 1925.[61]

Amery may have been encouraged to hasten his application to the Treasury because the cabinet was currently reviewing the problems of unemployment once more, and thanks to Cunliffe-Lister the merits of colonial development as a remedy were again being aired. It is noticeable, however, that in the memorandum Cunliffe-Lister submitted to the cabinet, emphasis was firmly placed on the long-term advantages of the policy. 'Hitherto', he wrote, 'there has been a tendency year by year to approve specifics, often expensive and uneconomic, because they were obvious temporary palliatives in a passing emergency'. What was really needed was a policy which while affording some immediate relief would also lead to an increase of normal trade. 'I am convinced that nationally the most remunerative expenditure we can incur is in the development of markets which will be complementary and not competitive. Africa fulfills this condition in a peculiar degree.' Hence he urged a policy of railway construction particularly in cotton growing areas and endorsed the recommendations of the Committee on Industry and Trade. On 7 August the cabinet supported in general terms this method of promoting commerce, and requested the Secretary of State for the Colonies to prepare proposals for railway construction in Africa and other developments in the empire.[62] A similar request followed later from the Cabinet Committee on Unemployment which in October 1925 once again turned to colonial development as a source of relief.[63]

The problem was that the proposals emanating from the East Africa Commission were at this stage still being analysed individually by the colonial governments and geographical departments responsible for the five territories concerned.[64] The Colonial Office did not have detailed schemes ready for immediate cabinet sanction. This was certainly the view of the Treasury officials who in September and October 1925 reviewed and condemned the East African proposals which Amery had hastily submitted in August. The lack of detail was pinpointed and the need for further investigation stressed. 'The C.O. have made no attempt to sift the schemes at all; their idea apparently is to get the money and then proceed to decide how to spend it.' It was true that £10 million could be usefully spent in the area, but the Treasury wanted to ensure that only profitable schemes which 'would *pay their way*' should be assisted 'in these hard times'. Care must be taken to prevent local governments being overburdened by new liabilities causing future reliance on grants-in-aid. Accordingly it was suggested that the only acceptable scheme already planned in Tanganyika should be approved and financed separately. In brief, the Treasury were insisting that sanction should be given individually to each proposal on an *ad hoc* basis as it matured and that the Colonial Office should not be allowed to distribute credit from a large fund to ill-prepared colonial ventures.[65]

This attitude was embodied in a draft reply to Amery prepared by the Treasury staff and sent to Churchill for approval on 12 October. There was very little in Amery's scheme which was regarded as acceptable. To raise large loans as proposed before they were needed would have an adverse effect on the money market and could disrupt the Imperial government's other financial plans. Moreover, there was no reason why the Exchequer should adopt the commission's recommendation and pay the interest on loans for the first five years, since it was usual in development works for the interest to be paid initially out of the capital raised for the project. Furthermore, holding out the prospect of large loans would tempt colonial governments to submit immature plans. Proposals would have to be presented in detail and would have to be scrutinized by better advisers than those available in the dependencies, namely by city financiers. In brief, the Treasury concluded, the loan question should be postponed until surveys and assessments had been completed.[66]

In view of these critical observations and their implicit reflection on the financial competence of the Colonial Office and the colonial governments, it seemed likely that Amery's proposals would founder. The report of the East Africa Commission had been signed in April and it was already October and no progress had been made. But as in earlier cases examined, political pressures were responsible for the defeat of the Treasury hardliners. The draft letter refuting Amery's suggestions was not sent. On 13 October 1925 Amery button-holed Churchill for half an hour and 'got him I think into a more reasonable frame of mind'. Certainly something impressed the Chancellor. As he explained to his senior Treasury advisers, the £10 million loan project had a great deal of cabinet and outside backing. 'The Cotton industry, the Steel industry, the inevitable unemployed and the Imperial argument all combine.' In the face of this combination, Churchill accepted the need for the Treasury to finance reasonable schemes. He rejected Amery's terms however: 'We are not ready to take a block sum from the money market and leave the C.O. to look about for ways to get rid of it, which their patient industry would no doubt soon discover'. And of the weakness of the Colonial Office's arguments he had no doubts: 'Incidentally let me know what would be the effect of the expenditure of a £10m. Railway loan on the British steel works. I gather it would be almost negligible'. The position is clear: the £10 million loan had to be accepted even though it would have little immediate effect on unemployment. But to ensure that it was not spent unproductively the Treasury would enforce real restrictions on expenditure.[67]

Treasury officials were understandably unhappy with Churchill's decision. Once again they drew the Chancellor's attention to the inadequate economic and financial investigations which lay behind the projects.

Our argument is not that railway development is undesirable in East Africa, nor that it should be provided otherwise than by loan, nor that the loan should not be guaranteed by the Imperial Exchequer, but that the moment has not yet come when Parliament ought to be asked to give a guarantee of the Imperial Exchequer to railway loans in respect of schemes the out-turn of which so little is yet known.

Nor were they impressed by the unemployment benefits which Amery claimed. Following up Churchill's query it was calculated that the schemes would give reasonable help to the export of railway track, but that the present annual exports of iron and steel would increase by only 1% and the current exports of rolling-stock by only 2½%. Niemeyer reckoned that on a liberal estimate only 40% of the £10 million would be spent in Britain and this over five years. Furthermore, 'savings here are certainly far less than the loan demanded and even if there was no East African loan the money involved would certainly be employed, very likely on works more immediately effective here as regards unemployment .... The unemployment arguments therefore are not impressive'. However, since Churchill had consented to Amery's plans for political reasons, these financial and economic criticisms could not deflect him from his course.[68]

Accordingly Amery was free to draw up a memorandum for the cabinet, setting out the case for a £10 million East African development loan on the lines put forward by the East Africa Commission and endorsed by the Committee on Industry and Trade. There would be ample economic returns, he argued, helping the unemployed in Britain, both in the short-term since much of the money raised would be spent in Britain, but especially in the long-term with the increased production of raw materials in the colonies, especially of cotton. Furthermore, 'every pound of tropical produce grown in these territories increases the purchasing power of their inhabitants for British manufactured goods in return'. He concluded with a political point, that the plan would also make good the government's electoral pledge to promote imperial development and build new markets.[69] Having seen Baldwin in advance and settled one or two details with Churchill, Amery was able to win the cabinet's formal approval without difficulty on 23 October 1925. He announced this decision with appropriate rhetoric in a public speech in Bristol the same day. The scheme would, he claimed, help appreciably to reduce unemployment in this country. The omens were good. 'The development of the cotton industry in Uganda, for instance, had brought work to the makers of British bicycles of which the natives now ordered thousands a month'.[70]

The pressures which added political weight to economic arguments for colonial development are well illustrated by the exaggerated reception of Amery's announcement. The headline in the *Daily Dispatch* for 26 October 1925 exclaimed: '£10m Loan Welcomed. Lancashire Trade Boom. More Cotton'. The report referred to the approval of Lancashire traders, industrialists, trade unionists and politicians. The *Daily Dispatch* reckoned that the loan would secure the ultimate independence of Lancashire for raw materials thus giving greater security to her workpeople. Moreover, opening up great new colonial markets in Africa created possibilities at least equal to anything India afforded to the British producer. It would also stimulate iron, steel and engineering activities since 60% of the loan would largely be spent on rolling stock in England. Furthermore, it was a measure for national economy since the scheme would generate labour and wages in place of unemployment and doles. W. H. Himbury, General Manager of the British Cotton Growing Association, thanked Amery and Ormsby-Gore for their assistance in 'our joint movement', and R. H. Jackson, Chairman of the Empire Cotton Growing Corporation, Fred Holroyd, President of the Master Cotton Spinners' Associations and several Lancashire M.P.s talked enthusiastically of fresh orders for British workshops and cheaper supplies of raw materials, thus guaranteeing 'our great industry' and reducing 'our position of dependence on America'. One Manchester M.P., Edward Fielden, exclaimed wildly, 'We in Lancashire will take that 10 millions in both hands but we will only take it as an instalment of what is to come'.[71] It is worth emphasising that this loan was ostensibly for railway development in East Africa, not a gift to Lancashire, that the cabinet had so far only approved the loan in principle and that the East Africa Loans Act was not in fact to be passed until December 1926, fourteen months later.[72]

The reason for this delay was that neither the Colonial Office nor the East African governments were in a position to spend money. Much necessary preliminary surveying and planning had to be completed before construction could begin. The cabinet had agreed that no bill was necessary in the current parliamentary session, and this gave the Treasury the opportunity not only to postpone legislation but also, in their eyes, to repair some of the damage caused by the capitulation of the Chancellor and the cabinet to the principle of an

East African guaranteed loan. In subsequent negotiations with the Colonial Office over the drafting of a bill, the Treasury insisted upon Colonial Office adherence to particular terms. The principal issues concerned the payment of interest on the loans to be raised, the method of issuing the loans, and especially the role of an advisory committee in drawing up the schedule.

The East Africa Commission had recommended that the Imperial Exchequer should pay the interest for the first five years on loans raised by the territories because they were anxious not to over-burden local revenues by immediate debt liabilities.[73] This had been a Colonial Office stipulation since development works for the relief of unemployment were first debated in 1921. The £3,500,000 loan to Kenya and Uganda, free of interest for the first five years, was a recent precedent. The Treasury therefore naturally assumed that the Colonial Office would press for these generous terms, and they were not happy at the prospect of an additional burden being imposed on imperial finances. The commission's proposal was discussed by Treasury officials and rejected, partly on the grounds that colonial revenues were in any case probably adequate to sustain interest charges. But the Treasury also had little faith in the financial professionalism of colonial governments and the Colonial Office, and they feared that generous terms might tempt colonies into over-ambitious projects which would not be rapidly profit-making, and which would lead to debt liabilities after the initial five year period beyond the capacity of local revenues to bear. The Imperial government would therefore be obliged to step in and continue indirectly to finance colonial development with grants-in-aid. Alternative financial terms were therefore aired in the Treasury: interest for an initial period might be paid out of the capital raised, or, more harshly, the territories should at once meet the interest charges out of current revenue.[74]

The Colonial Office, following normal practice, had asked the Treasury to draw up the financial clauses of the guaranteed loans bill.[75] The terms finally produced merely stated that interest and sinking fund payments on the loans would rank as prior charges on the general revenues of the territory over whatever other charges were incurred by the colonial governments after the passing of the act.[76] Nothing specific was said about the method of interest payments. The intention evidently was that a territory could pay interest out of its revenues or out of the capital it raised as it thought best; hence the lack of specification. What was deliberately eliminated was the option of Imperial government payment of the interest for five years. But a further limitation had been accidentally incorporated. In 1927 when Tanganyika began preparations for raising a loan under the act, the Law Officers ruled that payment of interest out of the capital was not allowed because this use of the loan had not been specified in the schedule to the act. Interest would have to be paid at once out of the territory's revenue.[77]

The significance of this episode lies not so much in the accident of the bad drafting of the bill, but in the Colonial Office's apparent acceptance of the shift away from the generous terms proposed by Ormsby-Gore's East Africa Commission. The responsibility seems to lie with Amery. The memorandum which Amery put to the cabinet in October proposing the measure, was, according to a note written by Amery to Churchill, 'in conformity with the lines of our talk the other day'.[78] In the memorandum, Amery referred to the East Africa Commission's suggestion that the Treasury should pay interest charges for five years, but he continued, 'I hope however that the dependencies may be able to meet the interest charges from the outset', or alternatively that they might be met from the capital raised, the size of the loan being increased for that purpose.[79] Why did Amery offer such a concession? The answer must lie in the nature and purpose of the memorandum. It was drawn up with Churchill's approval for submission to the cabinet, and it is probable that in order to win agreement for the principle of the guaranteed loan, Amery accepted a compromise with the Chancellor. This was Amery's first piece of major development legislation and he may have underrated the Treasury's ability to force him to stick to the terms of his memorandum. In his eagerness to get Churchill's co-operation he may have overplayed his hand. There is also some indication that Amery precipitated action on the bill before the required terms had been thought out, because, unexpectedly, the Crown Agents refused to incur liabilities for ordering materials for colonial development schemes on the strength of cabinet approval of only the principle of a bill. They wanted the bill to pass through Parliament first, or at least required the Treasury and the Colonial Office to agree on specific terms.[80] The consequent haste resulted in carelessness. It was later a fundamental criticism of the East Africa Loans Act, and one used to explain the failure of the territories concerned to take up the facilities offered, that they were obliged under the act to face immediate charges upon their revenues.[81]

While Amery and the Colonial Office seem to have accepted without protest the Treasury's stance on interest payments, they made a curious fuss about the method of raising the loans. The Crown Agents normally arranged the issuing of loans raised by colonial governments on their own credit, and when the Colonial Office asked the Treasury in October 1925 to draft the guaranteed loans bill, Amery stipulated that the Crown Agents should have sole responsibility for raising the guaranteed loans as and when required. Faced with Treasury objections, Sir Samuel Wilson, the permanent under-secretary, claimed there were precedents for this procedure and he warned Niemeyer that he would call at the Treasury to press the case. 'I am writing in the meantime so that you may be prepared for me with all your artillery and in the meantime I will be digging in.' The guns the Treasury trundled up were formidable. Moreover, the Colonial Office's defences were flimsy. Research in the Treasury records revealed that the precedents quoted by the Colonial Office were false. Therefore Niemeyer and his colleagues insisted upon adherence to a principle: loans guaranteed by the Imperial government were raised on British government credit, hence their attraction in the market, and they constituted British and not colonial government loans and must be issued accordingly by the Treasury through the Bank of England and not by the Crown Agents. Niemeyer added that if the loans were not issued through the Bank of England this would seem odd in the City and the loans would suffer, and that in any case a Crown Agents issue was more expensive than one through the Bank of England.[82]

Amery and Wilson refused to accept these arguments and pushed this ostensibly minor and technical matter to a cabinet decision. In March 1926, nearly four months after the Treasury had first disputed the Colonial Office proposal, the Colonial Office put their case in a paper for the cabinet. The Treasury drafted a counterblast. The arguments employed on both sides are instructive. The Colonial Office disparaged the significance of the Imperial government guaran-tee. They argued that the Secretary of State would watch over the financial interests of the British taxpayer, that the loans were raised primarily on the security of colonial government revenues, that the guarantee only added the additional security of Treasury support, that even if there were no guarantee the Imperial government could not allow a British colony to default and that, finally, 'the effect of the guarantees on the credit of the Imperial Government may be regarded as negligible; the total amount involved being so small as compared with the obligations of that Government'. The Treasury were not impressed by this interpretation. A guaranteed loan was not raised on the security of colonial revenues but on the credit of the British government, and the Treasury did not regard as insignificant the addition of several £ millions of new guaranteed stock to their market responsibilities. The conflict between the two departments resulted in the inevitable victory of the more prestigious office. At a cabinet meeting on 31 March 1926 Amery added the arguments that the Crown Agents needed the commission they would earn and that the issue of guaranteed loans by them would raise the general attractivenes of all loans they issued. But the cabinet accepted the Treasury's case that all stocks for which the Imperial government were responsible by guarantee or otherwise should be issued in the ordinary manner to which the money market was accustomed, that is, through the Bank of England. Amery recorded, 'Winston's dramatic appeal to "fundamental principle" was pompously upheld by Austen [Chamberlain]'.[83]

Lurking behind Amery's attempt to help Crown Agents' finances lay his more important desire to achieve administrative independence in the handling of the development loans. The Colonial Office and the Crown Agents, as the Treasury were aware, usually worked hand-in-glove. Amery wished to have behind him the sanction to raise guaranteed loans up to £10 million free from close Treasury supervision. That was why the Treasury insisted on adherence to the normal procedures which gave them control over the issuing and managing of the loans. The Treasury had been forced to give way on the cabinet-approved general policy of East African development, but they were determined to exercise their authority to check Amery's freedom of action. This is also clearly demonstrated in the protracted struggle over the advisory committee.

When the Colonial Office formally asked the Treasury on 31 October 1925 to draft the terms of the East African guaranteed loans bill, they candidly admitted that it was not possible to append a detailed schedule of the works to be carried out. The essential pre-liminary studies in most cases had not been completed. Therefore they asked for a schedule to be included which would describe only in general terms the type of work to be undertaken. The Colonial Office believed there were precedents for such a 'vague schedule'.[84] This was utterly unacceptable to senior staff in the Treasury who dismissed the precedents as inapplicable. They suspected, correctly, that Amery was attempting to obtain primary responsibility for assessing and approving East African development schemes as they matured, and they believed that such power would be abused, accidentally or otherwise, by a Colonial Office they regarded as professionally doubtful in financial matters.[85] That was why Niemeyer privately arranged for the appointment of an independent advisory committee. Ever since the East Africa Commission had reported in July 1925 he had been unofficially in contact with Sir James Currie, director of the Empire Cotton Growing Corporation, and Sir George Schuster, formerly a business director and member of the Trade Facilities Advisory Committee and currently Financial Secretary to the Sudan government. Evidently both men were regarded as 'sound' on financial matters. On 22 October 1925 Currie and Niemeyer exchanged letters airing the idea for an advisory committee to assess the development projects to be financed by the guaranteed loans to which Churchill had just agreed. Niemeyer suggested that proposals should be vetted by a small committee made up of 'one of your cotton people' plus a City expert or railway engineer, under the chairmanship of Schuster. 'We must get this business out of the hands of my Colonial Office brethren', he concluded. On 30 October Currie wrote to Ormsby-Gore, sending a copy of his letter to Niemeyer. Following Niemeyer's line, he recommended that an *ad hoc* committee should be set up to consider East African development plans. He claimed that the Treasury would simply accept its conclusions 'and would not submit your projects to further examination'. He even obligingly offered some names for the committee: Schuster, R. H. Jackson, chairman of the Empire Cotton Growing Corporation, and Brigadier-General Hammond, a consultant on railway engineering. The Colonial Office fell for this proposition. On 6 November Sir Samuel Wilson wrote to Niemeyer to propose such a committee and to recommend, as three acceptable members, Schuster, Jackson and Hammond. Niemeyer replied on 10 November and agreed that such a committee ought to start preliminary investigations at once. Shortly afterwards he had the pleasure of informing Schuster about 'the great conspiracy'. He told him that he would receive 'a letter from the Colonial Office asking you to preside over a Committee ... to vet the Colonial Office scheme for applying their £10 million guaranteed loan. I am very pleased about this .... At present the Colonial Office simply see a blank spot in the centre of Africa and say "let there be roads – the cost we know not (nor whither we go): but the loan is always by us"'.[86]

The Colonial Office had been rather cleverly deceived. The advisory committee which Sir Samuel Wilson and his colleagues had in mind was different from that envisaged by Niemeyer and his team. Colonial Office staff thought of it as their agent. Wilson explained to Ormsby-Gore: 'What we have to remember is that the Committee is more or less camouflage and is really being set up in order to try and facilitate our getting Treasury approval to any proposals put forward by the C.O.'.[87] Initially it appeared to fulfil that function. It began its work early in 1926 and in March produced a report recommending a loan expenditure of £1,268,636 on railways and other works in Tanganyika, and the Treasury accepted the proposals without hesitation.[88] But on 20 May 1926 Niemeyer informed Wilson that in drafting the guaranteed loans bill he had consulted Sir George Schuster and they had agreed on the necessary terms. The draft bill was sent to the Colonial Office for their comments. One observation that could have been made was to note the remarkable way in which the Colonial Office's 'camouflage' was exposed as a Treasury trap. The bill included a written-in provision for a permanent advisory committee which had to be consulted before loan expenditure could be approved. The Colonial Office were indignant, since they regarded the Schuster committee as simply a temporary tool to be employed until the act was passed. It was merely 'set up to facilitate the passing of the Bill'. 'Surely the Committee is one set up by the Secretary of State to advise him, and not, as almost seems, a Committee set up by the Treasury to which to refer the Secretary of State's proposals'. It was too gross an intrusion into Colonial Office responsibilities and was rejected in their reply to Niemeyer.[89]

Heated exchanges sped around Whitehall. Niemeyer claimed, rather dubiously, that a permanent advisory committee was fundamental to the Treasury's initial agreement to the bill. The Colonial Office denied this assertion. When the Treasury described the terms they offered as generous, Sir Samuel Wilson replied, 'I cannot quite make out where the generosity came in as, so far as I can see, you wished to turn down all our suggestions but perhaps it is because you did not go so far as telling me that I was a "... fool"!' He minuted: 'This correspondence shows how difficult it is to discuss anything with Sir O. Niemeyer'. He began to wonder if it was worth proceeding with the guarantee idea: 'I am not at all sure that it will enable us to raise money on very much easier terms', and it would give the Treasury bureaucrats dangerous opportunities to interfere in 'our work'. He added, 'I am afraid it is sheer waste of time my trying to discuss anything with Sir O. Niemeyer. In his opinion "Sir O.N." is the only one who can do anything, and no one else has any right to hold views contrary to his!' Even Ormsby-Gore became pessimistic. He feared that a permanent advisory committee would lead to excessive delay, and except in the case of Tanganyika where schemes were already prepared, 'I am not at all sure whether as it stands the bill is of any value to us in East Africa'.[90]

Meanwhile, Niemeyer was unburdening his complaints on Churchill. By July 1926 the bill had been drawn up and the text had been accepted by the Colonial Office except for the clause on the statutory committee. Niemeyer explained that the bill sanctioned the granting of a guarantee only after the proposals had been vetted by this committee and that he attached great importance to its work. While the Colonial Office wished to dismiss the Schuster committee after it had drawn up a rough schedule to be incorporated in the bill, the Treasury insisted that the committee should be retained after the act had passed through Parliament in order to scrutinize individual projects to be financed under the act as they appeared. 'Mr. Amery', he concluded, 'is always trying to get away from any vestige of financial control and has financial ideas of his own which are frequently remote from financial facts'.[91]

Amery tried to appeal over the heads of Treasury officials by despatching on 8 July 1926 a personal letter to Churchill. He attempted to soothe Treasury fears by happily agreeing that the Secretary of State should of course refer projects to an advisory committee if he felt that would be helpful. But a statutory obligation to consult a committee before making any allocation, however small, would cause practical inconveniences and delays. This personal letter gathered an accretion of Treasury criticisms before being sent on to Churchill. Niemeyer explained the functions of the committee as he saw it. In the first stage, the committee was to approve schemes in general and authorize expenditure on the surveys and so on which were necessary in drawing up detailed schemes in the colonies. At the second stage, after local information had been gathered, the committee would consider whether to authorize expenditure on individual projects. If approved, the Treasury would then arrange for a guarantee to be given on the loans to be raised. This would complete the committee's work and they would not be involved if minor variations subsequently occurred. Amery, Niemeyer claimed, was trying to cut out the important second stage. Churchill's private secretary attached his interpretation of Amery's intentions to Amery's letter: 'Amery says that the function of the Committee is to bless provisionally certain projects in advance of surveys, local enquiries and then to fade away leaving him to settle the actual scheme by haggling with the Treasury and manufacturing public opinion'. Churchill had backed his officials at each stage of these exchanges and he did not let them down at this point. In reply to Amery he simply quoted the advisory committees set up by the Trade Facilities Act of 1921 and the Export Credits Act of 1920 as inescapable and valuable precedents.[92]

This drew from the Colonial Office a further indignant reply, drafted by Ormsby-Gore and Amery together. It was a mixture of political bluff and rather tactless criticism of Treasury behaviour. Amery threatened to abandon the 'publicly announced' decision to proceed with the bill 'if I am not to be allowed to work it on reasonable lines'. This would be a great disappointment in 'our party'. The government would have failed to implement their promises to assist the development of the African dependencies, 'but I am already receiving evidence from East Africa that rather than be faced with any more control or delays they would prefer to get ahead on their own'. Amery tended to imply that the colonies were doing Britain a favour by accepting Imperial government aid. This cut little ice with the Treasury since they were doubtful of the value of colonial development for relieving unemployment. But it was the stick Amery insisted on wielding.

I am afraid the Treasury has never yet grasped the idea that it is more profitable to spend money in keeping the industries in this country engaged in the production of rails, bridging material and locomotives than in paying for doles or unproductive relief schemes, or that the object of an Imperial guarantee should be to facilitate progress and not to find pretexts for making all progress impossible.

Churchill remained unimpressed. In reply he adopted Niemeyer's claim that the creation of a permanent advisory committee was an essential part of his original acceptance of the guaranteed loan plan.[93]

Amery made one last appeal but his attempt to mollify Churchill merely aggravated Churchill's advisers. He admitted that in his previous letter he might have been a little hasty, but 'your people' were obstinate on a matter 'where we had agreed in substance', and made him suspect that 'your subordinates, not you' wanted to subject every detail of expenditure to scrutiny leading to delay. Niemeyer did not like that and minuted so. Amery went on to admit that he might have done them wrong, for he now realised that the Treasury's proposal did not require constant reference to the advisory committee but only prior consultation before any loan was raised. 'Exactly', commented Niemeyer. But then Amery argued that between departments of the same government such a statutory committee was still unnecessary. While prepared to submit proposed programmes to a committee whenever a new instalment of the loan was to be raised, 'I really do object strongly to a statutory proviso set forth in detail which puts myself and the East African Government in the position of a private speculator bringing his schemes before an authority protecting the public interest'. Rather ingenuously he added that if Churchill therefore agreed that a statutory committee was not needed 'we could run it through Cabinet tomorrow'. A final line was particularly indiscreet. He would, Amery added, be really grateful 'if you'd include an extra £1½ million for Iraq railways'. '*No*' thundered Niemeyer, 'we can't go on extending guarantees'.[94]

Amery's letter prompted Niemeyer to draw up a final memorandum for Churchill. The Treasury, he stated, were not opposed to East African development; they had agreed 'at considerable damage to our general financial policy' to support the proposal. But to spend to advantage, full business advice was needed and this the committee would provide. Its work would be completed when it had reported to the Treasury on the viability of proposals. He stressed the value of the Trade Facilities Advisory Committee which had similarly considered the economic and financial advantages of projects put forward. Moreover, since the schedule to the East Africa loans bill was so vague, Parliament could be expected to challenge it, and the provision of an advisory committee was a necessary defence.[95]

Since deadlock still ensued between the departments the often threatened appeal to cabinet was made. The issue was a foregone conclusion. The Home Affairs Committee studying the bill had shown little sympathy for Amery but had reserved the matter for the cabinet. At the cabinet on 14 July, Amery gave way to the general view of his colleagues.[96] This success for the Treasury view is an interesting comment on the Secretary of State's authority. Although he had won cabinet approval for a colonial development policy, there was no challenge to the Treasury's financial omnipotence. Precedents and Treasury prestige far outweighed Amery's desire for departmental independence. A change in policy was easier to achieve than an alteration in administrative method.

A further five months elapsed before the bill became law. The Schuster Committee produced its second report outlining acceptable East African development schemes in the middle of July 1926. At the end of the month copies of the report were sent to the colonies concerned for their observations, and delays ensued awaiting replies.[97] The matter had by this stage become simply a problem for the Colonial Office and colonial governments. The financial resolution to the bill was introduced into the Commons on 21 July 1926, and the bill was given the Royal Assent on 15 December.[98]

4. CONCLUSION

The passage of the East Africa Loans Act, like the earlier agreement to provide an imperial loan of £3,500,000 to Kenya and Uganda, illustrates the substantial effect which the economic depression had on the making of colonial development policy. Metropolitan and colonial lobbies expressed not just the economic case for assisting development projects in East Africa as a way of encouraging Britain's export recovery. They had also picked up the political value of this cry. Ministers and party leaders were sensitive to the need to offer relief for unemployment, increasingly sensitive as the depression proved more than a temporary downturn and recovery was slow and incomplete. Unemployment featured prominently in election campaigns, and pledges were made which ministers felt obliged, to a certain extent, to honour. Hence the Labour government had no qualms in January 1924 about adopting as their own the scheme to assist Kenya and Uganda. Hence also the ability of Amery and Ormsby-Gore to exploit the anxieties of ministerial colleagues and win consent to the principle of an East African guaranteed loan. One Treasury official concluded that Amery was anxious to press on with his bill 'mainly, on political grounds, to placate Lancashire and show that the Conservatives have *done* something for the Empire'.[99]

The justification for assisting development schemes in East Africa had, however, shifted from that offered in the immediate post-war period. Supporters of the East Africa Loans Bill in 1926, like those who welcomed the £3,500,000 loan to Kenya and Uganda in 1924, regarded the long-term development of colonial markets and sources of supply as of at least equal value to the immediate stimulus they would give to British exports and employment. Long-term justifications were prominent in the memoranda Amery and Cunliffe-Lister had put to the cabinet. Interestingly, the East Africa Loans Act included provision for expenditure on scientific research, the benefits of which would necessarily be long-term. Similarly, in the House of Commons debate on the bill, Amery emphasised the value of East African development as a means of developing overseas markets and sources of supply and of removing a dangerous dependence on the United States. Other speakers took up this theme, so that while the value of immediate orders for iron and steel from railway projects was by no means ignored, there was a distinct shift from an emphasis on merely short-term gains towards an appreciation of the broader benefits of imperial economic development for Britain's long-term economic needs. 'East Africa', it was claimed, 'can in future become the Eldorado of the 20th century'.[100]

While the £3,500,000 loan to Kenya and Uganda and the East Africa Loans Act had similar origins and purposes, there were, however, important differences between the schemes. For one thing, the earlier measure constituted, for the time, a substantial financial concession by the Treasury, an effective and expensive departure from the rule of economy. The East Africa Loans Act on the other hand was in practice limited and unhelpful. Its terms were far less generous than those envisaged by the East Africa Commission. The Treasury had been unhappy with Churchill for conceding the principle of a £10 million guaranteed loan, but in subsequent negotiations, helped by Amery's miscalculations, they succeeded in limiting the price of this setback. In particular, there was to be no Imperial government subsidising of interest charges on colonial loans, and the inclusion of a statutory advisory committee in the administration of the scheme gave them remote control over the issuing of guarantees. The Colonial Office's inability to produce planned and costed schemes in 1925–26 contrasted with their presentation of mature development plans in 1923–24, and this weakness gave the Treasury their opportunity to reassert their control over the extent and destination of aid. As a result, Colonial Office staff were soon disillusioned with the measure. Sir Samuel Wilson was reluctant to proceed with the restrictive terms imposed by the Treasury, and even Ormsby-Gore, the author of the original proposal, reluctantly admitted in November 1926 'I doubt seriously whether the £10 million loan bill is worth proceeding with'.[101] Kenya soon decided not to raise a loan with an Imperial government guarantee lest it damage her credit status. By the end of December 1929 Schuster's committee had recommended guaranteed loans totalling only £6,680,020 and only £3,500,000 had been actually spent.[102]

The evidence shows that Amery alone was anxious to press on in spite of the terms of the East Africa Loans Bill. His impetuosity may be explained either as a blind enthusiasm for the cause of imperial development or by a sensitivity to the political pressures upon him and the Conservative government. But it is also essential to realise that the proposal represented for Amery a significant breach with the *ad hoc* responses of earlier colonial development schemes, like the £3,500,000 loan to Kenya and Uganda. What he was seeking was the creation of a colonial development fund, although admittedly reserved for East African interests, but nonetheless a large financial supply which he as Secretary of State would be at liberty to spend as and when schemes were prepared. He wanted to avoid constant begging for new funds from the Treasury and Parliament when need demanded. This £10 million was intended to form a general source of supply which would make the development of East African territories no longer subject to the budgetary considerations of the British government. Hence his attempts to secure the issuing of the loans through the Crown Agents and his campaign to demote the role and authority of the advisory committee which the Treasury had inserted into the scheme. In other words the East Africa Loans Act was intended to break with the Imperial government's restricted colonial development policy. It was a preliminary attempt by Amery to create a general colonial development fund.

NOTES

1. Minute by Skevington 7 Jan. 1921, T161/76/S.5954/1.
2. L.-J. L. Nthenda, 'H.M. Treasury and the Problems of Nyasaland Public Finances 1919 to 1940', Oxford D.Phil., 1972.
3. E. A. Brett, *Colonialism and Underdevelopment in East Africa*, London, 1973, pp.63-5; P. S. Gupta, *Imperialism and the British Labour Movement 1914–1964*, London, 1975, p.72.
4. Report of Colonial Office Economy Committee 27 July 1921, CO 431/148/Treas 39529; see above p.91.

5. Treas. to C.O. 15 Jan. 1921 and C.O. to Treas. 21 Jan. 1921, CO 536/115/Treas 2453 and T 161/76/S.5954/1.

6. C.O. to Governor 3 June 1921, CO 536/116/CO 27891; Deputy Governor Jarvis to C.O. 15 June 1921 and C.O. to Jarvis 21 June 1921, CO 536/112/Gov 30243; Jarvis to C.O. 24 June 1921, CO 536/116/Gov 31871.

7. C.O. to Treas. 29 Aug. 1921, CO 431/148/Treas 39529; Skevington to Batterbee 6 Sept. 1921, minutes by Batterbee and Bottomley, 12 and 13 Sept. 1921, CO 536/116/Treas 44835.

8. Bottomley to Skevington 24 Oct. 1921, CO 536/114/Gov 52231; see also minute by Bottomley, 7 Oct. 1921, CO 536/116/Treas 44835 and by Batterbee 1 Nov. 1921, CO 431/149/Treas 48997. For the Churchill memo. of 28 Sept. 1921 see above p.94.

9. For the background to the East African war liability see above p.73.

10. Minute by Bottomley 1 Dec. 1920, CO 536/103/Gov 54344; see also correspondence 4 Dec. 1920 – 27 Jan. 1921 on T161/76/S.5954/1.

11. Jarvis to C.O. 16 Aug. 1921, CO 536/113/Gov 41628 and Jarvis to C.O. 10 Nov. 1921 and Read to Treas. 28 Nov. 1921, CO 536/114/Gov 56509.

12. Minute by Skevington 4 Jan. 1922, approved by Headlam, Meiklejohn and Niemeyer, Barstow to C.O. T161/147/S.13303; for the repayment agreement reached with Kenya in September 1921 see above pp.81-3.

13. *Third Report of the Committee on National Expenditure*, Cmd.1584, 1922, p.10; memo. by Bottomley, Jan. 1922, CO 536/122/Treas 2111.

14. Minutes 16 Jan. – 2 Feb. 1922, and Bottomley to Treas. 4 Feb. 1922, CO 536/122/Treas 2111. Sutherland was acting under-secretary during the absence of Edward Wood on a tour of the West Indies; see *Looking Back, the Autobiography of the Duke of Sutherland*, London, 1957, p.101.

15. Jarvis to C.O. 7 March 1922, minute by Batterbee 9 March 1922, CO 536/118/Gov 11260.

16. Barstow to C.O. 16 March 1922, T161/147/S.13303.

17. Draft by Bottomley 3 May 1922, CO 536/122/Treas 12678; final version CAB 24/138/CP 4169, draft by Bottomley CO 536/120/Gov 39674.

18. Churchill to Horne 26 Aug. 1922, CO 536/120/Gov 39674.

19. Treas. memo. on CP 4169, minute by Headlam 30 Aug. 1922 and Headlam to Batterbee in C.O. 2 Sept. 1922, T161/257/S.27989/01; Bottomley to Batterbee 2 Sept. 1922, CO 536/122/Treas 44077.

20. Scott to C.O. 18 Aug. 1922, CO 536/120/Gov 39674; for the appointment of the sub-committee see above p.92.

21. Minutes by Bottomley, Read, Masterton-Smith and Stevenson, 28–29 Sept. 1922, CO 536/120/Gov 48246; minute by Bottomley 28 May 1923, CO 536/128/Treas 24694.

22. C.O. to Treas. 6 Dec. 1922, CO 536/120/Gov 52997; minutes by Cuthbertson and Headlam 8–9 Jan. 1923 and Barstow to C.O. 16 Jan. 1923, T161/197/S.18649/1.

23. Archer to C.O. 28 Feb. 1923, minutes by Seel, Bottomley and Ormsby-Gore, 13–27 March 1923, C.O. to Treas. 29 March 1923, CO 536/124/Gov 11001; memo. of 30 April 1923, minute by Cuthbertson 9 May 1923, Barstow to C.O. 15 May 1923, T161/197/S.18649/1.

24. Minutes by Bottomley and Ormsby-Gore 28 and 29 May 1923 and Read to Treas. 31 May 1923, CO 536/128/Treas 24694; Barstow to C.O. 19 June 1923, T161/197/S.18649/1.

25. Minutes by Batterbee and Bottomley 1 and 3 March 1923, Read to Treas. 29 March 1923, CO 536/121/Gov 4436; Barstow to C.O. 8 May 1923, minute by Bottomley 9 May 1923, CO 536/128/Treas 23270; Read to Treas. 31 May

1923, CO 536/128/Treas 24694; Archer to C.O. 21 June 1923, CO 536/125/Gov 31305.

26. Archer to C.O. 25 July 1923, minute by Bottomley, CO 536/126/Gov 37469; Read to Treas. 17 Aug. 1923, CO 536/126/Gov 39192; minutes by Penson 17 and 30 Aug. 1923, Cuthbertson to Bottomley 2 Oct. 1923, T161/197/S.18649/2.

27. Parkinson to Penson 11 Sept. 1923, CO 536/128/Treas 42393.

28. Archer to C.O. 17 Oct. 1923, Bottomley to Cuthbertson 13 Nov. 1923, CO 536/126/Gov 50907; minutes by Cuthbertson and Skevington, 14-17 Nov. 1923, Cuthbertson to Bottomley 16 Nov. 1923 and Headlam to Read 21 Nov. 1923, T161/197/S.18649/2.

29. Read to Headlam, 23 Nov. 1923, minutes by Bottomley, Read, Ormsby-Gore and Devonshire 10 Dec. 1923 – 1 Jan. 1924, Devonshire to Neville Chamberlain 4 Jan. 1924, CO 536/128/Treas 55494.

30. Memo. by Cuthbertson, minutes by Cuthbertson and Headlam, 7 Jan. 1924 and draft reply to Devonshire, T161/197/S.18649/2.

31. CO 533/288/CO 5409; CO 533/275/Gov 9258; CO 533/276/Gov 11251; CO 533/276/Gov 13195.

32. CO 533/303/CO 25338; CO 533/296/Gov 39987; CO 533/301/CA 50693; CO 533/284/Gov 62264.

33. CO 533/293/Gov 8413, Gov 16485, Gov 26073.

34. CO 536/121/Gov 4434; CO 536/126/Gov 49943.

35. Oldham Chamber of Commerce to C.O. 26 Sept. 1923, minutes by Bottomley, Read and Stevenson 16-19 Oct. 1923, CO 536/129/MI 47526. In Dec. 1923 Oldham Chamber of Commerce pressed the Colonial Office to describe their plans for Uganda and in Jan. 1924 the M.P. for Stockport called at the office to enquire, CO 536/129/MI 61780.

36. Memo. by Bottomley 23 Oct. 1923, CO 323/911/CO 51934; minute by Parkinson, 28 Aug. 1923, CO 323/910/CO 46434; see also minute by Bottomley 19 Oct. 1923, CO 536/129/MI 47526.

37. See above p.109.

38. Coryndon to C.O. 7 Nov. 1923, CO 533/298/Gov 54115; Denham, governor's deputy to C.O. 17 Nov. 1923 enclosing memo. by General Manager of the Uganda Railway, CO 533/298/Gov 60500.

39. Coryndon to C.O. 1 Dec. 1923 and minute by Machtig 5 Dec. 1923, CO 323/901/Gov 58934.

40. Minutes of Unemployment Committee 18 Dec. 1923, Howarth to Machtig 20 Dec. 1923, Machtig to Howarth 29 Dec. 1923 and memo. CU 610, 31 Dec. 1923, CO 323/912/CO 63020.

41. Minutes by Cuthbertson, Headlam and Niemeyer, 3-4 Jan. 1924, T161/1057/S.27769/1.

42. Minutes of 72nd meeting of Committee on Unemployment, 8 Jan. 1924, CO 323/929/MO 1900; Report of Committee on Unemployment, 9 Jan. 1924, CAB 24/164/CP 15.

43. Ormsby-Gore to Devonshire, 11 Jan. 1924, CO 533/319/CO 3309; the Treasury were aware that the financial assistance sought by Ormsby-Gore was substantially greater than that available under the Imperial Economic Conference terms, the latter being estimated at about £80,000, memo. by Meiklejohn 11 Jan. 1924, T161/1057/S.27769/1. The Treasury had reasserted their claims upon the revenue of the Uganda Railway on 4 Jan. 1924, CO 533/323/Treas 608, and see above pp.78-9, 82.

44. Cabinet minutes 11 Jan. 1924, CAB 23/46/CAB 3(24)5.

45. Memo. by Meiklejohn and minute by Guinness, 11 Jan. 1924, T161/1057/S.27769/1.

46. Devonshire to N. Chamberlain 14 Jan. 1924, CO 533/319/CO 3305.

47. Minutes by Cuthbertson and Meiklejohn 14-15 Jan. 1924 and memo. by Skevington 14. Jan. 1924, T161/1057/S.27769/1.

48. N. Chamberlain to Devonshire 18 Jan. 1924, minute by Headlam 1 Feb. 1924, *ibid.*; Ormsby-Gore to Devonshire 18 Jan. 1924, Devonshire to N. Chamberlain 19 Jan. 1924, CO 533/319/CO 3305; Barstow to C.O. 18 March 1924, CO 536/134/Treas 13161 and 13163 and CO 533/323/Treas 13158 and 13159. For the final settlement of the war debt and Uganda Railway debt see below pp.255-7.

49. Memo. by Read for Thomas 25 Jan. 1924, CO 533/319/CO 3305; Arnold to Webb 30 Jan. 1924, CO 323/920/BT 4556; Report of Unemployment Committee 7 Feb. 1924, CAB 24/164/CP 83; cabinet minutes 8 Feb. 1924, CAB 23/47/CAB 11(24)4; *Hansard* HC, vol.170, cols.185-211, 1068-94, 25 Feb. and 3 March 1924.

50. Minutes by Parkinson, 28 Aug. 1923, CO 323/910/CO 46434; by Read 19 Oct. 1923, CO 536/129/MI 47526; by Niemeyer 4 Jan. 1924, T161/1057/S.27769/1.

51. J. H. Thomas, *Hansard* HC, vol.170, col.196, 25 Feb. 1924; minute by Bottomley 26 Feb. 1924, CO 533/308/Gov 9297.

52. Minute by Ormsby-Gore 11 Jan. 1924, memo. by Read 25 Jan. 1924, and Explanatory Note 16 Jan. 1924, CO 533/319/CO 3305; J. H. Thomas, *Hansard* HC, vol.170, col. 196, and Amery col. 1075, and see also Harris, col.1072 and Gorman, col.1085, 3 March 1924.

53. Deputation to Thomas 4 April 1924, CO 533/319/CO 17103; discussion in Commons and announcement of membership of committees, *Hansard* HC, vol.172, cols.351-95, 8 April 1924, vol.175, cols.70-1, 23 June 1924, cols.930-1, 30 June 1924, vol.176, col.2500, 4 Aug. 1924; Gupta, *Imperialism and the British Labour Movement*, pp.72-7. The other members of the commission were Major A. G. Church M.P.(Lab.) and F. C. Linfield M.P.(Lib.).

54. *Report of the East Africa Commission*, Cmd.2387, 1925, espec. pp.10, 18-22, 182.

55. CO 533/342/MI 18441, MI 24662, MI 32641; CO 533/341/HC 29813, HL 30014, HC 30015, HC 34722; CO 533/344/I 25408; CO 533/339/CO 34117; see also M. F. Hill, *Permanent Way. The Story of the Kenya and Uganda Railway*, 2nd ed. Nairobi, 1961, p.457.

56. *Memorandum on Transport Development and Cotton Growing in East Africa*, Cmd.2463, 1925. For Ormsby-Gore's evidence see CO 533/342/MI 20166.

57. F. W. S. Craig, *British General Election Manifestos 1918–1966*, Chichester, 1970, p.30; memo. by N. Chamberlain for Unionist Party Leader's Conference, 1924, Worthington-Evans papers, Mss.Eng.Hist. c.895; see also resolution passed at Party Conference Oct. 1925, Baldwin Papers, vol.48.

58. Amery to Milner 13 Nov. 1924, Milner Papers 209; Milner to Amery 5 Jan. 1925, Amery Papers, Box 54, Folder C; see also Amery to Baldwin 28 Jan. 1924, Baldwin Papers, vol.42.

59. See, for example, minute by Cuthbertson 3 Oct. 1924, T161/1057/S.27769/1.

60. Amery to Churchill 16 July 1925 and Churchill to Amery 20 July 1925, T161/478/S.27798/1.

61. Amery to Churchill 7 Aug. 1925, minute by Bottomley, CO 533/340/CO 36430.

62. Mema. by Cunliffe-Lister 27 July and 6 Aug. 1925, CAB 24/174/CP 366 and CP 389; cabinet minutes 5 Aug. and 7 Aug. 1925, CAB 23/50/CAB 43(25)12 and CAB 44(25)6.

63. Minutes of 89th Meeting Cabinet Committee on Unemployment, 7 Oct. 1925, CAB 27/191.

64. CO 533/339/CO 27083 and subsequent papers.

65. Mema. by Cuthbertson and Barstow, 29 Sept. and 1 Oct. 1925, T161/478/S.27798/1.

66. Draft reply to Amery, submitted to Churchill 12 Oct. 1925, *ibid.*

67. J. Barnes and D. Nicholson, eds., *The Leo Amery Diaries*, vol. 1, London,

1980, 13 Oct. 1925, p.421; Churchill to Barstow and Niemeyer 13 Oct. 1925, T161/478/S.27798/1.
68. Mema. by Barstow and Niemeyer 19 Oct. 1925, *ibid.*.
69. Memo. by Amery 15 Oct. 1925, CAB 24/175/CP 434.
70. *Leo Amery Diaries*, 19, 21 and 23 Oct. 1925, pp.423-4; cabinet minutes 23 Oct. 1925, CAB 23/51/CAB 50(25)7; *Bristol Times and Mirror*, 24 Oct. 1925, Amery Papers, Box G.100; see also *The Times*, 24 Oct. 1925.
71. CO 533/340/CO 36430.
72. The measure was merged with another scheme to provide a guarantee for a loan to Palestine of £4,500,000: hence the act's full title was the Palestine and East Africa Loans Act, 16 and 17 Geo.5, Ch.62.
73. *Report of the East Africa Commission*, Cmd.2387, p.182.
74. Memo. by Barstow 1 Oct. 1925, draft letter to Amery sent to Churchill 12 Oct. 1925, memo. on East African Railways, n.d., T161/478/S.27798/1; minutes by Hardman, Cuthbertson, Stocks 3–5 Nov. 1925, T161/478/S.27798/2.
75. Strachey to Treas. 31 Oct. 1925, CO 533/340/CO 48492.
76. Niemeyer to Wilson enclosing draft bill, 20 May 1926, CO 533/353/Treas 4427 and Palestine and East Africa Loans Act, 1926, clause 2(c).
77. T161/256/S.27798/03, espec. Law Officer's Opinion 9 Dec. 1927.
78. Amery to Churchill 15 Oct. 1925, T161/478/S.27798/1.
79. Memo. by Amery 15 Oct. 1925, *ibid.*, and CAB 24/175/CP 434.
80. Minutes by Strachey 28 Oct. 1925 and Amery 29 Oct. 1925, CO 533/340/CO 48492; minutes by Stocks 5 and 10 Nov. 1925, T161/478/S.27798/2.
81. See, for example, W. Graham, 'The Finance of East African Development', *Empire Review*, 44 (Nov. 1926), 437-40.
82. Strachey to Treas. 31 Oct. 1925, CO 533/340/CO 48492; Niemeyer to Wilson 21 Nov. 1925, Wilson to Niemeyer 26 Jan. 1926, minute by Young 27 Jan. 1926, Niemeyer to Wilson 29 Jan. 1926, T161/478/S.27798/2.
83. Mema. by Amery and by Treasury 24 March 1926, CAB 24/179/CP 129 and CP 130; cabinet minutes 31 March 1926, CAB 23/52/CAB 14(26)7; *Leo Amery Diaries*, 31 March 1926, p.448.
84. Strachey to Treas. 31 Oct. 1925 and minute by Green 28 Oct. 1925, CO 533/340/CO 48492.
85. Minutes by Hardman, Cuthbertson, Stocks and Phillips 3–19 Nov. 1925, T161/478/S.27798/2.
86. Correspondence of Niemeyer with Schuster, Currie and Wilson 2 Aug.–23 Nov. 1925, Niemeyer Papers, T176/20.
87. Minutes by Wilson 25 Nov., Strachey 15 Dec. and Wilson 18 Dec. 1925, CO 533/340/CO 52785.
88. First Interim Report of Schuster Committee, 18 March 1926, minute by Green 18 March 1926, CO 533/352/CO 2745; minutes by Hardman 7 April 1926 and Stocks 8 April 1926, and Treas. to C.O. 12 April 1926, T161/478/S.27798/01/1.
89. Niemeyer to Wilson 20 May 1926, minutes by Bottomley, Machtig, Strachey 24–26 May 1926, Wilson to Niemeyer 3 June 1926, CO 533/353/Treas.4427.
90. Niemeyer to Wilson 15 June 1926, minutes by Bottomley, Machtig, Strachey, Wilson 17–22 June 1926, Wilson to Niemeyer 28 June 1926, minutes by Ormsby-Gore and Wilson 7 July 1926, CO 533/353/Treas.5199.
91. Niemeyer to Churchill 3 July 1926, T161/256/S.27798/02.
92. Amery to Churchill 8 July 1926, CO 533/353/Treas.5199; minutes by Niemeyer and Grigg 9 July 1926, Churchill to Amery 10 July 1926, T161/256/S.27798/02.
93. Amery to Churchill 12 July 1926, Churchill to Amery 12 July 1926, CO 533/353/Treas.5199.
94. Amery to Churchill 13 July 1926, T161/256/S.27798/02.

95. East African Loan Committee, memo. by Niemeyer 13 July 1926, *ibid.*.
96. Minutes of Home Affairs Committee 5 July 1926, *ibid.*; cabinet minutes 14 July 1926, CAB 23/53/CAB 46(26)11.
97. *Report of the East African Guaranteed Loan Committee*, Cmd.2701, 1926; CO 533/352/CO 5662.
98. *Hansard* HC, vol.198, col.1321; *Hansard* HL, vol.65, col.1708; 16 and 17 Geo.5, ch.62.
99. Minute by Stocks 10 Nov. 1925, T161/478/S.27798/2.
100. *Hansard* HC, vol.198, cols.1321-66 espec. 1325-6, 1343, 1346; vol.200, cols. 1271-1334, 1521, 1984-2045, 2327-2406, 2437, 2589 espec. 1288-9, 1997, 1999-2000; *Hansard* HL, vol.65, cols.1534, 1611-31.
101. Minutes by Wilson 7 July 1926, CO 533/353/Treas.5199 and by Ormsby-Gore 22 Nov. 1926, CO 533/350/Gov.7732.
102. *Report of the East African Guaranteed Loan Committee 1926–1929*, Cmd.3494, 1930.

VII

THE COLONIAL DEVELOPMENT
ACT 1929

1. *THE ORIGINS OF THE COLONIAL DEVELOPMENT BILL*

Amery's continued tenure of the Colonial Office in the 1920s enabled him to apply lessons learned from his negotiations over the East Africa guaranteed loans in subsequent initiatives. The need to do so was for Amery all too apparent, since he remained convinced that imperial economic development was the only answer to Britain's economic problems. Although a backlog of orders in heavy industry after the General Strike allowed unemployment to dip briefly below 10%, Britain did not greatly benefit from the recovery in world trade during 1927–29. It could therefore be less easily claimed that the trade cycle was merely at a temporary nadir, nor was there much sign that the return to the gold standard had been of advantage. A structural economic problem was exposed, to confirm Amery's earlier analysis of the long-term difficulties from which the country was suffering. As he put it in a memorandum to the cabinet in July 1928, 'Hard facts are beginning to compel us to realise that our troubles are neither temporary nor due to purely external causes, but are fundamental and inherent in our own national policy'.[1] Accordingly Amery continued to press for the extension of tariff protection with imperial preferences and the sustained funding of empire settlement programmes.[2] Moreover, Baldwin's government had set up an Empire Marketing Board in 1926 with a nominal annual grant of £1 million. Its purpose was to encourage an increase in the consumption of imperial products by financing research into problems of production and marketing, by providing information services and by conducting publicity campaigns for imperial goods. The financial arrangement for the spending of the E.M.B.'s grant was of particular importance to Amery. Although the size of its annual grant was fixed only after negotiations with the

Treasury, the money obtained came under the control of the Secretary of State for spending at his discretion, without being subject to close Treasury scrutiny. Frequently in the past Amery had toyed with the idea of a colonial development fund: the virtues of the E.M.B.'s fund in his eyes renewed the attractions of the idea, particularly in contrast with the vexatious control retained by the Treasury over the guaranteeing of loans to East Africa.[3]

The political need to tackle the economic problem was also apparent to Amery and others in the Conservative party. A general election was due in 1929 and the government's failure to find a solution to unemployment left it vulnerable to criticism. In June 1928 cabinet ministers discussed the subject once again; as Amery commented, 'the steady increase of unemployment this summer is giving them all furiously to think'. Likewise in October 1928, the party's concern was expressed by Sir Montague Barlow, a former Conservative Minister of Labour, in a letter to Baldwin circulated to cabinet ministers: the rising unemployment figures alarmed him since 'widespread industrial irritation is apt to find expression through the Ballot Box to the detriment of the Government in power'.[4] Moreover, in 1928 and 1929 the Labour and Liberal parties published their programmes for tackling the depression and appealed for electoral support. *Labour and the Nation* proposed the establishment of an Employment and Development Board drawing on an annual Treasury grant to ensure that 'the national estate is scientifically developed and that useful employment is found for those who at present must endure the misery of involuntary idleness'. The Liberals' comprehensive report *Britain's Industrial Future* and their bold manifesto *We Can Conquer Unemployment* described several radical measures including large-scale domestic public works to push the economy into recovery.[5]

It was necessary for Conservative ministers to discover alternatives. The Industrial Transference Board set up in 1928 devised schemes to encourage the migration of unemployed workers from the depressed areas to assumed opportunities elsewhere in Britain or in the dominions.[6] At the same time Churchill was pressing upon his colleagues a scheme for the de-rating of industry and agriculture to encourage new investment.[7] Amery, however, was determined that the imperial development option should not be ignored. Even the Labour and Liberal parties had observed in some of their statements that the development of the empire's economic resources would help Britain's economic recovery,[8] but Amery was anxious to identify the

Conservative party with this particular platform. The Conservatives had reiterated their commitment to empire development at their party conference in October 1926, and Sir Montague Barlow urged the promotion of colonial development schemes in his letter to the Prime Minister in October 1928.[9] Amery's problem was to transform these general sympathies of the party and many of his cabinet colleagues into a specific decision to commit a substantial grant to a colonial development fund. The Treasury and the Chancellor were bound to resist such claims upon their resources. Churchill, determined to finance his de-rating scheme, was additionally concerned to restrain expenditure elsewhere. At a cabinet meeting in July 1928, 'Mr. Churchill emphasised the impossibility of financing measures for dealing with unemployment without taxation, the nature of which he indicated and which he thought the Cabinet was unlikely to desire before a General Election'.[10] Faced with this kind of obstacle and aggravated equally by Churchill's dogged allegiance to free trade principles, Amery repeatedly complained to Baldwin about Churchill's obstructionism, and even proposed a cabinet reshuffle to put himself or Neville Chamberlain into the Treasury.[11] 'If Winston could only be induced to go away and wage war somewhere something might perhaps be done.'[12]

Amery's opportunity to revive the case for a colonial development fund followed when on 1 October 1928 the Minister of Labour reported to the cabinet a further deterioration in employment prospects.[13] This seems to have persuaded Baldwin to set up an Inter-Departmental Committee under Sir Warren Fisher, the permanent secretary at the Treasury, to consider fresh measures for dealing with unemployment. On 12 October the secretary of this committee blithely explained to the Colonial Office that 'what is wanted is something that will be rapid in action, and give the maximum amount of employment, if possible away from the distressed areas', and he inquired if anything could be done 'with development in the Colonies and Protectorates, particularly railways and bridges? – assuming you get Treasury approval?'[14]

This naive request for immediate short-term relief for unemployment by colonial development fell on unenthusiastic ears. As Sir Gilbert Grindle, deputy under-secretary, minuted, 'We have had such appeals before'.[15] Permanent staff had not as a rule been enthusiastic about them. Nothing had changed. The minutes on the proposal and the memorandum eventually drafted remained cautious, even hostile. On the one hand it was doubted if development could be quickly accelerated to help the unemployed, and on the other it was stressed that unless lavish assistance was provided by the Imperial government there was a danger of overburdening colonial revenues by expediting development schemes to suit metropolitan needs. 'There seems to be a real danger to the Colonies in pressing on development works too fast', concluded Sir Henry Lambert from the Crown Agents' Office. It was admitted that 'all this practically amounts to a profession of incapacity to do anything', and the tone of this comment was incorporated in Grindle's minute of 29 October 1928 which summed up Colonial Office reaction for Amery. He explained that they had been asked to expedite matters before 'in return for somewhat elusive financial assistance .... The Treasury do not seem to realise that it is no assistance, but a distinct burden to a solvent Colony to undertake any work until it is economically sound to do so'. When developments were economically sound, and staff and labour were available, 'no solvent Colony experiences any difficulty in raising the money for them. The only opening, therefore, for such deals as the Treasury contemplate is in grant-aided Protectorates, and, if it is not to constitute a burden on the Protectorate, it must take the form of an increase in the grant in aid for a definite purpose'.[16]

It is striking that the Colonial Office permanent staff uniformly expressed disillusionment with and distrust of proposals to link colonial development and the relief of British unemployment. It is equally striking that Amery rejected their views. He was determined to make the most of the opportunity presented by the unemployment crisis and the approaching general election to circumvent orthodox obstruction to government expenditure and to present a case for colonial development as a long-term solution to Britain's economic needs. 'I think the Memo and Sir G. Grindle's minute of 29/10 much too negative', he minuted. 'Surely there is a good deal to be done if Treasury will fairly and squarely pay (not lend) total interest for five years, or part interest for longer period, or if T. Facilities were revived on reasonable basis.' Development accelerated by imperial financial assistance would stimulate other projects and thus provide a continuous flood of purchases in British markets. On 9 November at a meeting with Ormsby-Gore, Sir Samuel Wilson and Grindle, Amery insisted on adopting a positive response, in spite of the continued scepticism of his advisers. The Inter-Departmental Committee were to be told that a more generous trade facilities scheme should be adopted, but in addition 'I should send in a personal letter to Winston to say that I could do a great deal if I were given my money to play with but could not possibly do anything on existing lines held up all the time'.[17]

Amery despatched his letter to Churchill on 26 November 1928. It repeated arguments now rather worn from past usage. The Colonial Empire could be of value in easing unemployment in Britain; colonial governments already spent substantial amounts of money in Britain purchasing stores and materials for public works; development increased local purchasing power to Britain's advantage. More could be done to help the unemployed, but only if the Imperial government offered generous financial assistance. 'The truth is that the attempts the Government have hitherto made to combine Colonial development with relief of unemployment led to little but correspondence, committees and delay.' The £10 million guaranteed loan scheme for East Africa with its unattractive terms was one such disappointment. Colonial governments could not be left to shoulder debt charges, and therefore 'if you want to come to business you must offer, on loans raised in approved cases for development, payment of the whole interest, say for a period of five years, and possibly half or three-quarters interest for a longer period till the revenue from the development comes in to the Colony'. The novelty lay in Amery's proposal to establish a colonial development fund to meet such charges on schemes 'undertaken with the definite view of providing markets for the home manufacturer and employment for home labour'. A sum of £500,000 a year should be allocated for this purpose, with unspent balances at the end of each year being carried forward to the next. Moreover, drawing on his experience of the Empire Marketing Fund, Amery insisted that the Secretary of State must have a free hand in the control of this fund. 'It is the principle of the "block grant" for which I am asking.'[18]

Perhaps suspecting an initially unfavourable response from the Treasury, Amery also took pains to put his case to cabinet colleagues. He sent a copy of this letter to Baldwin, and added a note explaining that 'Four years bitter experience have convinced me that any attempt to help the employment situation here by accelerating Colonial development is hopeless as long as matters are left to the Treasury, which is at bottom against all expenditure, whether on development or on anything else'. He pressed home his request for a block grant, because 'It is only on E.M.B. lines i.e. if the Treasury can make no saving by holding up things, that any progress is possible'. He sent another copy to Steel-Maitland, the Minister of Labour, with further observations on the need for a long-term strategy. 'The real trouble is that you cannot do anything if your idea is only to start urging colonial development during a panic, and expect results within six months. The only way is to have a continuous policy of development and that you cannot have with the present attitude prevailing in the Treasury.'[19]

Amery would need to win such allies, for his scheme was savaged by the Treasury officials who examined it. Not only were there strong doubts about the effectiveness of colonial development as an immediate relief for unemployment, but it was also argued that expenditure on colonial development would divert resources from domestic investment and actually damage Britain's economic recovery. There were no idle funds available for investment in the colonies; indeed, 'there is great competition for capital required for productive enterprises – the present rates of interest are evidence of that – and capital funds diverted to Mr. Amery's purpose will only diminish the supply for other more immediately profitable undertakings'. Moreover, Amery's insistence on generous terms of aid filled the Treasury with apprehension since they felt that schemes not paying their way in the short-term were likely to be commercially unsound. On the other hand, they reckoned that schemes likely to be quickly profitable needed only such modest assistance as a guarantee of interest on loans to be raised. But their scorn was principally directed at Amery's appeal for a free hand in the expenditure of money from his colonial development fund.

Mr. Amery wants to sweep away all restrictions, relieve the Colonial Government of all share in the financial risk for the first five years at least, and possibly more, abolish Treasury control, and substitute the 'block grant' system borrowed from the E.M.B., with himself in sole control, unhampered, apparently, even by an advisory committee. The idea is so preposterous that it is hardly necessary to argue it seriously .... The scheme is sheer financial immorality, a temptation to the Colonial Governments to embark on premature and ill-conceived enterprises by financial inducements which blind them to the ultimate risk.

Churchill did not spend much time on this issue. In a curt reply to Amery he argued that the scheme was impossible since Parliament would not tolerate the absence of Treasury control, nor did he feel grants to aid immature colonial enterprises would help unemployment in Britain. Furthermore the cost of Churchill's de-rating scheme for industry was all the Exchequer could bear at the moment.[20]

The response of the Colonial Office permanent staff to this rebuff was confined to a single minute: 'It seems clear from this unpromising reply that there is no prospect of Treasury approval of anything in the nature of the creation of a Colonial Development Fund on a substantial basis'.[21] But Amery must have complained personally to Churchill of the way in which the Treasury was obstructing colonial development since the Chancellor requested details of his accusations. These Amery supplied on 28 February 1929. He argued that his department and the Treasury had different objectives, and that in order to avoid friction and delay the block grant system was essential,

under which the department responsible for the policy can carry it out both expeditiously and economically .... I have had the experience now for some years of contrasting the efficiency, expedition and real economy of the work of the E.M.B. and the remarkable results it has achieved with comparatively small outlay, as compared with the work either of the Overseas Settlement Office or of the Colonial Office in connection with colonial development, and while admitting that conditions are not in every respect the same, I am also certain that in both the two latter cases far more could have been done and far better results achieved if I had had the same amount of money to spend under my own control.

He concluded that 'check and criticism by another department which is not interested in promoting a policy, but instinctively disposed to limit expenditure, may result, possibly, in some reduction of the amount actually spent but certainly in a reduction of the efficiency with which the money is spent'. Following this general condemnation of Treasury activities, he then listed examples of what he felt to be unwarranted Treasury restrictions on development financing, the terms of loans, advisory committees, delays and false economies. And he rounded off this attack by a further appeal for a single large block grant to cover migration, the E.M.B. and grants-in-aid to colonies.[22]

Churchill was disturbed by this attack on Treasury practices. He minuted to his advisers: 'If the facts in this letter are correct, they constitute a very serious criticism on the work of the Supply Department of the Treasury'. A full report was ordered. This was rapidly supplied by Cuthbertson who proved to Churchill's satisfaction that Amery's facts were, to say the least, incorrect. The Colonial Office were condemned as professionally incompetent. Whereas Amery had accused the Treasury of obstructing the progress of one particular East

African railway scheme, Cuthbertson unequivocally asserted that 'the project was put forward on grossly misleading figures, bad enough to be termed fraudulent in the commercial world'. Amery had demanded sole responsibility for the expenditure of a block grant. Cuthbertson replied:

As regards the proposal to make the Department which is responsible for policy, responsible also for finance, whatever might be said for it in some quarters the Colonial Office would be one of the last offices to be entrusted with the dual charge. There is not a glimmering of financial sense in the place, and it is the lack of it which occasions these letters from the Minister and the failure to frame proposals on financially acceptable lines.

Churchill ordered a reply based on Cuthbertson's researches to be drawn up and sent to Amery: copies were also sent to Baldwin, Neville Chamberlain, Cunliffe-Lister and Worthington-Evans.[23]

Given this virtually public humiliation of the Colonial Office at the hands of the Treasury, it is indeed remarkable that this did not conclude discussions on a colonial development fund. However, in these months before the general election the government was increasingly concerned with the unemployment problem. Treasury officials might unfurl the banner of orthodoxy against heretical proposals, but cabinet ministers were undoubtedly conscious that it would be their heads on the political chopping-block in the event of electoral defeat, while the permanent staff soldiered on under new generals. The thought had occurred to Sir William Joynson-Hicks, the Home Secretary. In February 1929, after consulting Baldwin, he expressed to the cabinet his fears about unemployment and the forthcoming election. Existing policies were proving inadequate, and he urged the cabinet to adopt a strategy of imperial development to stimulate industrial recovery. He envisaged not just immediate relief for unemployment but also long-term trade benefits. To finance development works in the empire the government should guarantee a publicly subscribed loan and pay the interest charges on such a loan for an indefinite period. 'I am aware that in many quarters the raising of such a loan would be regarded as an abuse of Government credit and as a concealed measure of inflation', but there would be savings on unemployment relief and a net increase in national revenue. Above all, however, he stressed political need. The opposition could claim that the Conservatives had allowed unemployment to rise from just over one million when they took office to over one and a half million by the end of 1928. Electoral defeat was bad enough, but the unemployment policies being proposed by Labour and the Liberals were also dangerous and economically damaging.[24]

The Colonial Office examined this proposal and concluded at once that like Amery's plan it would simply be rejected by the Treasury. They were not, however, much disturbed by this prospect. 'In solvent colonies', Grindle observed, 'development proceeds far more rapidly without Treasury assistance than it does with that very Greek gift'. It was uniformly agreed that if aid was to be given it must be on Amery's block grant principle. As Wilson put it, 'No scheme which entails Treasury control will result in anything', but as Ormsby-Gore concluded 'I doubt whether you will ever get any help worth having in Imperial development with the present Chancellor of the Exchequer'.[25]

However, other political antennae were sensing the value of Joynson-Hicks' suggestion. The Minister of Labour, Steel-Maitland, drew up a supporting memorandum. From the political standpoint, he argued, there was ample justification for such a development policy. 'What, however, must be the features of the programme if it is to make a bright enough fly for us all to go a-fishing with in murky water?' The answer must be something imaginative, which would show national resources being developed, and something which would generate extra employment within three months. Road-making in Britain was one idea, but the construction of railways in East Africa was another. 'It is obvious, however, that the moment a "bold dramatic policy" begins to crystallize into actual schemes the economic aspects of the problem force themselves upon our attention. The Treasury is like nature itself: *Expellas furca, tamen usque recurret.* It is both right and fortunate for us all that this should be so'. In spite of this apparent obsequiousness, Steel-Maitland went on: 'After eight years of financial orthodoxy and eight years of unabating unemployment, ought we not to ask for a reasoned proof, for some foundations of belief that the financial policy by which we guide our steps is right?' Would it not be possible to give a fillip to public confidence and start the trade cycle back on the up-grade? He proposed a re-examination of the government's present credit, gold standard and bank rate policies.[26]

This, after a fashion, he got. Churchill, now in his fifth year as Chancellor, put orthodox Treasury views to the cabinet in his riposte to Joynson-Hicks and Steel-Maitland. It was argued that such a development scheme would either inflate banking credit or increase taxation and therefore push up prices. Moreover, expenditure on colonial development or road construction would be ineffective since 'the resources directed by the government to the employment of extra labour [would be] taken away from the resources of private persons, the investment of which would have led to the employment of labour at other points'. Furthermore, 'if the capitalist system is sound, private enterprise is more likely than the government to direct investment to purposes which are economically justified and will tend to increase the wealth of the community'. In addition, overseas investment might have a detrimental effect on the exchanges and therefore on the gold standard. The deduction the Treasury drew from the failure of earlier colonial development measures like the Trade Facilities Act and the East Africa Loans Act was that commercially sound schemes were simply not available in the colonies: more generous terms would merely foster uneconomic proposals. Churchill concluded that 'It is to be hoped that we shall not let ourselves be drawn by panic or electioneering into unsound schemes to cure unemployment and divert national credit and savings from the fertile channels of private enterprise to State undertakings mainly fomented for political purposes'.[27]

It is unlikely that Amery was happy with the way the cabinet handled the papers laid before it on 26 February. After a short discussion, 'the PM said he had to go to an early dinner' and with that it was decided to hand over the memoranda of Joynson-Hicks, Steel-Maitland and Churchill to a cabinet committee for examination. At least this gave Amery the opportunity to catch the ear of colleagues. On the following day he had a long talk with Neville Chamberlain, partly 'about my ideas for securing freedom from Treasury control as the first condition of any money allotted to Empire development'. He also wrote to Baldwin, criticising the Treasury's negative attitude and urging the Prime Minister to adopt a more positive policy of empire development for the general election. He cited the E.M.B. as an example of what could be achieved when freed from Treasury control, and then proposed a radical plan, the establishment of an Empire Marketing and Development Fund charged with £2,500,000 a year to spend on colonial development projects and empire trade promotion. This 'represents the reasoned conclusion of four years experience of the present futile and exasperating system'. Determined to press his message home, Amery cornered Baldwin the following week, renewed his request and, in addition, repeated his claim that 'the thing that would help us most in the country would be shifting Winston from the Exchequer'.[28]

Baldwin was never an easy man to push into quick decisions. On 13 March 1929 he postponed the creation of the promised cabinet committee until the return of the Chancellor and Minister of Labour from abroad.[29] Amery, however, was determined not to allow the issue to cool. Rather cunningly, wearing his other hat as Secretary of State for the Dominions, he submitted a memorandum to the cabinet entitled 'An Employment Policy for the Election'. The public, he claimed, were insisting on a solution to the unemployment problem. He conceded that the cost of any effective policy would exceed what might be available in a normal budget, and he accepted that for the present neither tariff duties nor increased taxes were acceptable. Therefore he suggested that the normal budgetary provision for debt redemption should be reduced and the saving diverted to investment in home and colonial development schemes. Predictably, he recommended for the latter the creation of a colonial development fund operating on the model of the E.M.B. under the direct control of the Secretary of State for the payment of interest charges on loans raised for colonial projects. Initially only £200,000 was needed but the amount should grow to £1 million a year, although this might include the £250,000 already spent annually by the Treasury on grants-in-aid to backward territories. What Amery desired was a commitment to a long-term empire development strategy.[30] Once again Baldwin managed to postpone decisions. At a cabinet meeting on 26 March he concluded that there was no time for discussion. He proposed to consult colleagues and raise the subject again after the Easter recess.[31]

Meanwhile, the Colonial Office completed their preparation of a memorandum to submit to the cabinet committee when and if it was set up to examine the Joynson-Hicks, Steel-Maitland and Churchill papers. The gist of this had been determined by Ormsby-Gore in reaction to the Treasury's assertion that colonial development gave no immediate assistance to the unemployed in Britain. The justification, he said, lay not in immediate orders of goods for public works in the colonies, but in 'the increase of complementary trade between raw material producing countries and an industrial country .... These countries are new and growing markets and anything which hastens or enlarges their economic expansion redounds permanently to the benefit of the industries of Great Britain.' He insisted that 'the benefits of public expenditure on colonial development must be regarded as indirect — and it should be the policy of the Conservative party to emphasise that the only *cures* for unemployment are indirect, i.e. the development of new oversea markets for the absorption of the ordinary products of private enterprise in Great Britain'. Hence he saw a case for assisting colonial public health schemes, scientific agriculture and educational developments as well as railway building. This long-term policy was also at the heart of Amery's thinking. In its final form the Colonial Office memorandum firmly rejected the Treasury assertion that private enterprise was more likely than government to direct investment to profitable avenues, 'and that therefore we live in the best of all possible worlds, in which unemployment is a blessing in disguise'. They proposed a plan akin to that put forward in the abortive letter sent to Churchill back in November 1928; 'the ideas in it may win more sympathy from other ministers', one official minuted. A colonial development fund should be set up with eventually £1 million a year to be administered by a board under the direction of the Secretary of State and used partly in lieu of the grants-in-aid currently issued by the Treasury but mainly to meet the interest charges for several years on development works in the colonies. The cabinet committee never was established, and so in April this document was presented directly to the cabinet by Amery, this time as Secretary of State for the Colonies.[32]

Meanwhile, other activities were drawing the attention of ministers to colonial development policy. On 12 March a group of employers associated with Lord Melchett held a conference with the General Council of the T.U.C. of which Ben Tillett was chairman. This Conference on Industrial Reorganisation and Industrial Relations recommended increased expenditure on migration, the reinstitution of trade facilities with more liberal conditions, an extension of export credits, the creation of a development fund for important national schemes and the creation of a Crown Colonies Development Committee. The Prime Minister, obviously concerned, responded by reconstituting the Inter-Departmental Committee on Unemployment with Sir Warren Fisher as chairman for the purpose of examining these proposals and also those that Lloyd George and his economist advisers had put forward in their Liberal Party manifesto *We Can Conquer Unemployment*. The Colonial Office were asked by this committee to give their views on the Melchett-Tillett report.[33] In response the Colonial Office decided to explain once more why the Trade Facilities Acts had been ineffective, to describe the Treasury's refusal to improve the terms of the scheme and to press again for the establishment of a colonial development fund supplied with up to £1 million a year. They despatched a memorandum on these lines to the committee on 27 March 1929.[34]

The following week this document surfaced as part of yet another cabinet paper, one of the items included in the Inter-Departmental Committee's report to Baldwin on the Melchett-Tillett proposals and *We Can Conquer Unemployment*. Accompanying it was a memorandum from the Ministry of Labour which also endorsed the idea of increased capital investment in the crown colonies, perhaps involving the payment of interest or the guarantee of capital and interest by the Imperial government. Much more remarkable was the contribution of the Treasury. They began in orthodox fashion by denouncing the financial aspects of the Liberal Party's proposals and by criticising the Melchett-Tillett suggestion of extending trade facilities. 'The effect of Government guarantees is exactly the same as additional Government borrowing on the gilt-edged market, tending to raise Government interest rates and ultimately general industrial rates.' They also appeared to question the value of accelerating colonial development. Referring to the minimal colonial response to the 1924 Trade Facilities Act they concluded that 'it is very doubtful, therefore, whether there is any genuine demand for facilities of this kind'. But then unexpectedly they conceded that colonial development was 'intrinsically attractive and there are advantages in diverting investment … from foreign to Empire countries'. Of course, there were caveats to this approval: easy terms might lead to ill-advised expenditure; the immediate impact on British exports would be small since good schemes took time to plan and half the capital required would be spent locally; this capital might be diverted from more productive investments at home. They also argued that the Colonial Stock Acts already helped colonies to raise the capital they needed. Nevertheless, they acknowledged that if colonies could not raise their capital independently, imperial assistance might be offered. They favoured the extension of the guaranteed loan system recently employed in East Africa, amended to lengthen the period for repayment and, more importantly, to allow the payment of interest out of capital during the construction period. But even more surprisingly they agreed that as an alternative the establishment of a colonial development fund should be considered. The fund should not receive a fixed annual sum as a block grant such as Amery had in mind, but should be given sufficient funds as required up to a maximum 'such as the finances of the year can afford'. Moreover, schemes would have to be approved, not just by the Secretary of State, but by 'a body of business men' acting as commissioners. 'Such a project has, *prima facie*, a good deal to commend it.'[35]

While the Treasury's tentative sketch for a colonial development fund clearly did not conform in its details to the proposals put forward by the Colonial Office, it was still a curious departure and it demands explanation. It was evident that the idea of such a fund was no longer just a preoccupation of Amery. Since the time of his first initiative in November 1928, the concept had gained other supporters within ministerial circles and outside. Political pressures on the Treasury were increasing. But the final erosion of their opposition resulted from their examination of a proposal for a colonial development fund from yet another quarter.

The Commission on Closer Union of the Dependencies in Eastern and Central Africa had been appointed in November 1927 as part of Amery's strategy to create a united white-settler dominated colony in the area. The report, signed in October 1928 and presented to Parliament in January 1929, included a review of communications problems. The commissioners concluded that development was imperative and that 'a mere policy of laissez-faire is not adequate to the requirements of the situation nor a worthy method of discharging the responsibilities of the Imperial Government'. Moreover, the terms of the East Africa Loans Act were condemned as too rigid, evidently the conclusion of Sir George Schuster, one of the commissioners and chairman of the advisory committee set up by the act. More substantial aid was needed. The guaranteed loan system could be improved by allowing the Imperial government to pay the initial interest charges. The Imperial government could also raise colonial loans on terms analogous to those of the Local Loans fund and these could be advanced to colonial governments free of interest. Or, alternatively, a colonial development fund could be formed to provide grants or possibly loans to meet interest charges. The commissioners did not, however, contemplate leaving expenditure from this fund to the discretion of the Colonial Office or even the Treasury since they 'do not normally possess the qualifications and experience necessary to take decisions of this kind'. Accordingly they proposed to devolve this responsibility on to a board made up of businessmen and, perhaps, one Treasury representative.[36]

These proposals had received only passing mention in the Colonial Office as late as March 1929. The Inter-Departmental Committee requested their comments on 2 April, but a Colonial Office report was not available in time to affect the decision-making on the principle of a colonial development fund.[37] It was otherwise with the Treasury. Consideration of the commission's recommendations began in January 1929. Initially, only in comparison with Amery's request for a block grant was any merit seen in the proposals.[38] The commissioners' claim that the state should accept responsibility for economic development was looked upon with suspicion; the financial implications were too dangerous.

Already the perpetual drain involved in the supply of capital for telephones, for local municipalities, for the unemployment fund and for other purposes goes far to neutralise the effect of the sinking fund and is perpetually defeating the hoped for improvement in Government credit. Great new commitments for Colonial development must be looked upon therefore with the utmost caution.

Moreover, expenditure on colonial development did depressingly little to assist trade in Britain since the bulk of expenditure was in the colonies. Indeed, aiding colonial development in the colonies amounted to subsidising schemes at the expense of the British taxpayer, 'when home enterprises equally promising, and of more importance to our trade, simply cannot obtain capital'. Of the commission's recommendations the best that could be said was that an extension of the guaranteed loan system was the least objectionable. The 1926 act could be amended to allow interest to be paid out of capital and to extend the period for repayment. However, by the end of March 1929 the Treasury were also considering the possibility of more liberal assistance. They turned to another of the commission's recommendations for a colonial development fund, and considered financing such a fund up to a maximum set by the state of national finances. They were also evidently mollified by the plan to use a board predominantly of businessmen to ensure the efficient use of funds, and they concluded that with such a safeguard an acceptable scheme might be devised.[39] These terms were then gingerly incorporated in their response to the Inter-Departmental Committee's request for observations on the Melchett-Tillett report. It is clear from this acceptance of the principle of a colonial development fund that by March 1929 the Treasury reluctantly accepted the need to make some concessions to prevailing political opinion and saw the advantage to be gained by suggesting terms which contained suitable safeguards against excessive and unwise expenditure: a limited fund and administration through a board of commissioners.

The Inter-Departmental Committee's report to the cabinet contained no conclusion and recommendations of its own, beyond a condemnation of the Liberal Party's proposals as needing a 'Mussolini regime' for their implementation.[40] But ministers must have been struck by the Treasury's apparent conversion to the concept of a colonial development fund and perhaps impressed by Amery's sustained advocacy of such a plan. On 10 April 1929 the cabinet agreed that imperial development should be accepted as a plank in the government's policy, and on 17 April Baldwin confirmed to his colleagues that such a commitment would be included in the major policy speech he was to make the following day. The Prime Minister must have been finally moved to this decision by the letter he had recently received from the Chancellor. 'So far as your declarations ... are concerned,' Churchill wrote, 'I should promise definitely *if we are returned* to provide a fund for Imperial development either by direct use or capitalisation.'[41]

Churchill had not minuted on the papers dealing with the proposals of the Commission on Closer Union, but sensitive to political pressures he had become aware of the strong feeling in favour of a colonial development policy in the cabinet and in interested sections of the electorate. His support paralleled both in its unexpectedness and in its essentially political basis his previous decision to accept the £10 million East Africa guaranteed loans scheme. With the Chancellor's agreement therefore, on 18 April 1929 Baldwin pledged the government to the creation of a colonial development fund.[42] The pledges did not commit the government to any detailed proposals, and this lack of precision only further serves to indicate the rapidity of the last stage of the Imperial government's decision-making and the influence an imminent general election at a time of high unemployment had upon that decision.

2. DRAFTING THE COLONIAL DEVELOPMENT BILL, APRIL–JULY 1929

While these political pledges were being made the permanent staff of the Colonial Office and the Treasury continued to debate the justifications for and the terms of the proposed new scheme. Naturally

Colonial Office and colonial government enthusiasm for new development legislation would depend on the degree of aid offered and its method of administration. The financial attractiveness of the measure would depend upon the arrangements, firstly, for raising capital and, secondly, for paying interest. A choice would have to be made between the several alternatives mooted in the various proposals put forward. Colonies could be left to raise capital under the Colonial Stock Acts, or they could be assisted, particularly where those acts were inapplicable, by Imperial government guarantees. The Commission on Closer Union and the Treasury had favoured this idea. The commission had also suggested that capital could be raised instead by the Imperial government, as under the Local Loans procedure, and advanced to colonies. There was also the possibility of capital being provided from a colonial development fund. It was generally accepted that many colonies could not afford to meet interest payments at once from their revenues, and that was why the Commission on Closer Union and the Treasury suggested that an amended guaranteed loan system should allow interest to be paid initially out of capital. But there were, for the Imperial government, more expensive alternative suggestions involving their payment of interest charges. Joynson-Hicks had favoured that approach, and by March 1929 the Treasury appeared ready to accept the suggestion of Amery and the Commission on Closer Union that an annually-supplied colonial development fund might be used to meet interest payments, by grant or loan. Disagreements remained, however. There was a wide gap between Amery's idea of a block grant leaving administrative responsibilities solely in the hands of the Secretary of State and the proposal of the Commission on Closer Union preferred by the Treasury that the vetting of schemes should lie in the hands of a body predominantly of businessmen. It is evident that the political commitment made by Baldwin on 18 April 1929 was based on no unanimity as to the terms of the proposed legislation. More than three months were to pass before the Colonial Development Act was passed.

The impression that Conservative pledges to create a colonial development fund were hasty political responses to election needs is supported by the singular lack of progress in settling the details of proposed legislation in the remaining two months of the government's life. Neither Amery nor Churchill commented on the relevant departmental papers during this period. Neither Colonial Office nor Treasury were given any directives by their political chiefs. Both departments betrayed a marked lack of enthusiasm for the proposed fund.

In spite of Amery's earlier eager advocacy, Colonial Office permanent staff remained oddly hesitant in their examination of the scheme. In April 1929, departmental heads reviewed once again without much enthusiasm the potential for colonial development schemes as a way of relieving unemployment in Britain. It was argued, for example, that the development of Uganda and Kenya could not be hurried, and the idea of accelerating public works in Nigeria was opposed. It was unwise to sanction schemes in anticipation of the 'ordinary programme'. The abiding anxiety was that overburdened colonial revenues would result.[43] Colonial Office staff were cautious even in their assessment of the Commission on Closer Union's proposals. They disliked the idea of extending the guaranteed loans system: this inevitably allowed the Treasury the right to interfere, since 'the nature of the guaranteed loan involves a possible charge on Home funds which the Treasury have a statutory duty to avoid'. The idea of a development fund was greeted more sympathetically, but any increase in the public debt of colonies was a cause for concern and therefore it was argued that the initial assistance with interest payments must be in the form of grants and not just loans. The Colonial Office also wanted to assist development schemes in the colonies, even if like the building of schools and hospitals, they were not directly remunerative. Moreover, they wanted aid to be given 'without undue preference being given to schemes likely to alleviate unemployment'. The development of colonies not the relief of unemployment was their primary concern.[44] Similarly the Crown Agents also worried about the danger of overburdening local revenues and subjecting colonies to Treasury financial control. Reviewing the Commission on Closer Union's proposals, they were doubtful about the chances of creating a satisfactory development fund, and preferred to help territories raise capital by extending the Colonial Stock Acts to cover protectorates and mandated territories and by allowing interest to be paid out of capital. Their model for development was still the traditional one. 'The wonderful development of the West African Colonies during the last thirty years had been effected without financial guarantees from the British Government and without (it is believed) their having once had to pay interest on their loans out of capital.'[45] In brief, the permanent staff at the Colonial Office and the Crown Agents remained sceptical of the idea of a development fund which took the relief of unemployment in Britain as its immediate target.

Treasury analysis of the development fund idea had reached a few conclusions before the Conservative government fell. Schemes would have to be vetted by a committee of financial and business experts, and without their approval no aid should be offered. Aid should not be given, as the Colonial Office proposed, to non-remunerative schemes offering no return for British trade and employment. Most officials also finally agreed that largely for practical reasons the use of guaranteed loans should be avoided. There was support for the suggestion that the Imperial government could advance capital for development projects from the Local Loans Fund. But the need for a colonial development fund remained in dispute. Such a fund, with a limited annual provision, might be a useful method of financing initial payments on loans raised, but alternatively money might be voted by Parliament as needed. Indeed, one senior official argued that if an expert committee concluded that a scheme would be commercially successful then capital should simply be raised by guaranteed loan allowing interest for a maximum of five years to be paid out of capital.[46] It is worth remembering that ministers had already committed the government to some form of development fund. It is evident that Treasury staff were not agreed upon the terms of any new assistance to colonial development and that their normal reluctance to commit government revenue had not disappeared.

Lacking directives from above, matters were allowed to drift through April and May. One flurry of activity accompanied attempts to incorporate a reference to a colonial development fund in the Conservative party election manifesto. In his public speech of 18 April 1929 Baldwin had referred to an independent commission which would advise the government on development schemes, but its powers were left unspecified. At the beginning of May, Neville Chamberlain had drafted a paragraph for the election manifesto which had proposed that the Secretary of State for the Colonies should chair this body. The Treasury objected to this apparent concession to Amery's thinking. Amery attempted to stiffen Chamberlain's resolve in a private letter. 'I have no doubt that what the Treasury wants is a committee of eminent business men very anxious about their reputation who will be precious careful before they ever authorise anything.' He envisaged frustrating delays. What was needed was an organisation like the E.M.B., 'the experts available for consultation but the decision and the driving power supplied by a minister anxious to get on with the work .... Do help me to press Stanley on this point'. But Baldwin chose instead to bury the conflict in indecision, and the cabinet on 6 May 1929 agreed to omit all reference to the machinery which would administer the proposed colonial development fund.[47] Electoral defeat followed, and on 4 June 1929 Baldwin's government resigned. Labour's assumption of office introduced a new political initiative and accelerated the departmental negotiations. The Labour party came to power with a general commitment to tackle the unemployment problem, and there were well-placed enthusiasts like J. H. Thomas who regarded colonial development as part of the solution.[48] Amery anxiously drew Thomas's attention to the proposal to create a development fund and was relieved to discover that 'he is very keen on my idea'.[49] The eagerness with which Labour picked up unfinished Conservative proposals in June 1929 was similar to their behaviour in January 1924. On both occasions uncompleted colonial development proposals were unhesitatingly adopted by the new ministers. The Labour government's contribution to the passage of the Colonial Development Act lay in the speed and energy with which the nebulous Conservative proposal was turned into legislative form.

At the first cabinet of the new government held on 10 June, J. H. Thomas, Lord Privy Seal with special responsibilities for unemployment, explained that he had already arranged with Sir Warren Fisher for the permanent heads of government departments to be at his disposal for the purpose of forming a committee in connection with that problem.[50] At the first meeting of this Inter-Departmental Committee on Unemployment, held on the following day, Thomas announced the formation of a separate Committee on Oversea Development and Migration to deal amongst other matters with colonial development suggestions. He also made it clear that financial and other objections were not to hold up practicable proposals.[51] The Committee on Oversea Development and Migration met for the first time on 13 June with Thomas in the chair. The Conservative government's proposal for a colonial development fund was taken up at once, and Thomas requested negotiations to be completed in time to pass legislation before the August recess. The Colonial Office should prepare a memorandum setting out proposed schemes, their cost, suggested means of finance and, in addition, the amount of employment they would provide in Britain. This is important. Thomas had told the committee that 'he attached great importance to stimulating development projects such as the production of cotton and other products within the Empire and other indirect ways of providing employment at home'. But his interest in colonial development evidently coupled immediate short-term unemployment relief with expectations that it would be a long-term solution to Britain's economic problems.[52]

Following Thomas's firm directive, the Colonial Office at once set about defining their terms for an acceptable colonial development fund scheme. Their memorandum, sent to the Oversea Development and Migration Committee on 20 June 1929, dealt with financial arrangements. They pointed out that colonies could raise capital under the Colonial Stock Acts, and the question of extending the acts to cover protectorates, protected states and mandated states was under consideration and was, it was implied, essential. Moreover, the loans authorised under the East Africa Loans Act of 1926 had not been exhausted, and therefore amendments were needed to enable those facilities to be fully used. Furthermore, a colonial development fund should allow small grants of capital to be made to poorer territories. These suggestions would cater for the problems of raising capital for development works. However, there remained the question of interest charges. Since the purpose of the scheme was to induce colonies to undertake works, with which they would otherwise not at present burden themselves, in order to accelerate the revival of industry at home, it was essential that there must be an element of free gift to the territory. This should take the form of a contribution of the whole or part of the interest on a loan for a certain number of years. Either a free grant of interest should be given from the colonial development fund, or the amount needed might be lent at low interest rates. In return for these terms, the Colonial Office would accept the need to administer the scheme on the advice of a statutory committee. Colonial Office staff perhaps accepted such a committee as unavoidable in view of the Treasury's known views and their previous insistence on a statutory committee in the case of the East Africa Loans Act. Lord Passfield, the new Secretary of State, found it acceptable: there was no Amery in office to defend the last ditch.[53]

The Treasury, however, were still critical of the proposal because they regarded it as irrelevant to the unemployment crisis.

The most obvious criticism on the Colonial Office Memo is that the scheme is for the most part quite unrelated to the problem of providing direct and immediate relief of unemployment in Great Britain .... The bulk of the fund ... will be spent on laying the broad foundations of future colonial prosperity, and cannot be expected to have any direct effect on industry and commerce at home for many years to come.

It was admitted that 'no doubt the creation of such a Fund is an act of wise and far-sighted policy, which will repay us in due course', but would not this attempt to accelerate development encourage unsound finance? Was it not better to study the government's other relief schemes before committing the Treasury? The only urgency was to finance the Trans-Zambesi bridge scheme, the concession for which was due to expire shortly, and a one clause bill to cover this require-ment was all that was needed. Moreover, certain suggested services in the new proposal seemed to overlap with the E.M.B.. Would it not be wise to combine the two schemes with a maximum allowance of £1½ million? If the fund was created it should be used simply to advance interest on capital borrowed from other sources, and with few exceptions ultimate repayment ought to be a *sine qua non*.[54]

Several Treasury officials were evidently still not enthusiastic about the proposal and wished to postpone further action. But Thomas was anxious for immediate legislation, and at a second meeting of the Oversea Development and Migration Committee on 24 June, he requested the Colonial Office, the Treasury and Parliamentary Counsel to prepare a bill. The officials obeyed these instructions and a draft based substantially on the Colonial Office's memorandum was completed by 26 June.[55]

One clause of the draft deserves special analysis. It proposed to extend the Colonial Stock Acts to protectorates, protected states and mandated territories. Since the colonial development fund was accepted by Colonial Office and Treasury as primarily designed to facilitate the payment of interest on loans, the problem of raising capital was an open question. The Colonial Stock Acts were con-sidered a sufficient inducement for the colonies, and the East Africa Loans Act, to be amended in the new bill so as to allow the payment of interest out of capital for the first five years, provided some facilities for the East African protectorates. The extension of the Colonial Stock Acts, however, would cater for their subsequent needs and also for territories outside that area.

It will be recalled that the Colonial Office had pressed without success for this extension in 1919—20.[56] The proposal had been aired again briefly and without effect in 1922 and 1926, but in June 1928 Amery launched yet another campaign to persuade the Treasury to change their mind, 'with a view to dispensing with the necessity of securing Imperial Government guarantees'. Unofficial contacts with the Treasury that summer were not encouraging and the subject was suppressed until the spring of 1929. By then Treasury officials had become increasingly conscious of the practical problems associated with calling repeatedly on Parliament to guarantee loans raised by dependent territories which were not covered by the Colonial Stock Acts. Accordingly they agreed to incorporate a clause in the Colonial Development Bill which would extend the acts to cover protectorates, protected states and mandated territories. It was a reluctant concession, but as one Treasury official observed, this option was less objectionable than further guarantees and the Chancellor might not be opposed.[57]

He was not. Indeed, when the draft bill and explanatory comments were submitted to him, Snowden added no minutes to the paper. His officials still argued that colonial development was only remotely related to unemployment and that its only justifications lay in the creation of future markets for British goods. Only the needs of the Trans-Zambesi bridge were urgent and for this a single-clause bill would suffice and other matters could be postponed until the autumn. But Snowden did not respond: presumably he was impressed by the need for some urgent action by the government in the face of the unemployment problem they had inherited, and the draft bill was allowed to go forward.[58]

The final stages in the bill's preparation were completed with sustained rapidity. Revised draft clauses were available on 29 June,[59] and were considered and approved at the third meeting of the Oversea Development and Migration Committee on 1 July. On 3 July the cabinet decided that to meet urgent requirements several bills, including the Colonial Development Bill, should be introduced into Parliament as soon as they had been approved by the cabinet's Home Affairs Committee and without further confirmation, as was normal, by the full cabinet. The Financial Secretary's memorandum on the bill was submitted to the committee on the same day. The Treasury again explained that, though the bill was expressly intended to promote commerce and industry in Britain it was not expected to have much immediate effect. Indeed, 'the Bill is primarily based on a far-sighted policy of Imperial development as one of the surest foundations of prosperity at home'. But this emphasis on the long-term impact of the measure did not deter the Home Affairs Committee. They passed the bill on 4 July with minor modifications.[60] Thomas had advised the Commons of the unemployment measures he intended to introduce and had included a sketch of the Colonial Development Bill in the debate on the King's Speech on 3 July.[61] On 10 July the Treasury issued a memorandum explaining the financial resolution,[62] and this resolution was considered in committee on 12 July and 15 July. The debate on the second reading occupied 17 July and the bill was considered in committee on the following day. It was read for the third time on 19 July and taken to the Lords where it passed in three days with the minimum of debate to be given the Royal Assent on 26 July 1929.[63]

3. *CONCLUSION*

The bill, which received only minor amendments during its legislative progress, dealt with three matters. In the first place it empowered the Treasury, with the concurrence of the Secretary of State for the Colonies and on the recommendation of an advisory committee, to advance money to any territory for the purpose of aiding and developing agriculture and industry 'and thereby promoting commerce with or industry in the United Kingdom'. This could be done by capital grants or by defraying for a maximum of ten years in whole or in part the interest on any loans raised for these purposes. Such advances could be either grants or loans. The fund would be sustained by a maximum grant of £1 million per year. Repayments of advances went to the Exchequer, thus preventing the creation of a revolving fund. The second section of the bill amended the Colonial Stock Acts. The third allowed the interest on loans raised under the East Africa Loans Act of 1926 to be paid out of capital for a maximum of five years and lengthened the period for the repayment of the loans from forty to a maximum of sixty years.[64]

The act contrasts in a number of respects with colonial development measures previously examined. In the first place the terms of aid were, by contrast with earlier proposals, generous. The Colonial Stock Acts were extended at last, and the initial burden of interest payments on capital raised was to be eased by grants or loans from the Colonial Development Fund. The act showed unprecedented flexibility in its terms. Secondly, unlike the East African Protectorates Loan Act of 1914, the Uganda Development Loan, Kenya's independent loan, the £3,500,000 loan to Kenya and Uganda and the East Africa Loans Act, the terms of the act made it more than the *ad hoc* response to particular colonial needs. It shared with the Trade Facilities Acts the distinction of being available to all colonies in the empire. It contained no restricted schedule of proposed works. Indeed, it encouraged more than the usual development of communications. The fund could also be used for improvements in agricultural production and marketing, for the development of fisheries and forestry, of water supplies and water power, of mineral resources and electricity, and for the promotion of scientific research and public health. It supported a programme of general imperial development much wider in scope than the Trade Facilities Acts, the Empire Marketing Board, the Empire Settlement Act and *ad hoc* colonial development proposals. The only explicit limitation resulted from a government pledge by Sir Oswald Mosley during the debate on the bill that it would not be used to finance educational developments.[65]

The wide scope of the act reflects its origins. To only a very small extent was it the fruit of any particular colonial need. To some degree it was made possible by Amery's desire to amend the failed East Africa Loans Act. The investigations of the Commission on Closer Union in Eastern and Central Africa had led to a proposal for a general colonial development scheme. But for the most part the act reflected the peculiar economic and political situation in Britain. By 1928–29 politicians turned instinctively to colonial development as one feature of their unemployment policies. Prime Ministers, Ministers of Labour, Presidents of the Board of Trade, and other ministers especially concerned with the continuing high level of unemployment clutched at the suggestion. It was politically essential to offer solutions to the crisis, and there had developed by 1928–29 a broad consensus in favour of the type of suggestion embodied in the Colonial Development Act. During the debate on the bill Churchill remarked: 'I cannot feel that any serious difference will arise between the Conservative Party and the Government upon the general method of treating' these schemes. Amery agreed: 'We on this side naturally welcome the compliment paid to our election programme in the adoption of something that was an important item in it'. Baldwin accepted that the importance of this emergency legislation warranted its rapid passage. Sir Herbert Samuel similarly claimed that the bill merely followed the ideas contained in the Liberal Party's book *Britain's Industrial Future*. In brief, the bill was, as Lunn, the parliamentary under-secretary at the Colonial Office, described it, a 'non-controversial measure'.[66] As indicated, the necessity of making pre-election pledges forced the Conservative government into commitments. In the urgency of post-election victory Labour politicians were forced to honour them.

It is important to notice, however, that the justifications for colonial development as a cure for unemployment had continued to develop. The parliamentary debates indicated that some members continued to emphasise the short-term value of the policy as a means of providing immediate relief from distress. Thomas spoke to them when he introduced the bill. It could be defended as a measure for colonial development, he confessed, 'but I am mainly concerned at this moment, because I believe that these changes will enable much work to come to this country when it is especially necessary'. Mosley, who was assisting Thomas in this campaign against unemployment, agreed with this interpretation. And Passfield in the House of Lords declared: 'Your Lordships will perhaps allow me to remind you that the principal motive for the introduction of this measure is connected with the lamentable condition of employment in this country, and this is an attempt to stimulate the British export trade'; he spoke of inducing the colonies to increase their development commitments 'for our advantage'. Other members agreed. 'The genesis of this Bill is the necessity for dealing with unemployment at home', said Captain Ronald Henderson, and Hilton Young commented that 'many of us on these benches put this Measure in the forefront of our programme in the campaign against unemployment'. Commitments that the money would be spent where possible in Britain reemphasised this conclusion.[67]

But there was also considerable agreement that the bill would have a long-term value. It is clear from the Colonial Office minutes that that office did not favour colonial development schemes as an immediate cure for unemployment, and the Treasury consistently rejected the idea that immediate relief would be forthcoming. As noted, the Financial Secretary in July 1929 could defend the bill only as a long-term solution to Britain's economic needs. Amery, Ormsby-Gore and Thomas had also expressed similar views during the preparation of the bill. During the parliamentary debates the long-term value of the proposal achieved prime recognition. Ormsby-Gore, for example, favoured the bill as a practical step to help both operatives and industry in this country, and at the same time to start a flow of permanent trade by opening up undeveloped countries and thereby advancing in the standard of living populations at present on a low economic standing in the world, whose standing can be heightened and purchasing power increased by providing them with the necessary facilities.

Churchill did not feel it had much prospect of affecting the problem of unemployment, but that this and Thomas's other schemes might lead to Empire and domestic development. Hilton Young agreed that it was not just the immediate purchases of capital goods that mattered but the later buying of consumer goods. The Earl of Plymouth took up the point in the Lords. It was, he argued, a point of controversy what effect the money spent in the Colonial Empire would have on unemployment. But since the colonies were large importers of British goods, Britain could only benefit from an improvement in colonial standards of living. In the Commons Lord Eustace Percy felt that so long as stress was laid on employment figures any colonial development policy would be weak since the Treasury would prefer to allocate money for expenditure in this country. He felt the justification for an active colonial development policy lay in the unemployment figures ten or fifteen years hence. 'The only way to ensure a prosperous country at that period is by Colonial development on an active scale carried out on the calculation of eventual if deferred profit.' The government argued along similar lines: 'The scheme is based', said Lunn, 'primarily on a far-sighted policy of Imperial development, but it will no doubt mean a good deal in prosperity to some industries at home'. Thomas too stressed the great importance of constructive development: he argued that it was feasible to grow everything in the empire.[68] We have met these arguments before: they are the neo-mercantilist platitudes of the 1880s, the 'economics of siege' during the First World War, and once again the refuge of an economy in distress. Sir Robert Hamilton accurately observed a changed attitude towards the colonies. 'It is not many years', he said, 'since a Prime Minister of this country spoke of these Colonies as being a millstone round our necks. Today the Lord Privy Seal has spoken of Crown Colonies as a lifebuoy which will bring safety to the old country.'[69] The continuation of economic depression into the late 1920s had forced a wider acceptance of the view that generous imperial assistance for colonial development would provide more than just immediate overseas demand for British goods but also long-term security for

Britain's economy. It was this calculation, plus the political necessity of offering some solution to the unemployment problem, that overcame the Treasury's reluctance to approve expenditure on colonial affairs, especially in a time of economic depression.[70]

NOTES

1. Memo. by Amery 2 July 1928, CAB 24/196/CP 210. See also S. Constantine, *Unemployment in Britain between the Wars*, London, 1980, pp.3, 5-16, 57.
2. See, for example, Amery's letters to Baldwin, 22 March, 11 July, 24 Sept., 1 Oct. 1928, Baldwin Papers, vol.30; memo. by Amery 20 June 1928, CAB 24/195/CP 198.
3. For the E.M.B. see L. S. Amery, *My Political Life*, vol.2, London, 1953, pp.346-56.
4. J. Barnes and D. Nicholson (eds.), *The Leo Amery Diaries*, vol.1, London, 1980, 27 June 1928, p.552; Barlow to Baldwin 26 Oct. 1928, copy in CO 323/1016/51165.
5. Labour Party, *Labour and the Nation*, London, 1928; Liberal Party, *Britain's Industrial Future*, London, 1928 and *We Can Conquer Unemployment*, London, 1929.
6. Cabinet minutes 7 Dec. 1927, CAB 23/55/CAB 60(27)1 and 4 July 1928 CAB 23/58/CAB 36(28)5; *Report of the Industrial Transference Board*, Cmd.3156, 1928; K. J. Hancock, 'The Reduction of Unemployment as a Problem of Public Policy 1920–1929', *Ec.H.R.*, 15 (1962), 328-43.
7. Churchill to Chamberlain 18 Oct. 1927, N. Chamberlain papers, NC 7/9/12 and subseq. letters; H. Pelling, *Winston Churchill*, London, 1974, pp.318-19.
8. P. S. Gupta, *Imperialism and the British Labour Movement 1914–1964*, London, 1975, pp.84-6; *Britain's Industrial Future*, pp.367, 376-8; see also Lord Amulree's proposal for a colonial development fund in a letter to J. H. Thomas, 20 Jan. 1929, Amulree Papers, Mss.Dep.c.385, and a similar plan by the Liberal M.P. F. C. Linfield published as a Supplementary Memo. to the *Report of the East Africa Commission*, Cmd.2387, 1925, pp.189-192.
9. Resolutions ... passed at Annual Conference, Oct. 1926, Baldwin Papers, vol.48; Barlow to Baldwin 26 Oct. 1928, CO 323/1016/51165.
10. Cabinet minutes, 4 July 1928, CAB 23/58/CAB 36(28)3; see also mema. by Churchill calling for reductions in government expenditure 30 Jan. and 6 Feb. 1928, CAB 24/192/CP 20 and CP 31.
11. *Leo Amery Diaries*, 7 April 1927, p.503, 24 April 1928, p.542, 27 Feb. 1929, pp.589-90, 4 March 1929, p.590; Amery to Baldwin, 10 April 1927, a 23-page handwritten protest, Baldwin Papers vol.28 and Amery to Baldwin, 11 March 1929, Baldwin Papers vol.36.
12. Amery to Steel-Maitland, 30 Nov. 1928, Amery Papers, Box G.89.
13. Cabinet minutes 1 Oct. 1928, CAB 23/55/CAB 45(28)6.
14. Jones to Grindle 12 Oct. 1928, CO 323/1016/51165.
15. Minute by Grindle 12 Oct. 1928, *ibid.*; see also papers of Inter-Departmental Committee, CAB 27/378. For the most recent sceptical response to such a proposal see reactions to an inquiry from the Industrial Transference Board in Feb. 1928, CO 323/977/50330 and S. Constantine 'The Formulation of British Policy on Colonial Development 1914–1929', Oxford D.Phil. thesis, 1974, pp.332-6.

16. Mema. by Boyd, Lambert to Grindle, 20 Oct. 1928, minutes by Allen, Machtig, Green, Vernon, Grindle, 22–29 Oct. 1928, *ibid.*. The Treasury, of course, had not offered any terms: the invitation to submit plans had merely come from an Inter-Departmental Committee of which the permanent secretary at the Treasury was chairman.
17. Minutes by Amery, n.d., Wilson 9 and 22 Nov. 1928 and by Grindle 21 Nov. 1928; Grindle to Jones 13 Nov. 1928, *ibid.*; *Leo Amery Diaries*, 9 Nov. 1928, pp.570-1.
18. Amery to Churchill 26 Nov. 1928, T161/291/S.33978.
19. Amery to Baldwin 26 Nov. 1928, and see also C.O. to Ministry of Labour 3 Dec. 1928, CO 323/1016/51165; Amery to Steel-Maitland 30 Nov. 1928, Amery Papers, Box G.89.
20. Minutes by Cuthbertson, Waterfield, Upcott and Hopkins, 18 Dec. 1928–21 Jan. 1929, Churchill to Amery 23 Jan. 1929, T161/291/S.33978.
21. Minute by Boyd, 8 Feb. 1929, CO 323/1064/61526.
22. Amery to Churchill, 28 Feb. 1929, T161/297/S.34608.
23. Minute by Churchill 1 March 1929, memo. by Cuthbertson 2 March 1929, minutes by Upcott, Hopkins and Churchill, 12–20 March 1929, memo. by Upcott 25 March 1929 and minute by Churchill 27 March 1929, *ibid.*.
24. Joynson-Hicks to Baldwin 31 Jan. 1929, Baldwin Papers, vol.12; memo. by Joynson-Hicks, 7 Feb. 1929, CAB 24/201/CP 27.
25. Minutes by Boyd, Grindle, Wilson and Ormsby-Gore, 12–25 Feb. 1929, CO 323/1064/61526.
26. Memo. by Steel-Maitland 16 Feb. 1929, CAB 24/201/CP 37.
27. Memo. by Churchill, 25 Feb. 1929, covering note by Treasury 23 Feb. 1929, CAB 24/202/CP 53.
28. Cabinet minutes, 26 Feb. 1929, CAB 23/60/CAB 9(29)4; *Leo Amery Diaries*, 26, 27 Feb., 4 March, and see also 22 Feb. 1929, pp.589-90; Amery to Baldwin 27 Feb. 1929, Baldwin Papers, vol.98.
29. Cabinet minutes, 13 March 1929, CAB 23/60/CAB 11(29)13; minute by Boyd 13 March 1929, CO 323/1064/61526.
30. Memo. by Amery, 18 March 1929, CAB 24/202/CP 87.
31. Cabinet minutes 26 March 1929, CAB 23/60/CAB 13(29)8.
32. Minute by Ormsby-Gore 7 March 1929, memo. by Boyd, Draft A, Colonial Development in Relation to Problems of Unemployment, minute by Vernon 19 March 1929, CO 323/1064/61526; memo. by Amery 10 April 1929, CAB 24/203/CP 110.
33. *The Times*, 13 March 1929 and Fraser to Wilson 20 March 1929, CO 323/1064/61526; minutes of 6th meeting Inter-Departmental Committee on Unemployment, 14 March 1929, CAB 27/378. For the Melchett–Tillett talks see A. Bullock, *The Life and Times of Ernest Bevin*, vol.1, London, 1960, pp.392-405.
34. Minute by Boyd 21 March 1929, memo. B on Melchett–Tillett Report 21 March 1929, minute by Boyd 26 March 1929, CO 323/1064/61526.
35. Report by Inter-Departmental Committee, 2 April 1929, CAB 24/203/CP 104. Those portions of the report dealing with *We Can Conquer Unemployment* were subsequently published as *Memoranda on Certain Proposals relating to Unemployment*, Cmd.3331, 1929; see also cabinet minutes 1 and 6 May 1929, CAB 23/60/ CAB 19(29)2 and CAB 20(29)2.
36. *Report of the Commission on Closer Union of the Dependencies in Eastern and Central Africa*, Cmd.3234, 1929, espec. pp.171-9. For the origins of the commission see *Leo Amery Diaries*, 13 April, 30 May, 8, 9, 13, 29 June, 4, 6 July 1928, pp.504, 507-15.
37. For reception of report see *ibid.*, pp.575-581; and for C.O. reaction to financial

proposals see minute by Bottomley 22 March 1929 and by Grindle 23 March 1929, CO 323/1064/61526; and for Inter-Departmental Committee's request see minute by Blaxter, 3 April 1929, *ibid.*.

38. Memo. by Hopkins for Churchill, 21 Jan. 1929, T161/291/S.33978.
39. Note on Financial Proposals in Hilton Young Report, 25 Feb. 1929, minute by Upcott 25 Feb. 1929, memo. by Upcott 28 March 1929, T161/291/S.33978/01.
40. Fisher to Baldwin 2 April 1929, covering letter to Report of Inter-Departmental Committee, CAB 24/203/CP 104.
41. Cabinet minutes 10, 11 and 17 April 1929, CAB 23/60/CAB 15(29)4, CAB 16(29)2, 5 and appendix, CAB 17(29)1.
42. *The Times*, 19 April 1929, copy on T161/291/S.33978/01.
43. Minutes of Group Council meeting, 18 April 1929, CO 323/1064/61526.
44. Memo. on Loan Proposals of Commission on Closer Union, sent to Inter-Departmental Committee, 12 April 1929, *ibid.*.
45. Ezechiel to Bottomley 10 April 1929, enclosing Notes on Hilton Young Commission Report by the Crown Agents, *ibid.*.
46. Minutes by Waterfield n.d., Hale 22 April 1929, Ismay 25 April 1929 and Phillips n.d., T161/291/S.33978/01.
47. *Leo Amery Diaries*, 3 May 1929, p.595; Amery to N. Chamberlain 4 May 1929, N. Chamberlain Papers, NC 7/2/41; cabinet minutes 6 May 1929, CAB 23/60/CAB 20(29)3; see also Draft of P.M.'s Election Address 7 May 1929, CAB 24/203/CP 141 and F.W.S. Craig, *British General Election Manifestos 1918–1966*, Chichester, 1970, pp.44-5.
48. See the correspondence on colonial development between Thomas and Sir William MacKenzie, in Jan. and March 1929, Amulree Papers, Mss.Dep.c.385. and Gupta, *Imperialism and the British Labour Movement*, pp.84-6.
49. Amery to Thomas 4 June 1929, Amery Papers, Box G.90 and *Leo Amery Diaries*, 4 and 5 June 1929, p.597.
50. Cabinet minutes 10 June 1929, CAB 23/61/CAB 22(29)4.
51. Minutes of Inter-Departmental Committee meeting, 11 June 1929, CAB 27/389.
52. Minutes of Committee on Oversea Development and Migration, 13 June 1929, CAB 27/382.
53. Memo. by C.O. 20 June 1929, O.D.M. 6, *ibid.*; Grindle to Upcott, 19 and 22 June 1929, T161/297/S.34609/1. The origins of this memo. are obscured by the curious and annoying 'weeding' and destruction of the relevant C.O. files, CO.61479 and 61480, see C.O. register CO 378/52.
54. Memo. by Waterfield 22 June 1929, minute by Upcott 24 June 1929, T161/297/S.34609/1.
55. Minutes of Committee on Oversea Development and Migration, 24 June 1929, CAB 27/382. Upcott to Parliamentary Counsel 24 June 1929 and Graham-Harrison to Upcott 26 June 1929, T161/297/S.34609/1.
56. See above pp.74-5.
57. CO 323/946/CO 4133; CO 323/1014/51044; CO 323/1034/60250; memo. by Phillips, 28 June 1929, T161/297/S.34609/1. For further details see Constantine, 'The Formulation of British Policy on Colonial Development', pp.375-8.
58. Hopkins to Snowden and mema. by Upcott and Phillips 27–28 June 1929, T161/297/S.34609/1.
59. Graham-Harrison to Phillips, 29 June 1929, *ibid.*.
60. Minutes of Oversea Development and Migration Committee, 1 July 1929, CAB 27/382; cabinet minutes, 3 July 1929, CAB 23/61/CAB 27(29)5; memo. by Financial Secretary 3 July 1929, CAB 26/12/H.A. 7; minute of Home Affairs Committee, 4 July 1929, CAB 26/12/HAC(29)3.
61. *Hansard* H.C., vol.229, cols.91-109, 3 July 1929.

62. *Memorandum explaining the Financial Resolution of the Colonial Development Act*, Cmd.3357, 1929.
63. There were only three speakers on the measure in the House of Lords, *Hansard* H.L., vol.75, cols.174-90, 270.
64. 20 Geo.5 ch.5.
65. *Hansard* H.C., vol.230, col.722, 18 July 1929.
66. *Hansard* H.C., vol.229, cols.112, 1262, vol.230, cols.471, 485, 782. See also W. Graham, President of Board of Trade, to Amery 13 June 1929, Amery Papers, Box G.90.
67. *Hansard* H.C., vol.229, cols.91-109, 260, 1255, 1257, 1261, 1282; *Hansard* H.L., vol.75, cols.175-6.
68. *Hansard* H.C., vol.229, cols.115, 1256, 1282, 1295, vol.230, cols.475, 481-3; *Hansard* H.L., vol.75, cols.183-4. For a similar emphasis on expected long-term benefits see leading article in *The Times* 17 July 1929, p.17.
69. *Hansard* H.C., vol.229, col.1277.
70. This interpretation is similar to that expressed by I. M. Drummond, *British Economic Policy and the Empire 1919–1939*, London, 1972, pp.50-1 and accordingly differs from those based only on published material put forward by E. R. Wicker, 'Colonial Development and Welfare, 1929–1957: The Evolution of a Policy', *Social and Economic Studies*, 7 (1958), 170-92, B. Niculescu, *Colonial Planning: A Comparative Study*, London, 1958, pp.58-60 and D. J. Morgan, *British Aid – 5. Colonial Development*, O.D.I., London, 1964, pp.15-16 who seem to argue that the object of the policy was to improve colonial economies and living standards primarily as ends in themselves. Morgan has since modified his view, see his *Official History of Colonial Development*, vol.1, *The Origins of British Aid Policy 1924–1945*, London, 1980, pp.37-42.

VIII

COLONIAL DEVELOPMENT
POLICY IN THE 1930s

1. *THE COLONIAL DEVELOPMENT ADVISORY COMMITTEE*

The operations of the Colonial Development Act in the 1930s require analysis for several reasons. For one thing, after 1929 most colonial government requests for imperial assistance towards their local development costs were directed towards the Colonial Development Fund. It is true that until its closure in 1933, the Empire Marketing Board continued to play a part in financing research into problems of colonial production and provided some help for the advertising and marketing of colonial products in Britain. Grants-in-aid were also distributed, but mainly to balance the budgets of colonial adminis-trations, to ease the hardships caused by natural disasters or to solve such particular problems as the burden imposed on Nyasaland by the financing of the Trans-Zambesia Railway.[1] But, by contrast, the establishment of the CDF on a permanent footing with an annual grant and unusually wide terms of reference made the measure of central significance in the 1930s. Moreover, in introducing the bill in the House of Commons ministers had spoken in a mood of jaunty optimism about its stimulating effect: Thomas envisaged a consequent annual expenditure on colonial development projects of up to £40 million a year, and Mosley claimed that 'If that fund is used to the full extent, very great orders on a very great scale can be given to this country'.[2] It is pertinent to ask whether these hopes were fulfilled. Furthermore, since colonial development policy in the 1930s was largely synonymous with the operations of the Colonial Development Act, it is obviously important to see whether in practice it adhered to the intentions of its originators. As the previous chapter indicated, the explicit purpose of the measure was to encourage colonial develop-ment in order to stimulate British industry and commerce and thus ease the burden of unemployment at home, either immediately or in the long-term. Metropolitan advantages took priority. It is not inconceivable that in the peculiar circumstances which prevailed in Britain and in the colonies in the 1930s, interpretations of the act were modified and its functions and objectives were altered. Whether such modifications took place and whether policy was in effect therefore changed are among the questions which this chapter will consider.

After the passage of the act, the first task of the Colonial Office and the Treasury was to work out the administrative arrangements whereby applications for expenditure from the CDF could be processed. The act stipulated that while it was the Treasury who actually issued money from the fund, with the concurrence of the Colonial Office, they could do so only on the recommendation of a specially-appointed committee. Accordingly, requests by colonial governments for assistance from the CDF were scrutinised initially by the Colonial Office permanent staff before being passed on with their observations to the CDAC. After due consideration the committee's recommendations were simultaneously laid before the Colonial Office and the Treasury for their approval. It is apparent from this procedure that in spite of its title as the Colonial Development *Advisory* Committee, the statutory role which the committee was given by the act meant that in practice it exercised a considerable amount of independent authority. It is true that the Colonial Office, with the blessing of the Treasury, actually selected the members of the committee. CDAC discussions were also monitored by the presence at its meetings of a secretary appointed from the Colonial Office and by the attendance of a senior man as a liaison officer, Sir Gilbert Grindle, the deputy under-secretary, until February 1930 and Sir John Campbell, the Colonial Office's financial adviser, thereafter. Moreover, the act did allow the Secretary of State to reject CDAC recommendations, and in practice this power was occasionally used to force the committee to review the terms of the assistance it was proposing to offer a colonial government.[3] Nevertheless, the CDAC did operate as a semi-autonomous body which could not be forced to accept Colonial Office suggestions. Certainly, Colonial Office officials believed the CDAC was largely beyond their influence. They felt it was rather more susceptible to Treasury direction. It is true that the Treasury were able to affect the committee's activities to some degree by control over the annual grant to the fund and by the power of veto over CDAC recommendations which they could and occasionally did exercise.[4]

Even so, the committee still retained a good deal of independent discretion and was by no means simply a mouthpiece of the Treasury. To a considerable extent, therefore, the operations and interpretations of the Colonial Development Act were left to the CDAC; in a sense, government departments abdicated their responsibility to a non-departmental statutory body.

Membership of this committee was therefore of critical significance.[5] The original six members were evidently chosen primarily because of their combination of business experience and interest in imperial economic affairs. The chairman, Sir Basil Blackett, had been a Treasury official from 1904 to 1922, latterly as controller of finance, and then from 1922 to 1928 Finance Member of the Government of India. But by 1929 he was primarily a businessman, the director of a number of companies including De Beers, Eastern and Associated Telegraph Co. Ltd., and Cables and Wireless Ltd.. In 1929 he became a director of the Bank of England. His interest in public health measures in the colonies reflected his work as President of the British Social Hygiene Council, an organisation concerned with the combat of venereal disease in the empire. Blackett died in 1935 after a motor accident and was succeeded as chairman by another member of the committee, Sir Alan Rae Smith, whose business experience was as a senior partner in a firm of chartered accountants. Sir John Eaglesome served in the Public Works Department in India before moving to West Africa in 1900 and becoming Director of Railways and Public Works in Nigeria from 1912 to 1919. He had also served on Milner's abortive Colonial Development Committee in 1919. He became President of Leeds Chamber of Commerce in 1933. Sir Felix Pole gained his business experience as General Manager of the Great Western Railway from 1921 to 1929 and as chairman of Associated Electrical Industries Ltd. thereafter. He visited the Sudan in 1923–24 and again in 1930–31 to report on transport services for the Sudanese government. He was the least assiduous member in his attendance, missing 70 of the 125 meetings held.[6] Sir Richard Jackson was Chairman of the Lancashire Indian Cotton Committee and of the Empire Cotton Growing Corporation, and he had also served on the East African Guaranteed Loan Committee until its operations were subsumed by the CDAC in 1929. He resigned owing to ill-health in December 1937. Finally, and unique among the original group was Ernest Bevin, General Secretary of the Transport and General Workers' Union since 1921, appointed by the Labour government primarily as a sop to those backbenchers anxious to ensure that proper labour conditions were observed in colonial development projects. Bevin was not without his interest in imperial economic affairs, at this time seeing empire markets as assets to help Britain's economic recovery, but since he resigned in September 1931 he made little impression on the CDAC's work.[7] His successor was more typical, Sir Edward Davson, Chairman of the British Empire Producers' Organisation, a former chairman of the Federation of Chambers of Commerce of the British Empire and a man of considerable business experience. He was also a member of the Imperial Economic Committee and of the Empire Marketing Board, a trustee of the Imperial Institute, and a governor of the Imperial College of Tropical Agriculture. He was to be a government adviser on colonial trade at the Ottawa Conference in 1932. Another new member who joined the committee in 1935 was Sir George Schuster, chosen for his apparently good credentials as a former member of the Trade Facilities Advisory Committee and the East African Guaranteed Loan Committee. He had been Finance Secretary to the Sudan Government from 1922 to 1927, the first Economic and Financial Adviser at the Colonial Office 1927–28, a member of the Commission on Closer Union in Eastern and Central Africa which in 1928 had recommended, among other things, the creation of a colonial development fund, and Finance Member of the Government of India from 1928 to 1934. He was, however, a poor attender and resigned in December 1938.[8] Slightly different in character were the final two appointments made. Sir Alan Pim joined in 1935 having retired from the Indian Civil Service in 1930. As chairman of a number of financial and economic commissions between 1932 and 1937 he obtained first-hand knowledge of conditions in Swaziland, Zanzibar, Bechuanaland, British Honduras, Basutoland, Kenya and Northern Rhodesia. A similar colonial rather than primarily business experience was the background to Sir John Chancellor's appointment in 1937. He had been Governor of Mauritius 1911–16, of Trinidad 1916–21 and of Southern Rhodesia 1923–28 and High Commissioner in Palestine 1928–31. He was, however, in the 1930s a director of the British South Africa Company and the Imperial Continental Gas Association. The CDAC as a body therefore retained throughout its history roughly the same general complexion. It remains to be seen how the combined business, imperial and administrative experiences of these decision-makers affected the way they approached their responsibilities.

2. *FINANCIAL RESTRAINTS*

Fundamental to an understanding of the way the CDAC operated is to recognise that the Imperial government's apparent commitment to a sustained programme of colonial development coincided with the onset of world economic depression. The year 1929 proved to be the peak of the trade cycle. In the United States a decline in consumption, intensified by the bursting of the Wall Street stock market boom in October, devastated business confidence, reduced levels of domestic investment and cut real income. American demand consequently fell and this exacerbated the already worrying problems of the world's primary producers. The resulting fall in the sales of manufactured goods, the collapse of the international gold standard and the increase in trade restrictions ushered in an era of depressed levels of international trade and high unemployment.[9]

One immediate effect of the depression in Britain was a revived anxiety about the budget. The financial restraints on government activities which had accompanied the earlier downturn in the economy after 1920 were again operated. As government revenue fell and the burden of unemployment payments rose, the government struggled to maintain a balanced budget by economies in expenditure elsewhere. The broad consensus in favour of this orthodoxy was epitomised by the parliamentary pressure which persuaded the Labour government in March 1931 to appoint Sir George May as chairman of a Committee on National Expenditure to investigate possible economies in government expenditure. When, ultimately, the Labour government split and fell over proposals to cut unemployment benefit, the succeeding National government under Ramsay MacDonald with Neville Chamberlain as Chancellor pressed on with a package of public expenditure cuts. This regime of tight control and close scrutiny of all items of government expenditure was unlikely to relax much even when the depression bottomed out in 1932 and cyclical recovery slowly began. There remained substantial claims on government revenue for social services, especially for unemployment and housing, and increasingly for rearmanent. Orthodoxy still insisted that the road to economic recovery was to avoid burdening private enterprise by high taxes and public borrowing.[10] In these circumstances it was, then, inevitable that the funding of the Colonial Development Act would come under close scrutiny.

On 1 August 1929 when the CDAC met for the first time, Blackett was confident that the £1 million a year notionally available would be easily spent.[11] The committee began its work on the assumption that money would be transferred from the Treasury to the CDF for the current financial year 1929–30. Disillusionment came quickly: there was to be no grant that year. They were further alarmed to hear in March 1930 that the vote for 1930–31 was only to be for £750,000: already the committee had committed themselves to an expenditure of £438,691. The chairman acquiesced only on the understanding that a supplementary estimate would be presented if the committee found it necessary.[12] The chances of such additional funding were however rendered remote as the government's financial crisis deepened. In December 1930, the Treasury were urging the Colonial Office to try and restrain the CDAC from making long-term commitments. The £1 million Blackett demanded of the Treasury for 1931–32 was cut to £750,000,[13] and in June 1931 he had to go before the Committee on National Expenditure to defend the very survival of the CDF. His argument that no immediate savings could be achieved by abolishing the fund because commitments for expenditure over the next two or three years had already been made may have had some effect, but the May Committee still recommended in its report in July 1931 that a maximum of £750,000 not £1 million should be issued in 1932–33.[14] In their anxiety, the Treasury urged the CDAC to limit their activities even before the cabinet had given its approval.[15] It was later agreed by Treasury and Colonial Office that the estimate for 1932–33 should be further reduced to £700,000: economy was necessary to make room for the increased grants-in-aid needed by colonial governments suffering from the depression. Given the commitments already made that meant that only about £80,000 of the grant for 1932–33 had been unallocated by January 1932, before the financial year had even begun. To top it up unspent balances for 1931–32 were carried over: this would still only allow fresh expenditure of about £200,000.[16] A similar operation was carried out for the financial year 1933–34. The Treasury allowed the balance from the previous year's grant to be carried forward and provided just £400,000 in the estimates. It was calculated that because of existing commitments less than £150,000 would be available to fund new applications during the year.[17] For 1934–35 a total provision of around £800,000 was agreed upon, but again this included money carried over from the previous year, and only £500,000 was put in the estimates leaving an estimated £100,000 or so available for new schemes.[18] The partial upturn in the economy by this time was allowing the Chancellor to take some of the pressure off government expenditure (for example, the 10% cut in unemployment benefit was restored in 1934), and the CDF estimate for 1935−36 was put at its highest figure so far, £900,000.[19] Even so, the committee were obliged to limit the assistance they could offer to Newfoundland that year, and they refused help to an Empire Air Mail Scheme largely on the grounds that the fund was so heavily committed already that money for new schemes was limited.[20] £900,000 was also provided for 1936−37 but only £500,000 for 1937−38, and the committee's request of £850,000 for 1938−39, allowing only £157,000 for new schemes, ran into trouble. In the event only £650,000 was allocated.[21] As a result of the cut, the committee calculated in December 1938 that there would be no balance to carry forward at the end of the year. Commitments for 1939−40 already totalled £500,000 and the committee wanted £300,000 in addition for new schemes. In fact only £750,000 was voted for the CDF that year.[22] A worthwhile scheme in Jamaica had to be turned down partly on the grounds that the grant to the CDF for the year was insufficient to meet the cost.[23] The final estimate was £600,000 for 1940−41, but this was mainly to be transferred to Colonial Development and Welfare schemes after the Colonial Development and Welfare Act was passed in July 1940.

It is then clear that in spite of apparent intentions in 1929 to supply the CDF with up to £1 million a year, this ambition was never realised. The total amount of money actually transferred from Treasury to CDF came to £6,650,000.[24] Even excluding 1940−41 when the fund's operations were being restricted in the war, the average allocation was £645,000 per year, not £1 million. The commitments which the CDAC made to finance projects over a number of years ensured that substantial amounts of money would have to be provided annually by the Treasury to honour those obligations, but little was made available each year to fund new schemes.[25] The CDAC felt their activities were being affected, and some proposals were undoubtedly rejected, reduced or less generously financed because of these limitations.[26] As in the 1920s, British budgetary considerations continued to restrict Imperial government expenditure on colonial development.

3. *APPLICATIONS AND TERMS OF AID*

However, budgetary needs alone do not explain the limited funding of the CDF during the 1930s. After all, in most years, the CDAC did not commit all the money at their disposal. Hence their ability to carry funds forward into the next financial year. Such a situation followed because the number of acceptable applications from the colonies was less than the legislators had hoped and expected.

Following the passage of the Colonial Development Act in July 1929, the colonies, protectorates and mandated territories were invited by the Colonial Office to submit applications to the CDAC.[27] It had obviously been the hope of those who devised the act that the fund would induce colonial governments to embark on a considerable number of large and expensive development schemes. Such had been the gist of Thomas's remarks to the CDAC at their first meeting in August 1929.[28] But by January 1930, with unemployment once more beginning to rise, Thomas became increasingly disappointed by the modest response of the colonies to the CDAC's invitations. His anxiety was transmitted to Blackett, and in a formal letter to the Colonial Office the CDAC pointed out that except for a few large public works already earmarked for expenditure under the East Africa Loans Act, ambitious schemes had not been submitted by colonial governments, and the CDAC for the most part had been handling only small projects.[29] In response the Colonial Office sent another despatch to each colonial administration, reminding them of the extraordinary opportunity presented by the existence of the CDF:

We have been so accustomed in the past to the financial difficulties which have hitherto delayed the economic development of the Colonial Empire that it has been difficult to adjust our minds to the entirely new situation created by the Colonial Development Act.[30]

The results still could not be described as spectacular. Thanks to Dr. Meredith's labours we have a good deal of ready information about applications to the CDAC.[31]

In the ten financial years from 1929 to 1939 the committee received 822 applications from 48 different colonial administrations plus a few general submissions. While virtually all colonial governments put in requests, half made only ten applications or less over these years. Although the pattern is not entirely consistent the largest numbers of applications came from the West Indies (Jamaica made 35 applications, Antigua 39, British Guiana 62) and from East and Central

TABLE 1

Applications to CDAC 1929–39

Year	(1) No. of Applications	(2) No. accepted excluding those later abandoned	Cost of (2) £
1929–30	62	46	5,379,327
1930–31	177	110	2,996,683
1931–32	86	43	423,796
1932–33	48	38	347,763
1933–34	55	40	2,136,631
1934–35	96	82	1,619,133
1935–36	91	73	1,016,245
1936–37	69	60	1,258,668
1937–38	61	54	930,475
1938–39	77	71	1,178,052
Total	822	617	17,286,773

Source: from D. G. Meredith, 'The British Government and Colonial Economic Development' Table 3.2, p. 92, with correction. Based on *Interim and Annual Reports of the Colonial Development Advisory Committee*, 1929–39.

Africa (Tanganyika made 55 applications, Kenya 33, Nyasaland 39). This suggests that those regions which even in the 1920s had been in most financial need turned to the CDF for assistance, and the richer, relatively self-sufficient territories in West Africa and the East appealed but rarely to the CDAC.[32]

Moreover, the total cost of the schemes accepted by the CDAC came to only £17,286,773 by March 1939. In only two or three years were even moderately high totals reached and the figures were always far below the £40 million a year originally envisaged by the optimistic Thomas.[33] Few of the schemes submitted involved large amounts of expenditure. The average was less than £30,000. Only thirteen projects cost more than £200,000, only three £1,000,000 or more of which the £3,062,354 to be spent on the Zambesi Bridge was outstandingly the largest, and almost the earliest, scheme submitted.[34]

This disappointing response may, of course, partly reflect the poor quality of some colonial administrations. There was a feeling in the CDAC that colonial governments did not have the staff, the expertise or possibly the energy to detect opportunities for local development.[35] But in the main what determined colonial responses to the

CDF was the world economic depression. The CDAC admitted that economic conditions inevitably deterred colonial governments from putting schemes forward.[36] In the early 1930s colonial development was envisaged primarily as the construction of a basic economic infrastructure in a territory and the encouragement of the production of primary goods for export. But the sharp reductions in the export value of most primary products from 1929 discouraged this process. Even when prices began their slow recovery after 1934, the market for primary goods was scarcely buoyant. At no time before the Second World War could most colonial producers be optimistic about the future demand for their products.[37] It was then natural for colonial governments to be hesitant about embarking on large-scale projects designed to stimulate increased output for an apparently saturated market. This discouraging economic scene helps explain the unexpectedly small amounts of CDF money which went into immediately productive projects. As Table 2 shows, little was spent encouraging agriculture, fisheries and forestry. Even the assistance given to internal transport and communications looks less impressive when set against the £3,500,000 loan to Kenya and Uganda or the £10 million guaranteed loan for East Africa discussed in earlier chapters.

Colonial governments also had a more immediate reason in the depression of the 1930s to be hesitant about making applications to the CDF. They were anxious about the effect which accelerated development works might have upon colonial government finances. Most colonial administrations in the 1930s were dependent on excise and customs duties for between 30% and 50% of their annual revenue. The fall in export values in the depression therefore had an immediate and catastrophic effect upon a number of them. In many cases government revenue fell by about 40% between 1929 and 1933. Although there was a slow recovery to a new peak around 1937, government revenue per head remained low, often lower even in the later 1930s than in the previous decade.[38] Constrained by the attempt to keep annual budgets in balance, colonial governments were forced to cut back on expenditure, especially in the early 1930s.[39] Those governments as in the West Indies which still could not balance the books were thrust back upon imperial grants-in-aid. This was unsatisfactory not only to colonial administrations but to the Colonial Office and Treasury who for their different traditional reasons were anxious to keep colonies financially self-sufficient.[40] Not surprisingly then,

TABLE 2
Analysis of Assistance Recommended by CDAC 1929–40

Category in Section 1(1) of Act	Annual Percentage											Total Percentage	Total Assistance Recommended £
	1929–30	1930–31	1931–32	1932–33	1933–34	1934–35	1935–36	1936–37	1937–38	1938–39	1939–40		
a) Agricultural Development etc.	1	5	3	13	1	7	5	2	3	14	18	6	534,118
b) Internal Transport and Communications	44	49	8	43	10	31	39	32	21	21	5	30	2,658,290
c) Harbours	5	–	1	–	37	6	5	–	–	3	–	5	474,245
d) Fisheries	–	–	1	–	–	9	3	–	6	3	–	2	156,630
e) Forestry	–	2	3	2	–	3	–	1	6	–	1	1	106,640
f) Surveys	3	1	–	3	2	9	4	–	–	4	1	3	253,375
g) Land Reclamation and Drainage	–	1	6	–	–	–	14	21	4	13	7	5	444,100
h) Water-supplies and Water-power	1	7	20	8	8	9	8	15	27	9	8	10	923,417
i) Electricity	–	3	–	3	–	–	–	–	–	–	11	2	163,608
k) Mineral Resources	37	–	–	–	30	–	–	–	–	–	3	9	770,050
l) Scientific Research etc.	2	11	9	14	4	7	8	2	8	23	1	7	597,654
m) Public Health	7	18	44	5	7	4	8	25	31	10	40	16	1,460,338
o) Miscellaneous	–	2	5	9	–	13	5	2	–	3	5	4	332,618
													£8,875,083

Source: *Interim, Annual and Final Reports of the Colonial Development Advisory Committee, 1929–40.* Amounts totalling less than 1% not included.

all parties were extremely sensitive when colonial governments applied to the CDAC: much would depend on the aid provided.

The act stipulated that CDF advances could be made 'either by way of grant or by way of loan, or partly in one way and partly in the other'. Moreover, aid could be given to defray 'in whole or in part, during a period not exceeding ten years from the raising of the loan, the interest payable by the Government on any loan raised' for development projects,[41] thus encouraging colonies to borrow the capital required themselves in return for help with interest payments. The terms of the act were therefore flexible, and the alacrity with which colonial governments would apply to the CDF would then depend on the generosity or otherwise with which the CDAC interpreted their brief. From the beginning the committee adopted one principle which however well-motivated probably reduced the attraction of the fund. As they put it in their final report, they had 'always attached importance to substantial participation by the Colonial Government where practicable in the financial obligations involved in any scheme. It has seemed to them that the live interest thereby secured locally in the effective and economical carrying out of a scheme was a matter of real importance'.[42] Although some territories were given more generous assistance when the CDAC reckoned they lacked the resources to meet even part shares of the financial burden of colonial development projects, the CDAC's ruling must have served as a deterrent to colonial governments contemplating applications.

Initially the CDAC were encouraged by Thomas to think of using the fund primarily to pay part of the interest for ten years on public loans raised on the open market by colonial governments. The expenditure of £40 million a year which he envisaged flowing from CDF aid of £1 million a year was calculated on the astonishingly optimistic basis of colonies being able to raise their own loans at 5% and being able to meet half the interest payments, the CDF meeting the other half.[43] The previous history of colonial development had shown that only a few colonial governments at the best of times could raise loans so cheaply and meet such interest payments so easily, and in the depression circumstances were less propitious. Moreover, the Colonial Office was particularly hostile to imperial financing of colonial development projects by the temporary grant of interest payments alone. As one official put it: 'We ought to be careful how far we encourage Governments to embark on large schemes involving a heavy burden after the period of assistance is over'.[44] The Colonial Office believed that such onerous terms were discouraging colonial applications to the CDF. As Table 3 shows, few colonies accepted aid on such a basis.

TABLE 3

Type of Assistance Recommended by CDAC 1929–39
(excluding schemes later abandoned)

	Grants £	Loans £	Grants of Interest £
1929–30	200,435	580,200	556,145
1930–31	670,818	329,119	185,948
1931–32	205,466	15,225	–
1932–33	137,351	118,444	7,560
1933–34	137,007	320,732	275,662
1934–35	435,214	649,187	–
1935–36	447,778	421,066	–
1936–37	505,987	304,058	–
1937–38	492,571	288,317	–
1938–39	565,973	59,905	–
Totals	3,661,249	3,086,253	1,025,315

Source: Based on figures in D. G. Meredith, 'The British Government and Colonial Economic Development', appendix 3, with corrections.

The largest single grant of interest was £500,000 to Nyasaland in 1929–30 but it is significant that the loan itself was raised under the East Africa Loans Act.[45]

The Colonial Office were also worried when the CDAC proposed to finance colonial development projects by loans from the CDF. The burden of interest and debt repayments might still threaten colonial budgets.[46] This was, for example, the reason why the Colonial Office opposed the terms of a CDAC loan offered to Sierra Leone in 1930. The permanent under-secretary reported that 'the Dept. here is naturally very frightened of taking the risk of Sierra Leone being landed in 5 years time with a debt of £500,000 which is practically ¾ of its annual revenue'. Colonial Office criticism obliged the committee to improve their terms.[47] It was also found necessary when British Guiana's budget balance was in jeopardy in 1936 for the CDAC to consider converting some of their earlier loans to the colony into grants.[48] Nevertheless, the committee continued to provide much of their aid in the form of loans, as Table 3 shows. Meredith may be right to point out that 80% of these loans were on easy terms, usually free of interest for the first few years and at fairly low rates thereafter. It is also true that debts to the CDF were for almost all colonies outweighed, often substantially outweighed, by external public debts. But nevertheless the prospect of interest and loan repayments evidently worried the Colonial Office and colonial governments. Abbott calculates that repayments actually added up to 36.9% of all loans paid out, and as will be shown in the next chapter, the cancellation of some debts to the CDF was regarded as sufficiently pressing to be incorporated in the Colonial Development and Welfare Act in 1940. Accumulated CDF debts per head of population were by 1940 often high even in territories where revenue per head was low.[49] It is highly probable that concern about such debt burdens persuaded some colonial administrations to restrict their applications to the CDAC.

It was in fact apparent from the start that the Colonial Office wished to persuade the CDAC to provide free grants rather than loans.[50] Table 3 shows that most assistance was provided in this fashion, the percentage varying from year to year but becoming higher in the later 1930s. The CDAC, however, often decided that even when a grant should be given it would only meet half the cost of the project. For example, in 1929 a request from Jamaica for a £10,000 grant to purchase harbour lights was met by an allocation of only £5,000, and at the same meeting Sierra Leone's application for a grant of £14,800 to build a jetty was met with a grant of £7,400.[51] Such responses may well have discouraged those colonial administrations who lacked surplus revenue from submitting applications, and certainly in a few cases such terms led governments to abandon projects proposed.[52]

Another characteristic of the CDAC's terms for assistance proved a more formidable deterrent. As a general rule the committee would not finance what they regarded as the normal administrative responsibilities of a colonial government. Such a restriction was publicised in their reports, and Blackett spelt out the message at a meeting with colonial governors at the Colonial Office in 1930.[53] In practice this meant turning down, for example, an application by Trans-Jordan for a grant to build a hospital because this curative service was deemed to be a normal government duty. Likewise, while Nigeria was given a grant to clear an area and resettle the population as part of a campaign against sleeping sickness, the cost of treating the infected was regarded as a normal administrative burden.[54] The CDAC operated a tight definition which regarded replacement costs as falling outside their brief, so that, for example, they refused to pay for a new government steamer for the Solomon Islands.[55] Likewise, temporary help to ease an industry in distress was also barred if aid was thought unlikely to lead to permanent improvement.[56] Perhaps not surprisingly, aid would not be given if the committee felt that a colony was capable of financing the scheme itself.[57] What the CDAC therefore in general rejected were schemes which were deemed not to fall within their definition of new development works. Mainly they would meet all or only part of the capital costs involved, for example, in the construction of roads or hospitals, the cost of surveys or specific medical investigation, or, especially after the closure of the E.M.B. in 1933, the cost for a limited period of specific research projects.[58]

But even if the full capital costs of development projects were met by the CDF this did not mean that a colonial administration would necessarily escape all financial burdens. As the Colonial Office pointed out, 'in practically every case a service financed by a free grant will involve a recurrent charge for staff and maintenance'.[59] The new hospital, railway, road or waterworks more often than not involved recurrent administrative charges falling upon a colony's budget. Occasionally, especially in the worst period of the depression in the early 1930s when colonial governments were most under stress, the CDAC were prepared to give some temporary help towards these charges.[60] But the general and well-publicised rule was that such expenses had to be borne by the colonial administration. Blackett told the Colonial Office Conference in 1930: 'We have felt it is not the function of the Fund normally to provide, in addition to the initial cost, any contribution towards the permanent maintenance of a service'. Indeed, a further part of his message was that the committee would only agree to finance a project if they were confident that 'the Colony is going to be in a position to carry the burden of that maintenance'.[61] This was reiterated in the committee's report in 1931, and in their final report they admitted that 'they have been obliged, by the interpretation which has been placed upon the Act, to reject schemes where there has appeared no reasonable ground for anticipating that the colonies concerned would be in a position to meet from their own resources the subsequent necessary cost of maintenance and upkeep'.[62] The Select Committee on Estimates in 1932 had pressed the CDAC to stick to this rule, and the Treasury were always at hand to check that territories could run services inaugurated by capital grants without running into deficit.[63] The Colonial Office too, similarly fearing unbalanced budgets and consequent dependence on Treasury grants-in-aid, carefully scrutinised projects like the construction of a medical school and teaching hospital at Kampala in order to check that Uganda's budget could bear the inevitable recurrent charges.[64]

This reluctance to use the CDF to provide more than the capital costs of new development did not, of course, deter governments from applying to the committee. But it is highly likely that they were at least partly deterred by the tendency to leave colonial budgets to meet recurrent costs as well as by the terms of assistance offered (loans, half-grants). As in the past it would be those colonial governments with the greatest needs who would find the limitations of the Colonial Development Act most discouraging.

4. *COLONIAL DEVELOPMENT AND METROPOLITAN NEEDS*

There was one further characteristic of the act which also perhaps deterred some colonial governments from applying to the CDAC. It stipulated that advances would be made for the purpose of agricultural and industrial development in the colonies, 'thereby promoting commerce with or industry in the United Kingdom'. As already demonstrated, the origins of the act lay in the political need felt by British ministers to offer some solution to the unemployment problem. However, it has been argued that this emphasis upon colonial development as a solution to high levels of unemployment in Britain was in practice ignored. Wicker regards the emphasis on the needs of the unemployed as at best secondary to a concern for colonial development as such. More recently Meredith writes that the CDAC 'placed very little weight on [the reduction of unemployment in Britain], which is surprising in view of the purpose of the Act'. Rampersad also concludes that the CDAC in practice was not blinkered by the need to ease the problem of unemployment in Britain and that the encouragement of colonial development *per se* was of equal importance to the committee.[65]

Such conclusions are by no means unreasonable deductions from analysis of the work of the CDAC, as the figures in Table 4 show.

TABLE 4

Projects Approved by CDAC: Estimated Proportion of Expenditure in UK 1929–39

Year	Percentage of expenditure in UK
1929–30	40.6
1930–31	41.0
1931–32	36.6
1932–33	25.7
1933–34	49.9
1934–35	21.8
1935–36	21.5
1936–37	18.7
1937–38	17.0
1938–39	11.5

Source: *Interim and Annual Reports of the Colonial Development Advisory Committee*, 1929–39.

The committee reckoned that the total cost of approved schemes by the end of this ten year period came to £17,275,238, but this involved an expenditure in the United Kingdom of only £5,785,355, or 33.5%.[67] Meredith also concludes that schemes were not rejected simply on the grounds that expenditure in the United Kingdom was insufficient. Indeed, he estimates that 52.3% of the cost of the schemes actually rejected by the committee would have been spent in the United Kingdom.[68] Clearly the immediate placing of orders in Britain was not the sole criterion which influenced CDAC decisions.

Nevertheless the act's apparent emphasis on metropolitan economic advantage cannot be lightly dismissed. Unemployment remained an inescapable political problem after 1929. Even in that year, on average, 10.4% of the insured workforce were unemployed, and the world depression rapidly pushed the total to 22.1% in 1932. Slow recovery later in the decade still left 10.8% out of work in the peak year 1937. Moreover, the concentration of unemployment, particularly long-term unemployment, in the depressed export industries was well-known. Public works in the colonies would provide some relief for iron and steel workers, engineers, coal miners.[69]

Certainly when the CDAC began their work they could not but be aware of the problem of unemployment and the political needs of their masters to provide some relief for it. J. H. Thomas attended the first meeting of the committee and announced that 'I want you to keep in mind the immediate effect on employment'. At least one member, Eaglesome, was equally aware of the urgency: 'Coming from the north-east coast as I do, they are anxious about getting some orders'.[70] Moreover, in the telegram and despatch which informed the colonial governments of the terms of the act, attention was drawn to the benefits to British industry, commerce and employment which accelerated colonial development projects were expected to bring.[71] Because some administrations were not giving full details of estimated expenditure in the United Kingdom when they submitted applications to the CDAC, Blackett requested the Secretary of State in November 1929 to send another despatch to the colonies reminding them of this obligation.[72] The committee also saw fit in their third published report in 1932 to remind applicants that after a project had been sanctioned 'no reduction in the rate or scale of expenditure in the United Kingdom should be authorised without prior reference to themselves'.[73] The CDAC took note of the percentage in their deliberations. They observed, when giving their approval, that a public health scheme in Antigua to cost £12,000 would result in an expenditure in Britain of over £4,000 and that a drainage scheme in Sierra Leone costing £60,500 would result in expenditure in Britain of £24,000. They requested further information about a road programme in St. Vincent since no orders were to be placed in the United Kingdom, and when it was discovered that a housing scheme in Montserrat would result in proportionately less expenditure in Britain than a comparable project in Antigua the committee demanded an explanation and granted assistance only when revised plans increased the expenditure in the United Kingdom.[74] A big scheme for railway and harbour developments in Sierra Leone was welcomed by Blackett because it was 'of value as providing employment in this country'. The director of the company involved was interviewed by the CDAC and asked point blank whether in return for a £500,000 loan from the CDF he would agree that orders of not less than £340,000 should be placed in Britain within a given period. Again, in response to a request from Nyasaland for a grant of £180,000 a year for four years, the chairman wanted some reassurance 'that it would involve the placing of orders in the United Kingdom of such amounts and such a nature, and at such dates, as to make it at least probable that the resulting relief to British unemployment would directly and indirectly be a sufficient recompense to the British taxpayer'.[75] It is true that this curiosity about immediate expenditure in Britain is more apparent from the records in the earlier years of the CDF than later. But information detailing the amount of expenditure expected in Britain had to accompany each application throughout the 1930s, and this information was collected and totals published in the annual reports of the CDAC as a reminder of the act's function.

Also constant through the decade was the operation of an imperial preference clause in contracts financed by the CDF. To use more recent terminology, tied aid was a well-established tradition in government purchasing, in spite of Britain's public adherence to the principles of free trade. Colonial administrations invariably employed the Crown Agents whenever they placed orders for public works abroad, and the Agents observed the principle of imperial preference laid down at the Colonial Conference in 1902 and confirmed at the Imperial Economic Conference in 1923.[76] There were few departures from this rule, except in the case of mandated territories where such discrimination was illegal. Similarly, whenever the British government provided financial assistance to help British exporters and development overseas, as under the Trade Facilities Acts in the 1920s, a clause in the agreements required recipients of aid to place contracts with British companies. The CDAC, evidently preoccupied with their duty to help British commerce and industry, quickly took up the matter. At their third meeting, in discussing a proposal to help Nyasaland, Blackett 'observed that if a grant were made, it would be necessary to make some stipulation that any contract signed should contain provision for the placing of orders in this country'.[77] A suitable clause to insert in CDF regulations governing all advances was then discussed at the next meeting. It was agreed to follow Trade Facilities Act practices and to insist that colonial development projects financed in whole or in part by the CDF should use British materials and British manufactured goods (made where practicable out of British materials) and should be shipped in British vessels and be insured by British companies.[78] The legality of such restrictions in the case of mandated territories was questioned by the Colonial Office and the Treasury, and the committee themselves later recognised that to insist on the use of British shipping would breach international law. The Crown Agents were also concerned that in the absence of foreign competition there was a tendency for higher prices to be charged. But with only minor modifications giving the Crown Agents some discretionary powers, the CDAC's proposals were accepted.[79] The ruling was firmly impressed on the colonies by a circular despatch of 11 July 1930: when colonial governments carried out CDF projects themselves, orders would have to be placed with the Crown Agents who would make contracts in the United Kingdom, and when private companies acted for colonial governments a clause in their contracts must ensure the use of British plant and machinery, made where possible from British material, and the use of British insurance companies.[80] At the same time the 'Buy British' policy was publicly announced in April 1930 in the first published report of the CDAC:

Placing of Orders in the United Kingdom and use of British Materials. The Committee understands that all orders for the Colonies are placed by the Crown Agents, and that it is the invariable practice of the Crown Agents to buy British goods only, when available. The Committee has, however, thought it desirable in accordance with the general policy in the matter of Government grants to public works, to make it an express condition of assistance from the Colonial Development Fund that, save in exceptional circumstances all orders for imported materials, etc., should be placed in the United Kingdom; and that the plant machinery and materials, etc., be of British origin and manufacture.[81]

This was no paper regulation: the CDAC allowed very few exceptions to the rule and were always alert to attempts to deviate from it. Even when on one occasion in 1937 both the Colonial Office and Treasury agreed that Nyasaland should be allowed to purchase foreign railway material as being substantially cheaper, the CDAC vetoed the proposal. In 1939 the possibility that foreign machinery might be used in a rice industry development in British Guiana drew a committee warning. Again they stipulated in 1939 that all material imported for the construction of a hotel in Antigua should be British. The committee confirmed in their final report that the principle of ensuring that orders were placed in the United Kingdom had been consistently followed.[82]

There were besides, especially in the early years, plenty of external observers to remind the committee of this duty. In the House of Commons, for example, the government was repeatedly asked to state the size of orders placed and the amount of employment created in Britain by expenditure from the CDF.[83] But the pressure was particularly intense when Britain's economic problems reached a crisis in 1931. The Treasury considered the 'Question of Suspending or Curtailing Colonial Development Fund Schemes in the Interests of Economy'. It was noted that some schemes inevitably gave more help to Britain than others, and it was suggested 'that the assistance available for new schemes should be confined to those which are likely to give the greatest benefit to this country in relation to the amount of assistance required'.[84] This was precisely the attitude taken by the May Committee itself which reported in July 1931 that 'on reviewing the schemes which have so far been assisted we find that in a fair number of them the element of benefit to the trade and industry of this country which is an essential condition of advances under the Act, is somewhat remote', and it recommended that aid should only be given to schemes giving the 'greatest and speediest benefit to this country in the near future'.[85] The Treasury and the new National government endorsed this strategy and the message was passed on to the CDAC and, as significantly, via a circular despatch to the colonies themselves. They were told by J. H. Thomas that while the CDF would not be absolutely restricted to financing schemes of short-range development only, 'the attention of the Colonial Development Advisory Committee has been invited to the desirability of concentrating their recommendations on schemes which are likely to give the greatest and speediest benefit to this country'.[86] It is therefore unlikely that colonial officials could have been unaware that the purpose of the Colonial Development Act remained unchanged. Meredith is probably right to conclude that this pressure explains the increased proportion of the costs of schemes approved by the CDAC which was spent in the United Kingdom in 1933–34.[87]

But it is also apparent from Table 4 that the proportion had been dwindling until that time and it was to decline to still lower levels thereafter. Low and diminishing expenditure in the United Kingdom from CDF-assisted projects does not, however, indicate a change in the objectives of colonial development policy but rather a shift in the techniques for securing them. The CDAC remained loyal to their brief. Indeed, it is of considerable importance to emphasise that the committee chose to be guided by a strategy which had become the consensus by the later 1920s, the notion that the value of colonial developments was essentially as a long-term solution to Britain's economic problems rather than as a short-term emergency programme. The debates on the Colonial Development Bill described in Chapter VII make that clear. The arguments and decisions of the CDAC confirm its perpetuation through the 1930s.

The May Committee's request that CDF money should be spent only on schemes likely to produce immediate benefits to British manufacturers led to protests by the CDAC, not on the grounds that this was an unwarranted attempt to wring metropolitan advantages out of colonial development, but because such an emphasis would deprive the CDF of a 'great deal of its value'.[88] The long-term strategy had been made clear to the CDAC at their first meeting. Grindle had reminded members that in the debate on the bill Thomas had argued that immediate benefits alone were not desired and that the committee should take into account the indirect benefit of colonial development work, increased trade betwen the colonies and Britain. Lord Passfield, the Secretary of State, echoed this: 'If we can increase the productivity of the African natives they will buy more things from us'.[89] The CDAC took the message to heart. Discussing in 1929 a proposal for the CDF to finance an ecological survey of Northern Rhodesia, the chairman conceded that this type of expenditure would not create immediate additional orders for goods or services in this country to any appreciable extent but that the future of the territory was promising and its development would lead to greater purchases in the United Kingdom. His colleagues agreed that such work would 'lead to increased trade with this country'.[90] The CDAC made their philosophy perfectly plain in their first published report:

The Committee had not regarded itself ... as being definitely tied down to recommending only such schemes as would be likely to have the effect of providing immediate orders for British goods and materials. On the contrary, it has been unwilling to interpret its functions narrowly, and in framing its recommendations ..., it has envisaged a long-range policy of Colonial development.[91]

The message was also relayed to the colonies. The letter sent to governors in the spring of 1930, urging them to submit applications, went out of its way to stress that

the attitude of the Advisory Committee towards applications is not governed by a narrow view of the unemployment problem here. The Committee is ready to entertain applications which involve little actual purchase of material in this country, or even none, if the object to which it is proposed to devote the money is one which may be expected to promote the development of the Colony, and thus indirectly to add to its wealth and consequent purchasing power to the general benefit of the trade of the Empire.[92]

Shortly afterwards, Blackett had an opportunity to put these views directly to the governors at the Colonial Office Conference. He did urge them to consider large projects likely to bring in immediate orders to the United Kingdom and help the unemployed, but 'I think we shall get more, do more, to help British industry and British commerce if we take a long view of the future and of the development than if we try simply to go after spectacular shop window cases which bring immediate large employment to this country'. He argued revealingly that 'what the Fund is meant for ... is that it should develop the heritage of the British Empire and the Colonial portions of it, not simply and solely because we are Trustees, not from purely altruistic motives, but with a view to making the states belonging to the British Empire productive in future generations'.[93]

The chagrin of Blackett and his colleagues is then understandable when the narrow views of the May Committee were endorsed by Treasury and cabinet in 1931. It is, however, apparent that these restraints did not prove permanently binding. Blackett asserted the value of colonial development as a long-term investment before the Select Committee on Estimates in 1932, and in 1934, for example, we find the CDAC approving grants for road construction in British North Borneo even though previous experience had shown that direct benefits to British trade would not be great.[94]

Most revealing of the CDAC's beliefs and behaviour is their handling of applications for help with public health projects. The promotion of public health was one of the purposes upon which the act stipulated CDF money could be spent, and the colonial governors had their attention drawn to this in the circular despatch of 10 August 1929.[95] The immediate advantage to Britain of aiding such work was apparent when it involved hospital-building or other public works for which imports from Britain were needed.[96] But it was the long-term advantages which were repeatedly stressed. Blackett was particularly keen on public health improvements. He told the Colonial Office's medical adviser that the promotion of public health in the colonies 'was an essential part of any ordered system of Colonial development', and he told the governors at the Colonial Office Conference that 'Medical and sanitary services, public health services, are likely to be one of the most fruitful ways of spending the Fund, taking a long view of the meaning of Colonial Development'.[97] The sentiment and at least part of the motivation was echoed by Lord Passfield at the same meeting: 'We can see the enormous advantage that there would be in getting the indigenous population free from hookworm, and a number of other things like that, which are always pulling them down in the way of production, and if they increase their production they will increase their orders for cotton cloth, or something else, which will be twice blessed'.[98] As a consequence of this concern,

Passfield set up a committee, including Blackett, to consider how the CDF could be used to promote public health. They agreed in their report in June 1930 that perhaps £100,000 a year might be spent on this work, mainly on capital outlay, in the initiation or improving of services, and possibly for paying for visiting specialists. 'That the health of the people is a primary factor in the economic development of a territory is not open to question.' The committee recognised that malnutrition reduced the capacity for work, depressed living standards and prevented the proper development of resources. A circular despatch from Passfield urged colonial governors to submit suitable schemes.[99]

In their first published report the CDAC made much of public health measures as part of their long-range policy. 'Wise expenditure on public health', they said, 'is essential to economic development'. Attention was drawn to aid given for re-housing schemes, venereal disease clinics, a medical expert's visit, tuberculosis investigations, the establishment of a medical school and for water and sanitation work. Similarly in their second report they explained that they were anxious to raise health standards overseas even though no immediate expenditure resulted in the United Kingdom, because 'its economic justification is to be sought ... in the consequent improvement which may be anticipated in the productive capacity of the populations affected, resulting in increased purchasing power'.[100]

Following the financial crisis of 1931, the May Committee and the Treasury attempted to dissuade the CDAC from financing such schemes and there was certainly some tightening up on expenditure for this purpose.[101] Sir John Campbell reported in March 1934 that 'the CDAC has lately been very much less liberal as regards "medical" and "health" grants than they were originally (this under Treasury pressure, to a considerable extent, I think)'. There is some evidence that when Blackett died in 1935 his successor as chairman was less enthusiastic about such work. Certainly Campbell thought that 'Sir Alan Rae Smith has never been very keen on these "health" grants; and we know that the Treasury dislikes them'. That month the Treasury did persuade Rae Smith to withdraw approval of aid for a native medical service in Zanzibar.[102]

Nevertheless, items continued to meet with CDAC approval. The extension of medical services in Northern Rhodesia in 1937, for example, was recognised to be a potentially large drain on CDF resources, but a grant was made because 'the general health of the populations was a very important factor in the economic development of the territory'. One of the largest commitments made by the CDAC, a free grant of £207,974 over seven years, was approved in January 1938 for tsetse research in Tanganyika, and the building of accommodation for trainee doctors at a Nyasaland hospital was financed against the initial opposition of the Treasury. One of the committee's very last decisions in July 1939 was to endorse a plan for medical training and research in Uganda at a cost of £240,000. Echoing the governor's own justification, the CDAC argued in their letter of recommendation to the Colonial Office and the Treasury that 'if the productivity of the East African territories is to be fully developed and, with it, the potential capacity of those territories to absorb manufactured goods from the United Kingdom, it is essential that the standard of life of the native should be raised, and to this end the eradication of disease is one of the most important measures'.[103]

The committee's interest in public health schemes was therefore sustained. Circumstances, including pressure from the May Committee and the Treasury, explain the fluctuations shown in Table 2 in the percentage of CDF money allocated to such work. But the comparatively high total for public health, plus the amounts spent on scientific research and surveys whose value to the British economy was also essentially long-term, helps explain the perhaps unexpectedly low percentage of total expenditure incurred in the United Kingdom by CDF-aided schemes. However, such expenditure does not show that the metropolitan advantages from colonial development were ignored by the CDAC in reaching their decisions.

5. CONCLUSION

As indicated in the previous chapter, the Colonial Development Act departed in several respects from earlier colonial development measures. But in spite of the fanfare which accompanied the establishment of a regularly provisioned Colonial Development Fund with unusually flexible and wide-ranging terms, the act is better seen as perpetuating through the 1930s a policy substantially evolved during the 1920s. For one thing, the CDAC could only respond to plans submitted by colonial governments. An attempt was made by the CDAC to widen their own terms to allow them to propose development schemes to colonies, but the Colonial Office, true to their traditions, insisted that initiatives must come from colonial governments.

As the committee recorded in their final report, they 'have been limited to making recommendations only on schemes specifically referred to them'.[104]

It followed that the Colonial Development Act continued the *ad hoc* project-based tradition of earlier measures. Drummond is right to argue that assistance was provided within a conceptual framework.[105] This envisaged the construction of economic and social infrastructures and the undertaking of scientific research as a way of stimulating primary production, increasing colonial purchasing power and consequently benefiting British industry, commerce and employment. But the CDAC found themselves handling colonial development projects not programmes. They reported that 'although the Committee have, where that was practicable, asked for comprehensive programmes of development to be submitted and programmes of this nature have on some occasions been prepared, they have had, as a general rule, no comprehensive picture of a colony's needs'. A package of proposals was submitted by Nyasaland and Tanganyika, but for the most part colonial governments did not, the Colonial Office would not and the CDAC could not draw up coherently assembled programmes.[106]

Furthermore, as in the past, expenditure on colonial development was fixed within narrow financial limits dictated by British budgetary priorities. The size of the CDF allowance accordingly fluctuated in an inverse relationship with colonial needs, tending to be lowest when the financial resources of colonial governments were most pressed. The terms upon which aid was granted also smacked of the grudging assistance of the 1920s. While cash grants certainly came more readily than in the past, the pressure on colonies to accept half grants or loans limited the attractiveness of the CDF. Finally, it was unlikely that a CDAC heavily representative of British business interests would have overlooked the legislation's emphasis on metropolitan economic benefit. Blackett's personal interest in public health measures and the presence in the later 1930s of Pim and Chancellor scarcely diluted that preoccupation. Besides, the terms of the act and outside pressures existed to remind the committee of their duties. The CDAC therefore stuck to their brief. Whatever the undoubted value of aid to the colonies themselves, the primary function of the Colonial Development Act was to ease the economic difficulties of the United Kingdom. That a long-term strategy was preferred was not a deviation from the act's function but integral to the concept of colonial development policy as it had evolved by the late 1920s.

As evidence of these traditional characteristics of the Colonial Development Act accumulated, discontent began to grow. The *ad hoc* nature of aid, the terms of aid, the metropolitan bias and the limited range of services upon which CDF money could be spent were being criticised by the later 1930s. In 1937 Lord de la Warr, Under-Secretary of State for the Colonies, was arguing that 'the time has come when we should consider the widening of an interpretation of the word "Development" in the Colonial Development Act'. In an argument for extending expenditure to include education, he claimed that 'the real "development" needed in Africa today is not the investment of large sums of capital but the improvement of the human capital'.[107] In April 1939 Sir Bernard Bourdillon, Governor of Nigeria, claimed in a long despatch to the Colonial Office that 'the Colonial Development Act as a measure for promoting long-range large-scale development throughout the Colonial Empire, was doomed to failure from the outset'. He criticised the limited amount of money in the fund, the practice of giving aid as loans at a time when the burden of public debt on the colonies was already so severe, the provision of grants which covered only a portion of the total cost of schemes and the failure of the CDAC to provide help to meet recurrent expenditure. He concluded that no real change of policy had occurred in 1929, that the regime of *ad hoc* assistance remained, and that 'the "doctrine of individual self-sufficiency" has never been abandoned'.[108] Even the CDAC in their final report were critical of the limited powers they had under the act, such as their lack of power to initiate schemes and especially their inability to meet long-term recurrent expenditure. 'This restriction', they recognised, 'has limited the value of the Act in those territories whose finances were weakest and where the need for assistance was, therefore, the most felt'.[109] It appears then that the basic colonial development policy operated at the end of the 1920s had not changed, but that there was a growing feeling by the end of the 1930s that it should. Why this was the case and whether changes were later effected form the subjects for the next chapter.

NOTES

1. See Table 6 below p.273.
2. *Hansard* H.C., vol.229, col.1259, 12 July 1929 and col.260, 4 July 1929.
3. See, for example, C.O. responses to CDAC proposals for Sierra Leone in 1930 described in D. G. Meredith, 'The British Government and Colonial Economic Development with particular reference to British West Africa, 1919–1939', Ph.D. thesis, University of Exeter, 1976, pp.204–16.
4. For the first occasion see, minutes of 33rd meeting CDAC, 26 Nov. 1930, CO 970/1; see also D. J. Morgan, *The Official History of Colonial Development*, vol.1, *The Origins of British Aid Policy, 1924–1945*, London, 1980, pp.51-2.
5. As Amery recognised, see his plea that it should not just be a body of businessmen in the debate on the Colonial Development Bill, *Hansard* H.C., vol.229, col.1270, 12 July 1929. For biographies of members see *Who Was Who* and *D.N.B.*.
6. Meredith, thesis, p.121. After the first year, in which meetings were usually held fortnightly, the committee settled down to a pattern of monthly meetings, see minutes CO 970/1-3.
7. A. Bullock, *The Life and Times of Ernest Bevin*, vol.1, London, 1960, pp.440-7.
8. His appointment was nevertheless a little odd. Campbell had opposed his appointment, see his minute 12 April 1938, CO 137/820/68845, and because of his financial proposals when in India the Treasury too regarded him with distrust, see I. M. Drummond, *The Floating Pound and the Sterling Area 1931–1939*, Cambridge, 1981, p.48.
9. For a review of the literature see P. Fearon, *The Origins and Nature of the Great Slump 1929–1932*, London, 1979.
10. D. H. Aldcroft, *The Inter-War Economy: Britain 1919–39*, London, 1970, pp.298-322.
11. Minutes of 1st meeting CDAC, 1 Aug. 1929, CO 970/1.
12. Minutes of 17th meeting CDAC, 26 March 1930, and 18th meeting, 9 April 1930, CO 970/1; CDAC to Treas. 26 March 1930 and Treas. to CDAC 4 April 1930, CO 323/1100/71261.
13. See Treas. letter and minutes, *ibid.*; minutes of 36th meeting CDAC, 25 Feb. 1931, CO 970/1.
14. Minutes of 40th meeting CDAC, 24 June 19: l, CO 970/1; Committee on National Expenditure, *Report*, Cmd.3920, p.134: the minority report recommended the provision of the full amount, p.250.
15. Waterfield to Blackett, 15 July 1931, T161/486/S.34609/0209; minutes of 41st meeting CDAC, 22 July 1931 and 42nd meeting 2 Sept. 1931, CO 970/1. The Labour cabinet agreed to this cut in national expenditure and it was endorsed by the National Government in *Memorandum on the Measures proposed to Secure Reductions in National Expenditure*, Cmd.3952, 1931, p.8.
16. Treas. to C.O., 5 Oct. 1931, CO 323/1153/81241/17; minutes of 45th meeting CDAC, 20 Jan. 1932 and 46th meeting 2 March 1932, CO 970/1; *Third Interim Report of CDAC*, Cmd.4079, pp.5-6. In fact only £600,000 was actually issued to the CDF.
17. Minutes of 55th meeting CDAC, 22 Feb. 1933, CO 970/2; *Fourth Interim Report of CDAC*, Cmd.4316, p.4.
18. Minutes of 63rd meeting CDAC, 29 Nov. 1933, CO 970/2; *Fifth Annual Report of CDAC*, Cmd.4634, p.10.
19. Minutes of 75th meeting CDAC, 30 Jan. 1935, CO 970/2; *Sixth Annual Report of CDAC*, Cmd.4916, p.13.
20. Minutes of 79th meeting CDAC, 29 May 1935, and 81st meeting, 24 July 1935, CO 970/2. Admittedly applications by Newfoundland totalled over £1 million.

21. Minutes of 103rd meeting CDAC, 15 Dec. 1937, and 105th meeting, 23 Feb. 1938, CO 970/3; *Ninth Annual Report of CDAC*, Cmd.5789, p.22.
22. Minutes of 113th meeting CDAC, 20 Dec. 1938, CO 970/3; only £500,000 was actually paid into the CDF.
23. Minutes of 116th meeting CDAC, 28 March 1939, CO 970/3.
24. For further details of amounts transferred see annual *Appropriation Accounts* and annual *Abstract Account of CDF with Report by Comptroller and Auditor-General*. The total amount paid out of the fund was £6,523,193.
25. G. C. Abbott, 'British Colonial Aid Policy During the Nineteen Thirties', *Canadian Journal of History*, 5 (1970), 81 and 'A Re-examination of the 1929 Colonial Development Act', *Ec.H.R.*, 24 (1971), 75 wrongly claims that re-payments by colonies of CDF loans went back into the CDF: section 1(8) of the act required them to be repaid to the Exchequer. See also annual *Abstract Account of CDF*.
26. See, for example, *Third Interim Report of CDAC*, Cmd.4079, p.4.
27. Circular telegram, 7 Aug. 1929, and circular despatch, 10 Aug. 1929, CO 323/1063/61480/1, reprinted as Appendix 1(a) and (b) in *First Interim Report of CDAC*, Cmd.3540, pp.20-4.
28. Minutes of 1st meeting CDAC, 1 Aug. 1929, CO 970/1.
29. Minutes of 15th meeting CDAC, 19 Feb. 1930, *ibid.*; CO 323/1100/71261/2.
30. Model letter drafted late Feb. 1930, *ibid.*, sent with minor modifications by each geographical department, for example, see CO 825/7/73036.
31. Details of applications for 1939−40 were not published by the CDAC and hence analysis is based on the period 1929−39 only. The total cost of schemes cited from Meredith's thesis differs slightly from those in D. G. Meredith, 'The British Government and Colonial Economic Policy, 1919−39', *Ec.H.R.*, 28 (1975), 490.
32. See Meredith, *Ec.H.R.*, (1975), Table 2, p.490 for the figures and for a slightly different conclusion, pp.489-92. Interestingly, Uganda had unusually buoyant government revenues for East Africa at this time and made little use of the CDF, E. A. Brett, *Colonialism and Underdevelopment in East Africa*, London, 1973, p.136.
33. In its final report covering the period up to July 1940 the CDAC calculated a total expenditure on schemes of only £19,284,536, *Eleventh and Final Report of CDAC*, Cmd.6298, p.8.
34. For a list of large schemes see Meredith, thesis, p.103.
35. *Eleventh and Final Report of CDAC*, Cmd.6298, p.9.
36. *Second Interim Report of CDAC*, Cmd.3876, p.10; *Third Interim Report*, Cmd. 4079, p.4; *Fourth Interim Report*, Cmd.4316, p.4.
37. J. F. Munro, *Africa and the International Economy, 1800−1960*, London, 1976, pp.150-2 and fig.1, p.148; Brett, *Colonialism and Underdevelopment in East Africa*, p.136; A. G. Hopkins, *An Economic History of West Africa*, London, 1973, pp.184-5.
38. Meredith, thesis, pp.33, 44-5 and appendix 1.
39. For the effect on recruitment to the Colonial Service see Sir Ralph Furse, *Aucuparius: Recollections of a Recruiting Officer*, London, 1962, p.241 and figures in appendix 1.
40. For C.O.-Treas. talks in 1931 on how to keep colonies solvent see T161/493/S.36290.
41. Section (2) and section 1(1)(n).
42. *Eleventh and Final Report of CDAC*, Cmd.6298, pp.7-8; see also Campbell's comment recorded in minutes of Group Council meeting, 6 March 1930, CO 323/110/71261/2.
43. Minutes of 1st meeting CDAC, 1 Aug. 1929, CO 970/1.

44. Minute by Bottomley, 8 Feb. 1930, and see also Wilson to Passfield, 22 Jan. 1930 and minute by Grindle 8 Feb. 1930, CO 323/110/71261/2.
45. *Report of the East Africa Guaranteed Loan Committee 1926–1929*, Cmd.3494, 1930, p.10; *First Interim Report of CDAC*, Cmd.3540, Table C, p.29.
46. Minutes of Group Council meeting, 6 March 1930 and C.O. to CDAC 11 March 1930, CO 323/1100/71261/2.
47. The episode is described in Meredith, thesis, pp.204-16.
48. Minutes of 92nd meeting CDAC, 28 Oct. 1936, CO 970/2.
49. Meredith, *Ec.H.R.*, (1975), 488-9, 491; Abbott, 'A Re-examination of the 1929 Colonial Development Act', pp.78-9; see also *Tenth Annual Report CDAC*, Cmd.6062, Table C, for loans per head of population.
50. Minutes of Group Council meeting, 6 March 1930, and C.O. to CDAC, 11 March 1930, CO 323/1100/71261/2.
51. Minutes of 9th meeting CDAC, 27 Nov. 1929, CO 970/1; see also minutes 94th meeting CDAC, 27 Jan. 1937, CO 970/2.
52. Meredith, thesis, p.93.
53. *First Interim Report of CDAC*, Cmd.3540, p.16; *Second Interim Report*, Cmd.3876, p.4; Colonial Office Conference, Misc.No.416, CO 885/32, p.39; *Colonial Office Conference 1930. Summary of Proceedings*, Cmd.3628, p.13.
54. Minutes of 99th meeting CDAC, 23 June 1937 and 94th meeting 27 Jan. 1937, CO 970/2.
55. Minutes of 26th meeting, 24 July 1930, CO 970/1; see also *First Interim Report of CDAC*, Cmd.3540, p.16 and *Second Interim Report*, Cmd.3876, p.4.
56. *First Interim Report of CDAC*, Cmd.3540, p.16; *Eleventh and Final Report of CDAC*, Cmd.6298, p.7; see, for example, minutes of 15th meeting CDAC, 19 Feb. 1930, CO 970/1.
57. *First Interim Report of CDAC*, Cmd.3540, pp.15-16. For Treasury involvement in one such case see minutes of 33rd meeting, 26 Nov. 1930, CO 970/1.
58. *Fifth Annual Report of CDAC*, Cmd.4634, p.8; minutes of 62nd meeting CDAC, 25 Oct. 1933, CO 970/2.
59. C.O. to CDAC, 11 March 1930, CO 323/1100/71261/2.
60. See Blackett at C.O. Conference in 1930, Misc.No.416, CO 885/32, pp.40-1; *Second Interim Report of CDAC*, Cmd.3876, pp.10-1; *Eleventh and Final Report*, Cmd.6298, p.7. Morgan, *The Origins of British Aid Policy*, p.58 cites three examples.
61. CO 885/32, p.40.
62. *Second Interim Report of CDAC*, Cmd.3876, p.4; *Eleventh and Final Report*, Cmd.6298, p.7. For one late example see minutes of 116th meeting CDAC, 28 March 1939, CO 970/3.
63. *First Report of the Select Committee on Estimates*, 1932, para.12; minutes of 42nd meeting CDAC, 2 Sept. 1931, CO 970/1 reveals one example.
64. See minutes on CO 536/204/40251.
65. E. R. Wicker, 'Colonial Development and Welfare 1929–1957: the Evolution of a Policy', *Social and Economic Studies*, vol.7 (1958), 174-8; Meredith, *Ec.H.R.*, (1975), 487; D. G. M. Rampersad, 'Colonial Economic Development and Social Welfare: the Case of the British West Indian Colonies, 1929–1947', Oxford D.Phil. thesis, 1979, pp.52-3, 56.
66. These figures differ slightly from those given by Meredith, *Ec.H.R.*, (1975), 488.
67. *Tenth Annual Report of CDAC*, Cmd.6062, Table A(1), p.38. The total cost of approved schemes is as given by the committee and therefore differs slightly from the corrected figure calculated by Meredith and cited in Table 1 above, p.203.
68. Meredith, *Ec.H.R.*, (1975), 488.

69. S. Constantine, *Unemployment in Britain between the Wars*, London, 1980, pp.3-25.
70. Minutes of 1st meeting CDAC, 1 Aug. 1929, CO 970/1. The government published three white papers in Dec. 1929, March 1930 and Dec. 1930 which included estimates of the expenditure in the U.K. and the man-years of employment created by the CDF: *Statement on Works Approved for Grant in Connection with Unemployment*, Cmd.3449, 1929, *Statement on Works Approved for Government Financial Assistance in Connection with Unemployment*, Cmd.3519, 1930, *Statement of the Principal Measures taken by H.M. Government in connection with Unemployment*, Cmd.3746, 1930.
71. Circular telegram, 7 Aug. 1929, and circular despatch 10 Aug. 1929, CO 323/1063/61480/1, reprinted as Appendix 1(a) and (b) in *First Interim Report of CDAC*, Cmd.3540, pp.20-4.
72. Minutes of 8th meeting CDAC, 20 Nov. 1929, CO 970/1; circular despatch to colonies, 28 Nov. 1929, CO 323/1063/61480/1.
73. *Third Interim Report of CDAC*, Cmd.4079, p.6.
74. Minutes of 6th meeting CDAC, 30 Oct. 1929, 8th meeting 20 Nov. 1929, 10th meeting 4 Dec. 1929, 12th meeting, 8th Jan. 1930, CO 970/1.
75. Minutes of 2nd meeting CDAC, 11 Sept. 1929, and 3rd meeting, 25 Sept. 1929, *ibid.*.
76. *Papers Relating to a Conference between the Secretary of State for the Colonies and the Prime Ministers of Self-Governing Colonies*, Cd.1299, 1902, p.4; *Imperial Economic Conference, Summary of Conclusions*, Cmd.1990, 1923, p.6.
77. Minutes of 3rd meeting CDAC, 25 Sept. 1929, CO 970/1.
78. Minutes of 4th meeting CDAC, 9 Oct. 1929, and 6th meeting 30 Oct. 1929, *ibid.*.
79. T161/980/S.34783; CO 323/1035/60279.
80. Copy on T161/980/S.34783 and CO 323/1079/70279; see also minutes of 23rd meeting CDAC, 11 June 1930, CO 970/1.
81. *First Interim Report of CDAC*, Cmd.3540, p.11.
82. CDAC to Treas. 1 May 1937, T161/980/S.34783; minutes of 96th meeting CDAC, 24 March 1937, CO 970/2, of 114th meeting, 28 March 1939, and of 116th meeting, 28 March 1939, CO 970/3; *Eleventh and Final Report of CDAC*, Cmd.6298, p.7.
83. *Hansard* H.C., vol.231, col.1749, 12 Nov. 1929; vol.235, cols.1949–70, 24 Feb. 1930; vol.247, col.339, 22 Jan. 1931; vol.265, col.383, 27 April 1932; vol.267, col.1085, 22 June 1932; vol.297, col.331, 30 Jan. 1935.
84. Memo. by Skevington, 18 June 1931, T161/486/S.34609/0209.
85. *Committee on National Expenditure, Report*, Cmd.3920, 1931, p.134.
86. Waterfield to Blackett, 15 July 1931, T161/486/S.34609/0209; Treas. to C.O. 5 Oct. 1931, circular despatch 27 Oct. 1931, CDAC to C.O. 30 Oct. 1931, CO 323/1153/81241/17; *Memorandum on the Measures proposed to secure Reductions in National Expenditure*, Cmd.3952, 1931; *Third Interim Report of CDAC*, Cmd.4079, 1932, p.4.
87. Meredith, *Ec.H.R.*, (1975), 488.
88. Minutes of 41st meeting CDAC, 22 July 1931, and see 42nd meeting, 2 Sept. 1931, CO 970/1.
89. Minutes of 1st meeting, 1 Aug. 1929, *ibid.*; see also memo. by Thomas, 23 Oct. 1929, CAB 24/206/CP 287 and by Passfield 22 Nov. 1930, CAB 24/216/CP 392, p.31.
90. Minutes of 4th meeting CDAC, 9 Oct. 1929, 5th meeting 16 Oct. 1929, CO 970/1; for a similar case, see 8th meeting, 20 Nov. 1929, *ibid.*.
91. *First Interim Report of CDAC*, Cmd.3540, p.17.
92. Model letter, Feb. 1930, CO 323/1100/71261/2.
93. Misc.No.416, CO 885/32, p.41.

94. *First Report from the Select Committee on Estimates*, 1932, q.408; minutes of 73rd meeting CDAC, 31 Oct. 1934, CO 970/2; see also the committee's defence of their long-term strategy following an investigation into the effect of the act on unemployment in Britain, *Fourth Interim Report of CDAC*, Cmd.4316, pp.4-5.
95. This clause, 1(1)m, had been added to the bill in committee to clarify its original intentions, *Hansard* H.C., vol.230, cols.722, 518, 710; circular despatch, CO 323/1063/61480/1, reprinted in *First Interim Report of CDAC*, Cmd.3540, appendix 1(b), p.21.
96. See, for example, minutes of 6th meeting CDAC, 30 Oct. 1929, CO 970/1.
97. Minutes of 13th meeting CDAC, 22 Jan. 1930, *ibid.*; Misc.No.416, CO 885/32, p.41; see also minute by Campbell, 16 March 1934, CO 111/714/35031/1.
98. Misc.No.416, CO 885/32, p.42.
99. Report of the Colonial Development Public Health Committee, 24 June 1930, Misc.No.413, CO 885/32; circular despatch, 16 Sept. 1930, CO 854/78.
100. *First Interim Report of CDAC*, Cmd.3540, pp.17-18; *Second Interim Report*, Cmd.3876, 1932, p.5.
101. See especially Waterfield of Treasury to Blackett, 15 July 1931, T161/486/S.34609/0209.
102. Minutes by Campbell, 16 March 1934, CO 111/714/35031/1, 2 Dec. 1935, CO 295/590/70127; minutes of 84th meeting CDAC, 18 Dec. 1935, CO 970/2.
103. Minutes of 94th meeting CDAC, 22 Jan. 1937, CO 970/2; of 107th meeting, 27 April 1938, 108th meeting 18 May 1938, and 119th meeting, 18 July 1939, CO 970/3; CDAC to C.O. and Treas., 8 Aug. 1939 and Governor's despatch, 22 April 1939, CO 536/204/40251.
104. See exchange between Blackett and Grindle, minutes of 1st meeting CDAC, 1 Aug. 1929, CO 970/1; *Eleventh and Final Report of CDAC*, Cmd.6298, p.9.
105. I. M. Drummond, 'More on British Colonial Aid Policy in the Nineteen-Thirties', *Canadian Journal of History*, 6 (1971), 191-3.
106. *Eleventh and Final Report of CDAC*, Cmd.6298, p.9; on Nyasaland see Morgan, *Origins of British Aid Policy*, pp.52-6 and on Tanganyika see Brett, *Colonialism and Underdevelopment*, p.136 and *Sixth Annual Report of CDAC*, Cmd.4916, pp.6-7.
107. Memo. by Lord de la Warr, n.d. [1937], CO 852/118/15279/5.
108. Bourdillon to C.O., 5 April 1939, CO 852/214/15201/17.
109. *Eleventh and Final Report of CDAC*, Cmd.6298, pp.8-9.

IX

THE COLONIAL DEVELOPMENT
AND WELFARE ACT 1940

1. *THE COLONIAL QUESTION IN THE LATER 1930s*

During the 1930s the idea that the Colonial Empire should be made to serve the economic interests of the metropolis in a period of economic depression and high unemployment continued to affect government policies and retained much popular political support. The CDAC adhered to their original brief, and the flows of colonial trade were in some cases further affected by the Ottawa tariff agreements of 1932 and by the imposition of quotas on Japanese textile imports into the colonies in 1934.[1] Cunliffe-Lister as Secretary of State for the Colonies from 1931 to 1935 retained his belief in the value of colonial products and markets as assets for the metropolitan economy and endeavoured to encourage their development.[2] Outside government, Amery and other enthusiasts in such organisations as the Empire Economic Union and the Empire Industries Association maintained their campaign for greater imperial economic unity.[3] It is, however, striking that this justification for increased imperial expenditure on colonial development was overlaid in the later 1930s by fresh anxieties and new proposals.

For one thing, participants to the debate on government economic policy began to show more interest in proposals for domestic-oriented recovery. The Liberal election programme of 1929, *We Can Conquer Unemployment*, had aroused considerable attention, and the same was true of Oswald Mosley's unorthodox plans put to government as the Mosley Memorandum and to the public in his resignation speech in May 1930. The essence of these schemes was reiterated with more frequency and greater sophistication as the decade unfolded, in Lloyd George's New Deal platform of 1935, in the Labour Party's economic proposals, in Harold Macmillan's *The Middle Way* in 1938, by non-party bodies like the Liberal and Democratic Leadership group and amongst economists by Keynes whose *General Theory* was published in 1936. The virtues of government domestic demand management even had some influence over Treasury monetary policy.[4] The attention given to proposals for easier credit and reflationary fiscal policies, including large-scale public works programmes at home, at least partly reflected the apparent failure of policies which had envisaged an export-led recovery. The staple export industries remained depressed. Experience had also demonstrated that stimulating exports by imperial economic development effected little immediate improvement in employment prospects. The government's own estimates could claim only modest amounts of new work created as a direct result of the Colonial Development Act. As an economic strategy, colonial development lost some of its appeal since it could at best be regarded as a long-term solution.

But at the same time Britain's long-term possession of a Colonial Empire was being increasingly questioned. Critics of empire had, of course, existed for many years, and especially since the beginning of the century, but until the later 1930s such dissenters remained a fringe group of marginal influence.[5] Most British observers were satisfied with colonialism because the economic and other advantages accruing to Britain were supposed to be balanced by equivalent gains to colonial peoples in the form of improved material standards of living and the grafting of certain western qualities onto their indigenous cultures. As J. H. Oldham put it in 1924, 'the European Powers are in Africa primarily from economic, not humanitarian motives. Their object is the development of their own industries and trade, but the benefit may be reciprocal'.[6] It was the standard assumption of advocates of colonial economic development in the 1920s that a natural harmony existed between the interests of the British and colonial economies and that British colonial rule inevitably brought progress. This easy optimism was to be seriously challenged in the 1930s.

The inevitability of improvement was rudely shattered by the world economic depression. Its effects were felt not just on the prices colonial producers received for their labour and therefore on their living standards. It affected also colonial government revenues and therefore the quality of government social and development services. Appointments to the colonial service sank dramatically in 1931 and 1932, including massive falls in the numbers of medical, educational, agricultural and veterinary specialists recruited by colonial governments.

Recovery was slow and never picked up to the rate of appointments made in the 1920s until after the Second World War.[7] For much of the 1930s social and economic conditions in the colonies were arguably worse than they had been in the previous decade, not better. Some observers felt that matters were only made worse when the Imperial government broke with free trade traditions at Ottawa in 1932. The preferential agreements may have affected only part of the Colonial Empire and in some cases may have been defensible in terms of protecting those colonies' markets elsewhere in the empire, but the imposition in 1934 of quotas on cheap Japanese imports of textiles into the Colonial Empire in the interests of Lancashire hardly seemed compatible with the concept of natural harmony. Opposition to the quotas in some colonies only increased concern at home, particularly among sections of the Labour and Liberal parties where Cobdenite ideals lingered longest.[8]

Contemporaries also correctly believed that economic problems lay at the root of many, though not all, of the outbreaks of social and political unrest which troubled colonial authorities in the later 1930s. There were strikes and riots in the West Indies in 1935 and more serious disturbances in 1937 and 1938. A strike in the Northern Rhodesian copper mines in 1935 resulted in some deaths when the police opened fire. In 1937 there was trouble on sugar estates in Mauritius and a cocoa hold-up in the Gold Coast and Nigeria by peasant farmers protesting at low prices. Jewish immigration into the British mandated territory of Palestine led to conflict with the Arabs, strikes and serious riots in April 1936 and simmering disorder thereafter.[9]

Social and economic problems and disturbances in the colonies inspired or provoked the publication in Britain of a large number of Imperial government reports into colonial conditions. They fuelled public concern. There were reports on the riots in St. Kitts, Trinidad and Northern Rhodesia which exposed underlying economic distress, low wages, underemployment, poor standards of living and harsh labour conditions.[10] There was a series of investigations by Sir Alan Pim between 1932 and 1937 into the financial and economic circumstances of a number of troubled territories: Swaziland, Zanzibar, Bechuanaland, British Honduras, Basutoland, Kenya and Northern Rhodesia.[11] Some general problems also received particular attention. J. H. Thomas, briefly restored as Secretary of State for the Colonies in 1936, was inspired by recent League of Nations' studies of nutrition and public health to initiate an enquiry into standards of nutrition and related government activity in each colonial territory. The material collected was remitted by the new Secretary of State, Ormsby-Gore, to a high-powered sub-committee of the cabinet's Economic Advisory Council chaired by Earl de la Warr, the under-secretary. It was to labour at its task over the next two and a half years before producing a two-volume report which both exposed the low living standards of Britain's colonial subjects and urged a more positive role for government in their improvement. Another series of studies of labour conditions in various territories was begun by the Colonial Office's newly-appointed Labour Adviser in 1938.[12]

At the same time further interest in colonial affairs was aroused by the revival of Italian imperialist ambitions in North Africa and by German demands for the return of the colonies taken from them by the Treaty of Versailles in 1919. The possibility of appeasing Nazi Germany by colonial concessions was given serious consideration by the British government on several occasions between 1936 and 1938. Rumours of this provoked lively public controversy which obliged opponents of restoration to define and defend the virtues of British colonial rule.[13]

Public interest in colonial questions explains and partly reflects the large number of private studies of colonial issues published in the later 1930s. The social and economic problems of the West Indies and the inadequacies of colonial and Imperial government policies were analysed in Professor W. M. Macmillan's *Warning from the West Indies*, published in 1936 and as a Penguin Book in 1938. The work was even received with considerable interest by Colonial Office staff. A similar impact was made by his *Africa Emergent* in 1938.[14] Leonard Barnes also produced a series of critical studies of colonial conditions and government policies beginning in 1935.[15] Also in 1935 Lord Hailey, a former Governor of the United Provinces in India, began work on a massively detailed review of colonial problems and practice in Africa on behalf of the Royal Institute of International Affairs. Although this too was an unofficial investigation, the prestige of the R.I.I.A., of the author and of the members of the Africa Research Survey Committee who supported him, plus the thorough-ness of the report, made the publication of *An African Survey* in November 1938 a major event.[16] Discussion of colonial issues was not, however, confined to scholarly volumes but was aired in journals, magazines and the newspapers. For example *The Political Quarterly* produced a special number on the empire in 1938, and in the same year *International Affairs* discussed 'The Colonial Problem'.[17] The riots in the West Indies were widely reported in the popular press as well as in the weeklies, and the general tone of comment was expressed by *The Times*: 'Recent events in the West Indies have shaken the complacency with which most people in this country have been accustomed to regard the Colonial Empire ... they have created an uneasy suspicion that economic and social improvements may be just as badly needed in other parts as well'.[18]

Greater concern with colonial conditions was also shown by the House of Commons. Ministers were subjected to repeated questioning, especially after the riots in the West Indies and on the subject of Germany's colonial claims. The Secretary of State for the Colonies was pressed to provide the House with more information on colonial affairs.[19] While critics of government policy were evident on all sides, it was the Labour Party which in the late 1930s asserted itself as a rather better organised, better informed and better led critic of colonial matters. Interest still did not run deep in the party as a whole, but several Labour M.P.s led by Arthur Creech Jones, a future Secretary of State for the Colonies, and supported by the experts recruited to the party's Advisory Committee on Imperial Questions, did keep the Colonial Office under constant pressure. Questions asked primarily concerned labour problems and social conditions in the empire and came thick and fast following the West Indian disturbances and the government reports on them. Summing up the effects of recent revelations Creech Jones told the House of Commons in 1938, 'During the last few years our own complacency in Colonial administration has been rudely shocked'.[20]

What gave an added edge to the debate on colonial conditions was the international dimension. Article 22 of the Covenant of the League of Nations asserted that colonial administrations in the mandated territories were to serve the interests of the inhabitants. It is true that the British government claimed that honouring this obligation involved no departure from the principles of British colonial trusteeship practised elsewhere in the Colonial Empire, and for most of the inter-war years the influence of the League on colonial policy is shadowy and hard to detect. But with the concern about colonial conditions aroused by the depression, riots and German colonial claims, some observers and even some Colonial Office staff felt that British colonial policy was failing to measure up to the standards of good government laid down by the Permanent Mandates Commission and the International Labour Organisation. An unprecedented sensitivity to international, including American, criticism of British colonial rule can be detected by the end of the decade.[21]

One effect of disillusionment with the fruits of British colonial rule was a disenchantment with the doctrine of protective trusteeship. The notion that British colonial administration ought primarily to preserve colonial peoples from too harsh a collision with western values and economic changes seemed to be an excuse for tolerating stagnation, even regression. Besides, the ideal of perpetuating indigenous virtues seemed irrelevant to a society as in the West Indies which had for so long existed within an essentially western culture and which in the 1930s was in deep distress. Demands therefore grew for a more constructive form of trusteeship which would repair the neglect, stimulate economic recovery and improve social conditions. This was the message of W. M. Macmillan, of Lord Hailey, of Creech Jones and, most significantly of the Colonial Office itself.[22]

In the later 1930s the Colonial Office showed it was receptive to new views and outside influences and accepted the idea of constructive trusteeship. For example, the Colonial Empire Marketing Board was established in October 1937 to assist the economic recovery of the colonies by promoting their products in Britain and overseas.[23] Ormsby-Gore as Secretary of State informed the Board at its first meeting that 'it is now the settled policy of all United Kingdom Governments to be guided in their Colonial policy by the doctrine of trusteeship .... We fully accept the position that it is our duty to advance to the fullest possible degree the interests of the Colonial territories under our charge'. The CEMB, he concluded, 'is merely one item in the programme of Colonial development'.[24] Labour Party and TUC pressure was responsible for other innovations, especially the Secretary of State's decision in 1937 to appoint a Labour Adviser to the Colonial Office and the department's efforts to persuade colonial governments to introduce appropriate legislation governing conditions of labour and trade union rights.[25] Similarly the TUC's recently formed Colonial Advisory Committee visited the Colonial Office in June 1938 and thereby initiated discussions which ultimately produced a plan to establish a Social Services department in the Colonial Office. Officials were by then sympathetic to such an innovation. The permanent under-secretary observed that it would 'be very useful in co-ordinating the work of social services which is going to be more and more important as time goes on'.[26] The influence of recent debates on colonial issues is fully revealed in the letter which the Colonial Office despatched to the Treasury seeking authorisation for the new department:

At the present time it is a matter of the highest political importance that His Majesty's Government should be able to show unassailable justification for its claim that it acts as a beneficial trustee for its subject peoples, and that there is urgent need for us to undertake an effective forward movement in developing the progress of social services, including the improvements of labour conditions, nutrition, public health, education, housing and so forth, in the Colonial Empire.[27]

It was inevitable that the same debates and similar anxieties would also focus attention in the late 1930s on the operations of the Colonial Development Act. Macmillan, for one, urged the Imperial government to be more generous in shouldering the financial costs of a constructive development policy in the colonies.[28] As Lord Hailey was later to put it, 'I sometimes wish that we could place our hands on our hearts a little less, and set them to explore our pockets a little more'.[29] How the Colonial Office, and the Treasury, would respond to this invitation remains to be considered.

2. MALCOLM MACDONALD AND THE WEST INDIES

In May 1938 a cabinet reshuffle brought Malcolm MacDonald back to the Colonial Office as Secretary of State. It was a crucial appointment for although he was only 36, he was already a politician of considerable experience. As the son of Ramsay MacDonald, the first Labour Prime Minister and later leader of the National Government, Malcolm MacDonald was brought up in a highly political home. He contested his first general election in 1923 at the age of 22 and became an M.P. in 1929. Moreover, he had been parliamentary undersecretary at the Dominions Office from 1931 to 1935 and had been in the cabinet for six months as Secretary of State for the Colonies in 1935 and since then as Secretary of State for the Dominions.[30] This experience had made him aware not only of the current debate on general colonial and imperial questions but had given him some detailed knowledge of colonial conditions and problems. He had recently been concerned with the economic and social difficulties of Swaziland, Basutoland and Bechuanaland, the High Commission territories in South Africa for which the Dominions Office was responsible. They revealed in microcosm many of the troubles of the Colonial Empire as a whole. Later, in retirement, he claimed that even in 1935 he had been convinced that British colonial policy needed substantial revision. Certainly when he returned to the Colonial Office on 16 May 1938 he was determined to inaugurate a more active development policy. Genuinely disturbed by the evidence of social and economic distress in the empire, MacDonald was also sensitive to domestic and international criticism of Britain's behaviour as a colonial power. What remained to be determined was the precise nature of a new initiative and whether he could persuade Treasury and cabinet to finance it.[31]

It was just as well that he was no novice and had the basis of a new policy in mind, since he had scarcely got his feet under his desk when decisions concerning the West Indies were required of him. At the beginning of May the disturbances in the West Indies worsened with outbreaks of violence in Jamaica.[32] This intensified the press and parliamentary concern about the islands already fuelled by the troubles in Trinidad and Barbados in 1937 and by the recent publication of the reports of inquiries into those disturbances. Labour M.P.s especially raised questions in the House of Commons, and in May 1938 demands were increasing for the appointment of a Royal Commission to investigate economic and social conditions throughout the West Indies.[33]

The West Indian department of the Colonial Office set about reviewing the political and economic conditions of the region, prompted initially by the new disturbances and latterly by parliamentary demands for a Royal Commission. They briefed the new minister in a long memorandum on 20 May 1938. The permanent staff reflected a pessimistic orthodoxy. They recognised that disturbances had occurred primarily because of the depressed state of the local economy, and they acknowledged that only Imperial government financial help could restore local prosperity. But though they contemplated requesting imperial aid for the suffering sugar industry, they claimed that 'it is doubtful if such a case could be made out, and still more doubtful if, however, it were presented, the Chancellor would listen to it. Past concessions have been hard enough to win'. They argued that 'large-scale improvements in the West Indies could not be effected without very heavy further expenditure from United Kingdom funds, which present financial conditions would not be likely to permit', and they therefore concluded that it would be dangerous to accede to the demands for a Royal Commission since it would 'raise hopes doomed from the outset to disappointment: and the consequences in the long run might be most unfortunate'. The department then fell back upon a defence of the various piecemeal schemes currently being introduced by local governments: they were in effect recommending that most traditional of colonial development policies, gradual improvements financed out of local colonial revenues.[34]

If it is striking how pessimistic and orthodox this departmental response was, it is equally noticeable how officials not wedded to the departmental structure rejected it. Sir Frank Stockdale had been appointed Agricultural Adviser to the Colonial Office in 1929, and he brought to the post and to this discussion practical knowledge of West Indian conditions, having served there in government agricultural departments before the First World War. He proposed a number of new approaches including the settlement of smallholders on the land and assistance for the cocoa and rice industries, and concluded that because the solution to the economic problems was urgent the appointment of a Royal Commission 'might be useful'.[35] This was vigorously endorsed by Sir John Campbell, the Economic and Financial Adviser at the Colonial Office. He was certain that financial assistance from the Imperial government had to be obtained in order to generate improvements in the West Indies. He was also quite explicit about the justification for such aid at this time: he was concerned about the possible repercussions of the West Indian disturbances on international opinion, especially in conjunction with the simultaneous bitter dispute over British policy in Palestine. He feared that the view might too readily be gained that there was something fundamentally wrong with British colonial rule. He was particularly perturbed by the American tendency to judge British colonialism by conditions in the neighbouring West Indies: 'One sees signs of a growing interest in the administration of these territories on the part of Americans, reflected in the American magazines. The W. Indies are, to some considerable extent, the British shop-window for the U.S.A. I am afraid it is not a very striking exhibit'.[36]

MacDonald's response to this divergence of opinion in the office was to summon a meeting of senior officials under his chairmanship. The participants included his under-secretary Lord Dufferin, Sir Cosmo Parkinson, the permanent under-secretary, Sir Henry Moore, assistant under-secretary but until recently Governor of Sierra Leone,

Clauson, assistant secretary in charge of the Economics department set up in 1935, Stockdale, Campbell and, as representatives of the West Indian department, Beckett, the assistant secretary and three of his principals. On 31 May 1938 the earlier departmental response was brushed aside, and it was agreed that a cabinet memorandum should be drafted recommending the appointment of a Royal Commission.[37] Fresh and more alarming news of disorder in Jamaica may have helped sway the decision,[38] but from what is known of MacDonald's intentions on taking office it is probable that he endorsed in any case the arguments of Stockdale and Campbell. In particular he shared the latter's anxiety about international criticism of British colonial rule. Moreover, MacDonald may have been swayed by Campbell's suggestion that the appointment of a Royal Commission might actually be a valuable political lever to prize open the imperial coffers and obtain development funds. It might be a more effective technique than mere departmental lobbying of the Treasury. The problem facing MacDonald in seeking to initiate a new policy was after all the perennial one of persuading the Treasury to release money to sustain it. And as Campbell had noted, 'What one may call the normal arguments available to the Dept. and the S/S are most unlikely to lead to anything material; but if there were a considered recommendation from a R. Comm. on the point that would presumably carry great weight'.[39]

The memorandum drafted by the Colonial Office described the economic problems of West Indian agriculture, pointed out that the consequent inadequate revenues of colonial governments prevented the self-financing of improvements in local welfare services, and argued that to improve local agricultural production and local social services imperial aid was therefore needed. Social welfare as well as economic prosperity were evidently the twin objectives of the new proposals. Moreover, assistance from imperial funds must be on a scale much greater than the existing system of grants-in-aid. The Colonial Office recommended the appointment of a Royal Commission to investigate these matters and to devise a long-term policy of reconstruction. It was argued that such a strategy would actually defuse present criticism of government policy at home and in the colonies and that future expenditure would be more acceptable to Parliament and taxpayer if based on the recommendations of a Royal Commission. It was, however, made clear that accepting the appointment of a Royal Commission did imply providing subsequently

whatever financial assistance was necessary to implement such recommendations: failure to take action would lead to further unrest
in the colonies. However, the crucial justification for substantial
imperial expenditure in the West Indies was that 'any further, steady
deterioration will prove very damaging to Great Britain's reputation
as a Colonial Power. It is ... imperative that, at a time when the
"colonial question" is being ventilated at home and abroad, we
should ourselves be as far as possible above reproach'.[40]

The memorandum was sent in draft form to the Treasury for their
comments, but it was never formally circulated to other ministers as
a cabinet paper. MacDonald had to react to domestic as well as international criticism of the government's colonial policy: the decision-
making process was accelerated when a parliamentary question asking
if the Secretary of State was going to appoint a Royal Commission
was submitted by a Labour M.P. for answer on 14 June 1938, the
day on which the Colonial Office estimates were also due to be
debated. MacDonald wanted to deflect criticism and avoid the impression that the government was capitulating to Labour pressure,
and he therefore wrote to the Chancellor on 10 June and urged
him to accept at once the appointment of a Royal Commission.[41]
Treasury officials were inevitably concerned at the potential cost of
their concession. They feared that the Exchequer was being asked to
meet with 'a blank cheque' whatever a Royal Commission proposed.
But in the event they capitulated. They recognised that the political
implications of the West Indian situation made acceptance unavoidable. Sir Richard Hopkins, second secretary, reluctantly conceded that
'I do not see how we can refuse to contemplate a Royal Commission
in view of recent happenings nor can we hope that such a Commission will result in anything other than more demands on the
Exchequer'.[42] Consequently, on 13 June, MacDonald obtained the
concurrence of the Chancellor and later of the Prime Minister, and
he was therefore able to announce the appointment of a Royal Commission on the West Indies when he introduced the Colonial Office
vote the following day.[43] The decision was only endorsed by the
cabinet at its meeting on 15 June. On that occasion 'the Chancellor
of the Exchequer agreed that, notwithstanding the probability that
a Royal Commission would result in proposals involving increased
expenditure, the course proposed by the Colonial Secretary was the
right one'.[44] The arguments and strategy of the Colonial Office had
proved remarkably successful. The Imperial government had agreed

to abandon the policy of self-financed development in the West Indies and to accept a commitment to finance whatever social as well as economic improvements a Royal Commission ultimately recommended.

3. REVIEWING THE COLONIAL DEVELOPMENT ACT

On the following day, 16 June 1938, MacDonald requested his staff to draw up a memorandum on the operations of the Colonial Development Fund.[45] This instruction shows that the Secretary of State was by no means solely concerned with conditions in the West Indies. While problems there were of pressing importance, he evidently wished to review colonial development policy more generally and to do so quickly, a month after taking office. Indeed, having achieved an initial success with a new policy for the West Indies, MacDonald seemed determined to exploit it.

On 27 June 1938 he chaired the first meeting of a departmental committee which with certain changes of personnel was to discuss this question on several occasions before the eventual drafting of the Colonial Development and Welfare Bill. The importance MacDonald attached to colonial development is indicated by the seniority of those present, who included not only Dufferin but the permanent under-secretary, Parkinson, the deputy under-secretary, Shuckburgh, all three assistant under-secretaries, Bottomley, Tomlinson and Moore, the assistant secretaries of the Economics, General and East Africa departments, Clauson, Calder and Dawe, plus a battery of five Colonial Office advisers including Campbell and Stockdale. In his opening remarks MacDonald made his reasons for reviewing and improving colonial development policy at this time perfectly plain. Although he spoke of 'our responsibility as trustees for the peoples of the Colonial Empire', arguments of political expediency predominated: 'Colonial affairs had come into particular prominence lately and the eyes of the world were upon us'. If the present inadequate policies were continued Britain's reputation as a colonial power would suffer irretrievable damage. The meeting then readily agreed on the inadequacy of the Colonial Development Act.

While it was generally accepted that the Colonial Development Advisory Committee performed a useful function, the machinery for initiating colonial development schemes was thought to be inadequate. Proposals were aired to appoint a planning officer in the Colonial

Office and to send officials overseas to help colonial governments draw up schemes. Parkinson raised a major issue when he 'drew attention to the restriction placed by legislation on the operations of the Colonial Development Fund in that it must be applied to schemes calculated to promote industry in or commerce with the United Kingdom'. It is true that Campbell reckoned that in practice this principle had been 'considerably watered down in its application by the Committee', but Moore, perhaps reflecting on his earlier career as a colonial governor, nevertheless argued that the stipulation 'had acted as a great deterrent to Colonial Governments in putting forward schemes'. Further criticism was aimed at the restrictive terms of the act which limited the assistance that could be given for the expansion of social services. Money could not be spent on education in the colonies although the importance of this for economic and social development was now widely recognised. The CDAC's unwillingness to meet the increased recurrent administrative costs normally a consequence of an expansion of social services was another considerable handicap to poorer colonies. The enlarged concept of colonial development clearly embraced much more than the development of a colony's economic resources. Finally, the size of the Colonial Development Fund was too small. MacDonald had already mentioned a figure of £7 or 8 million a year to the Chancellor as indicative of the true scale of needs. A 'show down' with the Treasury was, he felt, inevitable. MacDonald wanted to submit a paper to the cabinet after the summer recess, so the meeting decided to set up a departmental committee under Lord Dufferin to draw up proposals.[46] What was evidently needed were not just detailed legislative plans and perhaps changes in Colonial Office organisation but also the formulation of arguments to overcome the inevitable Treasury objections to greater expenditure on the Colonial Empire.

Dufferin's committee was also a high-level one: Parkinson, Shuckburgh, Tomlinson, Moore, Campbell, Stockdale, Clauson, Calder and Dawe. And it acted quickly, meeting on 1 and 4 July 1938. Dufferin explained that it was necessary to finalise proposals by 20 September in order to make them part of the government's legislative programme in the autumn parliamentary session, as MacDonald at this stage intended. The committee readily agreed that the operations of the Colonial Development Act needed amending in order to cover expenditure on social welfare. Attention focussed therefore on the practical problems of how best to combine imperial assistance for development works with aid to meet consequent recurrent running costs. In the end, three options were outlined. The first and most radical envisaged the abolition of the existing grants-in-aid system and its replacement by an enlarged CDF allowing for expenditure on development works and on administrative costs. It was, however, admitted that the Treasury would hardly relish an increase in imperial expenditure coupled with a diminution of Treasury control. The Colonial Office were also unhappy at ceding too much authority to an independent CDAC. Second, and more practical, was a plan to amend the existing act to allow it to cover expenditure on medical and educational services and to persuade the Treasury to be more generous with grants-in-aid to cover recurrent administrative expenses. Third was a complex scheme to classify colonies according to the state of their needs and finances, the poorest to be given CDF money for development and administrative needs, middling territories to be given aid on the basis of shared costs, and the rich being left with the existing system.[47]

The rapid progress made so far was then checked. Henceforth policy-making was to be buffeted by the worsening international crisis. On the 20 July 1938 an alarmed Chancellor of the Exchequer explained to his cabinet colleagues that unavoidable rearmament costs required economies in civil expenditure in order to maintain the government's financial stability.[48] It is not explicit in the documents but quite probable that these financial circumstances persuaded MacDonald to postpone immediate consideration of the colonial development proposals. At all events at the end of July he put the issue to one side and instructed his staff to bring it up again in September with a view to submitting a definite scheme to the cabinet in October. The delay was unfortunate, for September brought the Czechoslovakian crisis, the Munich agreement and increased government worries about defence. MacDonald felt obliged to postpone yet again his approach to the cabinet because, as he later explained, 'the Chancellor of the Exchequer had presented the Cabinet with an alarming picture of the country's financial position and at the same time there had been need of greater expenditure on armaments. It had seemed an unpropitious moment to ask for a few more millions for the Colonial Empire, so the scheme had been set on one side'.[49] Evidently at this time one political need cancelled out another.

There was at least some feeling among the permanent staff in the Colonial Office that as a result of the international crisis, this country 'will probably be neither as able nor as willing to act the rich uncle to the Colonial Empire as we were all, I think, hoping in the summer'.[50] But MacDonald was not to be put off indefinitely. He summoned another high-level meeting in the office on 9 December 1938, and reminded his staff of the political need for a more vigorous colonial development policy. 'In future', he argued, 'criticism of Great Britain would be directed more and more against her management of the Colonial Empire, and it was essential to provide as little basis as possible for such criticism'. In a sentence he personally added to the minutes of the meeting he went on: 'It was an essential part of her defence policy that her reputation as a Colonial power should be unassailable'. It was central to MacDonald's case that extending Britain's colonial development policy would not weaken the country at a time of international trouble, but would actually strengthen it. Therefore definite proposals should be formulated. He would then try and persuade the Chancellor 'that Colonial development would be of no less importance over the next ten years than any other branch of policy'. A discussion followed on the amount of money that might be needed to finance the new policy. MacDonald believed that as much as £10 million a year might be needed for an enlarged CDF, but he admitted that it would be bad tactics to frighten the Treasury by asking for too much at first, and he agreed with Campbell's proposal to limit the request to £3 million, substantially less than the figure talked about back in June. He also decided that a scheme should be prepared incorporating the second and third of the three options outlined in July, namely to widen the terms of the Colonial Development Act to cover social services and to relax the Treasury's grant-in-aid procedures on the one hand and to classify colonies' claims for imperial aid according to their needs and resources on the other.[51]

During succeeding months some of the impetus seems once again to have been lost. MacDonald was probably sidetracked by the problems of Palestine early in 1939.[52] The required memorandum outlining proposals was not in fact ready until March. The principal intentions at this stage were to retain but enlarge the CDAC, to encourage colonial governments to initiate development schemes partly by administrative improvements in the Colonial Office, to widen the terms of the Colonial Development Act to legitimise expenditure on a wide range of social services as well as on economic projects, to increase the CDF to £3 million a year, to persuade the Treasury to be more generous in their use of grants-in-aid to meet recurrent costs, and to devise a system which would allow the degree of imperial aid to be varied according to local needs and resources.[53]

At this point another element was added to the proposals. *An African Survey* was published in November 1938. Lord Hailey intended to see his recommendations affect government policy, and on publication he requested a meeting with the Secretary of State. In particular he was anxious to see realised his plan for the creation in Britain of a research bureau, supported by a Treasury-supplied fund, able to co-ordinate and finance scientific investigation in Africa.[54] MacDonald was clearly sympathetic to the proposal, and following a meeting with Hailey on 5 December 1938 he authorised the office to draw up a scheme for submission to the Treasury. To be decided was the size of the fund to be requested, the links between this organisation and the CDAC, and how Hailey's proposals should relate to the larger scheme for widening the scope of the Colonial Development Act.[55] By March 1939 the plans had been drafted, amended and finalised and awaited MacDonald's consideration. A maximum of £500,000 a year should be paid into a Colonial Research Fund, and a Colonial Research Advisory Committee should be appointed and attached to the Colonial Office to advise the Colonial Office and the Treasury on the financing of suitable sociological and scientific research not just in Africa but throughout the Colonial Empire. The committee and the fund should be set up by Act of Parliament in order to ensure the provision of an annual sum, and this could best be achieved as part of the legislation now envisaged to extend the Colonial Development Act. The proposal did, however, make it quite clear that since the existing act was intended primarily to benefit the United Kingdom, it was not as it stood appropriate to govern the operations of the Colonial Research Advisory Committee. 'Although the research to be assisted by the fund would be of a practical nature and to the material advantage of the United Kingdom, it would be primarily in the interests of the colonial people themselves, and cover social and educational fields which have hitherto been considered outside the terms of the Colonial Development Act.' The new emphasis is significant. In justifying the policy the memorandum claimed that 'Measures for the advancement of the colonies are politic at a time when the general question of colonial responsibilities is under widespread criticism and when it is expedient for us to justify our position'.[56]

These proposals, like the general plans for a new colonial development policy, had to wait until May before MacDonald could find the time to consider them. Even then, at a meeting with Hailey on 25 May 1939, he explained that further delay must follow. To achieve success and obtain the powers and funding he was seeking, MacDonald wanted to choose the right moment for his initiative. He planned to link together the proposals for a Colonial Research Fund and the extension of the Colonial Development Fund, partly so that the Treasury would be aware of the whole picture, but especially because he was anxious to put forward a bold package which would strike the imagination of the government, Parliament and general public. He had also not forgotten the West India Royal Commission whose report he expected in August or September 1939 and whose revelations and recommendations he expected would give additional weight to his arguments when he approached the Treasury and the cabinet. These political advantages outweighed in MacDonald's mind the disadvantages of having to wait until the autumn session.[57]

Meanwhile, further discussions took place inside the Colonial Office to finalise the proposals to modify general colonial development policy. There was broad agreement about the purpose and nature of the new policy. As Clauson, head of the new Social Services department, put it: 'there have been two motives behind this proposal, the one a desire to avert possible trouble in certain Colonies, where disturbances are feared if something is not done to improve the lot of the people, the other a desire to impress this country and the world at large with our consciousness of our duties as a great Colonial Power'.[58] To achieve these ends it was agreed that, as one official put it, 'greater latitude should be given to the interpretation of the word "development", which would embrace social as well as material progress, and would include, for example, medical and educational services'.[59] It is true that there was some debate as to whether these welfare improvements would be a consequence of or should be an alternative to economic development, but it was certainly understood that, for whatever purpose, more substantial Imperial government assistance on more generous terms was essential. The traditional view that colonies should normally be financially self-sufficient and that the Imperial government could not be expected to meet recurrent expenditure such as the running costs of new development works was repeatedly criticised. 'It is now proposed that the aim of balancing Colonial budgets at all costs should give place to the aim of ensuring a reasonable standard of social and material welfare.'[60] Even the notion that the United Kingdom taxpayer should expect some economic advantage from his expenditure on colonial development should be abandoned.[61]

But in spite of the progress made in discussions over the past twelve months, there remained surprising disagreements about the particular proposals to be put to the Treasury. Debate was enlivened by the receipt of a long despatch from Governor Bourdillon of Nigeria who blasted the established notions of financial self-sufficiency and damned the Colonial Development Act for its inefficacy. He lamented the problems of poor territories like Nigeria which, burdened by debts, could not raise enough extra local revenue to meet the interest on new loans or to face the recurrent expenditure which development works often entailed. He concluded with a request for future development loans to be granted by the Imperial government if necessary at reduced interest rates and more originally with a proposal that the Nigerian Agricultural, Forestry, Veterinary, Geological Survey and Co-operative departments should be financed entirely by the Imperial government. The relief this would give to the colony's finances would allow for an expansion of educational and medical facilities, and thus both economic and social welfare in the territory would benefit.[62] The proposal drew the support of some of his fellow African governors, a flutter of minuting in the Colonial Office and finally the approval of one senior officer.[63] This proposal had to compete with another, that the Treasury should finance the expansion of colonial social services as part of the annual Colonial Office vote, while the CDF supported economic development projects.[64] But most senior men stuck to the earlier consensus to amend the Colonial Development Act in order to increase the size of the fund and to widen the terms for its disbursement.[65]

By mid-summer MacDonald was again bogged down in other work,[66] but another departmental meeting of senior staff was held on 31 July 1939 under Lord Dufferin's chairmanship to prepare clear and concrete suggestions for him. The major decision seems to have been reached without controversy: 'It was agreed to proceed with the proposal to approach the Cabinet for sanction to expand the Colonial Development Fund'. Appetites had increased; £10 million a year was now to be requested, in addition to £500,000 for Hailey's Colonial Research Fund. Major alterations in the terms of the Colonial Development Act were also proposed. One amendment would remove the restriction that expenditure must help in 'promoting commerce with or industry in the United Kingdom'. Others would widen its scope to allow for capital expenditure on medical and educational schemes. Recurrent expenditure on economic development projects was also to be allowed, though it was left for the Secretary of State to decide whether recurrent expenditure on expanded social services could also be financed by the act: the majority of officials seemed to favour it. It was also agreed that membership of the CDAC would have to be altered to cater for these new duties, but more radical was the firm agreement that the committee should lose its statutory right to veto schemes put to it. The CDAC was to become *only* an advisory committee and full authority was to be restored to the Secretary of State and the Colonial Office.[67]

One important factor determining the decision to initiate the new policy in the guise of amendments to the existing Colonial Development Act was tactical. The question which inevitably concerned the office at a time when military expenditure was taking priority and economies in civil expenditure were being sought was how to persuade the Treasury, cabinet and Parliament to provide large additional funds for the colonies. The motivation and objectives of the new proposals marked a real break with the past and might well provoke opposition. However, the Colonial Development Act had been a non-controversial measure enjoying support from both sides of the House since its introduction. Campbell therefore argued that the best line of approach was to propose modifications of an act which had been generally popular in political circles and had a good press. 'Major political influences', he reckoned, 'would be in favour of expanding it.'[68] This view was shared by others: one suggested that the word 'development' should be kept in the title of the new legislation in order 'to link up with the old Act'.[69] The aim was to slip through major changes partially in disguise. For similar tactical reasons it was decided not to frighten off the Treasury by urging them at this stage to consider writing off some of the colonial debts which were recognised as a handicap on territorial development.[70] Tactics also partly explain the proposal that Colonial Office staff should visit the colonies to ensure that development money was properly spent. Plans were currently well-advanced for the appointment of a commissioner to perform such a task in the West Indies. It was believed such schemes would 'sweeten the Treasury' and would increase the chances of obtaining money.[71]

The other asset which Colonial Office policy-makers believed they had at this time was increasing public and parliamentary concern about colonial issues and particularly Britain's conduct as a colonial power. The debate which had stimulated MacDonald's initial interest came to a head in 1939. Governor Bourdillon had written in April that

there are clear signs that a considerable section of the British public is rapidly awakening from the complacency, indeed the apathy, with which it has been accustomed to regard colonial problems, and is beginning to have an uneasy feeling ... that certain other powers have some justification for suggesting that they would have succeeded in doing more than we have done for the development of tropical Africa.[72]

Hailey had done much since the publication of *An African Survey* to explain its contents and spread its message, and in July 1939 the *Report on Nutrition in the Colonial Empire* was presented to Parliament. By this time too the report of the West India Royal Commission was thought to be imminent.

4. THE IMPACT OF WAR

The Secretary of State's strategy of launching his new policy at the appropriate moment seemed on the point of success. By the end of August 1939 a rough draft of a Colonial Research and Development Act had been prepared,[73] and there remained only a few details of the new proposals for MacDonald to settle. These he intended to resolve at a final meeting of the departmental committee in the first week of September 1939.[74] MacDonald seems to have been singularly unlucky in his timing. On 1 September the German attack on Poland began, and on 3 September Britain declared war. The scheduled committee meeting nevertheless took place on the following day. MacDonald admitted that in the changed circumstances he had initially thought that the new proposals could only be finalised and then laid aside until some future opportunity arose to present them to the government. But after thinking the question over, he saw clear political reasons for pressing on. For one thing, 'it was very important ... that we should keep the Colonies contented during the war'. The pre-war disorders in the West Indies and the fear of unrest elsewhere in the Empire had partly inspired the earlier discussions, and MacDonald evidently saw the military necessity of avoiding such disturbances in wartime by a policy of colonial improvement. Moreover, 'he felt that a big scheme of Colonial development, announced quite soon, would impress people here and abroad ... it would rob our enemies of their arguments that we neglected our Colonial Empire and were not fit to have it; and it would impress public opinion at home and in neutral countries'. An argument stressing the propaganda value of a constructive colonial policy in wartime and the need to appeal to neutral, especially American, opinion was obviously an elaboration of the pre-war political arguments MacDonald and his colleagues had tossed around. But he followed it up, even in this first week of the war, with arguments relating to the post-war world:

he thought it essential that we should maintain our reputation for sound Colonial administration in order to be able to meet or face with equanimity any ideas at the end of the war for redistribution of Colonial territories or placing them under mandate ... he thought it very possible that there would be a strong feeling that all Colonies should be placed under international control. We must be prepared to meet that demand by showing that our Colonies were well administered and that we were fit and able to hold them ourselves as mandates; that in other words there could be no question of their being transferred to any other Power.

Officials did not demur from these arguments, and it was agreed that a cabinet memorandum should be prepared which the Secretary of State could discuss with the Chancellor. In particular, approval was wanted for a plan to amend the Colonial Development Act by widening its terms of reference to allow for expenditure of up to £10 million a year on social services as well as on economic development and on recurrent charges as well as on capital costs. The CDAC should be expanded into a Colonial Development and Welfare Advisory Committee and should be given powers to initiate proposals as well as to consider schemes put forward by colonial governments and the Colonial Office, but it should only be an advisory committee and should lose its statutory powers of veto. At the same time a Colonial Research Advisory Committee should be created to supervise expenditure from a separate fund of up to £1 million a year. These ambitious proposals and supporting arguments were elaborated in a draft memorandum for the cabinet.[75]

Preparations were then rudely interrupted by the Treasury. It was not the new plans but the continued operation of the old Colonial Development Act which sparked off their intervention. The realisation that the CDAC intended to carry on as normal with its next meeting scheduled for 19 September aroused the indignation of the Treasury's permanent staff. One official minuted: 'I should have thought that it would be out of the question for us to finance new development schemes in the colonies at the present time. The case needs no arguing'.[76] The Colonial Office were then sternly addressed:

You will readily understand that the war has given rise to the gravest financial problems and that the utmost economy on all services not directly relevant to the prosecuting of the war has become of paramount importance. In this connection I have to write to you on the subject of Colonial expenditure. We are not unmindful of the importance which your Secretary of State attaches to social services and economic development in the Colonies, and we fear that what follows must come as a heavy disappointment to him. But first things must come first. The whole future of the Colonies, as of a number of other things which we have at heart, depends upon the successful outcome of the war. Here, as in other services at home, we shall have to resign ourselves to stand still now, that we may have the power to progress in future.

Following this uncompromising opening it was announced that the Treasury would not sanction any new expenditure from the CDF unless it directly assisted the conduct of the war, that existing schemes would have to be reviewed and possibly suspended, and that all colonial governments should be urged to reduce their expenditure and build up financial balances in the United Kingdom to help the war effort.[77]

This hardly appeared the opportune time to ask the Treasury to commit themselves to a new and more expensive development and welfare scheme, and it seemed to spell the final ruin of MacDonald's new initiative. He was not, however, deterred. His response was to short-circuit the normal inter-departmental haggling by speaking personally to the Prime Minister. No notes of this interview of 11 September 1939 survive, but from its consequences it is apparent that MacDonald's political arguments carried some weight, for he was authorised to put his plans to the Treasury.[78] With this backing, he briefly saw the Chancellor on the same day and arranged to put the Colonial Office's detailed proposals to him at a future meeting.[79] Acting as his own envoy, MacDonald had side-stepped the Treasury's initial veto and accelerated the decision-making process.

MacDonald led his delegation, Dufferin, Moore, Clauson and Eastwood, into the Chancellor's den on 18 September 1939. The Colonial Office case was well-prepared, a judicious blend of tactical appeasement and vigorous attack. Prior to the meeting the Colonial Office had softened up the Treasury by sending for their approval a draft of one of a series of telegrams they intended to send to colonial governments urging them to exercise economy in their expenditure, to increase their local taxes and to avoid importing materials from overseas.[80] At the meeting special reference to this gesture towards economy and good management was made, and it was strengthened by a further concession: MacDonald halved the money he was now requesting to £5 million per year for colonial development and welfare and £500,000 per year for colonial research. The limited effects which colonial development schemes had on requirements for foreign exchange, on British resources and on manpower were also stressed. On the other hand, the necessity for the new policy was given a full airing. Some reference was made to the economic value of the Colonial Empire in wartime, but the political arguments were acknowledged to be of greater weight: the need to avoid disturbances in the colonies which would drain military forces and reduce colonial production, the need to respond to the report of the West India Royal Commission expected soon, the need to woo neutral opinion by demonstrating a constructive colonial policy, the need to prepare for post-war criticism of Britain's role as a colonial power.[81]

The Chancellor at least did not flatly refuse to consider the proposals, but it was evident that the Treasury were not going to be easily satisfied. MacDonald and his colleagues were sent back to the Colonial Office to prepare a memorandum setting out their arguments in detail. Once again the Colonial Office staff concentrated on couching their request in the form most likely to win Treasury consent. Subtle shifts of emphasis were suggested by Dawe: 'The argument should be directed to show how expenditure will assist our war effort in men and material. It might also be well to play upon the fear of disaffection and the expense of coping with it'. On the other hand references to post-war problems would seem too much in the future and ought not to be so prominently displayed.[82] In the event the memorandum, a substantial document, was approved by the Secretary of State and despatched to the Treasury on 11 October 1939.

The central request was for legislation to widen the terms of the Colonial Development Act to allow for expenditure of both a capital and recurrent nature on social services as well as on economic development and for the creation of a Colonial Development and Welfare Fund and a Colonial Research Fund to be supplied with annual maximum grants of £5 million and £500,000 a year respectively. The Colonial Office tried to lessen the impact of their demands on the Treasury by proposing to include within the grant for the Colonial Development and Welfare Fund the money normally spent by the Treasury on grants-in-aid and the £1 million a year which it was understood the West India Royal Commission was about to recommend for improvement in that region. It was also suggested that the full amounts would probably not be needed by either fund during the war. Reassuring noises were made about the scant effect the new policy would have on Britain's war effort, and reference was made to the administrative steps to be taken by the Colonial Office to ensure the efficient expenditure of the monies provided. In justification of new commitments at this time, the Colonial Office pointed out that recent investigation had revealed, what was already well known, that the poor agricultural societies of the empire 'cannot out of their own resources provide in any adequate degree the services which are now normally a part of civilised government'. It was argued that public concern was already sufficient to require further action, and the West India Royal Commission was once again employed as a political weapon. It was asserted that their report would have to be published and that its revelations would certainly increase criticism of government policy. 'Rather than resist this pressure until we have reluctantly to give way to it, ... it would be wise to anticipate it and make an early announcement that we intend to increase the funds for colonial development and welfare.' But most emphasis in the memorandum was placed on arguments of wartime necessity. Following Dawe's suggestion, it was pointed out that aid for the colonies would stimulate their production of food and raw materials for the war effort and reduce their need for foreign exchange to buy foreign imports. Political imperatives were particularly strong. Unrest in the colonies, reflected in trade union activities, political movements, strikes and rioting, was fuelled by economic and social grievances which needed to be corrected. Moreover, 'in parts of the Colonial Empire the mere fact that white men are again fighting, with every manifestation of brutality, among themselves tends to lessen the respect for their rule and for the benefit it brings'. Failure to help the colonies might, then,

bring to the surface a latent criticism and dissatisfaction amongst colonial peoples which might manifest themselves in ways highly embarrassing to our cause in the war. A contented and loyal Colonial Empire will, from the point of view both of production and of prestige, be a distinct asset to us in our struggle; any growth of discontent or disloyalty would damage us seriously and help the enemy.

It would be particularly damaging if troops had to be used to suppress disturbances, since this would be readily exploited by enemy propagandists. Neutral opinion also had to be considered. The accusation of enemies, that Britain was a hypocritical and selfish imperialist power, needed to be countered, and

I can think of few things that would have a more reassuring effect in the neutral world (and particularly in the United States), or that would add more to our moral prestige, than an announcement that despite the burdens that are put upon us by the necessity of fighting the war, we are going as far as conditions permit to find some additional money for promoting the welfare of the many millions of peoples in the Colonial Empire for whom we are the trustees.

A constructive colonial policy might also strengthen Britain's hand when colonial questions came up for examination in the post-war peace settlement. This was a formidable array of essentially political arguments, an elaboration of those expressed before September 1939 and tuned to the immediate circumstances of the war.[83]

The Colonial Office were determined that the new initiative should not be further blocked or delayed and therefore in his covering letter to the Chancellor, with its familiar 'Dear John' opening, MacDonald concluded by asking Simon to agree to a joint submission of the proposal to the war cabinet, thus guaranteeing its acceptance. It was also suggested that a public announcement of the new policy should be made to coincide with the delayed publication of the report of the West India Royal Commission, now expected in four to six weeks time. This was a timely reminder to the Treasury of the commitment to expenditure they had already made when agreeing to the appointment of that commission back in June 1938, as well as drawing further attention to the political storm expected when the report was published.[84]

These were the first documents formally describing the new colonial development proposals to be sent to the Treasury. No personal reply was ever received from the Chancellor of the Exchequer, for the questions raised were handled throughout by his permanent officials. It is unfortunate that their initial reactions are obscured by the destruction of the relevant documents in an air raid in October 1940,[85] but it is highly unlikely that the Treasury were best pleased at the Colonial Office's pressing of this matter. Recent circulars to government departments had urged them to exercise all economy in public expenditure.[86] Nevertheless, the request was not met by an absolute stonewall. Treasury officials seem to have recognised that some concession was inevitable, perhaps impressed by the political arguments advanced and equally by the Prime Minister's decision of 11 September 1939 to allow the proposals to be put forward. Representatives of the two sides agreed after a two-hour meeting on 27 November 1939 that the Colonial Office should draft a public statement summarising the plans and their objectives, to be issued, as MacDonald had always intended, at the same time as the publication of the report of the West India Royal Commission. This decision represented a Treasury acceptance of the principle of a new policy. But over the following months they subjected the Colonial Office's proposals to close, detailed and procrastinating criticism. Before an agreed public statement was issued, staff in the two departments had gone over the ground in several exchanges of letters and papers and at five meetings between their representatives.

On several occasions the Colonial Office felt irritated and frustrated. In view of the expected imminent publication of the West India Royal Commission's report and MacDonald's desire to use that document as a launching pad for his own initiative, the Colonial Office were concerned by the Treasury's delay in replying to some of their submissions.[87] More serious was the feeling that as negotiations proceeded the distance between the two sides was growing greater. The Treasury wanted to reduce the extent and significance of the new departure, whereas the Colonial Office wished it to make a big impact on the public. And as Parkinson bitterly reflected, 'if we do not bring out a really satisfactory statement, the fault, as has happened before, will be with the Treasury, but it is the Colonial Office which will be blamed in Parliament and the press, as has happened before, and will have to bear the odium'. 'My only comment', added MacDonald, 'is that if we are not now going to do something fairly good for the Colonial Empire, and something which helps them to get proper social services, we shall deserve to lose the colonies and it will only be a matter of time before we get what we deserve'.[88]

Some of the issues separating the two sides were fairly minor.[89] The Colonial Office had envisaged the establishment of a Colonial Research Fund, supplied with up to £500,000 a year. Lord Hailey's public advocacy of this scheme was perhaps enough to ensure that the Treasury would have to accept the proposal, but they jibbed for a while at the amount of money involved, and they did in the end persuade the Colonial Office to abandon the idea of a statutory fund. Instead it was agreed that up to £500,000 a year as required should be voted for colonial research as part of the annual Colonial Office estimates. The Colonial Office had also intended to preserve the CDAC as a statutory committee, giving it powers to initiate development schemes but depriving it of its power of veto. It was thought to serve a useful political function. The Treasury, however, preferred to see it abolished, presumably disliking the independence which the committee had shown in the past. Since the Colonial Office had also intended to blunt its powers, they agreed to this concession without too much heart-searching. It was understood that the Secretary of State could appoint on his own authority an advisory committee for colonial development and welfare work and, indeed, another for colonial research, but these would not be mentioned in the new act and would not have statutory status.

The really tricky issues were a consequence of the Colonial Office's attempt to widen the concept of colonial development policy to embrace the provision of aid for social services. The Treasury argued that the emphasis should be on economic development, the bias originally of the existing Colonial Development Act. Following traditional reasoning, they claimed that economic development would increase colonial government revenues enabling them to finance expanded social services themselves. The alternative to this doctrine of financial independence they saw as putting 'the Colonies on the dole from henceforth and forever'.[90] Accordingly they wished to eliminate references to colonial welfare and aiding social services from the public statement of policy. For MacDonald and the Colonial Office this was intolerable. They agreed that economic development had to be encouraged, but it was against the doctrine of financial self-sufficiency that they were reacting. As MacDonald told Treasury officials, it was 'essential to get away from the old principle that Colonies can only have what they themselves can afford to pay for: they must have what a first-class Colonial power may reasonably be expected to provide'.[91] MacDonald incorporated this principle in the first draft of the public statement which he personally wrote. Parkinson told his opposite number in the Treasury that the emphasis was 'essential', and Dawe asserted that 'Politically the whole point is that we should be able to make a big thing of the "welfare" side'.[92]

What worried the Treasury was, of course, the expense. The Colonial Office wanted to tap imperial funds not just for capital costs but also for recurrent expenditure, and in the case of social services these were particularly heavy. The Treasury were willing to accept imperial aid for capital outlay, but were reluctant to concede that the Imperial government should finance recurrent costs indefinitely. Eventually, faced with Colonial Office insistence, they offered to finance a proportion of recurrent expenditure on certain services for a fixed period, and later they proposed that the CDF should continue to finance capital costs while colonial development and welfare money should be voted annually by Parliament to meet recurrent expenditure. They were only shifted from this position when the Colonial Office proposed to abandon the idea of any statutory fund. This was a surprising move. The Colonial Office had begun by favouring the idea of a Colonial Development and Welfare Fund, suitably increased in size and with wider terms for its disbursement. It would, they believed, give a greater sense of permanence to the government's commitment, it would be more reassuring to the colonies, it would make 'more of a splash' politically,[93] and by maintaining a continuity with the existing act it might make smoother the passage of the new legislation. But this also proved partly to be a tactical position from which MacDonald was prepared to withdraw, if he achieved his objectives by other means. From the beginning the Treasury preferred to see development money provided annually in the Colonial Office estimates and not paid into a separate fund. They had long memories and felt that separate funds, like the Empire Marketing Fund, were too independent and difficult to control. In this case they were also opposed to the creation of a fund which could subsidise recurrent expenditure since this might mean that grant-aided colonies would receive money from two different sources, contrary to established parliamentary practice. Hence they preferred to use a fund to meet capital costs and voted money to meet recurrent expenditure. The Colonial Office probably saw this as a device to allow for expenditure on economic projects but to restrict assistance for social services, since it would be the latter that would need extra support for recurrent costs from annually voted money. Therefore they offered, and the Treasury were obliged to accept, the abolition of the fund. Money for capital and recurrent costs would come from a single source, an annual parliamentary vote of the sum required up to a maximum of £5 million, which the Treasury agreed to provide for the next two years. The Colonial Office had won the main argument, since this money could be spent on welfare as well as on economic development, and nothing in the legislation would bar expenditure on recurrent costs.

Agreement on most items was secured at negotiations held on 26 January 1940, and a draft *Statement of Policy on Colonial Development and Welfare and on Colonial Research*, incorporating the final terms of the proposals and their supporting arguments, was put before the cabinet on 15 February 1940 together with an explanatory memorandum by MacDonald. By then the cabinet had already decided, against MacDonald's advice, that the full report of the West India Royal Commission was after all too damning an indictment of British colonial rule to be published in full in war-time,[94] but MacDonald explained that he now wished to publish their more acceptable recommendations and to issue at the same time, partly as a response to them, his *Statement of Policy*. In defence of the new initiative, MacDonald referred to the pre-war disturbances in the colonies and the growing criticism of British colonial rule, and argued that the outbreak of war only reinforced the need for a constructive policy since 'a continuance of the present state of affairs would be wrong on merits, and it provides our enemies and critics with an admirable subject for propaganda in neutral countries and elsewhere'. Further trouble in the empire and renewed criticism of British colonialism after the war might be expected unless action was taken at once. Political arguments, which MacDonald had employed from the beginning, evidently carried weight, and with minor modifi-cations the cabinet gave MacDonald the authority he needed to publish his *Statement of Policy*. 'The view was generally expressed that the proposals ... represented a very important and desirable development in British Colonial policy'.[95] The *Statement of Policy* and the *Recommendations of the West India Royal Commission* were issued on 20 February 1940,[96] arrangements were made to give the new policy wide publicity,[97] and the Colonial Office, Treasury and Parliamentary Counsel settled down to the business of drafting the Colonial Development and Welfare Bill.[98]

At this point another ingredient was added to the mix. During the 1930s, when colonial revenues fell in the depression, concern grew about the impact of debts on colonial administrations. In some cases interest and repayments formed a high and fixed burden which they found difficult to shoulder. It was one of the complaints of Governor Bourdillon in his appeal for extra assistance from the Imperial govern-ment.[99] While little could be done beyond conversion loans to reduce the weight of public debt, a reconsideration of outstanding colonial debts to the Imperial Exchequer was possible.[100] Some of these like Kenya's debt of over £5½ million for the construction of the Uganda railway, predated the First World War. Others, as noted earlier in Chapters IV and VI, were debts incurred by East African governments in that war whose terms for repayment had still not been settled with the Treasury. Colonial indebtedness had been exacerbated in the 1930s by the Treasury's practice of providing loans rather than grants-in-aid to some administrations hit by the depression. The CDAC had also provided loans rather than grants on many occasions. In 1933, in view of the financial crisis affecting a number of colonies, the Treasury decided to postpone the settlement of some of these debts, and repeatedly over the following years the decision was taken in view of financial circumstances to postpone demands for repayment. In 1938 the Treasury told the Colonial Office that they proposed to waive some of these debts, and indeed an agreement had been reached by the end of the year to cancel the Uganda Railway debt. In the first half of 1939 the Treasury embarked on a further substantial review. It was recognised that 'many of these debts have an obvious unreality',[101] since there seemed little prospect of them being repaid. However, political as well as financial reasons affected the Treasury. 'General remission of the kind proposed seems to me to be just towards a number of Colonies which as primary producers have keenly felt the effects of depression over a long period, and it is perhaps appropriate at a time when our merits as compared with those of Germany in colonial administration may soon be under the public eye'.[102] When the Colonial Office also raised the subject in 1939 they therefore found they were pressing at an open door. However, the problem was to find a suitable opportunity to introduce the necessary legislation to waive colonial debts. It occurred to officials in the Colonial Office and in the Treasury virtually at the same time that the Colonial Development and Welfare Bill being drafted early in 1940 was the handy mechanism to dispose of 'this grisly topic'.[103] Senior Treasury officials recognised that 'remission is the natural corollary of the new Colonial policy recently announced', since 'the plain man will say that if we have found it necessary to embark on a programme of grants to the Colonies of £5 millions a year, it is not reasonable to expect repayment of past debts'.[104] With this sensible argument the Chancellor agreed, and during March and April the two departments sorted out with remarkably good grace the debts which would be waived in the new legislation. They totalled £11,264,489. Since the Treasury were primarily writing off bad debts their actions do, perhaps, deserve no more than Clauson's grudging acknowledgement that they were 'not ungenerous', but it is nevertheless an indication of the new departure signified by the Colonial Development and Welfare Act of 1940 that the Treasury chose the occasion to resolve an issue that had troubled the Colonial Office and a number of colonial governments for most of the inter-war years.[105]

With this matter happily on the way to solution, other details of the bill were quickly resolved. One Colonial Office man wrote with an air of surprise to his opposite number in the Treasury, 'I think we can congratulate ourselves that we are keeping nicely step by step'.[106] The bill passed through the cabinet's Home Policy Committee on 30 April 1940 and was presented by MacDonald to the House of Commons on 2 May 1940, almost two years after he had returned to the Colonial Office with the intention of introducing such a measure.[107]

5. CONCLUSION

It was typical of the bad luck that dogged MacDonald's labours that the presentation of the Colonial Development and Welfare Bill coincided with Hitler's push westwards and the ending of the 'phoney war'. One result was the replacement of Chamberlain by Churchill as Prime Minister on 10 May 1940 and a consequent cabinet reshuffle which on 13 May took MacDonald from the Colonial Office to the Ministry of Health.[108] At least MacDonald was given the satisfaction of piloting his bill through its second reading on 21 May. The bill was then to proceed steadily through the legislative hoops to receive the Royal Assent on 17 July 1940, but the course of the war, and in particular the presence of German troops on the Channel coast from 20 May, gravely affected the Colonial Office's ability to put the new act into operation. Some participants in the debate in the House of Commons mocked the measure as 'still born' at a time when all national resources would have to be devoted to waging war.[109] With much of this the new Secretary of State, Lord Lloyd, concurred, and for a while he considered including a clause in the bill to suspend its operations until more favourable circumstances permitted. In the event the measure proceeded unaltered, but Hall, the new under-secretary, explained to the House of Commons that in view of the immediate needs of war there would be a lack of resources for extensive colonial development work and a lack of qualified people to man the proposed advisory committees. Likewise Lord Lloyd explained to the Lords that 'much that we had hoped to do under this Bill when it became law must wait for happier times'.[110] Lord Lloyd warned colonial governments of the limited circumstances in which Colonial Development and Welfare money could at present be employed, restrictions which were not eased until his successor took off some of the pressure in a further despatch in June 1941.[111] Although annual expenditure on Colonial Development and Welfare schemes then rose from £177,802 in 1940–41 to £2,806,456 in 1944–45 and on Colonial Research from a first allocation of £6,670 in 1941–42 to £58,345 in 1944–45, these totals were, of course, far less than the maximum sums envisaged in the legislation. It is true that by March 1945 total commitments, including future expenditure, had reached £23,571,258 for Colonial Development and Welfare and £414,128 for Colonial Research, but most of these pledges were made only late in the war.[112]

It would, however, be wrong to argue that the Treasury therefore in effect won their contest with the Colonial Office. In the circumstances what is remarkable is that a measure with the specific terms of the Colonial Development and Welfare Act was passed at all. In spite of its apparent pedigree leading back to the Colonial Development Act of 1929 it is less the continuity than the novelty which should be emphasised. The *Statement of Policy*, the *Recommendations of the West India Royal Commission*, the terms of the new bill and the debate upon them make it clear that this measure did not have metropolitan economic gains as its priority. The stipulation of the 1929 act, that its aim was to promote 'commerce with or industry in the United Kingdom', was specifically denounced in the *Statement of Policy*. Instead the new policy had as its 'primary purpose ... to promote the prosperity and happiness of the peoples of the Colonial Empire'.[113] MacDonald told the Commons that 'the Bill which we are discussing this afternoon breaks new ground. It establishes the duty of taxpayers in this country to contribute directly and for its own sake towards the development ... of the colonial peoples for whose good government the taxpayers of this country are ultimately responsible'.[114] Hence the novel emphasis upon the promotion of social services. Hence also the facility under the new measure to use Colonial Development and Welfare money to subsidise recurrent expenditure. This marked a much more substantial break with the traditional doctrine of colonial financial self-sufficiency than the aid given to meet the capital costs of development advanced by earlier legislation. As Creech Jones put it in the House of Commons, 'we abandon once for all the old principle that each Colony must be self-supporting'.[115] Even though imperial funding of research into colonial subjects was not new and had simply been substantially in abeyance since the abolition of the Empire Marketing Board in 1933, the inclusion of social as well as economic topics as fit matters for study was another innovation. It should also be noted that the *Statement of Policy* indicated that the new policy was to encourage governments to produce development programmes and not just individual schemes. Hall claimed that 'one of the most important features of the new development policy is its insistence on planned development, and the functions of the advisory committees ... will be to consider not only detailed schemes, but also comprehensive development programmes which the Colonial governments have been asked to submit'. Except in the West Indies little could be done to realise this ideal during the war, but the concept is another indication of the new thinking behind MacDonald's policy.[116]

The principal novelty behind the act lay, however, in its general purpose. Its objectives were not economic as in 1929. The apparent altruism behind the proposal and its reception by Parliament has led one historian to describe it as 'perhaps the first unselfish Act in British imperial history'.[117] Such altruism was not untinged with feelings of guilt, aroused by the colonial question in the 1930s. Rear-Admiral Beamish bluntly informed the Commons that 'this Bill makes up at least a little for what we have done so wickedly in the past'. Sir Richard Acland saw it as 'just a small repayment ... for all the advantages we have received'.[118] But there was a more substantial political objective to be secured. The 1930s were a watershed during which the morality of colonialism and the record of Britain's achievements were subjected to fierce criticism at home and from abroad. The stability of the empire was also threatened, initially from within by social disturbances and burgeoning nationalist movements, but later from outside with German, Italian and Japanese attacks and even from unsympathetic scrutiny by the United States. In these circumstances traditional justifications of colonial rule looked increasingly shoddy: protective trusteeship and the civilising mission in the colonies had sown economic stagnation, social unrest and political dissent. In response a new policy of constructive trusteeship with the explicit purpose of improving social conditions in the colonies was devised, as a method of removing legitimate grievances in the colonies, re-stabilising the empire and defusing criticism of British colonial rule. The emphasis on colonial development and *welfare* was, then, essentially a defensive operation, to provide a new justification which would legitimise the perpetuation of colonial rule. This was the essence of the arguments advanced by MacDonald to the Treasury and cabinet. They proved irresistible. The Treasury's concession of a Royal Commission on the West Indies and even their acceptance of a new Social Services department in the Colonial Office were forerunners of their capitulation before the political arguments in favour of a Colonial Development and Welfare Act. Necessity likewise obliged cabinet, and later Parliament, to concur.

It has been argued that the passage of the act was a product of war, in part a propaganda exercise to defend British colonial rule and ensure colonial support for the war effort.[119] Certainly the war provided an opportunity to assert the virtues of British colonialism. The passage of the act was a demonstration of good government in contrast with the blackness all around. It was a function forcefully signalled by *The Times*: it was

an outstanding illustration of the true nature of British Imperialism that, at a supreme crisis in the fortunes of the Mother Country, its legislators acknowledge without question the continuing duty to contribute from our own substance to the needs of the peoples whose interests we hold in trust. The contrast between that trusteeship and the evil doctrine of *Lebensraum* could not be more glaring.[120]

This helps explain why the outbreak of war, the crisis of May–June 1940 and the pressing need to devote energies and resources to immediate military needs did not prevent the passage of the Colonial Development and Welfare Act.

But it is also apparent that the policy was not devised after the outbreak of war. Nor was it a response, as has often been claimed, to the West India Royal Commission.[121] Johnson is correct to conclude that 'the report of the Moyne Commission did not provide the Colonial Office with startling revelations on colonial conditions ...., nor did it instigate a reconsideration of policy on colonial development'.[122] In the event MacDonald used the Royal Commission as he had always intended, as a political lever to prise open the Treasury's coffers and finance a policy already defined. It is, however, also probable, *pace* Johnson, that the new policy was not mainly formulated as a response to West Indian disturbances in 1937–38.[123] The implication of MacDonald's later reflections on this period is that the inspiration for his new initiative came not from any specific problem but from reflecting on the general colonial debate of the 1930s. Indeed, the West Indian crisis may have been an opportunity as much as a cause. In 1974 MacDonald said that 'this West Indian crisis helped me enormously to get not only my advisers in the Colonial Office to look with great favour on a fairly urgent review, but I think that it also helped me to get such Ministerial colleagues as I needed to say, ''Yes, this has become a political question which is quite critical and we must go into it in an energetic way'' .... So the West Indian crisis ... therefore speeded up, I think, the sort of movement which I was hoping to push anyways'.[124]

The origins of the Colonial Development and Welfare Act require some final observations. The initiative for the new measure came from a new Secretary of State, Malcolm MacDonald. It required a minister of determination and clarity of mind to propose a novel and expensive policy at a time when other demands on his time and on Imperial government revenues were so pressing. MacDonald was not deterred by the political obstacles repeatedly laid in his path. It is, however, noticeable that MacDonald had the complete co-operation of his permanent staff in the definition and advance of his policy. There is no sign of that tension between officials and Secretary of State which had sometimes accompanied earlier ministerial initiatives. The influence of the debates on the colonial question and of the new ideas of constructive trusteeship may be seen in the conversion of the Colonial Office itself and in the eager support which the permanent officials gave to MacDonald and his plans.

NOTES

1. D. J. Morgan, *The Official History of Colonial Development*, vol.1 *The Origins of British Aid Policy, 1924–1945*, London, 1980, pp.4-10; I. M. Drummond, *British Economic Policy and the Empire, 1919–1939*, London, 1972, pp.114-18, 136-7.
2. Viscount Swinton, *I Remember*, London, 1948, pp.64-102; A. Earl, 'The Political Life of Viscount Swinton 1918–1938', Manchester M.A. thesis, 1960, pp.235-266; the Swinton Papers are disappointingly thin on this period.
3. Lord Melchett, *Imperial Economic Unity*, London, 1930; Sir R. Hadfield, *Empire Development and Proposals for Establishment of an Empire Development Board*, London, 1935; L. S. Amery, *The Forward View*, London, 1935. The centenary of the birth of Joseph Chamberlain in 1936 was used to launch a new imperial campaign, L. S. Amery, *My Political Life*, vol.3, London, 1955, pp.200-5; see also Amery Papers, Box H.120, Folders A and B, Box H.121, Folder A and Box I.131, Folder A.
4. S. Constantine, *Unemployment in Britain between the Wars*, London, 1980, pp.74-6; S. Howson, *Domestic Monetary Management in Britain 1919–38*, Cambridge, 1975, pp.86-9.

5. B. Porter, *Critics of Empire*, London, 1968.
6. Quoted in R. von Albertini, *Decolonization, the Administration and Future of the Colonies, 1919–1960*, New York, 1971, p.549.
7. Sir R. Furse, *Aucuparius: Recollections of a Recruiting Officer*, London, 1962, p.241 and figures in appendix 1.
8. Morgan, *Origins of British Aid Policy*, pp.10-13; P. S. Gupta, *Imperialism and the British Labour Movement 1914–1964*, London, 1975, pp.231-7; K. Robinson, *The Dilemmas of Trusteeship*, London, 1965, pp.75-7.
9. R. Hinden, *Empire and After*, London, 1949, pp.136-7; M. Crowder, *West Africa under Colonial Rule*, London, 1968, pp.476-7; A. G. Hopkins, *An Economic History of West Africa*, London, 1973, p.255; H. Johnson, 'The West Indies and the Conversion of the British Official Classes to the Development Idea', *Journal of Commonwealth and Comparative Politics*, 15 (1977) (Cass), 55-6; M. J. Cohen, *Palestine, Retreat from the Mandate*, London, 1978, p.10; B. C. Roberts, *Labour in the Tropical Territories of the Commonwealth*, London, 1964, p.181; R.I.I.A., *The British Empire*, 2nd ed., London, 1938, pp.162-3.
10. *Leeward Islands: Papers relating to the Disturbances in St. Christopher (St. Kitts)*, Cmd.4956, 1935; *Trinidad and Tobago Disturbances, 1937, Report of Commission*, Cmd.5641, 1938; *Report of the Commission appointed to enquire into the Disturbances in the Copper Belt, Northern Rhodesia, Oct. 1935*, Cmd.5009, 1935.
11. See, for examples, Cmd.4114, 4368, 4586 and 4907.
12. For Thomas's despatch of 18 April 1936 and appointment of Nutrition Committee see CO 852/58/10/15282; for Proceedings and Memoranda of the Committee on Nutrition in the Colonial Empire see CAB 58/199; for report of committee in 1939 see Cmd.6050 and 6051; Roberts, *Labour in the Tropical Territories*, p.184; *Labour Conditions in the West Indies*, Cmd.6070, 1939.
13. For government discussions see Morgan, *The Origins of British Aid Policy*, pp.14-21, and for broader treatment W. W. Schmokel, *Dream of Empire: German Colonialism 1919–1945*, New Haven, 1964; M. Gilbert and R. Gott, *The Appeasers*, 2nd ed. London, 1967, pp.80-101; M. Perham, *The Colonial Reckoning*, London, 1961, pp.45-9; A. Crozier, 'Imperial Decline and the Colonial Question in Anglo-German Relations 1919–39', *E.S.R.*, 11 (1981), 207-242.
14. Albertini, *Decolonization*, pp.109-12; Gupta, *Imperialism and the British Labour Movement*, p.246; see also Bourdillon to C.O., 5 April 1929, para.8, CO 852/214/15201/17.
15. R. Pearce, *The Turning Point in Africa*, Frank Cass, London, 1982, pp.12-14.
16. For the origins of the work and membership of the research committee see Lord Hailey, *An African Survey*, London, 1938, pp.v-vii. The R.I.I.A. also published among other items *The Colonial Problem*, London, 1937, and *The British Empire*, London, 1937.
17. *The Political Quarterly*, 9 (1938); *International Affairs*, 17 (1938); see also *International Affairs* 15 (1936) for an article by Lord Lugard on German colonial claims.
18. *The Times*, 11 June 1938, p.11.
19. See, for example, *Hansard* H.C., vol.332, cols.766-860, 28 Feb. 1938; Morgan, *The Origins of British Aid Policy*, p.14; for official attempts to provide additional information see *The Colonial Empire in 1937–38*, Cmd.5760, 1938, and *The Colonial Empire in 1938–39*, Cmd.6023, 1939.
20. Gupta, *Imperialism and the British Labour Movement*, pp.225-254; Johnson, 'The West Indies', pp.57-60; N. R. Malmsten, 'The British Labour Party and the West Indies, 1918–39', *J.I.C.H.*, 5 (1977), 189-97; *Hansard* H.C., vol.337, col.151, 14 June 1938; see also Papers of Fabian Colonial Bureau, Box 2 file 6,

Royal Commission on West Indies 1937–39, file 7 Committee for West Indian Affairs 1938–40, Box 46 file 1, Labour Party Advisory Committee on Imperial Question 1936–1945, and material in Creech Jones papers.

21. Robinson, *Dilemmas of Trusteeship*, pp.19-21; Albertini, *Decolonization*, pp.6-8; J. M. Lee, *Colonial Development and Good Government*, Oxford, 1967, pp.28, 151-2; Roberts, *Labour in the Tropical Territories*, pp.241-3; Johnson, 'The West Indies', pp.58, 70.

22. Porter, *Critics of Empire*, pp.320-4; Albertini, *Decolonization*, pp.83, 107, 110; Lee, *Colonial Development*, pp.41, 47.

23. The plans go back to the summer of 1935, CO 852/21/15263 and T161/1185/S.40371/1, were discussed by an Inter-Departmental Committee in 1936, CO 852/56/15263, 15263/1 and 15263/4, and went to the cabinet for approval in April 1937, CAB 24/269/CP 119 and CAB 23/88/CAB 19(37)4.

24. Minutes of 1st meeting CEMB, 20 Oct. 1937, CO 852/115/15263/4.

25. Gupta, *Imperialism and the British Labour Movement*, pp.248-252; Roberts, *Labour in the Tropical Territories*, pp.176-189; Creech Jones Papers, Box 14, files 1 and 3. Major Orde-Browne took up his duties as Labour Adviser on 30 May 1938.

26. Parkinson to Sec. of State, 12 July 1938, CO 323/1536/1751.

27. Jeffries to Hale, 16 Dec. 1938, CO 866/33/1327; see also minutes of meeting in C.O., 9 Dec. 1938, CO 852/190/15606. The department began work on 1 April 1939.

28. W. M. Macmillan, *Warning from the West Indies*, London, 1936, pp.196-8.

29. Lord Hailey, 'Some Problems Dealt with in the *African Survey*', *International Affairs*, 18 (1939), 201.

30. Between Oct. 1938 and Jan. 1939 he combined his position at the C.O. with the duties of Secretary of State for the Dominions. For biographical details see obituary in *The Times*, 12 Jan. 1981. At present the Malcolm MacDonald papers remain closed.

31. C. R. Nordman, 'Prelude to Decolonisation in West Africa; the Development of British Colonial Policy, 1938–1947', Oxford D.Phil. thesis 1976, pp.9, 17; Morgan, *The Origins of British Aid Policy*, pp.xiv-xv.

32. Governor's telegrams and despatch, 2, 3 and 10 May 1938, CO 137/826/68868. The preparation of this section has been helped by the article by Johnson, 'The West Indies', *op. cit.*.

33. *Trinidad and Tobago Disturbances, 1937*, Cmd.5641, 1938; *Report of the Commission appointed to enquire into the disturbances which took place in Barbados on the 27 July 1937 and subsequent days*, Barbados, 1937; Johnson, 'The West Indies', p.60.

34. Memo. by West Indian dept. 20 May 1938, CO 318/433/71168.

35. Minute by Stockdale, 20 May 1938, *ibid.*.

36. Minute by Campbell, 23 May 1938, *ibid.*.

37. Minutes of discussions in Secretary of State's room, 27 May and 31 May 1938, *ibid.*.

38. Johnson, 'The West Indies', p.67; see telegram from governor, CO 137/826/68868.

39. Minute by Campbell, 23 May 1938, CO 318/433/71168.

40. Memo. for cabinet by Secretary of State, CO 137/827/68868/4; also on CAB 21/809, draft on CO 318/433/71168.

41. MacDonald to Simon, 10 June 1938, T161/853/S.43411.

42. Minutes of 7-9 June 1938, *ibid.*.

43. Minute by Creasy, 13 June 1938, CO 318/433/71168; *Hansard* H.C., vol.337, cols.93-4, 14 June 1938, and for MacDonald's reply to MacLean's question col.54.

44. Cabinet minutes, 15 June 1938, CAB 23/94/CAB 28(38)8. Membership of the West India Royal Commission was not announced until 28 July 1938, *Hansard* H.C., vol.338, col.3299.
45. Parkinson to Bowyer and Boyse, 16 June 1938, CO 852/190/15606.
46. Minutes of meeting held in Secretary of State's room, 27 June 1938, and see also memo. by Clauson, 20 June 1938, CO 852/190/15606.
47. Minutes of Departmental Committee on Colonial Development, 1 and 4 July 1938, note summarising discussions, Parkinson to Dufferin, 18 July 1938, *ibid..*
48. CAB 23/94/CAB 33(38)6. MacDonald was also busy with the Palestinian problem that summer, see Cohen, *Palestine*, p.67.
49. Notice of Meeting to discuss Colonial Development, 9 Dec. 1938, CO 852/190/15606; see also report of interview with MacDonald in 1974, Nordman, 'Prelude to Decolonisation', p.17.
50. Memo. by Clauson, 8 Nov. 1938, CO 852/190/15606.
51. Notes of Meeting to discuss Colonial Development, 9 Dec. 1938, *ibid..*
52. Nordman, 'Prelude to Decolonisation', p.17; M. MacDonald, *Titans and Others*, London, 1972, pp.90-1; the Round Table Conference occupied much of Feb. and March 1939, Cohen, *Palestine*, pp.74-82.
53. Amended memo. by Boyse, n.d. but following minute by Campbell of 16 March 1939, CO 852/190/15606.
54. Hailey, *African Survey*, pp.1629-33; Pedler to Creasy, 18 Nov. 1938, CO 847/13/47097.
55. Record of Discussion on Hailey's *African Survey*, 6 Dec. 1938, minute by Pedler, 6 Dec. 1938, minutes of meeting in C.O., 20 Dec. 1938, *ibid..*
56. Lord Hailey's African Survey: Proposals for a Colonial Research Fund, *ibid..*
57. Minutes of discussion 12 May 1939 and of meeting to discuss Colonial Research Fund, 25 May 1939, *ibid..*
58. Memo. by Clauson, 7 June 1939, CO 852/250/15606 Part 2.
59. Memo. by Bourdillon, 10 June 1939, *ibid..*
60. Memo. by Bourdillon, and see Parkinson to Dufferin, 14 July 1939, *ibid..*
61. Minute by Moore, 30 June 1939, though see the complaint by the ageing Shuckburgh, 1 July 1939, *ibid..*
62. Bourdillon to C.O., 5 April 1939, CO 852/214/15201/17.
63. Minutes and extracts from governors' letters, *ibid.*; Jardine of Sierra Leone to C.O., CO 852/215/15201/23; Mitchell of Uganda to C.O., CO 852/215/15201/48; Young of Tanganyika to C.O., CO 852/214/15201/21; memo. by Calder, 21 June 1939, CO 852/250/15606 Part 2.
64. Memo. by Clauson, 7 June 1939, *ibid..*
65. See, for example, minute by Moore, 30 June 1939, *ibid..*
66. Parkinson to Dufferin, 14 July 1939, *ibid..*
67. Minutes of meeting 31 July 1939, memo. by Calder 8 Aug. 1939, minutes by Clauson, Dawe and Parkinson, 11-21 Aug. 1939, *ibid..*
68. Minutes of meeting 31 July 1939, *ibid..*
69. Dawe to Parkinson 18 Aug. 1939, memo. by Calder 8 Aug. 1939, *ibid..*
70. Minutes of meeting 31 July 1939 and memo. by Calder 8 Aug. 1939, *ibid..*
71. The phrase is Lord Dufferin's, see Dufferin to Secretary to State, 19 Sept. 1938, CO 852/190/15606; see also comments by Campbell in meeting 31 July 1939, CO 852/250/15606 Part 2 and memo. by Orde Brown, 23 July 1939, CO 852/250/15606 Part 1.
72. Bourdillon to C.O., 5 April 1939, CO 852/214/15201/17.
73. Appendix to memo. by Calder, 8 Aug. 1939, CO 852/250/15606 Part 2: amendments to this draft had been subsequently suggested.
74. Parkinson to Secretary of State, 21 Aug. 1939, *ibid..*

75. Note of a Meeting, 4 Sept. 1939, and draft memo, Economic Development and Welfare, by Eastwood, CO 323/1698/7450 Part 1.
76. Inch to Hale, 5 Sept. 1939, T161/995/S.45149/1.
77. Barlow to Parkinson 7 Sept. 1939, CO 323/1698/7450 Part 1.
78. Minute by Eastwood, 14 Sept. 1939, *ibid.*. The importance of this meeting was confirmed by MacDonald in his interview in 1974 with Nordman, 'Prelude to Decolonisation', p.17.
79. Parkinson to Barlow, 12 Sept. 1939 and minute by Eastwood 14 Sept. 1939, CO 323/1698/7450 Part 1.
80. Parkinson to Barlow, 15 Sept. 1939 and subseq., *ibid.*. Morgan gives a precis of these documents, *Origins of British Aid Policy*, pp.72-3.
81. Based mainly on the notes of the meeting made by Hale of the Treasury, 19 Sept. 1939, T161/995/S.45149/1, but see also the brief prepared for MacDonald by Eastwood, 15 Sept. 1939, CO 323/1698/7450 Part 1.
82. Minutes by Dawe and Moore, 21 Sept. 1939, *ibid.*.
83. Colonial Development, Note for the Chancellor, *ibid.*.
84. MacDonald to Sir John Simon, 11 Oct. 1939, CO 859/19/7475.
85. See note of 28 Nov. 1940 attached to the few grubby surviving papers on T161/1079/S.45935/3.
86. Treas. circulars of 28 Sept. 1939 on CO 323/1698/7450 Part 2 and of 2 Oct. 1939 on T161/995/S.45149/1.
87. See, for example, Parkinson's reminder to Hale of Treasury, 28 Dec. 1939, CO 859/19/7475.
88. Minutes by Parkinson, 12 Jan. 1940 and by MacDonald, 14 Jan. 1940, *ibid.*.
89. The negotiations can be followed in the papers and minutes from 27 Nov. 1939 to 16 Feb. 1940 on CO 859/19/7475, CO 859/40/12901 Part 1 and T220/17.
90. Wilson of Treasury to Parkinson, 5 Jan. 1940, CO 859/19/7475.
91. Note on Colonial Development and Welfare, record of meeting with Treasury, 27 Nov. 1939, see also Outline of Statement of Policy, *ibid.*.
92. Parkinson to Wilson, 18 Jan. 1940, CO 859/40/12901 Part 1; minute by Dawe, 12 Jan. 1940, CO 859/19/7475.
93. Creasy to Hale, 11 Jan. 1940, *ibid.*.
94. The report was signed on 21 Dec. 1939, the cabinet discussed it on 30 Jan. 1940, CAB 65/5/WM 27(40)2. The full report was not published until Oct. 1945, Cmd.6607.
95. CAB 67/4/W.P. (G)(40)44; CAB 65/5/W.M. 42(40)2.
96. Cmd.6175 and Cmd.6174; *Hansard* H.C., vol.357, cols.1164-6.
97. CO 859/40/12901 Part 2.
98. See material on *ibid.*, CO 859/40/12901/C, C1 and C2 and T220/17.
99. Bourdillon to C.O., 5 April 1939, CO 852/214/15201/17; see also S. H. Frankel, *Capital Investment in Africa*, London, 1938, espec. table 37, p.182.
100. Much of the material is contained in T161/1057/S.22769/3, T161/1111/S.39540/1 and /2, CO 852/189/4, CO 852/245/15453/14, and CO 852/299/15453/14.
101. Hale to Barlow, 12 Jan. 1940, T161/1111/S.39540/2.
102. Hopkins to Fisher, 7 March 1940, *ibid.*.
103. Minute by Blunt, 30 Jan. 1940, T161/1111/S.39540/2; see also minute by Eastwood, 9 Feb. 1940, CO 852/299/15453/14.
104. Hopkins to Horace Wilson, and Barlow to Hopkins, 29 Feb. 1940, T161/1111/S.39540/2.
105. For the principles upon which the Treasury selected the debts for cancellation see minute by Caine, 12 April 1940, CO 852/299/15453/14; for a description of the debts see *Financial and Explanatory Memorandum of the Colonial Development and Welfare Bill*, and for a list see schedule to the Colonial Development and Welfare Act, 1940, 3 & 4 Geo.6. ch.40.

106. Creasy to Syers, 8 March 1940, T220/17.
107. Minutes of 14th meeting, CAB 75/4/HPC (40) and memo. by Secretary of State, 24 April 1940, CAB 75/7/HPC (40)88, copies on CAB 21/810 and CO 859/40/12901/C2; *Hansard* H.C., vol.360, col.914.
108. It has been suggested that Churchill's bitter opposition to MacDonald's Palestinian policy in 1939 explains this transfer and MacDonald's later removal from the cabinet to become High Commissioner in Canada in Feb. 1941, Cohen, *Palestine*, p.85.
109. Wedgwood, *Hansard* H.C., vol.361, cols.76-9, and see Schuster, cols.80-2.
110. See correspondence between C.O. and Treas., May–June 1940, T220/18; Hall, *Hansard* H.C., vol.361, cols.1205-6, 11 June 1940; Lloyd, *Hansard* H.L., vol.116, col.724, 2 July 1940.
111. Telegram and despatch from Lloyd to governors, 5 June 1940, CO 323/1755/7450 and 10 Sept. 1940, CO 859/41/12905/1; despatch from Lord Moyne, 5 June 1941, CO 859/81/12905/4, published as *Certain Aspects of Colonial Policy in War-time*, Cmd.6299, 1941.
112. *Annual Appropriation Accounts* 1940–41 to 1944–45, combining Colonial Development and Welfare schemes with Colonial Development and Welfare schemes in the South African High Commission Territories; *Reports on the Operation of the Colonial Development and Welfare Act*, 1940–42, Cmd.6422, 1942–43, Cmd.6457, 1943–44, Cmd.6532 and 1944–45, no command number.
113. Cmd.6175, pp.4-5, 8.
114. *Hansard* H.C., vol.361, col.45, 21 May 1940.
115. *Ibid.*, col.57.
116. *Ibid.*, col.1206, 11 June 1940; Cmd.6175, p.8; E. R. Wicker, 'Colonial Development and Welfare, 1929–1957: The Evolution of a Policy', *Social and Economic Studies*, 7 (1958), 182.
117. Gupta, *Imperialism and the British Labour Movement*, p.248.
118. *Hansard* H.C., vol.361, cols.103, 115, 21 May 1940.
119. This seems to be the implication of Pearce, *The Turning Point in Africa*, p.21.
120. *The Times*, 22 May 1940. This passage from a leading article was thought sufficiently apposite to be preserved in the Treasury files, T220/18.
121. Wicker, 'Colonial Development and Welfare', p.181; G.C. Abbott, 'A Reexamination of the 1929 Colonial Development Act', *Ec.H.R.*, 24 (1971), 79.
122. Johnson, 'The West Indies', p.76.
123. *Ibid.*, p.55. Rampersad, 'Colonial Economic Development', p.188, agrees with Johnson.
124. Interview given by MacDonald in 1974, Nordman, 'Prelude to Decolonisation', p.12; see also Morgan, *Origins of British Aid Policy*, pp.xiv-xv.

X

CONCLUSIONS: POLICIES AND POLICY-MAKING

1. *IMPERIAL GOVERNMENT EXPENDITURE ON COLONIAL DEVELOPMENT*

This study has been concerned with the nature and purpose of British colonial development policy in the period from the First World War to the passage of the Colonial Development and Welfare Act in 1940. Before offering some conclusions on the policy-making process and on the changing motives behind policy initiatives, it is useful to put expenditure on colonial development into a broader context.

The inter-war years may be seen as a time of transition in colonial development policy, lying between two contrasting periods. As described in Chapter II, only limited amounts of aid were granted to the colonies by the Imperial government before the First World War; a mere £1,400,000 was voted by Parliament in the forty years between 1875 and 1915, to which might be added about £12,000,000 made available to the dependencies as loans but not all taken up before 1914, nor subsequently in some cases.[1] By contrast the Colonial Development and Welfare Act of 1945 alone proposed an expenditure of up to £120 million over ten years and this maximum was raised to £140 million by the Colonial Development and Welfare Act of 1950. Other measures, such as the funding of the Colonial Development Corporation and later Colonial Development and Welfare Acts in 1955, 1959 and 1963, were to confirm this increased financial commitment to colonial development.[2] In order to determine whether policy was moving in that direction between the wars it is worth attempting to calculate the amounts of money allocated annually by the Imperial government for the development of the Colonial Empire. The amount of aid provided for public works, scientific research and other services in the colonies gives a reasonable indication of the extent to which the Imperial government felt itself to have an interest in, or to be responsible for, colonial development.

It is not possible to arrive at an absolutely accurate audit of expenditure, and the tables which follow must be used cautiously and with a clear understanding of the criteria upon which they were constructed. The intention has been to construct aggregates which represent maxima. Figures are drawn mainly from the appropriation accounts for which the Colonial Office and Dominions Office were responsible. It has not been possible to include the cost of work by other government departments which was known to be relevant to the business of colonial development. In particular, in the field of scientific research, an important and frequently stressed precondition for colonial development, the cost of much work was borne by the Imperial government. However, it often formed part of an expenditure on more general British services; thus the quota of imperial aid for specifically colonial development cannot be isolated, for example, in the work of Kew Gardens, the Department of Scientific and Industrial Research and the Department of Overseas Trade. Any under-estimation is probably more than compensated for by the inclusion in the following tables of expenditure on the Empire Marketing Board, on the Imperial Institute and under the Trade Facilities Act of 1924, whose interests covered domestic, Indian and dominions subjects as well as those of the colonies. It is frequently difficult to distinguish between these items. And finally the tables include the Imperial government's financial aid to colonial governments which took the form of grants-in-aid. Such assistance covered a variety of purposes, between which the estimates do not clearly differentiate. It is not always possible to distinguish aid for development from aid for other purposes including grants to help a colonial government meet the costs of ordinary administration. An Imperial government grant-in-aid to relieve a colony of some part of local administrative expenditure may have allowed a colonial government to divert some of its revenue into public works or other projects contributing to colonial development. It was a practice that His Majesty's Treasury frowned upon, but it would be dangerous to assert that it never happened. Only those items which are clearly designated as for the payment of governors' salaries and for military expenditure have been omitted. There are still some curiosities included; for example, the Imperial government paid Cyprus's share of the Turkish National Debt.

TABLE 5

Imperial Government Grants for Health, Education, Research
and Development 1918−40, in £

Description	1918−19	1919−20	1920−21	1921−22	1922−23
Tropical Diseases Bureau	500	500	1,000	1,000	1,000
Imperial Institute	2,500	2,500	2,500	10,000	10,000
Hong Kong University	300	300	300	300	300
Imperial Bureau of Entomology	500	500	500	1,000	1,000
West Indies Agricultural Dept.	4,519	5,430	6,961	8,600	5,017
Tropical Diseases Investigation	500	500	500		
Scientific Research, Development of Economic Resources		1,000	10,000	10,000	1,000
National Council for Combating Venereal Diseases			7,950	500	
Oil Exploration in Papua			15,000	35,000	
School of Tropical Medicine			1,000		
Capital Expenditure, Mesopotamia Railways				231,438	271,328
Maintenance of Iraq Railways					269,471
Medical Mission to Idrisi					113
TOTAL	8,819	10,730	45,711	297,838	559,229

Table 5 gives the annual expenditure by the Imperial government
between 1918 and 1940 on the empire's scientific, health, agricultural
and general research institutes, on certain educational facilities, and
on a few specific development projects. It also includes expenditure
under the Trade Facilities Act of 1924 and the Colonial Development
Act of 1929 and on the Empire Marketing Board. Table 6 provides
a survey of Imperial government grants or loans-in-aid to colonial
administrations, their amounts, purposes and the territories involved.
The tendency from 1921 onwards was for the Treasury to provide
loans rather than grants. The tables, incidentally, suggest alternative
case studies to those examined in this book, for example, the funding
of scientific research and grants and loans to other territories such
as Tanganyika. The annual totals on Tables 5 and 6 are added together
in Table 7 to give a reasonably accurate figure for the Imperial government's maximum contribution to colonial development between the
wars. It is not possible to quantify in financial terms the advantages
given to dependencies by the Colonial Stock Acts or by Imperial

TABLE 5 (cont.)

Description	1923–24	1924–25	1925–26	1926–27	1927–28	1928–29
Tropical Diseases Bureau: Bureau of Hygiene and Tropical Diseases	1,000	1,000	1,000	1,000	1,000	1,000
Imperial Institute and Imperial Mineral Resources Bureau	12,177	12,500	12,500	12,500	16,122	12,500
Hong Kong University	300	300	300	300	300	300
Imperial Bureau of Entomology	1,000	1,000	1,000	1,000	1,000	1,000
West Indies Agricultural College: Imperial Coll. of Trop. Agric.	4,000	3,000	2,000	18,000		
Scientific Research, Development of Economic Resources	2,000	2,000	2,000	2,000	2,000	2,000
National Council for Combating V.D.; British Social Hygiene Council			1,000	866	495	290
Kamaran Quarantine Station	22,335					
Pan-Pacific Scientific Congress	750					
Colonial Agricultural Scholarships				2,917	3,455	3,411
Empire Marketing Fund				500,000	400,000	500,000
Expenditure under Trade Facilities Act 1924				5,837	18,249	61,449
Pacific Health Conference				271	115	
Sleeping Sickness Commission				750		
TOTAL	43,562	19,800	19,800	545,441	442,736	581,950

government guarantees of loans raised, for example, by the Sudan, Palestine and some West Indian territories, in addition to those East African territories covered by the act of 1926. Contemporaries disagreed about their value, but they should perhaps be kept in mind.

Some observations may be offered. Allocations in any one year could obviously be significantly affected by the decision in a particular case to provide aid on a substantial scale, such as the £3,500,000 loan to Kenya and Uganda in the financial year 1923–24. Annual totals are, however, interesting. It can be seen from Table 7 that on average annual expenditure reached nearly £1,600,000 between the wars. This is a distinct increase on pre-war levels of help. Moreover, the annual awards are in general higher in the 1930s than in the 1920s,

TABLE 5 (cont.)

Description	1929–30	1930–31	1931–32	1932–33	1933–34
Bureau of Hygiene and Tropical Diseases	1,000	1,000	1,000	1,000	1,000
Imperial Institute and Imperial Mineral Resources Bureau	12,500	12,500	12,477	10,000	10,000
Hong Kong University	300	300	300	300	300
Imperial Bureau of Entomology	1,000	1,000			
British Social Hygiene Council	468	500	331	500	500
Colonial Agricultural Scholarships	4,343	4,500	4,500	3,466	3,036
Empire Marketing Fund	550,000	612,500	549,000	320,000	250,000
Expenditure under Trade Facilities Act 1924	61,449				
Antarctic Research	8,000	8,000			
Colonial Development Fund		750,000	750,000	600,000	400,000
Contribution to Institut Colonial International, Brussels		287	377	429	
West Indies Unemployment Relief Grants		74,529	123,833	56,520	
West Indies Food etc. Relief Grants		2,386			
TOTAL	639,060	1,467,502	1,441,818	992,215	664,836

substantially a reflection of the cost of funding the Colonial Development Act. Nevertheless, it may be safely concluded that Imperial government expenditure on colonial development between the wars remained noticeably limited. The cost of some of the items dutifully detailed in the estimates and appropriation accounts, and logged in Tables 5 and 6, may seem bizarrely small. Although average expenditure did grow between the wars, totals seem pale in comparison with the Imperial government's commitment in the Colonial Development and Welfare Act of 1940 to spend over the next ten years up to £5 million a year on development and £500,000 a year on research. Although the Colonial Development Act of 1929 did raise expenditure levels in the 1930s, large-scale obligations were only accepted during and after the Second World War.

This can be confirmed by some other comparisons. Expenditure on colonial development took only a small share of total Imperial government expenditure on the British Empire. If we add together

TABLE 5 (contd.)

Description	1934–35	1935–36	1936–37	1937–38	1938–39	1939–40
Bureau of Hygiene and Tropical Diseases	1,000	1,000	1,000	1,000	1,000	1,000
Imperial Institute and Imperial Mineral Resources Bureau	16,346	16,496	16,546	16,676	16,936	17,400
Hong Kong University	300	300	300	300	300	300
Imperial College of Tropical Agriculture	14,400	14,400	14,400	14,400	16,000	16,000
British Social Hygiene Council	400	494	500	500	363	253
Colonial Development Fund	500,000	900,000	900,000	500,000	650,000	500,000
East Africa Agricultural Research Sta., Amani	6,000	6,000	6,000	6,000	6,000	6,000
Colonial Agric. Service Fund Grant in Aid	1,587	1,773	1,917	2,240	2,212	2,109
Contributions to Imperial Econ. and Research Services	11,945	11,875	11,753	12,916	12,807	12,830
Grants to Dominions Govts' Institutes for Research	18,922	2,843	1,956			
Fishery Research Grant	5,000	2,544				
Testing and Marketing of Colonial Timbers		3,934	4,879	4,860	5,020	4,946
Conferences		508	591			
Hydrographic Surveys Palestine and Trans-Jordan				10,000	30,000	4,000
Colonial Empire Marketing Board				674	9,9093	26,360
Central Pool of Survey Instruments				457	348	6
Palestine Technical Mission				90	3,697	
Makerere College East Africa						100,000
TOTAL	575,900	962,167	954,842	570,113	753,776	691,204

GRAND TOTAL 1918–40 £12,294,049
Source: *Annual Appropriation Accounts* 1918–40

the administrative costs of the Colonial Office, Dominions Office and India Office, the expenditure on Overseas Settlement and on Colonial, Middle Eastern, Dominions, Irish, Indian and Burmese Services, plus the financing of the Colonial Development Fund, Empire Marketing Board, Imperial Institute and Trade Facilities Act we reach a total expenditure over the years 1918 to 1940 of £167,619,789, over

TABLE 6
Imperial Government Aid to Colonial Administrations 1918–40, in £

Territory	1918–19	1919–20	1920–21	1921–22	1922–23	1923–24	1924–25
Cyprus	50,000[1]	50,000	50,000	50,000	50,000	50,000	50,000
Western Pacific	10,199	7,703	7,633	17,922	13,442	13,650	15,259
St. Helena	8,000	3,800	2,900	3,200	3,000		7,000
Weihaiwei	4,000	7,900	20,000	8,000			
Somaliland	83,000	199,000	210,000	100,000	75,000	29,000	21,000
Tanganyika			180,000	914,000[2]	800,000[2]	750,000[2]	350,000[2]
Malta			250,000				
Nyasaland				100,000[3]	86,050	44,500	90,000
Uganda				250,000[4]	150,000	150,000	
S. Rhodesia				150,000[5]	150,000[5]		
Mesopotamia				1,087,500			
Trans-Jordan				80,000	90,000	150,000	14,850
Kenya					3,500,000[6]		
N. Rhodesia							138,000
Dominica						5,000[7]	
Leeward Is.						10,000[7]	
TOTAL	155,199	268,403	720,533	2,760,622	1,417,492	4,687,150	701,109

Territory	1925–26	1926–27	1927–28	1928–29	1929–30	1930–31	1931–32
Cyprus	50,000	50,000	50,000	92,800	92,800	92,800	92,800
Western Pacific	21,748	17,193	17,548	13,466	11,006	11,814	15,239
St Helena	4,000	2,500	2,500	2,000	2,000	6,000	12,000
Somaliland			21,000			44,000	31,000
Tanganyika	350,000[2]						
Nyasaland	110,000	120,000	50,000	40,000	60,000	113,000	119,500
Trans-Jordan	103,957	66,000	45,000	40,000	40,000	84,000	84,700
N. Rhodesia	100,000						
Dominica	8,449[8]	30,000[2]	8,500[9]	24,500[9]	11,000[2]	28,000[9]	40,045[9]
Leeward Is.				5,000[7]			
St. Lucia			17,500[10]	5,000	3,000	7,500	36,500
Aden			49,000	47,906	50,637	51,074	52,080
Swaziland				32,500[2]	38,000[2]	5,000[2]	32,000[2]
Antigua						5,000	27,500
British Guiana						50,000	220,000
Mauritius							5,000[7]
British Honduras							5,000[7]
St. Kitts-Nevis							10,000
TOTAL	748,154	285,693	261,048	303,172	308,443	498,188	783,364

TABLE 6 (cont.)

Territory	1932–33	1933–34	1934–35	1935–36	1936–37	1937–38	1938–39	1939–40
Cyprus	92,800	92,800	92,800	92,800	92,800	92,800	92,800	92,800
Western Pacific	15,591	15,108	15,846	13,557	11,086	10,953	11,531	10,972
St. Helena	8,500	7,500	3,000					1,000
Somaliland	11,000	16,000			26,500			
Nyasaland	79,000	64,000	54,000	80,168	90,439	190,000	206,000	165,000
Trans-Jordan	72,000	65,000	60,000	42,000	$97,572^2$	$51,009^2$	$272,009^2$	$512,009^2$
Dominica	$13,350^9$	11,000	26,000	8,000	12,500		5,500	20,000
St. Lucia	6,500		9,000	14,000			$30,000^7$	$22,000^{10}$
Aden	50,016	52,108	53,477	63,804	71,509	66,648	82,738	117,877
Swaziland	$29,000^2$	$30,000^2$	$61,500^2$	48,000	$34,000^2$	$43,300^2$	52,000	54,000
Antigua		$1,500^{11}$		6,000	1,000			
British Guiana	120,000	$100,000^{12}$			$62,360^2$	35,500		
British Honduras	20,000	20,000	57,000	25,000	27,500	$8,000^{11}$	$64,000^2$	$130,000^2$
Newfoundland	$166,570^{13}$	$634,000^{14}$	$348,759^{14}$	$369,680^{14}$	$406,075^{14}$		$320,000^2$	$1,150,000^2$
Cayman Is.	$1,000^7$							
Montserrat		15,000	6,000	$5,000^7$	$2,700^7$	$3,000^{11}$	$3,000^{11}$	4,750
Bechuanaland		177,000	$98,000^{10}$	50,000	60,000	25,000	35,000	$51,400^2$
Aden Protectorate							$4,100^2$	$8,800^2$
TOTAL	685,327	1,301,016	882,382	883,369	969,181	490,710	1,178,678	2,340,608

GRAND TOTAL 1918–40 £22,629,841

Source: *Annual Appropriation Accounts* 1918–40, excluding salaries, travel expenses, military expenditure and, where identifiable, other non-developmental expenditure.

All items are grants or loans-in-aid of local administrations except where otherwise indicated in the notes.

1. All Cyprus grants to meet share of interest on Turkish debt.
2. Includes grants and/or loans for development works.
3. All Nyasaland's allocations include aid to meet obligations under Trans-Zambesia Railway Company guarantee.
4. All Uganda's allocations are instalments of Development Loan.
5. Loan for development works prior to establishment of Responsible Government.
6. Loan for railway construction in Kenya and Uganda.
7. For repairs and relief of distress after natural disaster.
8. Includes cost of an economic investigation.
9. Includes aid for repairs and relief of distress after natural disaster and grants and loans for development works.
10. Includes aid for repairs and relief after natural disaster.
11. Loan for development works.
12. Includes grant for relief of unemployment.
13. To meet interest payments on external debt.
14. Includes aid to meet interest payments on external debt.

£7,600,000 a year. The bulk of this expenditure, particularly in the Middle East, was on military business. This excludes, of course, those other expenses of empire accounted for by other government departments, especially the Foreign Office, War Office and Admiralty.[3]

TABLE 7

Total Imperial Government Expenditure on Colonial Development
1918–39

	Expenditure on Colonial Development	% of G.N.P.
1918	164,018	0.003
1919	279,133	0.005
1920	766,244	0.013
1921	3,058,460	0.064
1922	1,976,721	0.047
1923	4,730,712	0.119
1924	720,909	0.018
1925	767,954	0.018
1926	831,134	0.020
1927	703,784	0.016
1928	885,122	0.020
1929	947,503	0.021
1930	1,965,690	0.045
1931	2,225,182	0.055
1932	1,677,542	0.043
1933	1,965,852	0.050
1934	1,458,282	0.035
1935	1,845,536	0.042
1936	1,929,023	0.042
1937	1,060,823	0.022
1938	1,932,454	0.038
1939	3,031,812	0.056

Total Expenditure £34,923,890
Average Annual Expenditure £1,587,450

Sources: Tables 6 and 7 and C. H. Feinstein, *Statistical Tables of National Income, Expenditure and Output of the U.K. 1855–1965*, Cambridge, 1972, averaging calculations based on figures of Gross National Product in tables 1 and 2, pp.T5-6, 8-9.

Expenditure on colonial development remained an insignificant item in the Imperial government's annual accounts. Central government expenditure was £1275 million in 1920, fell to around £700 million a year between 1923 and 1936 and then rose to £1409 million by 1939. Dominating these figures was the servicing of the national debt at a cost of around £300 million a year until the conversion loan of 1932 reduced the figure to just over £200 million a year. Military costs were cut from the immediate post-war peak of £520 million in

1920, but they remained around £110–140 million a year between 1923 and 1934 and rose again to £473 million by 1938.[4] One small indication of the limited expenditure on colonial development can be seen in a comparison between the average annual expenditure of under £1,600,000 on that item and central government expenditure on stationery and the maintenance of public buildings which rarely fell below £5 million a year in the 1920s.[5] Finally, with more recent methods of calculating the extent of official aid in mind, it is of interest to note from Table 7 that only once did expenditure on colonial development creep above 0.1% of G.N.P. and usually it was substantially less.

2. POLICY MAKERS

The purpose of these financial comparisons is not, it must be stressed, to condemn the past in the light of the present, nor, indeed, *vice versa*. The aim is to clarify the problem which now needs to be reviewed. How do we explain the limited amount of money spent on colonial development and in what circumstances were new commitments accepted?

The case studies examined show that Imperial government decisions to increase expenditure on the Colonial Empire were by no means the result of a ready consensus between policy-makers that such expenditure was invariably desirable and to be encouraged. Governments have a multiple and not a single personality. Behind the final bland public declaration of policy in the press, in the Commons or in election manifestos, lay a lather of collisions and conflicts between rival departments and ministers, usually resolved to some extent by compromise. There were, it has also been noted, occasional divisions of interest and purpose between ministers and their permanent advisers, particularly in the Colonial Office. It was, therefore, frequently the case that the success of a new initiative depended substantially though not completely upon the energy and persuasive power of the Secretary of State.

As Table 8 shows there were twelve different Secretaries of State in the years between August 1914 and the introduction of the Colonial Development and Welfare Bill into the House of Commons in May 1940. Traditionally, tenure of the Colonial Office was regarded by politicians mainly as a stop-gap appointment, usually carrying a place in the cabinet and hopefully acting as a step towards a political career

TABLE 8

Ministries, Secretaries of State for the Colonies, Chancellors of the Exchequer 1914–40

Ministry	Secretary of State	Chancellor
Asquith's Liberal Government (from 1910)	L. Harcourt	Lloyd George
Asquith's Coalition Government May 1915	A. Bonar Law	R. McKenna
Lloyd George's Coalition Government Dec. 1916	W. Long	A. Bonar Law
Lloyd George's Coalition Government Jan. 1919	Viscount Milner	A. Chamberlain
	W. S. Churchill (from Feb. 1921)	Sir R. Horne (from April 1921)
Bonar Law's Conservative Government Oct. 1922	Duke of Devonshire	S. Baldwin
Baldwin's Conservative Government May 1923	Duke of Devonshire	S. Baldwin
		N. Chamberlain (from Aug. 1923)
MacDonald's Labour Government Jan. 1924	J. H. Thomas	P. Snowden
Baldwin's Conservative Government Nov. 1924	L. S. Amery	W. S. Churchill
MacDonald's Labour Government June 1929	Lord Passfield	P. Snowden
MacDonald's National Government Aug. 1931	J. H. Thomas	P. Snowden
	Sir P. Cunliffe-Lister (from Nov. 1931)	N. Chamberlain (from Nov. 1931)
Baldwin's National Government June 1935	M. MacDonald	N. Chamberlain
	J. H. Thomas (from Nov. 1935)	
	W. Ormsby-Gore (from May 1936)	
Chamberlain's National Government May 1937	W. Ormsby-Gore	Sir J. Simon
	M. MacDonald (from May 1938)	

in higher circles. This pattern seems less apparent between 1914 and 1940. It was, perhaps, mainly a stopping-place for Bonar Law, Long, Passfield, Churchill and Devonshire, but the other occupants of the office brought an unusual degree of enthusiasm to the post. Harcourt's long tenure made him a competent and experienced minister with achievements in colonial development to his credit before the outbreak of the war. Milner thought highly of his work.[6] Milner himself brought to the office much administrative experience, having served under Cromer in Egypt and as Governor and High Commissioner in South Africa, and he had a deep concern for colonial development as a solution to the profound social and economic problems he discerned in Britain. Sir Ralph Furse rated him the greatest of the Secretaries of State he served.[7] There was, by contrast, nothing in J. H. Thomas's earlier career to suggest that he would have any profound interest in colonial matters, but he soon embraced the idea of colonial development as a solution to Britain's economic problems, and, as noted, he encouraged that cause later as Lord Privy Seal. Of Amery's passionate advocacy of imperial economic unity and development little more needs to be said. It was a cause he had espoused as a young man in the 1890s and to which he was wedded until his death in 1955. Similarly Cunliffe-Lister devoted much of his political energy to imperial economic affairs: his move to the Colonial Office in 1931 merely confirmed the interest he had shown previously as President of the Board of Trade. It was also appropriate that Ormsby-Gore should eventually take over the office in which he had energetically worked as under-secretary for several years in the 1920s. Finally, Malcolm MacDonald's move to the Colonial Office in 1938, after a brief appearance there in 1935, brought to the post another minister with remarkably clear ideas on colonial development policy and anxious to increase Imperial government expenditure upon it.

Given the unusual interest of the inter-war Secretaries of State in colonial affairs and particularly in colonial development, it appears even more unexpected that their energetic appeals for additional Imperial government expenditure met with such apparently modest results. It is true that in some cases the cause of tariff reform and empire settlement absorbed much of their attention and perhaps distracted them from the campaign for increased expenditure on colonial development.[8] But there were also substantial obstacles and handicaps which Secretaries of State faced when they did focus their attention on that goal.

It was suggested in Chapter II that one restraint on colonial development policy before 1914 was the structure of the Colonial

Office. Officials could draw on the advice of specialists in other government departments and in organisations outside government and on the Crown Agents and a few Colonial Office advisers and advisory committees. But on the whole the geographical division of responsibilities probably reduced the importance of economic and social questions in the eyes of the administrators and induced a conservative attitude towards colonial development. There is evidence to suggest that for much of the inter-war period similar inhibitions remained. The Colonial Office was by no means a static body between 1914 and 1940. Numbers grew from 192 in 1914 to 350 in 1929 and to 465 in 1939.[9] But for much of this period the structure of the office, the division of duties and the definition of business remained unchanged. As described in Chapter II, the main work of the Colonial Office in 1914 was handled by six geographical departments, each headed by a principal clerk, handling respectively the dominions, West Africa and the Mediterranean, East Africa, Nigeria, the West Indies and the Eastern territories. There was in addition an Accounts department, mainly dealing with the annual estimates, and a General department under the chief clerk which handled legal work, patronage, establishment and supposedly all matters of common interest. Otherwise each geographical department dealt virtually unaided with the full range of problems concerning their colonies. Supervising the office was the permanent under-secretary and two assistant under-secretaries whose duties were also divided essentially on geographical lines. By 1918 no structural changes had occurred, merely the appointment of a third assistant under-secretary to share in the geographical distribution. In 1920 the burden of work on each geographical department was reduced by further geographical division when the Eastern department was split into the Ceylon and Mauritius department and the Far East department, while the East Africa department shed responsibilities to a new Tanganyika and Somaliland department. In 1921 Britain's new Middle Eastern empire was passed into the care of the Colonial Office, and another geographical department under a fourth assistant under-secretary was created. In 1926 responsibility for the dominions was devolved on to a separate Dominions Office, but otherwise the Colonial Office remained virtually unaltered until 1929 when the previous Nigeria department was merged into a single West Africa department, Ceylon and the Mediterranean were linked into a single unit and Mauritius was returned to the Far East department. This reduced the geographical departments to seven, and the assistant under-secretaries, now numbering three, maintained their geographically-divided overlordships. There was to be one later geographical re-arrangement in 1932 with the merging of the Pacific and the Mediterranean in one department and the re-uniting of Ceylon and the Far East into an Eastern department.[10]

The effect of this method of distributing work was to ensure that the fundamental unit for the consideration of colonial affairs remained the colony. For most of the inter-war period and especially in the 1920s problems were defined by geographical frontiers. Substantially as a result, economic issues still tended to be swamped by the multitude of other colonial matters with which officials were confronted. The Colonial Office in the 1920s has been described as 'a heptarchy with the heads of the seven geographical departments going their own way (and basically not interested in economic development) and a General Department which did a few odd jobs like defence, postage stamps, etc. which could only be handled centrally'.[11] Cunliffe-Lister recalled that when he took office in 1931 'everything was in watertight geographical departments'.[12] The emphasis in this approach was for each department to consider all the problems affecting their particular territories and to discourage attempts to assess issues of possibly general relevance to the Colonial Empire as a whole.

This feature of office organisation was strengthened by one aspect of the method of promotion through the office hierarchy. There was a considerable continuity of service in a single department. E. R. Darnley was serving as a first class clerk in the West Indies department from 1911 having joined the Colonial Office in 1898. In 1919 he was made principal clerk of the department and he was still at its head in 1931, the year before he retired. In 1915 H. R. Cowell became a second class clerk in the Eastern department, graduated to a first class clerk in the same department in 1916, and took over the Ceylon and Mauritius section when the department was divided in 1920. In 1929 he remained head of the Ceylon and Mediterranean department in the reshuffle that year, and in 1932 he became head of the reunited Eastern department where he stayed until he retired in 1938. A. E. Collins joined the Colonial Office in 1894, headed the Eastern department from 1911, took over the other half, for the Far East, in the 1920 division and remained in charge until his death in 1926. A. J. Harding was a second class clerk in the Niger department in 1913, a first class clerk in the same department in 1915, took charge of the department from 1920 and left only in 1927 to take over the Middle East department. Finally, Sir Cecil Bottomley, who played a prominent role in many of the negotiations analysed in this study, joined the Colonial Office in 1901, was a first class clerk in the East Africa department in 1913 and then served as head of the department from 1918 to 1927 when he was made an assistant under-secretary with East Africa still part of his province. Occasionally senior officers were transferred from responsibilities in one department to deal with other territorial or general problems, and this seems to have become more common in the 1930s, but even these men generally spent several years with each department before being moved.[13] Moreover, most senior posts normally went to men who had made service in the Colonial Office a life-long career. It was rare for outsiders to be brought in. In 1929 eight of the nine departmental heads, called assistant secretaries since 1920, had served long periods in the office, a minimum of 18 years, a maximum of 34. In 1940 the same was true of twelve of the thirteen assistant secretaries, a minimum of 14 years, a maximum of 29.[14] As a result of such service, particularly concentrated in one or two geographical departments, the Colonial Office contained men of quite remarkable knowledge of a wide range of problems affecting their colonies, but it did not encourage a wider outlook embracing general colonial aims and needs.

Of course, the informal exchange of ideas and conclusions between the Colonial Office staff must be assumed, and there were occasional *ad hoc* inter-departmental committees bringing heads together for the discussion of general problems and proposals. But there is evidence to show that energetic ministers anxious to press on with the cause of colonial development were not entirely satisfied with the existing Colonial Office and modifications were attempted. When Amery first went to the Colonial Office as under-secretary in 1919, he seems at once to have realised that the bureaucratic structure could restrict the initiatives which he and Milner wished to launch. We find him considering the establishment of a Colonial Office Council at which ministers would meet and settle questions with departmental heads at regular meetings.[15] But more significantly, Amery was anxious to draw upon outsiders for the expertise he evidently found lacking within the office. For a while he toyed with the idea of 'using the Crown Agents for creating a real General Staff for Crown Colony development'.[16] There was, indeed, a good deal of communication between Colonial Office and Crown Agents between the wars as earlier chapters have shown, and Amery did attempt to protect the Crown Agents from Treasury attacks. There were also conscious attempts to widen the range and sources of advice for the Secretary of State. Milner's Colonial Development Committee, of which Amery was an enthusiastic member, tried to draw on the financial, business and technical advice of experts outside the Colonial Office, and this technique was later followed by the appointment of advisory committees to supervise the operations of the East Africa Loans Act and the Colonial Development Act, although it will be remembered that the particular powers with which these committees were endowed owed rather more to the Treasury than to the Secretary of State.

More acceptable to the Colonial Office were the additional committees in more traditional mould appointed between the wars to advise the Secretary of State on the technical matters which were increasingly important to programmes of colonial development and which seemed to lie beyond the competence of most Colonial Office staff. For example, the Advisory Medical and Sanitary Committee for Tropical Africa, set up in 1909, extended its brief to cover the whole Colonial Empire in 1922. It ran alongside the Colonial Medical Reseach Committee, established in 1927 to advise the Medical Research Council on appropriate projects, and merged with it in 1931 to form the Colonial Advisory Medical Committee. Similarly the Colonial Survey Committee of 1905 extended its scope to become the Colonial Survey and Geophysical Committee in 1935. There was an Advisory Committee on Native Education from 1923, a Colonial Advisory Council on Agricultural and Animal Health from 1929 and an Imperial Communications Advisory Committee also from 1929. There were in addition several new bodies with executive as well as advisory duties whose activities were advantageous to inter-war Secretaries of State: the Colonial Research Committee from 1919, the Imperial Bureau of Mycology from 1920, the Imperial Mineral Resources Bureau from 1923, the Committee for Research in the Falkland Islands from 1923, the Imperial Forestry Institute from 1924 and the more wide-ranging bodies like the Imperial Economic Committee from 1923, the Empire Marketing Board from 1926 to 1933, the Executive Council of the Imperial Agricultural Bureaux from 1933 and the Colonial Empire Marketing Board from 1937. Sir George Fiddes, writing of the advisory committees in 1926, concluded that the unofficial members ... are men in the front rank of their respective professions, and ... the Office thereby obtains the best advice from persons acquainted with the latest developments of medical and other sciences, in a way that it could not expect to do from any permanent technical staff appointed to perform similar duties.[17]

It was clearly possible for a former senior official to regard these committees as adequate for the needs of the Colonial Office. But their proliferation after the Second World War perhaps suggests that they remained too few in number and too restricted in scope between the wars to affect more than marginally the earlier course of colonial development policy.

A widening of the range of professional advisers to the Secretary of State was another indication of the lack of appropriate expertise within the Colonial Office after the First World War. In 1914 there was only a legal adviser and a botanical adviser. After the war Milner appointed an adviser on mineral questions but that post lapsed in 1922. Similarly Churchill established a commercial adviser in 1921 but that lasted only until 1923. Amery left a more secure legacy with the restoration in 1926 of the post of medical adviser, vacant since Chamberlain's day. Then in February 1927 Sir Samuel Wilson, the permanent under-secretary, set about an examination of the organisation of the Colonial Office. Amongst other things his investigatory committee concluded that more expert advice was needed on financial, veterinary, railway and forestry matters.[18] This report encouraged Amery to appoint in March 1927 a second committee, again under Wilson, to conduct a further review. The evidence gathered included a recommendation from Niemeyer in the Treasury who argued that the Colonial Office's work in the future would be increasingly involved with development matters and that neither the Colonial Office nor the Crown Agents were adequately equipped to handle such business: an adviser was needed. Wilson's second committee eventually discounted the need for veterinary, railway and forestry advisers but they did agree that an economic and financial adviser was urgently needed, and this appointment was made in 1928. They also identified the need for an agricultural adviser and the first appointment followed in 1929.[19] A fisheries adviser, seconded from the Ministry of Agriculture, was also on hand from 1928 to 1937, an adviser on animal health from 1930, and a labour adviser from 1938.[20]

While these increased sources of advice undoubtedly made the Colonial Office better-equipped in the 1930s than in the 1920s to handle the tasks which ambitious Secretaries of State set before them, they did not entirely resolve the problems created by distributing work predominantly in geographical packets. This issue was also examined in 1927 and 1928 by the two committees on Colonial Office reorganisation which Sir Samuel Wilson chaired. The first committee conceded that the pressure of work had in recent years increased very considerably, and that as a result 'there is no adequate opportunity for officers to study the bigger questions of policy or to do the more extensive reading which would render their work more valuable and less mechanical'. But while the committee condemned the tendency to work within tight geographical blinkers, they rejected the idea of the subject division of work. It was 'essential that there should be some staff in the Office ... in touch with all questions concerning the territory in question'. They argued that proper assessment of railway or other development schemes required knowledge of all other works in progress in the territory and a familiarity with the colony's financial and political situation.[21] The second committee returned to the issue only to be confronted by memoranda from three assistant undersecretaries, Grindle, Shuckburgh and Bottomley, asserting the traditional priorities of the geographical departments: 'the attempt to advise the Secretary of State on important questions without reference to the general complex of political, financial and administrative questions that make up the work and knowledge of a Geographical Department is bound to end in disaster'. Wilson had come to favour an enlarged general division because, as a sub-committee reported, 'there is, under the present system, some risk of the effective consideration of a question being impaired by the loss of time involved by the method of circulating General files in rotation to each of the separate geographical departments whose observations are needed'.[22] But Wilson hastened to reassure staff that full liaison between general division and geographical departments was, of course, essential. Amery too favoured retaining the pre-eminence of the geographical departments, and, accordingly, in 1928 the only change was to revamp the General department, dividing it into separate sections, one dealing with establishment and the Colonial Service, a second with pensions and civil research, a third with defence, finance, currency, transport and social hygiene, and a fourth with colonial development. It was this last section which handled the papers preliminary to the Colonial Development Act in 1929.[23]

This revision was still not found to be sufficient. In 1931 the first new separate subject departments were established, one dealing with recruitment and training and the other with the Colonial Service and establishment, and both within a new Personnel Division. This still left the handling of economic matters unaffected and apparently little improved. When in 1931 the economic blizzard and the Ottawa Conference thrust matters of trade and production into the forefront of office business, Cunliffe-Lister found it ill-prepared.

I found myself handicapped by an extraordinary absence of detailed knowledge .... There were no records or statistics of the amount which different countries took from the Colonies, the relative importance of these markets, or where the imports to the Colonies came from .... It appeared to be nobody's business to know about sugar, rubber, tin, tea, oilseeds or anything else as world commodities.

According to Cunliffe-Lister, his requests galvanised the economic section of the General department into action and *An Economic Survey of the Colonial Empire* running to 600 pages was rapidly produced.[24] But it was 1935 before the Economic department formally achieved independent status within the General Division in recognition of the importance of its work.[25]

This new subject department was an indication of the increased priority given to colonial economic developments in the early 1930s. By contrast the establishment of a separate Social Services department in 1939 is revealing of the preoccupation with welfare in the colonies in the later 1930s. A deputation to the Colonial Office from the Colonial Advisory Committee of the TUC in June 1938 stimulated internal office discussions on such a department. Malcolm Mac-Donald favoured the idea. In December 1938 the Secretary of State submitted his request to the Treasury for this extension of the office:

Mr. MacDonald considers that the present importance of social services in the Colonies is so great that he can no longer regard as satisfactory an arrangement under which these questions are dealt with as a mere section of the duties of a General Department .... The work which is envisaged for the new Department will be work which at present is only partially being done.

What obliged the Treasury to concede, 'in the face of the need for economy', was MacDonald's emphasis on the political urgency of justifying the Imperial goverment's claim in the late 1930s 'that it acts as a beneficial trustee for its subject peoples'.[26] As a result of this and other changes, the Colonial Office by 1940 could match their geographical division of seven geographical departments with seven subject departments, arranged into a Personnel Division and a General Division. It is entirely in keeping with this recognition of the need for bureaucratic reorganisation to tackle novel administrative problems that the *Statement on Colonial Development and Welfare* in February 1940 described the strengthening of the Economic department, the creation of the Social Services department, the appointment of a Business Adviser and the establishment of an additional assistant under-secretary as the necessary prerequisites for the launching of the new policy.[27] During and after the Second World War and in the thick of operating that policy, further extensive office developments were undertaken.[28] But until such bureaucratic reorganisation took place, it is probable that the Colonial Office's expertise and methods of work were unhelpful to the effective promotion of new colonial development initiatives.

Moreover, bureaucratic changes between the wars did not necessarily effect a transformation of the ideas and aims of Colonial Office staff. Some of their assumptions probably continued to restrict expenditure on colonial development by limiting its perceived objectives. The pre-First World War belief that the economic development of the Colonial Empire essentially meant an improvement in the production and export of primary products was scarcely altered between the wars. The complementarity between colonial primary production and metropolitan industrial exports was still assumed. Amery spoke for most when in 1929 he explained to the Commons: 'it is not very probable, or, indeed, very desirable in the interests of the populations themselves, that industrial development should be unduly accelerated' in the colonies. In the same debate, Ormsby-Gore reassured M.P.s that outside Singapore no industrial developments were contemplated in the Colonial Empire.[29] Few colonial governments submitted industrial development schemes to the CDAC in the 1930s and most of these were small and inexpensive food-processing projects. A Cabinet Inter-Departmental Committee on the Industrial Development of the Empire examined the issues involved in 1934 and recommended that colonial industries should not be 'artificially' encouraged and that conditions and hours of work in existing workshops and factories should be brought more into line with those in the United Kingdom in order to reduce competition from sweated labour. With these attitudes and proposals Colonial Office staff generally concurred, and the industrial processing of colonial products in the colonies and development of import substitution industries proceeded slowly, privately and with little deliberate Colonial Office financial assistance. For example, the Colonial Office in general refused to allow colonial governments to protect infant local industries against metropolitan competition by discriminatory tariffs.[30] In June 1939, the head of the Economic department placed agricultural improvement as the first priority in the Colonial Empire and regarded the development of subsidiary industries as only a later prospect,[31] and in May 1940 his successor agreed that the Colonial Development and Welfare Act like the Colonial Development Act should avoid 'subsidizing uneconomic secondary industries in the Colonies competing with United Kingdom manufacturers'.[32] One of the rare complaints came from Sir Henry Moore, former Governor of Sierra Leone but assistant under-secretary at the Colonial Office in 1939, who claimed that proposals to create secondary industries in the colonies had been poorly received by the CDAC, and who criticized the 'more or less unwritten rule that any proposals, whether in the field of industry or tariffs, which give rise to any conflict of economic interest, should be approached from the standpoint that United Kingdom trade interests must rank first, Dominion trade interests second, and those of the Colonial Empire last'.[33] Of course, the lack of positive assistance from the Colonial Office does not alone explain the slow development of industry in the colonies, but the prevailing views of Colonial Office staff and ministers partly accounts for the somewhat restricted perceptions they had between the wars of the needs and opportunities for expenditure on colonial development.

Amongst the Colonial Office staff's reasons for discouraging industrialisation and other radical economic innovations for much of the inter-war period remained their view that the consequences would be incompatible with their inherited notions of protective trusteeship. The duty of preserving native society from disruption was re-emphasized and re-publicized by Lord Lugard, especially in *The Dual Mandate*, and the message seems to have been happily accepted by most colonial officials. The interdependence between economic activities and cultural, social and political practices was also stressed by most academic anthropologists especially in the 1920s. Together these approaches encouraged the maintenance where practicable of versions of indirect rule and often discouraged policies likely to disrupt the cohesion of local society. Sir Andrew Cohen, commenting on the Colonial Office he knew in the 1930s, concluded that there was still more insistence 'on safeguarding African society than on helping

Africans to develop'.[34] Before 1914 such views had been another discouragement to increased expenditure on colonial development, and they continued to leave many Colonial Office staff suspicious of proposals to accelerate development programmes.

Not until the later 1930s did this restraint on colonial development policy begin to ease when the fruits of protective trusteeship were exposed to criticism and the years of benign neglect increasingly condemned. As suggested in Chapter IX, the shift towards a more constructive version of trusteeship in the 1930s, was partly provoked by economic depression, unrest in the colonies, the exposure of low nutrition standards and other matters which brought colonial conditions before public notice. But it is also probable, as Professor Lee has suggested, that Colonial Office assumptions were also affected by that contemporaneous expansion in the domestic role of the state in Britain.[35] The unsystematic but nevertheless extensive increase in the role of government as manager of the economy and provider of welfare services reflected and fuelled a lively debate on the legitimate responsibilities of the state. Increased state obligations for the unemployed, the poorly housed, the sick and the depressed areas in Britain seem to have opened Colonial Office eyes to the scope for improved welfare activities in the colonies. There was talk in the late 1930s of Britain's 'slum Empire', and we find one official in 1939 arguing that in exceptional circumstances a colony 'may have to be treated for a period of years like a derelict area in this country'.[36] The new sympathy in the Colonial Office for constructive trusteeship seems then to be a part of and a reflection of that simultaneous domestic drift towards economic and welfare planning. As Sir Keith Hancock put it, 'the Development and Welfare policy began to be born when the idealists of colonial trusteeship dissolved their time-hallowed partnership with the individualists and made a new one with the planners'.[37]

But this shift also required a modification in traditional Colonial Office views of their relationship with colonial governments, and this had only been partially accomplished by 1940. Between the wars, as before 1914, Colonial Office staff expected colonial development schemes to be initiated by colonial governments and they were reluctant to put forward proposals themselves or to embrace other metropolitan initiatives. Their notion of the decentralized empire and their own supervisory rather than initiatory role in administration and development was expressed, for example, during the discussion in

1928 on Colonial Office reorganisation. 'In many ways', it was explained, 'a policy of centralized control must prove to be incompatible with the policy of encouraging the free development of the Colonies as individual units'.[38] For this reason, as noted in earlier chapters, staff tended to be suspicious of development schemes originating in the metropolis. Advocates of more extensive colonial development policies had accordingly to convince an otherwise sceptical Colonial Office that the strings attached to their proposals would not deliver the colonies bound hand and foot to some grand metropolitan plan. The Colonial Office embraced with more sympathy proposals originating from colonial governments. Likewise the CDAC found that they were dependent on the energy of colonial governments in putting forward schemes for consideration and were denied the right to initiate schemes for themselves.

This dependence on colonial governments partly explains the interest of Secretaries of State in improving the quality of the Colonial Service. If development programmes were dependent for their planning and execution on colonial servicemen, then their numbers and range of expertise needed to be increased. Amery had particularly ambitious plans to create a unified Colonial Service out of the separate and independent services employed by virtually each portion of the Colonial Empire. But it was symptomatic of colonial government resistance to these centralising plans that, for example, they refused to contribute one-quarter of one per cent of their revenues to finance a single higher agricultural service. In 1929 Amery appointed a committee under Sir Warren Fisher which in the following year reported in favour of unifying the services and slowly, by the time of the outbreak of the Second World War, a more unified Colonial Service was achieved.[39] But the expansion and improvement of the agricultural, veterinary, medical, forestry and other scientific specialist services relevant to development work probably only increased Colonial Office reliance on Colonial Service initiatives. Moreover, it is doubtful if the visits by Colonial Office staff to the colonies, which Amery and Sir Samuel Wilson encouraged and which later Secretaries of State organised more systematically, made officials more willing to initiate action from London on their return.[40] Similarly the bringing in to the Colonial Office of former high-ranking staff from the colonies, like ex-Governor Wilson in 1925 and ex-Governor Moore in 1937, may have increased Colonial Office sympathy for and understanding of colonial government difficulties, but it was unlikely to increase Colonial Office desires to determine policy at the centre and impose it on the colonies. Amery attempted to inaugurate a regular series of Colonial Office Conferences at which colonial governors or other high-ranking officials could be, in part, persuaded to see and subsequently to follow the aims and objectives of the Secretary of State, but his first in 1927 was followed by only one more in 1930 before the idea fizzled out. Not until very late in the 1930s are there some signs that Colonial Office staff were prepared to accept a greater degree of responsibility in initiating the new development and welfare policy. In December 1938 when appealing to the Treasury for approval to set up the Social Services department, the Colonial Office commented: 'While the actual execution of developments ... must be carried out by the local staffs in the Colonies themselves, the initiative, inspiration and guidance must to a large extent be supplied from here'.[41] The *Statement of Policy on Colonial Development and Welfare* in February 1940 also hinted at a shift in the balance of Colonial Office and colonial government roles, speaking of the need to urge colonial governments to prepare development programmes and for co-operation in their planning and execution.[42] But even then it was denied that the Colonial Office intended to dictate policy, and this reflected the prevailing mood in the department, well-expressed in August 1939 by Parkinson, the permanent under-secretary, during discussions on the new policy:

It is essential to preserve the position of the Colonial *Governments* .... I am convinced that it is our duty in the Colonial Office to see that they are treated with the consideration they deserve .... It will be fatal if we ever allow ourselves to be forced into the position, or drift into the position, of attempting to govern any part of the Colonial Empire from Downing Street. The guiding principle must, I submit, be that the Colonial Office and the Colonial Governments *co-operate*.[43]

There was, of course, much good sense, political and economic, in this conception of the proper relationship between the Colonial Office and the colonies, but in spite of the modification which had taken place since before the First World War, these assumptions probably did act as a further discouragement to colonial development initiatives from the centre.

In brief, these ideas plus traditional notions of protective trustee-ship and of the limited objectives of policy, help explain the restricted expenditure on colonial development before 1940. Colonial Office structure and organisation of business helped to nurture and preserve these views. Only late in the period can alterations be clearly discerned. By the later 1930s structural changes in the Colonial Office reflected and encouraged new ideas on economic and welfare management. It is symptomatic that in the thick of policy-making in the late 1930s were the new Colonial Office Economic and Agricultural Advisers, Campbell and Stockdale, and to a lesser extent the new Labour Adviser, Orde-Browne. As shown in Chapter IX the negotiations were also handled by the new subject departments, Economic initially, Social Services subsequently. It is apparent that MacDonald, in contrast for example with Amery, found at his back a Colonial Office rather more willing and better equipped to applaud and assist his new initiative.

Of course, as several previous chapters have shown, the other major restraint on Imperial government expenditure on colonial development remained the Treasury. Treasury opposition broke Milner's patience, frustrated Amery's plans, muted the activities of the CDAC and threatened MacDonald's new policy. Colonial Office complaints, common before the First World War, hardly diminished afterwards. Sir George Fiddes, former permanent under-secretary, wrote with evident resentment in his study of the Colonial Office in 1926: 'Great as are the powers of the Secretary of State in his own sphere, he cannot add even a messenger to his staff, or increase the pay of any member, without the consent of the Treasury, which is only given after jealous and prolonged examination, and the presentation of an overwhelming case'. He claimed that 'an indispensable preliminary to progress in any territory is to free it from Treasury control'.[44]

The Colonial Office permanent and political staff seemed to imply at times that the Treasury were especially restrictive of expenditure on colonial affairs. It is true that the Treasury did respond to what with some justification they regarded as the Colonial Office's and Colonial Service's professional incompetence in financial matters by rigorous examination of Colonial Office claims for Imperial government expenditure. But the Treasury were equally reluctant to spend money on other government departments. The inter-war period is punctuated by inter-departmental conflicts over expenditure. The Treasury adhered throughout to orthodox budgetary principles, and considered it to be a primary duty to limit government expenditure. As before 1914, it was assumed that high expenditure, requiring consequent high levels of taxation or government borrowing, imposed a burden on private business which should be avoided. Chancellors between the wars invariably endeavoured to reduce tax levels and government claims on the money market from the unprecedentedly high levels to which they had been raised during First World War. But circumstances between the wars made the necessary reductions in government expenditure difficult to accomplish. Central government expenditure had been less than £200 million in 1913–14, but in each of the last two years of the war it was over £2,500 million, and although income tax had risen from 1s 2d in the £ to 6s in the £ by 1920–21 much of the war had been financed by borrowing, accumulating a total national debt of over £7,000 million. Annual interest payments on the debt which had been only £20 million in 1913 had risen to £325 million a year by 1920 and absorbed nearly one-third of the yield from taxation. Chancellors after the war were undeniably preoccupied with trying to reduce the size of the debt, the figure for debt repayments and the levels of taxation. They were further impressed by the need to do so by the onset of economic depression late in 1920 and the orthodox arguments which ruled that lower taxation, less government borrowing and reduced prices were the route to recovery. The second savage downturn in 1931 merely reinforced these priorities.[45]

Moreover, the Colonial Office never showed much sympathy with the basic Treasury problem: which of the many claims upon the finite resources of the Exchequer were most justified? This wider consideration necessarily affected the willingness of the Treasury to approve colonial development projects which, in themselves, might be economically viable. In the immediate post-war period the Treasury were subjected to requests for financial assistance from many departments, for example, for increased social services. Operating within the framework of orthodox financial policy the Treasury believed they could only allocate a limited amount of money to spending departments. Hence their request to the Colonial Office in 1919 for a complete programme of colonial development projects, and hence their annoyance when no such programme was provided. The Treasury felt they were being asked to distribute precious government resources without adequate information on the total needs of the Imperial government's departments. Later, when it was argued that colonial development would in fact help alleviate unemployment in Britain, the Treasury had still to judge whether expenditure on colonial development would be a more effective palliative for unemployment than a similar amount of expenditure on public works in Britain. Although the Treasury were able to see the long-term economic justifications for colonial development, the imminence of economic collapse persuaded them that they must give priority to short-term financial necessities. Later in the 1930s the claims of rearmament also competed for expenditure with proposals for colonial development and welfare.

It also remained true that the Treasury's basic theses were generally accepted by other government departments and politicians and were buttressed by much public and parliamentary support. The Treasury were not acting in defiance of the consensus. This was particularly true in the crisis years of 1921–22 and 1931–32 when the government was subjected to determined anti-waste campaigns. Reductions in government expenditure were demanded. The two Committees on National Expenditure under Geddes and May which resulted commanded a wide spectrum of parliamentary approval and inevitably strengthened the Treasury's hand. To this must be added the Treasury's prestige as a government department. Their authority, partially diminished in the necessary spending spree of the First World War, was restored after the war and confirmed by the appointment in 1919 of the Treasury's permanent secretary as head of the civil service.[46] The views of the Treasury and the Chancellor usually commanded the consent of other ministers. As we have seen, whenever the Chancellor insisted in cabinet on resisting the wishes of the Secretary of State for the Colonies he was always successful. Thus the Treasury obtained their desired administrative arrangements for expenditure under the Trade Facilities Act, the East Africa Loans Act and the Colonial Development Act. In brief, the Treasury's opposition and the continued widespread approval for orthodox budgetary policy acted as further restraints on the extent of Imperial government expenditure on colonial development up to 1940.

3. *POLICY-MAKING*

The limited expenditure on colonial development may be explained by the restraints analysed. But the figures provided earlier and the case studies examined in previous chapters indicate that those restraints were not insurmountable. The Colonial Office were not incapable of pressing home their arguments and the Treasury were not a total barrier to expenditure. Either Secretaries of State were able to convince the Treasury of the financial merits of Colonial Office proposals, or the Colonial Office plans drew sufficient political support inside the cabinet and outside in Parliament, party and public to force the Treasury into concessions. A review of policy-making between the wars will clarify the circumstances in which financial assistance was granted to the colonies.

Before 1914 it had been a subject for congratulation in the Colonial Office that the economic and social development of most colonies owed little to financial help from the Treasury. Imperial government loans and grants-in-aid invariably involved galling Treasury supervision of colonial finance. While the Treasury sought to avoid such expenditure, the Colonial Office and colonial governments were equally anxious to maintain the financial independence of the colonies. It followed that one of the major purposes of the Imperial government's colonial development policy before 1914 was to help territories lay down the basic economic infrastructure which would generate local prosperity and enable local governments to improve their income and finance future development projects unaided. This was the model of development illustrated and inspired by its success in West Africa.

Self-financed colonial development remained the ideal for Colonial Office staff after the First World War. However, the efficacy of such a strategy inevitably depended on the ability of colonies to raise their own capital. The sources for this were various, and the annual reports issued by colonial governments between the wars reveal their range. Firstly, territories were less inclined to turn to the Imperial government for assistance if private enterprise was tempted to invest locally. The attractiveness of colonies to private capital depended partly on the value of local markets, partly on the demands for local products and also upon the existence of an economic infrastructure through which these resources could be tapped. Thus in the 1920s and 1930s Palestine was helped by a considerable influx of Jewish capital, and Hong Kong was also sufficiently developed to attract private investment.[47] Secondly, revenue from local taxation, particularly customs duties, could provide colonial administrations with sufficient income to meet the needs of public works. Taxation, in other words, was a form of domestic capital formation. In 1927, the Government of Hong Kong reported with pride that the colony had financed 'its amazing developments during the past 30 years by means of its annual revenue and without recourse to borrowing'.[48] Thirdly, some colonial governments avoided imperial aid by drawing on local or regional financial resources. Small local loans were raised by many West Indian administrations, and the more prosperous territories of Southern Rhodesia, the Federated Malay States and the Straits Settlements raised larger ones. The governments of these last two territories also lent money to neighbouring governments.[49] Finally, relatively well-developed dependencies with a reasonable export trade and respectable credit were able to raise loans for further development on the London market. Between the wars this remained by far the largest source of loan capital for the Colonial Empire. As Table 9 shows, nominal loans on the open market between 1919 and the outbreak of war in 1939 totalled £144,957,693, much larger than the total expenditure by the Imperial government on colonial development. Except for the Colonial Stock Acts and the rare guaranteed loan act, such borrowing proceeded without Imperial government assistance. It lies behind most of the public works schemes embarked upon by colonial governments.[50]

Not all colonial administrations enjoyed such opportunities between the wars. That explains why the East African territories received most of the financial assistance provided by the Imperial government in the early post-war period. Kenya, Uganda, Nyasaland, Tanganyika and Northern Rhodesia at this time had underdeveloped local infrastructures and did not attract enough private investment. They could not provide their governments with sufficient revenue for self-financed public works, they could draw on only meagre local or regional capital resources and their credit did not allow them to rely confidently on the London money market. Accordingly, since they were regarded by their governments and the Colonial Office as having some economic potential and since they were or might easily become dependent on imperial grants-in-aid, they obtained much of the assistance for development which the Imperial Treasury grudgingly released after the First World War. This emphasis on meeting the financial needs of poorer dependent East African territories demonstrates that the assumptions of the West Africa model of development remained influential in the Colonial Office and in the Treasury. This was revealed in several of the case studies presented earlier in this study.

It was argued in Chapter III that the First World War programmes for imperial development aroused little enthusiasm amongst the permanent staff of the Colonial Office and that in any case even the

TABLE 9

Loans raised by Colonial Governments on London Market 1919—39

Date	Territory	Nominal Amount in £	%	Price	How Raised
1919 Oct.	Sudan	3,500,000	5½	95½	G.L.A.
1919 Nov.	Nigeria	6,200,000	6	100	C.S.A.
1920 Jan.	Gold Coast	4,000,000	6	100	C.S.A.
1921 Feb.	Sudan	2,880,000	5½	92	G.L.A.
1921 June & Oct.	Ceylon	6,000,000	6	97	C.S.A.
1921 Oct.	Nigeria	3,000,000	6	97	C.S.A.
1921 Nov.	Kenya	5,000,000	6	95	C.S.A.
1921 Dec.	Straits Settlements	5,155,000	6	97	C.S.A
1922 May	British Guiana	1,000,000	5½	99½	Independent
1922 May	Straits Settlements	4,200,000	4½	95	C.S.A.
1923 Jan.	Sudan	3,250,000	4½	93	G.L.A.
1923 March	Jamaica	670,000	4½	94	C.S.A.
1923 Oct.	Nigeria	5,700,000	4	88	C.S.A.
1924 Feb.	S. Rhodesia	3,000,000	5	98	C.S.A.
1924 May	Sudan	513,400	4½	95¼	G.L.A.
1924 Nov.	Sudan	1,500,000	4	86	G.L.A.
1925 Nov.	Gold Coast	4,628,000	4½	94	C.S.A.
1927 Jan.	Nigeria	4,250,000	5	100	C.S.A.
1927 Nov.	Kenya	5,000,000	5	99½	C.S.A.
1927 Nov.	Palestine	4,475,000	5	100½	G.L.A.
1928 March	Fiji	765,000	5	101	C.S.A.
1928 May	Kenya	3,500,000	4½	95	C.S.A.
1928 June	Tanganyika	2,070,000	4½	96½	G.L.A.
1928 Nov.	S. Rhodesia	2,000,000	4½	97	C.S.A.
1929 July	British Guiana	2,000,000	5	98	C.S.A.
1930 Jan.	Ceylon	1,250,000	5	99	C.S.A.
1930 Feb. & Nov.	Nigeria	4,650,000	5	99	C.S.A.
1930 Sept.	Ceylon	1,750,000	4½	95	C.S.A.
1930 Dec.	Kenya	3,400,000	4½	98½	C.S.A.
1930 Dec.	Sierra Leone	202,500	4½	97½	C.S.A.
1931 March	Gold Coast	1,170,000	4½	98	C.S.A.
1931 June	Sierra Leone	151,100	4½	100	C.S.A.
1931 July	Tanganyika	3,000,000	4	94½	G.L.A.
1932 Jan.	Uganda	2,000,000	5	96	C.S.A.
1932 Jan.	Mauritius	600,000	5	98½	G.L.A.
1932 Jan. & Feb.	N. Rhodesia	1,250,000	5	94-96¾	C.S.A.
1932 Feb.	Nyasaland	2,000,000	4½	97½	G.L.A.
1932 June	Cyprus	615,000	4	95	C.S.A.
1932 June	Jamaica	377,000	4	94	C.S.A.
1932 June	Tanganyika	500,000	4	98	G.L.A.
1933 Feb.	N. Rhodesia	1,097,000	3½	98	C.S.A.
1933 Feb.	Uganda	235,600	3½	97½	C.S.A.
1933 March	Trinidad	1,035,000	3½	98½	C.S.A.
1933 Aug.	Kenya	305,600	3½	98½	C.S.A.
1933 Oct.	S. Rhodesia	2,250,000	3½	98	C.S.A.
1933 Oct.	Jamaica	403,000	3½	99½	C.S.A.
1934 Jan.	Nyasaland	1,570,000	3	98½	G.L.A.
1934 May	British Guiana	175,400	3	96	C.S.A.
1934 June	S. Rhodesia	2,750,000	3¼	97½	C.S.A.
1934 June	Ceylon	800,000	3½	100	C.S.A.
1934 Sept.	Nigeria	4,188,000	3	97½	C.S.A.
1934 Nov.	Fiji	182,497	3	99	C.S.A.
1934 Dec.	Fed. Malay States	4,000,000	3	100	C.S.A.
1935 May	Gold Coast	602,000	3	101-102	C.S.A.

TABLE 9 (cont.)

Date	Territory	Nominal Amount in £	%	Price	How Raised
1935 Aug.	Trinidad	1,670,000	3	100	C.S.A.
1935 Nov.	S. Rhodesia	1,250,000	3	99	C.S.A.
1935 Dec.	Ceylon	4,500,000	3	100	C.S.A.
1936 Jan.	British Guiana	209,922	3	99	C.S.A.
1936 April	Jamaica	350,000	3	99	C.S.A.
1936 Aug.	Kenya	175,000	3	100	C.S.A.
1936 Dec.	Grenada	166,600	3	99	C.S.A.
1937 Aug.	Mauritius	301,800	3½	100¼	C.S.A.
1937 Nov.	Jamaica	850,000	3	92½-93½	C.S.A.
1937 Dec.	Sierra Leone	570,000	3½	101	C.S.A.
1937 Dec.	S. Rhodesia	2,250,000	3½	101	C.S.A.
1938 Feb.	Mauritius	177,000	3½	102¼	C.S.A.
1938 Feb.	Fiji	144,740	3	93½	C.S.A.
1938 April	Jamaica	340,000	3	98½	C.S.A.
1938 April	Sierra Leone	306,834	3	96½	C.S.A.
1939 Jan.	Jamaica	1,300,000	3½	99	C.S.A.
1939 April	Ceylon	1,015,000	3½	100-101½	C.S.A.
1939 April	Uganda	614,400	3½	98	C.S.A.
1939 July	Sudan	2,000,000	3¼	97	G.L.A.

Grand Total: £144,957,693

G.L.A. = Guaranteed Loan Act.   C.S.A. = Colonial Stock Acts.

Small subsequent issues to cover expenses of raising loans not included.

Sources: *Stock Exchange Year Books*, 1920, 1931, 1940; *Annual Colonial Reports*; *Annual Treasury List of Stock issued under Colonial Stock Acts* in Parliamentary Papers.

committed leadership of Milner and Amery could not get round the obstacle of the Treasury and the campaign for economy in government expenditure. What we do see, in Chapter IV, is a resumption on the pre-war *ad hoc* basis of Imperial government aid for the East African dependencies. Colonial governments' requests for the release of funds under the 1914 East African Protectorates Loans Act and the Imperial government's reluctant agreement to meet those obligations owed nothing to the visionary war-time schemes for creating the autarkic empire. The policy conformed precisely to that which, in spite of Joseph Chamberlain, had remained dominant before the war. It was the colonial governments who initiated the pressure for further Imperial government expenditure: it was not inspired by metropolitan needs. It was the East African territories, barely free from imperial grants-in-aid, that received this assistance. The primary purpose of this assistance was to provide the territories with the railways and harbours necessary to help them achieve financial self-sufficiency in the future.

In the period of post-war inflation, the inadequacy of the assistance provided caused the government of Uganda to propose a new scheme. The origins of the 1920 Uganda Development Loan and the reasons for the Imperial government's decision to provide further aid conform once more to the pre-1914 model. The financially vulnerable protectorate of Uganda was to be made financially secure by a further injection of a limited amount of Imperial government finance.

The same concept of the role of the Imperial government in promoting colonial development lies behind the negotiations leading to the first independent loan raised by Kenya on the London market in 1921. Colonial Office staff were anxious to restrain the colony's government lest it overburden local revenues with high interest costs and thus force the territory to lose its recently acquired independence of imperial grants-in-aid. The Treasury were equally anxious to avoid such a relapse. In addition they made it perfectly plain that they regarded their principal function to be that of maintaining a healthy *Imperial* government budget by demanding a settlement of Kenya's war debt to the Imperial Exchequer. Pressing the claim might have wrecked Kenya's attempt to raise its first London loan. However, the Treasury were equally anxious to encourage this step towards Kenya's future self-development. The concessions which the Treasury accordingly made to Kenya confirm the impression that the pre-war model was still dominating policy-making. Territories should be helped towards financial self-sufficiency by limited Imperial government encouragement.

From 1921 onwards, the onset of economic depression in Britain and the rise of the unemployment figures began to influence the arguments used in decision-making. But the traditional *ad hoc* aspects of policy were still influential. In Chapter VI, the initiatives leading to the Imperial government's £3,500,000 loan to Kenya and Uganda in 1924 were seen to stem mainly from the colonies. It was again the undeveloped East African territories, still potential burdens on the Imperial Exchequer, that received further assistance. And the negotiations were once more complicated by the Treasury's attempts to claim prior repayment of East African war debts. In 1924 the Treasury remained more concerned to limit the financial liabilities of the colonies to the Imperial Exchequer than to increase the economic assets of the colonies to the British economy.

This attitude was implicit even in the negotiations of 1925–26 leading to the East Africa Loans Act. On this occasion the objective of securing the future financial self-sufficiency of the East African territories was not explicitly stated. But it was once again the poorer East African territories that dominated Imperial government concern. And it is significant that the 1926 act encouraged those territories to raise capital on the London market and thus relieved the Imperial government of the duty of subsidizing their development with grants-in-aid.

The pre-war West Africa model of limited Imperial government assistance for colonial development therefore remained a powerful influence on policy-making. In the early 1920s the Colonial Office permanent staff framed their requests for Treasury financial aid in those traditional terms. It was primarily to secure the future financial self-sufficiency of the territories that the Treasury reluctantly acceded to those requests.

The onset of economic depression seriously modified both the objectives of British colonial development policy and the process by which decisions were made. Until the unemployment situation developed there was considerable agreement on the aims of policy between the few participants in policy-making. The Colonial Office permanent staff, the Treasury and the colonial governments accepted the basic principles of the West Africa model. The economic depression did two things. Firstly, it increased the number of people interested in colonial development. Secondly, it introduced new arguments, new concepts of the purpose of colonial development. The old consensus was shattered and policy-making became a more complicated struggle between rival advocates with quite different objectives.

The crisis confronting the governments of the 1920s was both economic and political. On the one hand they were forced to recognise their responsibility to help the economy recover. And on the other, the depression in industry and mass unemployment became a matter of major political importance. All political parties regarded the search for a solution to the unemployment situation either as their major political burden when in power or as a golden opportunity to obtain power. This preoccupation dominated the election manifestos. In a search for solutions, publicists and politicians of all parties turned to the idea of colonial development, initially as a short-term and later as a long-term cure for Britain's economic problems. In this way the imperial visionaries obtained the political allies with whose help they were able to override Treasury opposition to expenditure.

Changed attitudes were thus pioneered by politicians and not by bureaucrats.

While the Colonial Office permanent staff, the Treasury and the colonial governments demonstrated a continued loyalty to the earlier model of colonial development, Britain's domestic economic problems inspired politicians in the Colonial Office and also in the other departments of the Imperial government to reconsider the purpose of colonial development. Proposals for Imperial government expenditure on colonial development came from the Board of Trade, government committees on unemployment and other interested ministers. The apparent ineffectiveness of traditional Treasury policy as a cure for unemployment and the continuing political importance of finding a solution greatly contributed to the increase in cabinet support for a policy of colonial development. Instead of seeing that policy primarily as a means of achieving the financial self-sufficiency of the colonies, the Board of Trade, the Ministry of Labour and other interested parties began to see colonial development as a means of alleviating distress in Britain. Given the fact that colonial development in practice meant the building of railways, harbours, roads, bridges and other public works in the colonies, and also that the materials for their construction could and should be bought in Britain, then, it was argued, the acceleration of colonial development programmes would increase overseas demand for British goods especially in the distressed export industries. It followed that it might be necessary to offer a degree of Imperial government financial assistance to colonial governments in order to persuade them to accelerate their development schemes. A small Imperial government commitment should lead to significant colonial purchases of British products. The novelty of this proposal is that unlike the dominant pre-war model of colonial development it clearly regarded the economic interests of Britain, not the financial interests of the Imperial Treasury nor the interests of the colonies, as the main priority.

The weight of these new arguments at a time of serious unemployment was demonstrated in the negotiations concerning the Imperial Economic Conference which led to the Trade Facilities Act of 1924. Here was a colonial development scheme which was formulated on the initiative of the metropolitan authorities, which was not an *ad hoc* response to a particular colony's needs but was available to all the Colonial Empire, and which had as its objective the relief of British economic distress and not the achievement of colonial financial independence. It was a measure which, as described in Chapter V, was disliked by the Colonial Office permanent staff who resented subordinating colonial to imperial interests. It was also a measure whose inadequate terms rendered it singularly useless.

Nevertheless the argument which made the Imperial government accept the Trade Facilities Act did not expire with it. That colonial development might provide immediate short-term relief for unemployment was a powerful thesis in the making of subsequent commitments. While Colonial Office staff were anxious to obtain the £3,500,000 loan to Kenya and Uganda in 1924 as a means of ensuring the future financial independence of the territories, such generous terms of assistance were only obtained in the face of Treasury opposition because of those supporters who saw the proposed railways as a means of providing immediate relief for unemployment in Britain. The same type of argument was also helpful as described in Chapters VI and VII in ensuring the passage of the East Africa Loans Act and the Colonial Development Act. The latter in particular was strongly supported on the grounds that it would relieve unemployment in Britain. Hence it was not framed as a traditional *ad hoc* response to a particular colonial need but, like the Trade Facilities Act, it was open to all the Colonial Empire. Urgent metropolitan requirements ensured this departure from the earlier policy of limited assistance to colonies.

It is also apparent that this new theory of the value of colonial development was itself modified. The Trade Facilities Acts had been mainly concerned with colonial development as an immediate short-term relief for unemployment. The continuation of the depression encouraged those who saw in colonial development an essentially long-term strategy. Instead of calculating the value of colonial development in terms of the immediate purchases of steel rails and building materials, it was argued that the real value to the metropolis lay in the development of colonial purchasing-power and the increase in colonial supplies of raw materials. The imperial visionaries, who since the days of Joseph Chamberlain had been arguing that Britain's economic security lay in the better integration and development of the empire, found new supporters in the economic depression of the 1920s, particularly when earlier expectations of a rapid cyclical recovery had evaporated. The 1924 loan to Kenya and Uganda attracted more support for this reason. And the arguments on these lines were even more in evidence during the discussions leading to the East Africa Loans Act in 1926. That the strategy best suited to meet British economic needs was a long-term one helps explain the provision in that act for expenditure on scientific research. Similarly, the long-term strategy loomed most prominently in the discussions leading to the Colonial Development Act in 1929, and, as suggested in Chapter VIII, seems to have guided the Colonial Development Advisory Committee in their administration of the measure through the 1930s. It is this which gives the 1929 act real significance. While the idea of colonial development as an immediate relief for unemployment may have been important in ensuring the safe passage of the proposal through inter-departmental negotiations, cabinet and Parliament, the act emerges with a distinct and contrasting character. It was not an *ad hoc* response to a particular colonial problem. It envisaged more than assistance for transport improvements since it covered expenditure on public health and on scientific research as well. It committed the Imperial government to an increased financial contribution to colonial development and for an indefinite period. And it emphasised the long-term value of such work to Britain. The measure was symptomatic of an anxiety which encouraged those in authority to turn to the Colonial Empire for the relief of a British economy in distress.

The Treasury permanent staff were not convinced of the validity of these arguments. They were sceptical of the value of colonial development as a solution to the unemployment problem, particularly in the short-term. And they regarded its efficacy as a long-term cure as unproven and, besides, essentially irrelevant when pressing short-term financial needs should have priority. Hence their opposition to making the terms of the Trade Facilities Acts more generous, their hostility to the guaranteed loan proposal for East Africa, their opposition to the idea of a colonial development fund, and their determination during and after the financial crisis of 1931–32 to restrict the annual grant to the CDAC. But though unconvinced by the economic arguments advanced in support of these measures and alarmed at their potential drain on the Imperial Exchequer, they reluctantly bowed to the political arguments in their favour. Ministers had to offer solutions to the depression. Terms were agreed and financial assistance was provided.

At the end of the 1930s the Treasury were once again asked to open their coffers for expenditure on the colonies. But it was argued in Chapter IX that the purpose of the new initiative with its emphasis on colonial welfare was novel. It had, of course, been assumed earlier that the development stimulated by imperial funds would benefit the colonies by improving their economic infrastructure, their trade and their public services. However, although colonial development policy was expected to raise colonial living standards, this would mainly be a means to an end, an incidental by-product of a policy whose primary purpose was to ease the problems facing the British Treasury and the British economy. By the late 1930s such priorities were being questioned. Nutrition, health and other aspects of colonial living standards were being specifically examined and the quality of imperial and colonial administration criticized. The urgent need for improvement was asserted by numerous critics, and responsible ministers came to echo their observations. Lord Dufferin, under-secretary of state at the Colonial Office, explained in 1938 that 'the first object of Colonial development is to enable Colonial peoples to lead happier and fuller lives'.[51] But it is doubtful if disinterested benevolence is the principal explanation of the Imperial government's radical and expensive commitment to colonial development and welfare in 1940. Increased expenditure appears to have been proposed by the Secretary of State and accepted by the cabinet as a necessary political response to unrest in the colonies and criticism at home and overseas of British colonial administration. Economic advantages to Britain from accelerated development programmes now became the incidental though welcome by-products of a policy conceived for other purposes. By the later 1930s those responsible for the Colonial Empire appeared less than confident in the virtues of British colonial rule, its achievements and, significantly, its long-term stability. The arguments for colonial development and welfare were preoccupied with justifying the perpetuation of colonialism. The new policy was seen as a necessary defensive strategy at a time when critics within and enemies without appeared to threaten Britain's political control of the Colonial Empire.

It should, moreover, be noted that scarcely a reference was made before 1940 to suggest that the new policy would be a preliminary to decolonisation.[52] Although MacDonald is sometimes credited as the first Secretary of State to accept colonial independence as the ultimate objective of British colonial rule, such a faith had no bearing on the policy-making preparatory to the Colonial Development and Welfare Act.[53] The purpose of the policy-makers was not the preparation for political withdrawal and colonial self-government but the improvement and hence preservation of imperial rule. Although

British colonialism was on the defensive in the later 1930s, it was not in retreat. Colonial development and welfare policy is symptomatic of a determination to re-group, revive and restore Britain's moral authority and her political control over the Colonial Empire.

One distinguishing characteristic of the new policy was the unexpected ease with which the Colonial Office drew financially large concessions from the Treasury at an apparently unpromising time: resources were otherwise being concentrated on military needs. This may be explained partly by the better and more vigorous presentation of the case for colonial development expenditure by a reorganised and reinspired Colonial Office under an energetic Secretary of State. But it is also symptomatic of the Treasury's comparative weakness when their instinctively financial or economic arguments for economy were confronted by political arguments for expenditure. Treasury officials by the end of the 1930s were sensitive not only to general public criticisms of British colonial practices, but were aware of the effect of such criticisms on cabinet ministers. As in earlier cases, the Treasury were unable to deflect claims on the Exchequer once the political need for new commitments was accepted by the politicians.

The passage of the Colonial Development and Welfare Act in 1940 did not, of course, complete the concessions which the Treasury were obliged to make. Thereafter, the Treasury were to be repeatedly pressed to disgorge taxpayers' money for the satisfaction of colonial development policies. But the arguments that they subsequently found impossible to resist had for the most part already been previously rehearsed, in their essential characteristics, during the inter-war debates analysed in this study. For example, as several writers have shown, the need to defend British colonial rule against the criticisms of their American allies obliged the British government during the Second World War to honour the development commitments of 1940 and, indeed, to extend them in scope and cost.[54] After the war, in an increasingly hostile international environment, the political need to demonstrate the virtues of constructive trusteeship could not be denied. The argument for expenditure on colonial development as a justification and defence of colonial rule retained its potency. On the other hand, the post-war economic problems of Britain, particularly in the later 1940s, revived the appeal of colonial development as a way of increasing valuable supplies of food and raw materials from within the sterling area. The idea of colonies as imperial economic assets and of colonial development expenditure as a way of realising them continued to attract imperial policy-makers.[55] It is in this sense that the inter-war period may be seen as a unique period of transition in the history of colonial development policy, marking a departure from the limited aims and means prevailing in the period before 1914 and a step towards the definition and expression of policies which during and after the Second World War were more ambitious and, inevitably, more expensive.

NOTES

1. See above, p.12.
2. E. R. Wicker, 'Colonial Development and Welfare 1929–1957: the Evolution of a Policy', *Soc. & Econ. Studies*, 7 (1958), 176, 183, 187-9; D. J. Morgan, *British Aid – 5. Colonial Development*, O.D.I., London, 1964, and *The Official History of Colonial Development*, London, 1980.
3. *Annual Appropriation Accounts*.
4. A. T. Peacock & J. Wiseman, *The Growth of Public Expenditure in the United Kingdom*, 2nd ed., London, 1967, pp.184-5, 201.
5. Sir B. Mallet & C. O. George, *British Budgets, third series, 1921–33*, London, 1933, pp.558-9.
6. Milner to Ready, 2 Nov. 1919, Milner Papers 211; Milner to Harcourt 21 Jan. 1921, Milner Papers Add.Mss.Eng.Hist. c.700.
7. Sir R. Furse, *Aucuparius: Recollections of a Recruiting Officer*, London, 1962, p.56.
8. This seems to be supported by the much greater bulk of documents concerned with tariffs and settlement than with colonial development in the private papers of Amery and Swinton, and also of Neville Chamberlain and Baldwin. S. B. Saul makes a similar point on Joseph Chamberlain in 'The Economic Significance of Constructive Imperialism', *J.Ec.Hist.*, 17 (1957), 192.
9. Figures for staff at Colonial Office, from messengers to permanent under-secretary, in *Annual Appropriation Accounts*.
10. *Colonial Office Lists*.
11. Sir Gerard Clauson, who served in the Colonial Office from 1919 to 1951, letter to author, 14 July 1971.
12. Lord Swinton, *I Remember*, London, 1948, p.65.
13. The practice of keeping officers in one department for long periods was criticized in the Report of Committee on the Organisation of the Colonial Office 28 Feb. 1927, CO 885/29/Misc.No.382, p.8.
14. *Who Was Who; Colonial Office Lists*.
15. J. Barnes and D. Nicholson, eds., *The Leo Amery Diaries*, vol.1, London, 1980, 24 Aug. 1920, p.266.
16. *Ibid.*, 12 Feb. 1919, p.256, 15 Oct. 1919, pp.264-5, and Amery to Milner 12 Feb. 1919, Amery Papers, Box 54, Folder B.
17. Sir G. Fiddes, *The Dominions and Colonial Offices*, London, 1926, p.37.
18. CO 885/29/Misc.No.382, Report, 28 Feb. 1927.
19. CO 885/30/Misc.No.391, 1st Interim Report, 16 May 1927; Hopkins Papers, T175/14A.
20. *Colonial Office Lists*.

21. CO 885/29/Misc.No.382.
22. Even Grindle had acknowledged this weakness, see minute 26 June 1923, CO 323/903/BT 31274.
23. CO 885/30/Misc.No.391, report of sub-committee, second interim report 7 Nov. 1927, final report 30 March 1928, and Misc.No.392, papers by Grindle, Shuckburgh, Bottomley, C.O. to Treas. 14 May 1928 and Treas. to C.O. 19 May 1928; L. S. Amery, *My Political Life*, vol.II, London, 1953, p.338; Wilson to Hopkins 1 June 1928, Hopkins Papers, T175/14A.
24. Swinton, *I Remember*, pp.65-8.
25. *Colonial Office List* 1935.
26. Jeffries to Hale 16 Dec. 1938 and Hale to Jeffries 21 Jan. 1939, CO 866/33/1327; CO 323/1536/1751.
27. Cmd.6175, p.6.
28. J. M. Lee, *Colonial Development and Good Government*, Oxford, 1967, pp. 100-110; J. M. Lee & M. Petter, *The Colonial Office, War and Development Policy*, London, 1982, pp.59-65; Sir Cosmo Parkinson, *The Colonial Office from Within*, London, 1947, pp.53-83; *Colonial Office List* 1950.
29. *Hansard* H.C., vol.227, cols.1411, 1498-9, 30 April 1929.
30. D. G. Meredith, 'The British Government and Colonial Economic Policy, 1919–39', *Ec.H.R.*, 28 (1975), 493-8; E. A. Brett, *Colonialism and Underdevelopment in East Africa*, London, 1973, pp.266-81.
31. Memo. by Calder 21 June 1939, CO 852/250/15606 Part 2.
32. Minute by Caine, 7 May 1940, CO 859/40/12901 Part 3, though Shuckburgh, deputy under-secretary, commented 'But I take it that we should not necessarily accept the Board of Trade view of what is or is not an "uneconomic" secondary industry', n.d., *ibid.*.
33. Minute by Moore, 19 June 1939, CO 852/250/15606 Part 2.
34. Sir Andrew Cohen, *British Policy in Changing Africa*, London, 1959, p.18; see also B. Porter, *The Lion's Share*, London, 1975, pp.292-3.
35. Lee, *Colonial Development and Good Government*, p.39.
36. Draft cabinet memo. by Eastwood, Economic Development and Welfare of the Colonial Empire, CO 323/1698/7450 Part 1; memo. by Calder 21 June 1939, CO 852/250/15606 Part 2.
37. W. K. Hancock, *Wealth of Colonies*, Cambridge, 1950, p.56.
38. Memo. by C.O. & D.O. Branch of First Division Association, CO 885/30/Misc. No.392.
39. Amery, *My Political Life*, vol.2, p.339; C. Jeffries, *The Colonial Empire and its Civil Service*, Cambridge, 1938; R. Heussler, *Yesterday's Rulers*, Oxford, 1967; Furse, *Aucuparius, op. cit.*
40. Amery, *My Political Life*, vol.2, p.337; 3rd Interim Report of Committee on Colonial Office Organisation, 5 March 1928, CO 885/30/Misc.No.391; CO 885/29/Misc.No.381; K. Robinson, *The Dilemmas of Trusteeship*, London, 1965, p.37.
41. Jeffries to Hale 16 Dec. 1938, CO 866/33/1327.
42. Cmd.6175, pp.7-8.
43. Minute by Parkinson 21 Aug. 1939, CO 852/250/15606 Part 2.
44. Fiddes, *The Dominions and Colonial Offices*, pp.15, 121.
45. S. Constantine, *Unemployment in Britain between the Wars*, London, 1980, pp.46-51, 63-5, 68-70; D. Winch, *Economics and Policy*, Fontana ed., Glasgow, 1972, pp.73-154; H. Roseveare, *The Treasury*, London, 1969, pp.258-272.
46. M. Beloff, *Imperial Sunset*, vol.1, *Britain's Liberal Empire*, London, 1969, p.353; Roseveare, *The Treasury*, p.248.

47. Palestine, Col.No.12, 1924, p.3; Col.No.59, 1930, p.13. Hong Kong C.R.No.1203, 1922, p.3; No.1414, 1927, p.5; No.1472, 1928, p.3.
48. Hong Kong C.R.No.1414, 1927, p.3. See also, for example, Gold Coast C.R.No.1418, 1927–28, p.14; Gambia C.R.No.1444, 1928, p.6; Seychelles C.R.No.1560, 1930, p.19.
49. See, for example, Bahamas C.R.No.1285, 1925, p.9; Barbados C.R.No.1913, 1938–39, pp.40-1; Bermuda C.R.No.1409, 1928, p.7; Jamaica C.R.No.1550, 1930, p.8; Southern Rhodesia Year Book No.2, 1930, p.554; Federated Malay States C.R.No.1183, 1922, p.7, No.1784, 1935, p.109; Straits Settlements C.R.No.1140, 1921, p.12, No.1537, 1930, p.19 and No.1812, 1936, p.80; Kelantan C.R.No.1534, 1930, p.8. For other regional loans see Zanzibar C.R.No.1052, 1919, p.6; Seychelles C.R.No.1061, 1919, p.2; Basutoland C.R.No.1016, 1918–19, p.2.
50. To cite one case see the financing and construction of Takoradi Harbour, D. G. Meredith, 'The British Government and Colonial Economic Development with Particular Reference to British West Africa, 1919–1939', Exeter Ph.D. thesis, 1976, pp.140-88.
51. Royal Empire Society, *The Crucial Problem of Imperial Development*, London, 1938, p.79.
52. For brief hints at self-government as the ultimate goal of policy see Clauson to Parkinson 9 June 1939, CO 852/250/15606 Part 2, and minutes of C.O.-Treas. meeting 10 Jan. 1940, CO 859/19/7475.
53. C. R. Nordman, 'Prelude to Decolonisation in West Africa, the Development of British Colonial Policy 1938–1947', Oxford D.Phil. thesis, 1976, p.10, and M. MacDonald, *Titans and Others*, London, 1972, pp.240-1; but see also R. Pearce, *The Turning Point in Africa*, London, 1982, pp.23-4.
54. W. R. Louis, *Imperialism at Bay*, Oxford, 1977; Pearce, *The Turning Point in Africa*, pp.28-39, 65-6; Lee and Petter, *The Colonial Office, War and Development Policy*.
55. J. F. Munro, *Africa and the International Economy 1800–1960*, London, 1976, p.180; A. Wood, *The Groundnut Affair*, London, 1950; Morgan, *The Official History of Colonial Development*, espec. vol.2.

BIBLIOGRAPHY

1. PRIMARY SOURCES

A. MANUSCRIPT

1. *Public Record Office, London*
   Cabinet Papers
   Colonial Office Papers
   Treasury Papers
   Hopkins Papers
   Niemeyer Papers

2. *Bodleian Library, Oxford*
   Amulree Papers
   Milner Papers
   Worthington-Evans Papers

3. *Rhodes House, Oxford*
   Creech Jones Papers
   Fabian Colonial Bureau Papers

4. *University Library, Cambridge*
   Baldwin Papers

5. *Churchill College, Cambridge*
   Swinton Papers

6. *University Library, Birmingham*
   Neville Chamberlain Papers

7. *Rt. Hon. Julian Amery, M.P.*
   Leo Amery Papers

B. OFFICIAL PUBLICATIONS

1. *Colonial Office Lists* and *Dominions and Colonial Office Lists*

2. Annual reports on territories of the British Colonial Empire, issued as Colonial Reports, Colonial Office Reports, Foreign Office Reports, Stationery Office Publications or Command Papers together with *Southern Rhodesia Official Year Book*

3. *Hansard, Parliamentary Debates*, House of Commons and House of Lords

4. *Public General Acts*

5. *Annual Estimates, Supplementary Estimates* and *Appropriation Accounts* in Parliamentary Papers

6. *Annual Treasury List of Stock issued under the Colonial Stock Acts* in Parliamentary Papers

7. Other Parliamentary Papers:

Statistical Abstract for the British Empire 1899–1913, Cd.7827, 1915.
Recommendations of the Economic Conference of the Allies, Cd.8271, 1916.
Financial Facilities for Trade. Report to the Board of Trade by Committee Appointed to Investigate, Cd.8346, 1916.
Royal Commission on the Natural Resources, Trade and Legislation of Certain Portions of His Majesty's Dominions, Final Report, Cd.8462, 1917.
Resolutions passed by the Committee on Commercial and Industrial Policy on the Subject of Imperial Preference, Cd.8482, 1917.
Extracts from Proceedings and Papers laid before the Imperial War Conference, Cd.8566, 1917.
Final Report of the Committee on Commercial and Industrial Policy after the War, Cd.9035, 1918.
Imperial War Conference, 1918. Extracts from Minutes of Proceedings and Papers laid before the Conference, Cd.9177, 1918.
First Annual Report of the Colonial Research Committee, Cmd.1144, 1921.
Conference of Prime Ministers and Representatives of the United Kingdom, the Dominions and India, 1921, Summary of Proceedings, Cmd.1474, 1921.
Third Report of the Committee on National Expenditure, Cmd.1589, 1922.
Imperial Economic Conference, Summary of Conclusions, Cmd.1990, 1923.
Imperial Economic Conference, Record of Proceedings, Cmd.2009, 1924.
Report of the East Africa Commission, Cmd.2387, 1925.

Memorandum on Transport Development and Cotton Growing in East Africa, Cmd.2463, 1925.

Report of the East African Guaranteed Loan Committee, Cmd.2701, 1926.

Imperial Conference, 1926, Summary of Proceedings, Cmd.2768, 1926.

Colonial Office Conference, 1927, Summary of Proceedings, Cmd.2883, 1927.

Report of the Industrial Transference Board, Cmd.3156, 1928.

Report of the Commission on Closer Union of the Dependencies in Eastern and Central Africa, Cmd.3234, 1929.

Memorandum showing the Progress and Development in the Colonial Empire and in the Machinery for dealing with Colonial Questions from Nov. 1924 to Nov. 1928, Cmd.3268, 1929.

Memoranda on Certain Proposals relating to Unemployment, Cmd.3331, 1929.

Statement on Works Approved for Grant in Connection with Unemployment, Cmd.3449, 1929.

Report of the East African Guaranteed Loan Committee 1926–1929, Cmd.3494, 1930.

Statement on Works Approved for Government Financial Assistance in Connection with Unemployment, Cmd.3519, 1930.

Colonial Development Advisory Committee, First Interim Report, Aug. 1929 to Feb. 1930, Cmd.3540, 1930.

——, *Second Interim Report 1930–31*, Cmd.3876, 1931.

——, *Third Interim Report 1931–32*, Cmd.4079, 1932.

——, *Fourth Interim Report 1932–33*, Cmd.4316, 1933.

——, *Fifth Annual Report 1933–34*, Cmd.4634, 1934.

——, *Sixth Annual Report 1934–35*, Cmd.4916, 1935.

——, *Seventh Annual Report 1935–36*, Cmd.5202, 1936.

——, *Eighth Annual Report 1936–37*, Cmd.5537, 1937.

——, *Ninth Annual Report 1937–38*, Cmd.5789, 1938.

——, *Tenth Annual Report 1938–39*, Cmd.6062, 1939.

——, *Eleventh and Final Report, April 1939 to July 1940*, Cmd.6298, 1941.

Annual Abstract Account of Colonial Development Fund with Report by Comptroller and Auditor-General.

Colonial Office Conference 1930, Summary of Proceedings, Cmd.3628, 1930.

Statement of the Principal Measures taken by H.M. Government in connection with Unemployment, Cmd.3746, 1930.

Committee on National Expenditure, Report, Cmd.3920, 1931.

Memorandum on the Measures proposed to Secure Reductions in National Expenditure, Cmd.3952, 1931.

First Report from the Select Committee on Estimates, 1932.

Financial and Economic Situation of Swaziland, Cmd.4114, 1932.

Financial and Economic Position of Bechuanaland Protectorate, Cmd.4368, 1933.

Financial and Economic Position in British Honduras, Cmd.4586, 1934.

Financial and Economic Position of Basutoland, Cmd.4907, 1935.

Leeward Islands: Papers relating to the Disturbances in St. Christopher (St. Kitts.), Cmd.4956, 1935.

Report of the Commission appointed to Enquire into the Disturbances in the Copper Belt, Northern Rhodesia, Oct. 1935, Cmd.5009, 1935.

Trinidad and Tobago Disturbances, 1937, Report of Commission, Cmd.5641, 1938.

The Colonial Empire in 1937–38, Cmd.5760, 1938.

The Colonial Empire in 1938–39, Cmd.6023, 1939.

Report of the Committee on Nutrition in the Colonial Empire, Cmd. 6050 and 6051, 1939.

Labour Conditions in the West Indies, Cmd.6070, 1939.

West India Royal Commission 1938–39, Recommendations, Cmd.6174, 1940.

Statement of Policy on Colonial Development and Welfare, Cmd.6175, 1940.

Certain Aspects of Colonial Policy in War-time, Cmd.6299, 1941.

Report on the Operation of the Colonial Development and Welfare Act, 1940–42, Cmd.6422, 1943.

Return of Schemes under the Colonial Development and Welfare Act, 1942–43, Cmd.6457, 1943.

——, *1943–44*, Cmd.6532, 1944.

——, *1944–45*, 1945.

Report of the West India Royal Commission, Cmd.6607, 1945.

Colonial Development and Welfare, Despatch 12 Nov. 1945, Cmd.6713, 1945.

Report from the Select Committee on Overseas Aid, House of Commons Paper 299, 1970–71.

Colonial Development and Welfare Acts 1929–70. A Brief Review, Cmnd.4677, 1971.

C. OTHER CONTEMPORARY PUBLICATIONS

Amery, L. S., *National and Imperial Economics*, Westminster, 1923.

——, 'The Economic Development of the Empire', *United Empire*, 16 (1925).

——, 'Empire and Prosperity', *Criterion Miscellany*, 23 (1930).

——, *The Forward View*, London, 1935.

Associated Newspapers, *Life of Joseph Chamberlain*, London, 1914.

Baillie Hamilton, W. A., 'Forty-Four Years at the Colonial Office', *The Nineteenth Century and After*, 65 (1909).

Barnes, L., *Empire or Democracy?*, London, 1939.

Bigland, A., 'The Empire's Assets and How to Use Them', *Journal of the Royal Society of Arts*, 65 (1917).

——, *The Call of Empire*, London, 1926.

Brampton, Sir J., 'The Colonial Office from Within', *Empire Review*, 1 (1901).

Bruce, Sir Charles, 'The Colonial Office and the Crown Colonies', *Empire Review*, 11 (1906).

Cannan, E., *An Economist's Protest*, London, 1927.

Frankel, S. H., *Capital Investment in Africa*, London, 1938.

Frewen, M. 'The Structure of Empire Finance', *The Nineteenth Century and After*, 88 (1920).

Graham, W., 'The Finance of East African Development', *Empire Review*, 44 (1926).

Grice, J. Watson, *The Resources of the Empire*, London, 1917.

Hadfield, Sir R., *Empire Development and Proposals for Establishment of an Empire Development Board*, London, 1935.

Hailey, Lord, *An African Survey*, London, 1938.

Henderson, H. D., *Colonies and Raw Materials*, Oxford, 1939.

Labour Party, *Labour and the Nation*, London, 1928.

Leacock, S., *Economic Prosperity in the British Empire*, London, 1930.

Liberal Party, *Britain's Industrial Future*, London, 1928.

Lloyd-Greame, Sir P., *The Imperial Economic Conference*, National Unionist Association, Westminster, 1924.

Lugard, Sir F. D., 'The Crown Colonies and the British War Debt', *The Nineteenth Century and After*, 88 (1920).

——, *The Dual Mandate in British Tropical Africa*, London, 1922.

Macmillan, W. M., *Warning from the West Indies*, London, 1936.

——, *Africa Emergent*, London, 1938.

Melchett, Lord, *Imperial Economic Unity*, London, 1930.

Milner, Lord, *The Nation and the Empire*, London, 1913.

——, *Questions of the Hour*, London, 1923.

Ormsby-Gore, W., *The Development of Our Empire in the Tropics*, Nottingham, 1927.

Royal Empire Society, *The Crucial Problem of Imperial Development*, London, 1938.

R.I.I.A., *The Colonial Problem*, London, 1937.

——, *The British Empire*, 2nd ed., London, 1938.

Saunders, E., *A Self-Supporting Empire*, London, 1918.

Williams, H. G., *Imperial Rationalisation*, London, 1930.

Wilson-Fox, H., 'The Development of Imperial Resources', *Journal of the Royal Society of Arts*, 65 (1916).

——, 'The Development of the Empire's Resources', *The Nineteenth Century and After*, 82 (1917).

——, 'Payment of War Debt by Development of Empire Resources', *United Empire*, 9 (1918).

D. NEWSPAPERS AND PERIODICALS

The British Citizen and Empire Worker
The Economist
Empire Review
Fortnightly Review

International Affairs
Journal of the Royal Society of Arts
Nineteenth Century and After
Political Quarterly
Stock Exchange Year Book
The Times
United Empire

2. SECONDARY SOURCES

A. COLONIAL OFFICE AND COLONIAL DEVELOPMENT

Abbott, A. W., *A Short History of the Crown Agents and their Office*, London, 1959.

Abbott, G. C., 'British Colonial Aid Policy During the Nineteen Thirties', *Canadian Journal of History*, 5 (1970).

——, 'A Re-examination of the 1929 Colonial Development Act', *Economic History Review*, 24 (1971).

Albertini, R. von., *Decolonization, The Administration and Future of the Colonies, 1919–1960*, New York, 1971.

Arnold, G., *Economic Co-operation in the Commonwealth*, Oxford, 1967.

Bailey, R., *Promoting Commonwealth Development*, London, 1970.

Barnett, T., *The Gezira Scheme: An Illusion of Development*, London, 1977.

Baster, A. S. J., 'A Note on the Colonial Stock Acts and Dominion Borrowing', *Economic History*, 2 (1933).

Bauer, P. T., *Dissent on Development*, London, 1971.

Benians, E. A., Butler, Sir J. and Carrington, C. E., eds., *The Cambridge History of the British Empire*, vol.3, Cambridge, 1959.

Bhagwati, J. and Eckaus, R. S., eds., *Foreign Aid*, Harmondsworth, 1970.

Blakeley, B. L., *The Colonial Office 1868–1892*, Durham N.C., 1972.

Brett, E. A., *Colonialism and Underdevelopment in East Africa*, London, 1973.

Buckley, S., 'The Colonial Office and the Establishment of an Imperial Development Board: the Impact of World War 1', *Journal of Imperial and Commonwealth History*, 2 (1974).

Burley, K. H., 'The Imperial Shipping Committee', *Journal of Imperial and Commonwealth History*, 2 (1974).

Burton, A. M., 'Treasury Control and Colonial Policy in the Late Nineteenth Century', *Public Administration*, 44 (1966).

Cohen, Sir A., *British Policy in Changing Africa*, London, 1959.

Cross, C., *The Fall of the British Empire*, London, 1968.

Crowder, M., *West Africa under Colonial Rule*, London, 1968.

Drummond, I. M., 'More on British Colonial Aid Policy in the Nineteen-Thirties', *Canadian Journal of History*, 6 (1971).

——, *British Economic Policy and the Empire 1919–1939*, London, 1972.

——, *Imperial Economic Policy 1917—1939*, London, 1974.
Dumett, R. E., 'The Campaign against Malaria and the Expansion of Scientific, Medical and Sanitary Services in British West Africa, 1898—1910', *African Historical Studies*, 1 (1968).
——, 'Joseph Chamberlain, Imperial Finance and Railway Policy in British West Africa in the Late Nineteenth Century', *English Historical Review*, 90 (1975).
Ehrlich, C., 'The Uganda Economy 1903—1945' in Harlow, V., and Chilver, E. M., eds., *A History of East Africa*, vol.2, Oxford, 1965.
——, 'Building and Caretaking: Economic Policy in British Tropical Africa, 1890—1960', *Economic History Review*, 26 (1973).
Fiddes, Sir G., *The Dominions and Colonial Offices*, London, 1926.
Fieldhouse, D. K., 'The Economic Exploitation of Africa: some British and French Comparisons' in Gifford, P. and Louis, W. R., eds., *France and Britain in Africa*, New Haven and London, 1971.
Gaitskell, A., *Gezira: a story of development in the Sudan*, London, 1959.
Gann, L. H. and Guignan, P., *The Rulers of British Africa 1870—1914*, London, 1978.
Garner, J., *The Commonwealth Office 1925—68*, London, 1978.
Gupta, P. S., *Imperialism and the British Labour Movement 1914—1964*, London, 1975.
Hall, H. L., *The Colonial Office*, London, 1937.
Hancock, W. K., *Survey of British Commonwealth Affairs*, vol.2, *Problems of Economic Policy 1918—39*, part 1, London, 1940, part 2, London, 1942.
——, *Wealth of Colonies*, Cambridge, 1950.
Hardy, S. M., 'Joseph Chamberlain and Some Problems of the "Underdeveloped Estates" ', *University of Birmingham Historical Journal*, 11 (1968).
Hayter, T., *Aid as Imperialism*, Harmondsworth, 1971.
Heussler, R., *Yesterday's Rulers*, Syracuse New York, 1963.
Hill, M. F., *Permanent Way. The Story of the Kenya and Uganda Railway*, 2nd ed., Nairobi, 1961.
Hinden, R., *Empire and After*, London, 1949.
Holland, R. F., *Britain and the Commonwealth Alliance 1918—39*, London, 1981.
Hopkins, A. G., *An Economic History of West Africa*, London, 1973.
Hyam, R., *Elgin and Churchill at the Colonial Office*, London, 1968.
——, *Britain's Imperial Century 1815—1914*, London, 1976.
——, 'The Colonial Office Mind 1900—1914', *Journal of Imperial and Commonwealth History*, 8 (1979).
Jeffries, C., *The Colonial Empire and its Civil Service*, Cambridge, 1938.
——, Sir C., *The Colonial Office*, London, 1956.
——, *A Review of Colonial Research 1940—1960*, H.M.S.O., London, 1964.
Jessop, D., 'The Colonial Stock Act of 1900: A Symptom of the New Imperialism?', *Journal of Imperial and Commonwealth History*, 4 (1976).
Johnson, H., 'The West Indies and the Conversion of the British Official Classes to the Development Idea', *Journal of Commonwealth and Comparative Politics*, 15 (1977).

Kesner, R. M., 'Builders of Empire: the Role of the Crown Agents in Imperial Development, 1880–1914', *Journal of Imperial and Commonwealth History*, 5 (1977).

——, *Economic Control and Colonial Development. Crown Colony Financial Management in the Age of Joseph Chamberlain*, Oxford 1981.

Killingray, D., 'The Empire Resources Development Committee and West Africa 1916–20', *Journal of Imperial and Commonwealth History*, 10 (1982).

Knowles, L. C. A., *The Economic Development of the British Overseas Empire*, vol.1, London, 1924.

Kubicek, R. V., *The Administration of Imperialism: Joseph Chamberlain at the Colonial Office*, Durham, N.C., 1969.

Lee, J. M., *Colonial Development and Good Government*, Oxford, 1967.

——, ' "Forward Thinking" and War: the Colonial Office during the 1940s', *Journal of Imperial and Commonwealth History*, 6 (1977).

——, and Petter, M., *The Colonial Office, War and Development Policy*, London, 1982.

Louis, W. R., *Imperialism at Bay*, Oxford, 1977.

Low, D. A., *Lion Rampant*, London, 1973.

Malmsten, N. R., 'The British Labour Party and the West Indies, 1918–39', *Journal of Imperial and Commonwealth History*, 5 (1977).

Mansergh, N., *The Commonwealth Experience*, London, 1969.

McIntyre, W. D., *Colonies into Commonwealth*, London, 1966.

Meredith, D. G., 'The British Government and Colonial Economic Policy, 1919–39', *Economic History Review*, 28 (1975).

Morgan, D. J., *British Aid – 5. Colonial Development*, O.D.I., London, 1964.

——, *The Official History of Colonial Development*, 5 vols., London, 1980.

Morris, J., *Farewell the Trumpets*, Harmondsworth, 1979.

Munro, J. F., *Africa and the International Economy, 1800–1960*, London, 1976.

Niculescu, B., *Colonial Planning: A Comparative Study*, London, 1958.

North – South: A Programme for Survival. Report of the Independent Commission on International Development Issues, Pan ed., London, 1980.

Parkinson, Sir C., *The Colonial Office from Within 1909–1945*, London, 1947.

Partners in Development: Report of the Commission on International Development, London, 1969.

Pearce, R., *The Turning Point in Africa*, London, 1982.

Perham, M., *The Colonial Reckoning*, London, 1961.

Pim, Sir A., *The Financial and Economic History of the African Tropical Territories*, Oxford, 1940.

Ponko, V., 'Economic Management in a Free Trade Empire: the work of the Crown Agents for the Colonies in the 19th and early 20th Centuries', *Journal of Economic History*, 26 (1966).

Porter, B., *Critics of Empire*, London, 1968.

——, *The Lion's Share*, London, 1975.
Pugh, R. B., 'The Colonial Office, 1801–1925', in Benians, E. A., Butler, Sir J. and Carrington, C. E., eds., *The Cambridge History of the British Empire, vol.3, The Empire-Commonwealth 1870–1919*, Cambridge, 1959.
——, *The Records of the Colonial and Dominions Offices*, H.M.S.O., London, 1964.
Reese, T. R., *The History of the Royal Commonwealth Society 1868–1968*, London, 1968.
Roberts, B. C., *Labour in the Tropical Territories of the Commonwealth*, London, 1964.
Robinson, A., *Fifty Years of Commonwealth Economic Development*, Smuts Memorial Lecture, Cambridge, 1972.
Robinson, K., *The Dilemmas of Trusteeship*, London, 1965.
Saul, S. B., 'The Economic Significance of Constructive Imperialism', *Journal of Economic History*, 17 (1957).
Semmel, B., *Imperialism and Social Reform*, London, 1960.
Sinclair, K., 'Hobson and Lenin in Johore: Colonial Office policy towards Concessionaires and Investors 1898–1907', *Modern Asian Studies*, 1 (1967).
Snelling, R. C. and Barron, T. J., 'The Colonial Office and its Permanent Officials 1801–1914', in Sutherland, G., ed., *Studies in the Growth of Nineteenth Century Government*, London, 1972.
Turner, J. A., 'The British Commonwealth Union and the General Election of 1918', *English Historical Review*, 93 (1978).
Vail, L., 'The Making of an Imperial Slum: Nyasaland and its Railways, 1895–1935', *Journal of African History*, 16 (1975).
Ward, B., Runnalls, J. D., D'Anjou, L., eds., *The Widening Gap: Development in the 1970s*, New York and London, 1971.
Wicker, E. R., 'Colonial Development and Welfare, 1929–1957: the Evolution of a Policy', *Social and Economic Studies*, 7 (1958).
Will, H. A., 'Colonial Policy and Economic Development in the British West Indies 1895–1903', *Economic History Review*, 23 (1970).
Wilson, C., *A History of Unilever*, 2 vols., London, 1954.
Wrigley, C. C., 'Kenya: the Patterns of Economic Life, 1902–1945', in Harlow, V. and Chilver, E. M., eds., *A History of East Africa*, vol.2, Oxford, 1965.
Zwanenberg, R. M. A. van and King, A., *An Economic History of Kenya and Uganda 1800–1970*, London, 1975.

B. POLITICAL AND ECONOMIC BACKGROUND

Aldcroft, D. H., *The Inter-War Economy: Britain, 1919–1939*, London, 1970.
Ashworth, W., *An Economic History of England 1870–1939*, London, 1960.
Barnett, C., *The Collapse of British Power*, London, 1972.
Beloff, M., *Imperial Sunset*, vol.1 *Britain's Liberal Empire 1897–1921*, London, 1969.

——, 'The Whitehall Factor: the Role of the Higher Civil Service 1919–39' in Peele, G. and Cook, C., eds., *The Politics of Reappraisal*, London, 1975.

——, 'The Political Blind Spot of Economists, *Government and Opposition*, 10 (1975).

Booth, A. and Glynn, S., 'The Public Records and Recent British Economic Historiography', *Economic History Review*, 32 (1979).

Cohen, M. J., *Palestine, Retreat from the Mandate*, London, 1978.

Constantine, S., *Unemployment in Britain between the Wars*, London, 1980.

Craig, F. W. S., ed., *British General Election Manifestos 1918–1966*, Chichester, 1970.

Crozier, A., 'Imperial Decline and the Colonial Question in Anglo-German Relations, 1919–39', *European Studies Review*, 11 (1981).

Darwin, J., 'Imperialism in Decline? Tendencies in British Imperial Policy between the Wars', *Historical Journal*, 23 (1980).

Fearon, P., *The Origins and Nature of the Great Slump 1929–1932*, London, 1979.

Gilbert, M. and Gott, R., *The Appeasers*, 2nd ed., London, 1967.

Guinn, P., *British Strategy and Politics 1914 to 1918*, Oxford, 1965.

Hancock, K. J., 'The Reduction of Unemployment as a Problem of Public Policy, 1920–1929', *Economic History Review*, 15 (1962).

Heath, Sir T. L., *The Treasury*, London, 1927.

Hicks, U. K., *The Finance of British Government 1920–1936*, London, 1938.

Howson, S., *Domestic Monetary Management in Britain 1919–38*, Cambridge, 1975.

Hurwitz, S. J., *State Intervention in Great Britain*, New York, 1949.

Johnson, P. B., *Land Fit for Heroes*, Chicago and London, 1968.

Kennedy, P., *The Realities Behind Diplomacy*, Glasgow, 1981.

Lockwood, P. A., 'Milner's Entry into the War Cabinet', *Historical Journal*, 7 (1964).

Mallet, Sir B. and George, C. O., *British Budgets, second series, 1913–1921*, London, 1929.

——, *British Budgets, third series, 1921–1933*, London, 1933.

Marwick, A., *The Deluge: British Society and the First World War*, London, 1965.

Mowat, C. L., *Britain between the Wars*, London, 1955.

Northedge, F. S., *The Troubled Giant*, London, 1966.

Peacock, A. T. and Wiseman, J., *The Growth of Public Expenditure in the United Kingdom*, 2nd ed., London, 1967.

Peden, G. C., *British Rearmament and the Treasury 1932–1939*, Edinburgh, 1979.

Pollard, S., *The Development of the British Economy 1914–67*, 2nd ed., London, 1969.

Roseveare, H., *The Treasury*, London, 1969.

Rothwell, V. H., *British War Aims and Peace Diplomacy 1914–1918*, Oxford, 1971.

Sabine, B. E. V., *British Budgets in Peace and War 1932–1945*, London, 1970.

Schmokel, W. W., *Dream of Empire: German Colonialism 1919–1945*, New Haven, 1964.

Skidelsky, R., *Politicians and the Slump*, London, 1967.
Stubbs, J.O., 'Lord Milner and Patriotic Labour 1914–1918', *English Historical Review*, 87 (1972).
Tawney, R.H., 'The Abolition of Economic Controls, 1918–21', *Economic History Review*, 13 (1943).
Winch, D., *Economics and Policy*, Glasgow, 1972.
Wright, M., 'Treasury Control 1854–1914' in Sutherland, G., ed., *Studies in the Growth of Nineteenth Century Government*, London, 1972.

C. MEMOIRS AND BIOGRAPHIES

Amery, J., *The Life of Joseph Chamberlain*, vol.IV, London, 1951.
Amery, L.S., *My Political Life*, 3 vols., London, 1953–5.
Barnes, J. and Nicholson, D., eds., *The Leo Amery Diaries*, vol.1, London, 1980.
Bullock, A., *The Life and Times of Ernest Bevin*, vol.1, London, 1960.
Dictionary of National Biography.
Feiling, K., *The Life of Neville Chamberlain*, London, 1946.
Furse, Sir R., *Aucuparius: Recollections of a Recruiting Officer*, London, 1962.
Gollin, A.M., *Proconsul in Politics*, London, 1964.
Hewins, W.A.S., *The Apologia of an Imperialist*, 2 vols., London, 1929.
Long, W., *Memories*, London, 1923.
MacDonald, M., *Titans and Others*, London, 1972.
Middlemas, K. and Barnes, J., *Baldwin*, London, 1969.
Pelling, H., *Winston Churchill*, London, 1974.
Perham, M., *Lugard, The Years of Authority 1898–1945*, London, 1960.
Swinton, Viscount, *I Remember*, London, 1948.
Who Was Who.

D. UNPUBLISHED THESES

Burton, A.M., 'The Influence of the Treasury on the Making of British Colonial Policy 1868–1880', Oxford D.Phil., 1960.
Constantine, S., 'The Formulation of British Policy on Colonial Development 1914–1929', Oxford D.Phil., 1974.
Earl, A., 'The Political Life of Viscount Swinton 1918–1938', Manchester M.A., 1960.
Meredith, D.G., 'The British Government and Colonial Economic Development with particular reference to British West Africa, 1919–1939', Exeter Ph.D., 1976.
Nordman, C.R., 'Prelude to Decolonisation in West Africa: the Development of British Colonial Policy, 1938–1947', Oxford D.Phil., 1976.
Nthenda, L.-J.L., 'H.M. Treasury and the Problems of Nyasaland Public Finances 1919 to 1940', Oxford D.Phil., 1972.
Rampersad, D.G.M., 'Colonial Economic Development and Social Welfare: the Case of the British West Indian Colonies, 1929–1947', Oxford D.Phil., 1979.

INDEX